SHAPING THE
AMERICAN EDUCATIONAL STATE

SHAPING THE AMERICAN EDUCATIONAL STATE

STATE 1900 to the present

Edited and with Introductory Essays by
CLARENCE J. KARIER

THE FREE PRESS
A Division of Macmillan Publishing Co., Inc.
NEW YORK

Collier Macmillan Publishers
LONDON

Dedicated to Norma and our children

The Free Press
A Division of Macmillan Publishing Co., Inc.
866 Third Avenue, New York, N.Y. 10022

Collier-Macmillan Canada Ltd.

Library of Congress Catalog Card Number: 74-4647

Printed in the United States of America

printing number
1 2 3 4 5 6 7 8 9 10

Library of Congress Cataloging in Publication Data

Karier, Clarence J   comp.
   Shaping the American educational state, 1900 to
the present.

   (Urgent issues in American society series)
   Includes bibliographical references and index.
   1. Education—United States—History—Addresses,
essays, lectures. 2. Discrimination in education—
United States—Addresses, essays, lectures.
3. Euthenics—Addresses, essays, lectures.
4. Eugenics—Addresses, essays, lectures. I. Title.
I. Title.
LA205.K315   370'.973   74-4647
ISBN 0-02-917040-0
ISBN 0-02-917030-3 (pbk.)

ACKNOWLEDGMENTS

From a paper originally presented at the Center for Educational Policy Research, Harvard University, Spring 1972. See page *1*.

From *San Francisco Chronicle*, San Francisco, Cal., Wednesday Nov. 4, 1900. See page *25*.

From the *Madison Democrat*, Madison, Wisconsin, Wednesday morning, August 15, 1894. See page *28*.

From University of Chicago Archives: Presidents' Papers 1889–1925: Laughlin to Harper, August 6, 1894 [Box 44, Folder 21]. See page *31*.

From University of Chicago Archives: Presidents' Papers 1889–1925: Harper to Bemis, Jan. 2, 1894 [Box 8, Folder 17]. See page *32*.

From Division of Archives and Manuscripts, The State Historical Society of Wisconsin: Richard T. Ely Papers: Letter to Hamilton W. Mabie, Esq. from Richard T. Ely, August 24, 1895. See page *33*.

From University of Chicago Archives: Presidents' Papers 1889–1925. See page *37*.

From University of Chicago Archives: Presidents' Papers 1889–1925: Harper to Rockefeller, August 25, 1900 [Box 56, Folder 13]. See page *43*.

From University of Chicago Archives: William Rainey Harper Personal Papers: Gates to Harper, Dec. 14, 1903 [Box 9, Folder 2]. See page *43*.

From University of Chicago Archives: Presidents' Papers 1889–1925: Rockefeller to Harper, Dec. 26, 1903 [Box 56, Folder 16]. See page *45*.

University of Chicago Archives: Presidents' Papers 1889–1925: Harper to Rockefeller, Dec. 31, 1903 [Box 56, Folder 16]. See page *45*.

From University of Chicago Archives: William Rainey Harper Personal Papers: Gates to Harper, Nov. 9, 1904 [Box 9, Folder 3]. See page *46*.

From *Educational Review*, Jan. 1902, pp. 1–14. See page *52*.

From *AAUP Bulletin*, Vol. 25, No. 5, December 1939. See page *62*.

From the *New York Times* Magazine, March 27, 1949. © 1949 by the New York Times Company. Reprinted by permission. See page *95*.

Reprinted from *U.S. News & World Report*, May 19, 1969. Copyright 1969 U.S. News & World Report, Inc. See page *104*.

Noam Chomsky, "Some Thoughts on Intellectuals and the Schools," *Harvard Educational Review*, 36, Fall 1966, pp. 484–491. Copyright © 1966 by President and Fellows of Harvard College. See page *116*.

From Office of the White House Press Secretary, September 18, 1970. For release 6:00 P.M., Sunday, September 20, 1970. See page *124*.

Copied from unpublished manuscripts in the Brown University Library, "Education," by Lester Frank Ward, dated 1871–1873, pp. 127–180. See page *145*.

From H. H. Goddard, "Mental Levels and Democracy," *Human Efficiency and Levels of Intelligence*. (Copyright 1920 by Princeton University Press) pp. 95–107. Reprinted by permission of Princeton University Press. See page *165*.

From Lewis M. Terman, Virgil E. Dickson, A. H. Sutherland, Raymond H. Franzen, C. R. Tupper and Grace Fernall, *Intelligence Tests and School Reorganization*. (New York: World Book Co., 1923), pp. 22–29. Reprinted with permission from the author's heirs. See page *170*.

Reprinted with permission from *Educational Review*, November 1924, pp. 169–174. See page *175*.

Originally given as an address before the National Education Association, Oakland, California, July 2, 1923. The study summarized was made possible by a grant from the Commonwealth Fund of New York City. Reprinted with permission from *School and Society*, Vol. XIX, No. 483, March 29, 1924, pp. 359–364. See page *183*.

From Lewis Madison Terman, "Were We Born That Way?" *World's Work*, 44, 1922, pp. 655–660. Reprinted with permission of the author's heirs. See page *197*.

Carl C. Brigham, *A Study of American Intelligence* (Copyright 1922 by Carl C. Brigham), published by Princeton University Press, pp. 197–210. Reprinted by permission of Princeton University Press. See page *207*.

David Starr Jordan, "Closed Doors or the Melting Pot," *The American Hebrew*, September 26, 1924, p. 538 and 592. Reprinted by permission from *Jewish Week* and *American Examiner*. See page *215*.

Edward L. Thorndike, "Intelligence and Its Uses," *Harper's Monthly Magazine*, January 1920, pp. 227–235. Reprinted by permission of author's heir. See page *219*.

Copyright © 1920, by Minneapolis Star and Tribune Co., Inc. Reprinted from the April 1920 issue of Harper's Magazine by permission of author's heir. See page *238*.

Dick & Jane as Victims: Sex Stereotyping in Children's Readers (pamphlet). Women on Words and Images, Princeton, N.J., 1972, pp. 30–39. See page *244*.

From Edward A. Ross Papers, Division of Archives and Manuscripts, The State Historical Society of Wisconsin. See page *256*.

From Edward A. Ross Papers, Divisions of Archives and Manuscripts, The State Historical Society of Wisconsin. See page *257*.

From Edward A. Ross Papers, Division of Archives and Manuscripts, The State Historical Society of Wisconsin. See page *258*.

From Edward A. Ross Papers, Division of Archives and Manuscripts, The State Historical Society of Wisconsin. See page *259*.

From Gregory Mason, "An Americanization Factory," *The Outlook*, V. 112, February 23, 1916, pp. 430–448. See page *259*.

From Joseph H. Wade, District Superintendent, New York City Public Schools, "Education of the Immigrant," *U. S. Bureau of Education Bulletin*, No. 51, 1913, pp. 23–24. See page *268*.

From Marion Brown, "Is There a Nationality Problem in Our Schools?" *National Educational Association Proceedings*. (Chicago: University of Chicago Press, 1900), pp. 585–590. See page *269*.

First of a series of six articles, originally printed in *The New Republic*, October 25, 1922, pp. 213–215. Reprinted with permission of the Yale University Library, owner of the Walter Lippmann Collection. See page *283*.

Second of a series of six articles originally printed in *The New Republic*, November 1, 1922, pp. 246–248. Reprinted with permission of the Yale University Library, owner of the Walter Lippmann Collection. See page *286*.

Third of a series of six articles originally printed in *The New Republic*, November 8, 1922, pp. 275–277. Reprinted with permission of the Yale University Library, owner of the Walter Lippmann Collection. See page *290*.

Fourth in a series of six articles, originally printed in *The New Republic*, November 15, 1922, pp. 297–298. Reprinted with permission of the Yale University Library, owner of the Walter Lippmann Collection. See page *294*.

Fifth in a series of six articles, originally printed in *The New Republic*, November 22, 1922, pp. 328–330. Reprinted with permission from the Yale University Library, owner of the Walter Lippmann Collection. See page *296*.

Sixth in a series of six articles, originally printed in *The New Republic*, November 29, 1922, pp. 9–11. Reprinted with permission of the Yale University Library, owner of the Walter Lippmann Collection. See page *301*.

Lewis M. Terman, "The Great Conspiracy," *The New Republic*, December 27, 1922, pp. 116–120. Reprinted with permission of the author's heirs. See page *305*.

Walter Lippmann, "The Great Confusion," *The New Republic*, January 3, 1923, pp. 145–146. Reprinted with permission of the Yale University Library, owner of the Walter Lippmann Collection. See page *313*.

Russell Marks, "Race and Immigration: The Politics of Intelligence Testing." Copyright © 1974 by Russell Marks. Reprinted by permission of the Author. See page *316*.

Arthur R. Jensen, "How Much Can We Boost IQ and Scholastic Achievement?" *Harvard Educational Review*, 39, Winter 1969, 1–123. Copyright © 1969 by President and Fellows of Harvard College. Reprinted by permission of the publisher and the author. See page *342*.

Invited address presented to the XIXth International Congress of Psychology, London, England, July 30, 1969, and dedicated to Prof. Th. Dobzhansky on his 70th birthday. This work was prepared with the support of Mental Health Training Grant 1 TO1 10715–04 BLS for Research Training in the Biological Sciences. The author is Currently Professor of Psychology and Zoology, University of Illinois, Urbana Champaign. Reprinted from *Seminars in Psychiatry*, Volume 2, No. 1, February 1970, pp. 89–105. See page *348*.

This is the first publication of "Heredity, Intelligence, Politics, and Psychology," a paper given at the American Psychological Association, 1973. Copyright © 1975 by The Free Press. See page *367*.

Copyright © 1972 by Noah's Ark, Inc. (*Ramparts* Magazine). By permission of the editors. See page *393*.

This is the first publication of "Dysgenics—A Social-Problem Reality Evaded by the Illusion of Infinite Plasticity of Human Intelligence?" a paper presented at the American Psychological Association, Division 9, Society of Psychological Study of Social Issues, Symposium on "Social Problems: Illusion, Delusion or Reality," Washington, D.C., September 7, 1971. Copyright © 1975 by The Free Press. Many of these ideas were more fully extended in a lengthy debate which appeared in *Phi Delta Kappan*, January 1972 and March 1972. See page *409*.

From Henry E. Garrett, *The Citizen*, January 1970, p. 21. See page *418*.

Henry E. Garrett, *Breeding Down* (pamphlet), (Richmond, Virginia: The Patrick Henry Press, undated). See page *418*.

The author is further indebted to Russell Marks and Stephen Yulish for their invaluable research assistance on this book.

Contents

Chapter 6

Chapter 7

Chapter 8

Chapter 9

The Nature–Nurture Debate: Towards a False Consciousness 275

Chapter 10

Contributors

LESTER FRANK WARD, author of *Dynamic Sociology*, is considered the founder of the field of sociology in America.

EDWARD ROSS was a liberal sociologist who was fired from Stanford University for his anti-immigration speeches at the turn of the century. Later, as professor of sociology at the University of Wisconsin, he was actively involved in immigration restriction.

WILLIAM HARPER was president of the University of Chicago at the turn of the century.

DAVID STARR JORDAN was president of Stanford University at the start of this century.

RICHARD T. ELY was a leading liberal progressive professor of economics at the University of Wisconsin who was charged with activities unbecoming a university professor.

JOHN D. ROCKEFELLER was the multi-millionaire oil magnate who supported the founding of the University of Chicago.

F. T. GATES was executive secretary for John D. Rockefeller.

THEODORE ROOSEVELT was the twenty-sixth president of the United States.

RICHARD M. NIXON was the thirty-seventh president of the United States.

JOHN DEWEY was the leading American liberal educational philosopher during the first half of the twentieth century.

SIDNEY HOOK was professor of philosophy at New York University who actively led the anti-communist movements in the schools before and after World War II as well as the attack on the student New Left in the 1960s.

ALEXANDER MEIKLEJOHN was well known for his work as a founder of the experimental college at the University of Wisconsin and for his strong stand on academic freedom.

NOAM CHOMSKY is professor of linguistics at M.I.T. and is well known for both his work in linguistics and his anti-Vietnam War activities.

LEWIS M. TERMAN was professor of educational psychology at Stanford University who developed the Stanford–Binet I.Q. Test. He was also one of the leading figures in the testing movement in America.

H. H. GODDARD translated the Binet Scale in 1908 and later wrote *The Kallikak Family*. Professor Goddard was active in both the testing movement and the eugenics movement.

FRANK N. FREEMAN was an educational psychologist at the University of Chicago.

C. C. BRIGHAM was professor of educational psychology at Princeton, wrote *A Study of American Intelligence* (1923), and helped create the tests used to restrict immigration.

EDWARD L. THORNDIKE was professor of educational psychology at Columbia University and was perhaps the most influential educational psychologist in the first half of the twentieth century. His name appears on numerous books directed at teacher training as well as actual elementary and secondary curriculum.

PRESCOTT HALL was a lobbyist for the Immigration Restriction League.

JOSEPH H. WADE was district superintendent of the New York City Public Schools.

MARION BROWN was principal of City Normal School, New Orleans, Louisiana.

WALTER LIPPMANN was one of the leading liberal columnists and commentators of the twentieth century.

RUSSELL MARKS is a leading critic of the testing movement in American culture.

JERRY HIRSCH is professor of psychology and zoology at the University of Illinois. He has published widely in the fields of psychology and genetics, and is one of the more perceptive critics of Arthur Jensen's racial theories.

ARTHUR JENSEN is professor of psychology at the University of California, Berkeley, who became famous for his thesis about the heritability of intelligence and the inferior cognitive ability of black people.

LEON KAMIN, professor of psychology at Princeton University, has published widely and is a critic of the Jensen thesis.

HENRY E. GARRETT was chairman of the Psychology Department at Columbia University until his retirement. He then wrote racist pamphlets for the Patrick Henry Press that were used effectively to stir racial fears among white Americans in the 1960s.

WILLIAM SHOCKLEY, professor of engineering at Stanford University, was co-winner of the Nobel Prize in Physics for his work in developing the transistor. Later he became best known for his racial views which he termed, "raceology."

Preface

All history is written from a perspective that is invariably shaped out of one's existential present. As noted educator John Dewey once remarked:

> The slightest reflection shows that the conceptual material employed in writing history is that of the period in which a history is written. There is no material available for leading principles and hypotheses save that of the historic present. As a culture changes, the conceptions that are dominant in a culture change. Of necessity new standpoints for viewing, appraising, and ordering data arise. History is then rewritten.[1]

In this respect, history is a part of the living present and every new present generates a need to re-examine the past. If that past is to remain connected as a vital explanation for the living present, the questions the historian asks of the past are important not only for shaping his particular view of the past, but also for determining his contribution to the solution to present-day problems. Historical interpretation, thus, is inescapably bound up with the problems of the present as well as the possibilities for their solution. Here, the historian has a vital role to play. Hayden V. White has expressed this well.

> The contemporary historian has to establish the value of the study of the past, not as 'an end in itself' but as a way of providing perspective on the present that contributes to the solution of problems peculiar to our own times.[2]

History is an imaginative art in which pictures of the past are painted in the contemporary world by the historian out of the artifacts of the past. Much of what the historian creates, including chronology itself, is a consciously developed illusion. The historian writes his story of the past as if

---

[1] John Dewey, *Logic: The Theory of Inquiry*. (New York: Henry Holt and Co., 1938), p. 253.
[2] "The Burden of History," *History and Theory*, Vol. V, No. 2, 1966, pp. 111–134.

he lived in the past as an observer and recorder of events. He then moves the reader along from past to present, creating the illusion that he and the reader have been there. One can, of course, no more live in the year 1900 than in the year 2001 except in imagination. The verbal reconstruction of the past thus involves an imaginative, creative act. History, however, is more than pure fiction and illusion. A picture of the past leaves the world of fictional writers when the historian insists on documentary evidence to establish the validity of his story. Here, context, documentation and fair use of documents are important criteria for establishing the validity of his particular view of the past. Historical analysis, thus, involves both addressing the important problems of the present and past in such a way that the story of the past is functionally useful in understanding those problems, and the process of critically establishing the validity of the interpretation through documentary evidence. Historical writing must ultimately pass the test not only of social usefulness, but also of empirical creditability. Neither test, however, leads to certitude with respect to historical judgment. Both criteria rest on meaning and judgment being exercised in an existential moment of time. In this sense, there can no more exist a definitive history as there can exist a definitive present. There are, however, many pictures of the past that are judged more or less true and more or less useful by the living present.

This book was written with such concerns in mind. It was not intended to be definitive or, in any sense, to cover a field. It was written from a definite limited perspective of the present out of which emerged central questions and issues which, in part, guided the selection of materials. The reader, then, is invited to consider the assumptions of the author with respect to his present, consider the significance of the questions asked, and then to examine some of the key documents upon which the interpretation was based. Wherever possible, the documents are reproduced in their entirety, after the interpretation is presented, so that the reader might judge the context from which a particular quotation or interpretation was derived. The reader, then, is invited to make his own judgment of the past.

The author writes from a perspective of the present which holds that American society is not structured to enhance the dignity of man but unfortunately, is, structured to foster a dehumanizing quest for status, power and wealth. We live, I believe, in a fundamentally racist, materialistic society which, through a process of rewards and punishments, cultivates the quest for status, power and wealth in such a way so as to use people and institutions effectively to protect vested interests. A society, which took forty years to discover that its government was experimenting, in the interest of public health, with the syphilitic condition of its poor, repressed black people, seems a fairly racist society. Just as any social system which tolerates the infant mortality rates of its urban ghettos to exist as it does in America today is less than humane. The average American appears to live an insecure, pressurized social existence where success and failure is measured in terms of wealth and property, and where large numbers of people live on the brink of economic and social failure. Nurtured on a materialistic code of ethics and schooled to survive in a competitive economic system, the modern American has grown highly responsive to many forms of systems' management. He is, in many respects, manipulated from cradle to grave in both his needs and his desires. The spirit of rebellion which once seemed to surge through the American soul now appears only a faint afterglow of a strange past. The quest of the modern age is not for freedom but for security.

The social system, it seems, can satisfactorily manage and control virtually all human needs except one: the need to know, to feel and to control one's own social destiny through the acquisition and growth of personal strength and development. Unfulfilled in this fundamental experience which connects one's inner world with his outer social existence, many frantically attempt to escape the absurdity of their existence via drugs, alcohol, sex, sports and entertainment; while still others have come to accept these, often controlled avenues of escape as a way of life. The modern American is an insecure, alienated person. He is alienated from the possible fulfillment of his own socially creative self by a social system which controls and punishes through material rewards. Such a system is sustained by varying kinds and degrees of alienation. Perhaps the most significant kind is that which turns men away from critically examining their social system because they have come to believe that they cannot change that system. The successful life in this regard is that life which plays the system according to its rules and rewards and succeeds on those terms. This, it would seem, is a truly alienated person, fundamentally alienated from that part of his self which calls for the control of his own social destiny.

Modern society seems to cultivate this kind of alienation through its economic and social control system, which repeatedly threatens the very psycho-social existence of the person. Such a person, alienated from his socially creative self, can find little more than a strange utopian reverie in George Bernard Shaw's suggestion that, "Some men see things as they are and say, why? I dream things that never were and say, why not?" The truly alienated person who has come to believe that he cannot change the system under which he lives is not interested in seeing things as they are and asking why, or for that matter, even dreaming things that never were and asking, why not? This book is addressed to the nonalienated person who can still ask why. From a nonalienated perspective, one might ask not only why, but, indeed, how we got where we think we are.

The answer to that question is to be found, in part, in the emergence of the corporate liberal state which was conceived in the Wisconsin progressive tradition and nurtured in the new nationalism of men like Theodore Roosevelt, Herbert Croly, and Woodrow Wilson. The progressive liberals fostered the notion that the political state could be used as a positive vehicle to reconcile the competing interest of capital, labor and the public welfare. They further surmised that such conflicting interest could be reconciled by effectively rationalizing and stabilizing an ever expanding economy of production and consumption of goods and services. A part of that system came to include a vast compulsory elementary and secondary educational system, capped by the university. The university played a fundamental role in providing the expertise that created the theoretical and practical knowledge and trained manpower by which the system has been sustained and further developed. In return, the political-economic system invested heavily in a vast educational complex which, from kindergarten to graduate school, served to train producers and consumers, to manage labor supply and, more importantly, to teach those values necessary to maintain the kind of community now in existence. Reflecting on this purpose of schooling in the educational state, R. Freeman Butts succinctly argued:

> A public school serves a public purpose rather than a private one. It is not maintained for the personal advantage or private gain of the teacher, the proprietor or board of managers; nor does it exist simply for the enjoyment, happiness or advancement of the individual student or his parents. . . . Rather, the prime purpose of the public school is to serve the general welfare of a democratic society, by assuring that the knowledge and understanding necessary to exercise the responsibilities of citizenship are not only made available but actively inculcated. . . . Achieving a sense of community is the essential purpose of public education. This work cannot be left to the vagaries of individual parents or small groups of like minded parents, or particular interest groups, or religious sects, or private enterprises or cultured specialties.[3]

[3] R. Freeman Butts, "Assaults on a Great Idea," *The Nation*, April 30, 1973, p. 554.

Professor Butts was essentially correct. The educational state which emerged in the twentieth century did not exist simply for the enjoyment, happiness or advancement of the individual student, but rather to inculcate those social values which were necessary to maintain and develop the community as it has developed in present-day society. The fact that this community, today, is highly competitive, materialistic and racist ought to suggest some doubt, at least, about the kind of values the schools have been inculcating over the past few generations.

Rather than viewing schooling in the educational state as a failure, as many are prone to do, one might look at it from the standpoint of many of the "professional" educators who helped shape the educational state in the twentieth century, and then consider whether they were successful or not. From the standpoint of many of the leading psychologists instrumental in shaping the curriculum of the educational state in the first half of the twentieth century—who were themselves racist—the racial bias of the present-day schools would not appear as a failure, but as a tribute to the validity of their ideas as well as to their success as curriculum trackers and organizers. Contrary to the ideas of Christopher Jencks, Herbert Gintis and others, the central purpose of public education was not to equalize wealth or opportunity.[4] It was, however, designed to help fit people into a social system that was not necessarily their own choice. It fit people into that system by helping some barely to survive, others merely to exist, and still others to prosper. From the standpoint, then, of many of the shapers of the educational state in America, the schools were successful. They accomplished what they were designed to do.

Due to the limits of space, regretfully, many important educators, movements and concerns are necessarily left out of this book. One such group which deserves the attention of a separate book is that tradition which some educational historians have termed "child-centered." The tendency has been to picture the efficiency-society-oriented educators to which much of this book is addressed to be conservative, while the child-centered tradition is assumed to be radical. The thrust of both traditions has been in the direction of social control as well as social stability. To be sure, most of the educators examined in this book are more overt and direct, while the child-centered educators are more subtle and indirect; nevertheless, the social consequences of their efforts have often been the same. If one goes further and examines the rhetoric and practice of many chil-

---

[4] See Christopher Jencks, *Inequality: A Reassessment of the Effects of Family and Schooling in America.* (New York: Basic Books, 1972).

centered educators in both the nineteenth and twentieth centuries, the social control function of the "new" education often is obvious. This is clear when, for example, a nineteenth-century child-centered educator, such as Pestalozzi, would say, " 'the poor must be educated for poverty' for in order 'to enjoy the best possible state, both of soul and body . . . it is necessary to desire little and be content with still less.' " [5] Under the circumstances it was little wonder that Johann Gottlieb Fichte in his *Addresses to the German Nation* called for the rejuvenation of the Prussian nation along such child-centered Pestalozzian lines and that such an appeal received such electrifying and positive support by the aristocratic classes of Prussia. Here was an education which could meet the needs of the "new" Germany without threatening the class structure. Many of the American progressives, at the turn of the century, held this rejuvenated Germany as their ideal model.

In America at the turn of the century, Ann Keppel's study of rural educational reform seems to indicate that child-centered methods were consciously being used to keep the rural children rural.[6] Similarly, in the urban ghettos at the turn of the century child-centered techniques commonly were employed in the settlement houses and Americanization classes aimed at integrating the immigrant into American society.[7] The Progressive Education Association literature clearly reflects the concern for social efficiency and control. For example, the first of the Seven Principles of Progressive Education was: "Freedom to develop naturally." The meaning of this principle was explained as:

> The conduct of the pupil should be governed by himself *according to the social needs of his community*. This does not mean that liberty should be allowed to become license, or that the teacher should not exercise authority when it proves necessary.[8]

Many of the 1930 as well as 1970 progressive educators were, in fact, middle-class reformers, using child-centered techniques to improve the quality of education for middle-class children. Whatever technique was used, educational progressivism was much like political progressivism, i.e.,

---

[5] As quoted in Clarence J. Karier, *Man, Society, and Education*. (Glenview, Ill.: Scott, Foresman and Co., 1967), p. 224.

[6] See Ann Keppel, "Country Schools for Country Children," (Unpublished Ph.D. dissertation, University of Wisconsin, 1960).

[7] See Paul Violas, *A History of Urban Education in Twentieth Century America*. (New York: Putnam, expected publication date 1975).

[8] Patricia Albjerg Graham, *Progressive Education From Arcady To Academe*. (New York: Teachers College Press, Columbia, 1967), p. 29. Underlining for emphasis added.

a conservative thrust which in effect contributed to the maintenance of the social system. The emphasis of this book is not on the child-centered educators, however, but on those selected educators who more often saw themselves as rationalizing and engineering an educational system which they believed would openly and directly impose values on the young.

Given these concerns about the past in relation to the present, the author's perception of the present, and the role of the educational state in contributing to that present, the questions addressed were directed at those selected individuals who seemed to be instrumental in shaping what became the educational state in twentieth-century America. Two questions provide the thematic structure for the book. The first question concerns the role, function and responsibility of the professional in the educational state; the second raises the issues of how and why the system was rationalized in the minds of some key educational reformers in the twentieth century. If one finds the present educational system heavily racist and designed to protect class interest, it should not come as a surprise to find that many of America's educational leaders were also racist, interested in protecting the vested interests of the favored classes. This book was not designed to examine all of the developments in education in the twentieth century but to focus on these two selected issues which connect with the problematic present; to create an interpretation of the historical development of these issues in twentieth-century America; and to make available some of the key documents upon which the interpretation was based. The reader can then judge.

Note of Explanation to the Reader

On February 5, 1973, Sidney Hook granted permission for the author to reprint in its entirety his article, "Academic Integrity and Academic Freedom." Again, on February 8, 1973, Sidney Hook also granted permission for the author to reprint in its entirety his article, "A Plan to Achieve Campus Peace." And again, on April 3, 1973, Sidney Hook granted permission for the author to reprint in its entirety his article, "Academic Freedom and 'The Trojan Horse' in American Education" as it appeared in *Academic Freedom and Academic Anarchy*. All of these permissions required payment of fees for use of the articles. However, in a formal letter received by the publisher on February 6, 1974, while this book was in production, Sidney Hook withdrew his permissions to republish the above articles on the grounds that the selection of articles distorted his position.

The overall design of this book is basically twofold: first, to provide the reader with a critical interpretation of selected movements which have shaped the educational state in America, and secondly, to provide some of the key primary source documents that were used in the initial interpretation. Each document was to be reproduced in its entirety so as to avoid distortion as much as possible. It was thus assumed that the reader would be prepared to make his judgment as to the adequacy or inadequacy of the interpretation.

The author sincerely regrets the fact that Sidney Hook believed the selection of his articles distorted his position and, therefore, found it necessary to withdraw permissions to reproduce his articles. It should be clear to all, friend and critic alike, that one cannot deal with the liberal position on academic freedom as it developed over the past four decades in America without coming to grips with Hook's position. Understanding his role and his position is vital to understanding what took place. What remains, then, of the original selection of documents in this section of the book is, "The Real Crisis On the Campus" for which permission to reproduce was granted by *U.S. News and World Report* who control the copyright. In view of Professor Hook's objections to the author's selection of his articles the publisher went so far as to offer to include exactly the material that Professor Hook wanted in the book. However, despite this generous offer, he refused to reconsider his withdrawal of permissions. Under these circumstances, the author has taken the liberty of writing short, condensed summaries of each article he would like to have reproduced. These summaries should be taken not as an abstract or a paraphrase of what Sidney Hook said, but rather as the author's interpretation of what he thinks Hook said. In each instance, the reader is urged to consult the original and read it in its entirety before making a final judgment.

Because of these unusual circumstances, it is necessary, in this instance, to deviate from the format of the book by following an analysis of the period with summaries of some key documents. The author also would like to apologize for the inconvenience it may cause the reader who takes the time to find and read the original articles.

Introduction

The historian William Appleman Williams has suggested that the key to understanding the last 100 years of American diplomatic history is to be found in the concept of the frontier in America. He argued that the frontier was more than a social safety valve for the Eastern seaboard or a social equalizer for those who moved West. Rather, it was as the earlier frontier historian Frederick Jackson Turner put it "a gate of escape." [1] Through this gate passed the American social conscience, repeatedly escaping the discomfort of self-reflection and the implications that such reflections might have for social action. Combining the Puritan sense of mission with the enlightenment notion of progress, the American mind used the frontier to shield its social conscience while it legitimatized its actions from the slaughter of the American Indian in the nineteenth century to the slaughter of the Vietnamese in the twentieth century.

The frontier was, as Williams argued, an expansionist concept which always was moving forward to greater and greater heights and bigger and better things (better was most often defined in terms of efficiency). The solution to the problem of maldistribution of wealth and power lay, not in creating institutions that would redistribute the wealth and power, but in creating institutions that would create more wealth and power. More land, more property, more production, more trade, etc., were usually the easy solutions to very difficult internal problems. In this respect, the thesis which Williams developed in *The Contours of American History* makes sense, especially as he finds the frontier mentality at work in the vast worldwide, corporate apparatus this country has produced in the twentieth century. David Eakins further extended the frontier thesis by analyzing the way in which large corporate interests managed to bring U.S. foreign policy into a sympathetic relationship with their interests through the creation of private foundations such as the Brookings Institute, the National

---

[1] William Appleman Williams, *The Contours of American History*. (Chicago: Quadrangle Paperbacks, 1966), p. 377.

Industrial Conference Board, and the Twentieth Century Fund, which provided the research data and often the personnel who were instrumental in shaping American foreign policy.[2]

While Williams' extension of Turner's frontier thesis helps explain an American expansionist foreign policy, it only partially describes what took place within American corporate society itself. The part left out and indeed that which seems to add to the other half of the thesis is the emergence of the educational state in the twentieth century which, in effect, became a new frontier for many Americans. Turner sensed this when he said that in the twentieth century, "The test tube and the microscope are needed rather than ax and rifle in this new ideal of conquest." [3] Just as one of the controlling myths of the nineteenth century was the belief that westward movement would result in social mobility, so too, one of the central myths of the twentieth century is that schooling will result in social mobility. While some viewed the educational frontier as a vehicle of individual mobility, others saw it as a vehicle to enhance national power, and still others, to generate economic growth. This combination of beliefs accounts for the readiness of so many people to invest so large a share of their wealth and energy in a mass system of schooling.

In the seventy years between 1870 and 1940, the American population trebled, while the American high school population increased ninety times and the college and university population increased thirty times.[4] As this educational frontier emerged, a young man would more often be advised to go to college rather than to go West. Once fixed in the public mind as the center where social opportunities might be gained, the school became the major vehicle for social indoctrination as well as social control. Williams further suggested that the frontier thesis was,

> . . . fundamentally and extensively anti-intellectual in its direct impact and long range results. Having defined everything good in terms of a surplus of property, the problem became one of developing techniques for securing more good things from a succession of new frontiers.[5]

In the educational state, one also finds a passion for bigger and better schools again in terms of efficiency, as well as a strong inclination toward an objective product which is easily interchanged with property.

The business of the school was business. Vocational guidance and training took on the characteristics necessary to serve mass-production

[2] See David W. Eakins, "The Development of Corporate Liberal Policy Research in the United States, 1885–1965." (Unpublished Ph.D. dissertation, University of Wisconsin, 1966).

[3] Frederick Jackson Turner, *The Frontier in American History*. (New York: Henry Holt & Co., 1950), p. 284.

[4] Harvard Committee, *General Education in a Free Society*. (Cambridge, Mass.: Harvard University Press, 1945), p. 7.

[5] Williams, *The Contours of American History*, p. 374.

industries. When industries in the 1920s needed workers who would tire-lessly devote the major portion of their lives to serving a single machine, assembly line or company, the vocational guidance advocated by David Snedden was critical.[6] As the needs of industry within the recent decades shifted to that of workers who could adapt and change jobs with relative ease, so too, did the rhetoric and practices of vocational guidance and training shift to "career education" which supposedly prepared the young to shift occupations with relative ease. The business aspects of the schools were not restricted solely to areas of vocational guidance[7] and training, rather they permeated many aspects of the general curriculum. Whether it was the teacher in the progressive schools of 1920 or the "innovative" teacher of the 1970s who used a "contract system" for organizing class-room activities, the business implication could hardly be missed. The same was true of the "experimental" programs which substituted play money for grades. For many, the competition for grades was only a synthetic process which prepared the child for the "real" world of competing for dollars. Thus, in the minds of some, greater school achievement easily translated into greater acquisition of wealth and property. Similarly, just as the liberal reformer's solution to the problem of maldistribution of wealth was to increase the gross national product thus increasing the standard of living for a larger and larger middle class,[8] so too, real inequities in educational opportunity were usually met with a call for more schooling which would increase the achievement level for more and more children.

The middle-class quest for greater achievement was more a quest for property status and economic security than a quest for knowledge and intellectual growth. Just as much of the nineteenth-century Western frontier movement was motivated by materialistic interests which bore anti-intellectual consequences, so too, much of the twentieth-century educational frontier was motivated by materialistic interests which sim-ilarly culminated in strong anti-intellectual characteristics in American

[6] See Walter H. Drost, *David Snedden and Education For Social Efficiency.* (Madison: University of Wisconsin Press, 1967).

[7] Business organizations in many cities literally created and operated guidance pro-grams in the public schools. In some cases business association not only guided the pupils, but also at times enforced the compulsory education laws. Such was the case in 1913 when the Chicago Association of Commerce brought suit against the parents of a fifteen year old boy for not being in school. See Peter Sola, "Plutocrats, Pedago-gues and Plebes: Business Influences on Vocational and Extra Curricular Activities in the Chicago High Schools 1899-1925." (Unpublished Ph.D. dissertation, University of Illinois, Champaign-Urbana, 1972).

[8] This was essentially Horace Mann's and Herbert Croly's solution to the problem of maldistribution of wealth. See Lawrence A. Cremin, *The Republic and the School: Horace Mann on the Education of Free Men.* (New York: Teachers College Colum-bia, 1957), pp. 87-88. Also see Herbert Croly, *The Promise of American Life.* (New York: E. P. Dutton & Co., 1963).

education. "Growth" whether in the factory or the school was an expansionist term. As John Dewey put it,

> Since in reality there is nothing to which growth is relative save more growth, there is nothing to which education is subordinate save more education.[9]

This kind of expansionist thinking allows one to escape the more difficult but critical questions of growth and education for what?

As the school doorway became "a gate of escape," the net effect of much twentieth-century educational rhetoric involving a meritocratic system was to transfer the blame for repression onto the repressed. Here the Kerner Report is instructive. The Report clearly and decisively indicted white America as racist, but it failed to take the next logical step which would be to call for an effective educational program for the children of white Americans in order to eliminate that racism. Instead, the Report proposed special education for black children. The practical outcome of the Kerner Report was simply that the problem was not white racist attitudes, but rather black failure to meet sufficient standards to enter the meritocratic economic system. The burden of proof thus fell on black children.

The idea that a more thoroughly schooled population would be less inclined toward violent social revolution because they would then become better producers and consumers of wealth was clear to Horace Mann as early as 1848. Education, he argued, "does better than to disarm the poor of their hostility toward the rich; it prevents being poor." [10] Mann, of course, knew what Daniel Webster had earlier asserted, that education, indeed, was "a wise and liberal system of police by which property, and life, and the peace of society are secured." [11] While the many problems of poverty, crime and disease might be solved with an educated population, neither Webster nor Mann believed that the school could solve the social problems directly. On the educational frontier in the twentieth century, however, some viewed the schools as a place to solve every social problem from race relations to unemployment. In part, this was due to the growing strength of those who, from Helvetius to B. F. Skinner, saw education as a process of "discovering the wires by which the human puppet is moved," and in part, it was a necessary consequence of using the schools as a frontier vehicle for adults to escape the real problems of their present world. One might, in this sense, do as George S. Counts did in 1932 and "Dare the Schools Build a New Social Order," without seriously threatening the

[9] John Dewey, *Democracy and Education*. (New York: The Macmillan Co., 1916), p. 60.

[10] As quoted in Lawrence A. Cremin, *The Republic and the School*. (New York: Teachers College, Columbia, 1957), p. 87.

[11] As quoted in Clarence J. Karier, *Man, Society, and Education*. (Glenview: Scott, Foresman & Co., 1967), p. 51.

power structure of the society in which he lived. In many ways, it was frontier escapism to charge teachers and children with the task of social reconstruction when the economic and political power rested elsewhere. Counts, of course, was not a radical but a liberal reformer who in later years became famous for his anti-communist campaign in the schools a decade before Joseph McCarthy appeared on the scene. The questions that immediately present themselves are who shaped the policies which guided the educational state in twentieth-century America, and what was the relationship of those who determined policy to the liberal reformers and professional educators who managed the system to implement that policy?

Little historical evidence supports the notion of a conspiracy theory by which the educational side of the corporate liberal state has emerged; and even less evidence supports Michael Harrington's notion that this has been, on the whole, *An Accidental Century*. A preponderence of evidence seems to indicate that the major social philosophy of many of the corporate and educational leaders who stood for flexible, dynamic change was largely pragmatic, reflecting a good deal of John Dewey's instrumentalism. Although John Dewey and James B. Conant might disagree on many items, they would not disagree that the ultimate criteria for a true pragmatic test is, as William James and Randolph Bourne had pointed out earlier, *survival* of the system.

A brief examination of the value profile of many twentieth-century liberal education reformers reveals that while they generally held a basic enlightenment faith in scientific progress, they also feared the unruly, ignorant masses whom they believed generated the conflict and violence which they abhorred in their society. They furthermore believed that the way out of such social problems was to develop an expert professional leadership which could eliminate conflict and violence first, by scientifically rationalizing the social order and, secondly, by creating an overall educational system which would unite the school and the society. Most of these men assumed an ethic of enlightened self-interest which respected power and ultimately placed the highest value on survival. Considering that this combination of attitudes and values was put to the test of practice within the historic context of the last fifty years, one can understand how the educational state emerged. It is not necessary, then, to conjure up a conspiracy theory. In many respects, the educational state came to be the mirror image of the social and political philosophy practiced by the controlling classes of American society. This assumes that the ideas and values that men hold dear often make a difference in terms of social action.

It would, indeed, seem strange, if, for example, a country which had the necessary social values to lead the world in creating mass-production industries would not produce a mass system of education. Put another way, practical efficiency-minded America could hardly be expected to tolerate for very long an educational system which produced impractical and inefficient people. The schools not only help perpetuate those necessary attitudes toward work, wealth and success in a materialistic, competitive society, they also serve to rationalize and justify the current class system on the basis of meritocracy. A popular second-grade reader used in American schools today summarizes the lessons taught as follows:

What Did We Learn?
1. We go to school to learn about other people.
2. We learn that people look different from each other.
3. People speak different languages.
4. Some people have more than others, some have less.
5. Some people know more than others. Some know less.
6. Some people can learn a lot. Some people can learn only a little.[12]

The second-grade child learns that some people look different, speak differently, and some know more, learn more and have more wealth than others. The differences in wealth are associated with knowledge and ability and are treated as if they are as natural as differences in speech or appearance. If the second grader learns his lesson well, he has taken an important step in his socialization—the acceptance and justification of an economically determined meritocracy. The meritocratic principle, in this context, becomes an explanation and justification for differences in wealth, prestige, status, authority and power. The lower-class child, confronted with this kind of association, is being prepared for what comes later in his life. This child has to be controlled, his character shaped and his aspirations lowered according to the place society has prepared for him. Over and over again, the fear of the unruly masses appears in the literature of the eugenics, testing, guidance, settlement house and Americanization movements on the educational frontier in the first decades of the twentieth century. H. H. Goddard reflected a fairly common theme when in 1920 he said, "The disturbing fear is that the masses—the seventy or even eighty-six million—will take matters into their own hands. The four million or so of superior intelligence must guide and direct the masses." [13] This is no doubt what David Starr Jordan, President of Stanford University, had in mind two decades earlier when he said, "If collective action is to be safe, the best thought of the best men must control it." [14] Edward L.

[12] Lawrence Senesh, S.R.A. *Our Working World.* (Chicago: Science Research Associates, 1965), pp. 177–78.

[13] H. H. Goddard, *Human Efficiency and Levels of Intelligence.* (Princeton: Princeton University Press, 1920), p. 97. For a more current analysis of the way in which the testing process attacks the dignity of the lower-class person and thus locks him into the lower class see Richard Sennett and Jonathan Cobb, *The Hidden Injuries of Class.* (New York: Random House, 1973).

[14] David Starr Jordan, *The Care and Culture of Men.* (San Francisco: Whitaker & Ray Co., 1903), pp. 73–74.

Thorndike spoke of "the perfect power to breed the next generation" and "perfect freedom to regulate their careers." The educational state that emerged during the first three decades of the twentieth century was more than a manpower device through which producers and consumers might be trained for a productive adult life; more concisely, it made the protection of wealth and social power of the privileged classes more secure. The testing movement in addition to the meritocracy served to mask power in order to effectively immobilize any real revolutionary opposition. If a man truly believes that he has a marginal standard of living because he is inferior, he is less likely to take violent measures against that social system than if he believes his condition to be a product of social privilege. In 1965, the Russell Sage Foundation issued a report entitled, *Experiences and Attitudes of American Adults Concerning Standardized Intelligence Tests*, which indicated that lower-class respondents are more likely to believe that intelligence tests actually measure inborn intelligence.

While many might view the meritocracy as fixed by heredity and therefore advocate eugenic control as did Edward L. Thorndike; others like Lewis Madison Terman, seemed to catch the implication of their earlier racial superiority arguments in the burning bodies at Buchenwald, Dachau and Belsen, and began to shift from a less strictly racist position. In many ways the argument over heredity *v* environment is misleading. One can as easily accept a strong hereditarian position and still advocate political, economic and social equality as one might accept a strong environmentalist position and still argue for political, economic and social inequality. The hereditarian argument need not be socially conservative, and the environmentalist argument need not be socially liberal. The key point is that there is, in fact, no inherent logic, either in the mind of man or in the universe which predetermines that differences in intellectual ability necessarily should mean differences in social power. Why, for example, should one be more favorably rewarded because he happened to inherit a superior intelligence, or because he happened to be born into a superior social environment? Repeatedly, from Lewis M. Terman, Edward L. Thorndike, Arthur Jensen or Richard Herrnstein, psychologists have attempted to link ability with the social system in which they lived, and seldom ever questioned the principle meritocracy of itself. By failing to question the ideal assumptions upon which the meritocracy rested, such as the assumptions of equal opportunity and the inherent value of competition, and further to fail to question the hierarchy of values which undergird their own role as professional social science experts in the liberal society, they, in fact, became more often *Servants of Power*.[15] The question of whether the university professor as a professional expert in the

[15] See Loren Baritz, *The Servants of Power*. (New York: John Wiley Press, 1960).

educational state served power or truth is still a fundamental issue in American education today. Nevertheless, within the first half of the twentieth century the university and its "servants" had come to play a key role in the corporate liberal state.

By the beginning of the twentieth century Wisconsin progressives, following in the German tradition, set the pattern for the experts' involvement in reform. The intellectual resources of the university were used to solve social problems resulting from immigration, urbanization and industrialization. The important theme which appears in the educational literature of the first three decades of the century was social efficiency and managed social order. Increasingly, the representatives of the larger financial and corporate interests of American society came to believe that the way in which this social efficiency could be achieved was through application of the principles of the new liberals. While the old liberalism justified individualism and cutthroat competition, the new corporate liberalism which emerged in the thinking of such men as Herbert Croly, Richard Ely, Edward Ross, John R. Commons and others protected the basic structure of wealth and power in the "new order" by increasing the standard of living for a larger middle class. Herbert Croly expressed these sentiments when he suggested that progressive democracy was "designed to serve as a counter poise to the threat of working class revolution." [16] Similarly, the Wisconsin progressive, Richard Ely, defined his philosophy as "progressive conservatism."

The corporate liberal state which emerged by World War I included an array of bureaucratic regulatory agencies which cooperatively worked with business and labor to achieve that optimal balance of interests for all concerned. The logical thrust of corporate industry, as well as the progressive liberals who tended to dominate the new social sciences, was toward the development of a new scientific management to engineer socially for control and order.[17]

Whether it was John R. Commons, Edward A. Ross and Richard T. Ely at the University of Wisconsin; or Samuel Gompers and Andrew Carnegie in the National Civic Federation; or perhaps Jane Addams and Walter Rauchenbusch in the settlements of Chicago and New York, all thought and worked toward a larger, more orderly corporate society utilizing knowledgeable experts to ameliorate the many varied problems of that society. It is fairly common to find the same people involved with educational reform and uplift, also involved in municipal reform, trust regulation and immigration restriction. Old public institutions had to be reorganized to increase the effectiveness of administrative and bureaucratic

[16] James Weinstein, *The Corporate Ideal in the Liberal State*. (Boston: Beacon Press, 1968), p. xi.
[17] See Baritz, *The Servants of Power*.

functions at each level of government.[18] In the private sector, new organizations were created which effectively channeled corporate wealth toward the support of liberal progressive reform. Just as corporate wealth established foundations for research and policy study in the area of foreign policy, the larger financial interests moved to establish philanthropic foundations which profoundly influenced the development of American education. Philanthropic foundations became a major stimulus for political and educational reform.

The educational state, which thus emerged in America between 1900 and 1970 and which came to occupy the time and attention of the bulk of American youth from age 7 to 21, included the many boards and commissions from national, state and local levels of government, foundations and a large cadre of "professional" experts who generally accepted the basic assumptions upon which the system rested. In a very real sense, the educational state was the life system for the larger corporate liberal state which later emerged during the Cold War as a massive militarized system.

The educational state, as a life system for the larger corporate liberal state, served a vital process of supplying trained manpower for production and consumption, as well as perhaps the more important function of keeping large numbers of people off the labor market. In such a mass-production-oriented society, the schools were used to standardize the future citizen as interchangeable parts for an intricate production and consumption system. Testing, guidance and curriculum reform movements all helped to objectify and rationalize the child for his place within the system.

Under the guise of a meritocratic system, the "professional" experts served to stabilize and rationalize a class system based on privilege, status and economic power. These experts, as members of the newly "arrived" lower middle class invariably worked as servants of power within the educational state. Throughout the twentieth century, the complex of issues changed from decade to decade, but the moral problem of the professional as an educational courtier remained. Was it possible to serve truth and power without a conflict of interest or were there times when as a moral person the expert as advisor to those who wield power would be required to choose the hemlock? This was the dilemma of the university professor in the educational state.

---

[18] Increased efficiency in city, state and federal government often meant a corresponding decrease in political influence on the part of the poor and disinherited. See Samuel P. Hays, "The Politics of Reform in Municipal Government in the Progressive Era," Alexander B. Callon Jr., ed., *American Urban History*. (New York: Oxford University Press, 1969).

CHAPTER 1

Academic Freedom and Responsibility: The Role of the Professor in the Educational State

It is not to be expected that kings should philosophize and philosophers should become kings, nor is it to be desired, because the possession of power inevitably destroys the independent judgment of the reason. But in order that both parties may properly understand their functions, it is indispensable that kings or kingly peoples (those governing themselves according to the laws of equality) should not permit the class of philosophers to perish or to become mute, but should allow them to speak openly. And there need be no fears of propagandism in such a case because this class is by its very nature incapable of banding together and forming clubs.[1]

Immanuel Kant

The way in which men have conceptualized the "proper" relationship of knowledge to power and thought to action has profoundly shaped the ways in which they have rationalized their social system. Thus, Immanuel Kant conceived the role of philosopher and the role of king as functionally different and therefore, separate. Power, he argued, inevitably destroys the independent judgment of reason; therefore, philosophers should not engage in political action. His freedom to speak, however, must be protected by the king so that he can carry out his function of inquiry which,

---

[1] Quoted in Friedrich Paulsen, *The German Universities and University Study.* (New York: Charles Scribner's, 1906), p. 254.

in turn, will contribute to the well-being and harmony of the king and the state. Furthermore, Kant argued, the king would automatically be protected from radical "propagandism" by the philosopher's inability to organize and become politically effective. Kant had delineated the role of the nineteenth-century German university professor. That role cast the professor as both a creator of new knowledge and a servant of power.

More than most Western educational institutions, the German university profoundly shaped the course of Western civilization. Pushing back the frontiers of knowledge, the German university set the standard of creative excellence for generations of American and European students. This high creative productivity of both students and professors was usually attributed to the application of the principles of freedom of learning, *Lernfreiheit*, and the freedom of teaching, *Lehrfreiheit*. Just what these principles meant in actual practice in nineteenth-century Germany, and just how these principles were adopted to the American university is crucial in understanding much of the academic freedom dialog in twentieth-century America.

While most American students stood in awe of the great advances in scientific knowledge that resulted from the principles of *Lernfreiheit* and *Lehrfreiheit*, few noticed that both science and academic freedom were first nourished and cradled in an authoritarian class-oriented Prussian society. Repeatedly, American social theorists have confused the struggle for academic freedom and the quest for scientific truth with the struggle of people to gain economic, political and social freedoms. If there is, indeed, any inherent logical relationship between the concept of academic freedom and the social system it serves, that relationship is fundamentally elitist, not equalitarian. The idea of academic freedom is premised on the assumption that some people can think and create new knowledge while others cannot. Indeed, it is often argued that the thinker must be protected by the powerful from the less knowledgeable masses who, in an unreasoning moment, might destroy the goose that laid the golden egg.

Whether the principle of academic freedom is employed by a social system moving toward a more elitist or more equalitarian society, the justification of the practice is the same. It is invariably justified on the grounds of the presumed benefits which will accrue to that society. The principle of freedom to teach, in Germany, was grounded in the assumption that a special freedom was necessary in order to produce new knowledge. *Lehrfreiheit* was not, however, premised on the assumption that such a practice would lead to economic, political or social freedom. The principle of *Lehrfreiheit* did not include the right of the professor to belong to radical, political parties or to advocate unpopular causes publicly or privately. The aristocratic elite which ruled German society was protected against the activities of radical professors and students in a number of ways.

Since the faculty and students were members of the ruling class, they generally could be expected to identify the interests of the state with their own personal interests. Furthermore, as hired officials of the state, the professors were well screened to insure loyalty to the state, scientific objectivity, and noninvolvement in unpopular political action. For example,

> Minister Altenstein, in recommending Hegel for the chair left vacant since Fichte's death, assured King Frederick William III that the philosopher would mind his own business and refrain from participating in the political agitation of the day. He described Hegel's philosophy as moderate and scientific.[2]

G. Stanley Hall and many other Americans who studied at a German university found it to be the "freest spot on earth." While one can recognize that this might be true within the confines of the seminar walls, it should also be recognized that the university was also free from professors who advocated unpopular social and political causes. From the perspective of Kant and others who espoused the principle of *Lehrfreiheit*, this was as it should be, since they believed the roles of philosophers and kings were inevitably separated by function. The function of the king who wields power in practical political action, necessarily must be governed by virtues of conviction, consistency and force of action, colored by a realistic pragmatic opportunism. The scholar on the other hand must maintain, at all times, a theoretical indifference which allows him to pursue theory in accordance wherever the facts may lead. The advocacy role, then, of the man of action necessarily destroys the neutrality function of the scholar. Virtues for the philosopher, it was claimed, were vices for the king; conversely, virtues of the king were vices for the philosopher.[3] In Plato's *Republic*, the philosopher king, when viewing the brilliance of truth, was not and should not be involved in action. It takes years of practical experience, Plato argued, before such a man can properly rejoin his fellows in any leadership capacity in the practical world of action. In spite of such arguments, the German university professor was allowed to engage in politics and advocate popular political and social reforms. The prohibition against the advocacy role of the professor was apparently confined only to unpopular causes. When, for example, Johann Gottlieb Fichte, in his *Address to the German Nation*, called for an education which would fashion the will and moral character of the nation, he saw the university playing an advocacy role.

Freedom to teach, however, even in the theoretical sense, had its limitation. Anarchists, Marxists, and Social Democrats, viewed as enemies

---

[2] Frederic Lilge, *The Abuses of Learning*. (New York: The Macmillan Co., 1948), p. 24.

[3] See Paulsen, pp. 255–256.

of the state, were not allowed to teach in a German university of the nineteenth century. As Friedrich Paulsen put it,

> Suppose that a man had been convinced by his own reflection upon the nature of the state or by the eloquence of a Tolstoi, that the state as an institution of force was an evil, and ought to be destroyed. That, too, would unfit him for the office of a teacher of political science just as it would unfit a person to be a teacher of law if he looked upon the positive law as a foolish burden and a plague—always provided at least that the state is not inclined to abrogate itself and the law in case theory demands it.[4]

In the closing decade of the nineteenth century, when so many American professors were losing their academic positions because of their social, political and economic ideas, Dr. Arons, of the University of Berlin, was dropped from the faculty for belonging to the Social-Democratic party. While the faculty of the University of Berlin conceded that Dr. Arons would be unfit to teach if he taught in the social sciences, it was argued that as a professor of physics, he was of no political danger to the state. Nevertheless, the German Ministry of Education fired Dr. Arons on grounds that membership in the Social-Democratic party ". . . made him unworthy of the confidence which his calling demanded." [5]

Although Professor Paulsen and the faculty of the University of Berlin regretted the dismissal of Professor Arons and looked toward the day when a professor's private life as a Social-Democrat would be seen as non-threatening to the state when he taught physics, neither Paulsen nor the Berlin faculty could conceive of the University ever accepting a Social-Democrat as a professor in the social sciences. The academic freedom of the professor of social science was far more sharply circumscribed than that of the professor of physical sciences.

Thus, the limitations on freedom of inquiry at the German university were fairly clear. First, the professors and students were generally drawn from the aristocratic classes. Second, as hired officials of the state, the professors could not theoretically or practically support any causes which would undermine the authority of the state. Third, the role of the professor as a "scientific" inquirer producing new knowledge was so circumscribed that it prevented any advocacy role which would agitate the public peace and harmony of the state.

The professor's role, although necessarily apolitical, was not construed to make him inactive when it came to protecting the state. Thus, Professor Einstein could advocate the development of the atomic bomb in the interest of the protection of the state, without violating the traditional canons of academic freedom. In these terms, the scholar who worked for the state

4 *Ibid.*, pp. 246–247.
5 *Ibid.*, p. 251.

was involved directly with the social uses of knowledge. The issue, then, becomes not whether the professor has any responsibility in regard to the social uses of knowledge he has created, but what happens when his employer uses that knowledge for objectionable purposes. Is it morally incumbent upon the professor who, on the one hand, readily received honors and laurels from the state for the creation and application of knowledge because he had unique freedoms, to take especially strong stands against the social misuse of that knowledge because he also had a unique responsibility? This was the ethical situation which some atomic scientists keenly felt when they so desperately, frantically, but unsuccessfully attempted to prevent the use of the atomic bomb.[6]

With Hiroshima came the end of scientific innocence. The social implication of "pure" physical science was as devastating as an advocacy role of the social scientist. One of the key pillars supporting academic freedom was the idea of scientific neutrality. The Hiroshima holocaust shook that pillar. As Richard Hofstadter and Walter P. Metzger have pointed out, much of the rationale for academic freedom was based on the two principles of universalism and neutrality which made up a creed signifying, ". . . the brotherhood of man in science that is akin in aspiration to the brotherhood of man in God." [7] This presumably secular, scientific credo nurtured in the German university tended to supplant the basically seminary function of the American college in the latter half of the nineteenth century. The credo included an argument that a free public test of knowledge would result in a kind of scientific universalism which included a respect for evidence, tolerance, objectivity and honesty; while the value of neutrality cultivated by the scientific inquirer would transcend ideology and result in truth. It was this scientific credo which increasingly appeared, from Hiroshima to the Vietnam War, more as an act of faith than fact. The picture of the scientist laboriously producing better means of mass destruction under the guise of neutrality and the disinterested pursuit of truth stood as a tragic mockery to those who saw a potential for the brotherhood of man in science. Nevertheless, by the beginning of the twentieth century, the rhetoric involving the argument for academic freedom in America was charged with the scientific credo. The acceptance of that credo by university professors and the general public was slow and torturous.

One factor which contributed to a rather slow acceptance of the notion of the neutrality of the scientific inquirer was the fact that a practical-minded America usually held little respect for the ivory tower and often

[6] See Robert Jungk, *Brighter Than a Thousand Suns.* (New York: Harcourt Brace, 1958).

[7] See Richard Hofstadter and Walter P. Metzer, *The Development of Academic Freedom in the United States.* (New York: Columbia University Press, 1955), p. 366.

expected to see immediate results in terms of practical action. When that public found the professor "useful" it was usually in his capacity as an applied scientist. In general, it has been true that the theoretical scientist has been allowed a greater range of freedom than the applied scientist. The role of applied scientist is usually restricted by the immediate institution which finds his work relevant. Under the circumstances, such a role is hardly neutral.

A second factor which slowed the acceptance of the "scientific" credo was the fact that the role of the professor in the American college had traditionally been that of a shaper of moral character rooted in both a religious and classical tradition. The American college teacher was carefully screened more for the potential influence he might have on the character and personality of a student, than for his potential in creating new knowledge. John Dewey, in his article on "Academic Freedom" makes a significant distinction between the emergence of a university ideal and the sectarian college of the nineteenth century. Given the function of the earlier sectarian college (religious indoctrination), the hiring and firing practices were tightly controlled by the powers who governed the college. With the gradual emergence of the German university ideal, the scientific credo was increasingly employed to define the role of the professor and to rationalize the hiring and firing practices. In the older sectarian college, faculties were well screened for objectionable ideas. In this sense, the controlling leadership of the community was well protected from possible faculty radicalism. What was to be the nature of the screening device and what assurance and protection did the leadership of the community have against possible faculty radicalism at the new university? Quick answers were not easily forthcoming. Under the circumstances, careful screening of faculty for radical ideas and easy dismissal of faculty for advocating unpopular causes continued. Gradually, however, the scientific credo argument was effectively used to convince a large share of the governors of American educational institutions that objective scientific pursuit of truth would result in the muting of faculty radicalism. With that argument went the further notion that professors must organize into professional organizations not only to protect themselves from society, but also to rationalize and stabilize their condition of employment in order to protect society from the professor who might unscientifically agitate social questions. Interestingly, while Immanuel Kant saw professors as "incapable of banding together and forming clubs" and therefore politically powerless, American professors, under the leadership of John Dewey and others, by 1915 formed the American Association of University Professors (AAUP). Dewey, however, took great pains to point out that the organization was not to protect the immediate interest of professors under fire, but to organize a profession which could stabilize their condition of employment and set the guidelines for policing their own ranks. While the professionalization of faculty by way of the AAUP extended security against faculty radicalism to those who governed American institutions, the faculty, at the same time, gained security from arbitrary dismissal procedures.

The application of the German concept of *Lehrfreiheit* to the American university produced some peculiar stresses and paradoxes, which readily became apparent at the University of Wisconsin in the circumstances which surround the Ely case of 1894. Heavily influenced by the German concept of using the state to ameliorate the social condition arising from industrialization, the Wisconsin progressives used the university for doing research and proposing practical solutions for various economic and social problems. One of the main roots of the development of the liberal educational state runs through that institution to the German university. So extensively was the cooperative idea developed that eventually the University of Wisconsin slogan became, "The boundaries of the campus are the boundaries of the state." Given the function of the university as both a source of knowledge and an advocate of enlightened solutions to potentially controversial social problems, the role of the individual professor became that of not only a producer of knowledge but an advocate of "enlightened solutions." The critical point, here, is what really are "enlightened solutions." The definition is usually provided by the governors of the institutions in terms of the activities which strengthen the interests of those who manage and govern.

In the summer of 1894, Professor Ely was charged with believing in "strikes and boycotts, justifying and encouraging the one while practicing the other." Professor Ely was further charged with having:

> . . . threatened to boycott a local firm whose workers were on strike; to have said that a union man, no matter how dirty and dissipated, was always to be employed in preference to a nonunion man, no matter how industrious and trustworthy; to have entertained and advised a union delegate in his home.[8]

As a professor of economics in a period of acute economic and social conflict, it is not surprising to find Ely being charged with such crimes. What is surprising, however, is that he exonerated himself by testifying publicly that in spite of his sympathetic writings about the labor movement, he never counseled workers to strike, never threatened the use of a consumer boycott, never favored the closed shop, and never entertained a striker in his home. The latter charge was dropped when, during the testimony, it was proven that one of his students, not Ely, had entertained the striker.

[8] As quoted by Hofstadter and Metzger, *The Development of Academic Freedom in the United States*, p. 426.

Ely defined his philosophy as that of "progressive conservatism," which included a kind of limited Christian socialism based on the divine origin of the authority of the state. His beliefs further included an organic conception of the state made up of a natural hierarchy of classes which, in turn, supported a strong rationale for private property.[9] In public testimony he argued that on the whole he was "more conservative" than he had been in the past and that he was one of the first ". . . to examine exhaustively, to expose and to attack unsparingly, anarchy in the United States." [10] The investigation not only proved the original charges false, but essentially demonstrated the "conservativeness" and "safeness" [11] of his views.

This, then, was the Wisconsin Ely case, sometimes referred to as the "Magna Charta" of academic liberty. However, it was not so much the case, as the report of the Regents Investigating Committee, which echoed freely throughout the mythical ivy-covered halls of the twentieth century. The report read in part as follows:

> We feel we would be unworthy of the position we hold if we did not believe in progress in all departments of knowledge. In all lines of academic investigation it is of the utmost importance that the investigator should be absolutely free to follow the indications of truth wherever they may lead. Whatever may be the limitations which trammel inquiry elsewhere we believe the great State University of Wisconsin should ever encourage that continual and fearless sifting and winnowing by which alone the truth can be found.[12]

While Ely basked in the limelight of victory, few noticed the apparent contradiction between the rhetoric and the reality of academic freedom in the Wisconsin case. Stranger, still is the fact that in the midst of the conflict, Professor Ely had publicly testified that if the charges were, in fact, true, then they would ". . . unquestionably unfit me to occupy a responsible position as an instructor of youth in a great university." [13] Just why would Professor Ely consider himself unfit to occupy a responsible position as an instructor of youth if, in fact, those charges were true? How would those charges unfit him? What, then, was Professor Ely's own conception of his role as a teacher at a "great university?" Professor Ely was trained in the German university and had taught previously for eleven years at the first American model of the German university, Johns Hopkins. It is

[9] For Ely's beliefs, see Theron F. Schlabach, "An Aristocrat On Trial: The Case of Richard T. Ely," *Wisconsin Magazine of History*, Vol. XLVII; No. 21, Winter 1963–64.

[10] Merle Curti and Vernon Carstensen, *The University of Wisconsin*, Vol. I. (Madison: University of Wisconsin Press, 1949), p. 516.

[11] *Ibid.*, p. 526.

[12] *Ibid.*, p. 525.

[13] *Ibid.*, p. 516.

possible that the answer to these questions can be found in the German concept of *Lehrfreiheit*. While the German professor took pride in having academic freedom, he also conceived of himself as an agent of the state who would not espouse unpopular causes which, in any way, jeopardized the harmony and security of the state. If one assumes that Ely held the German concept of academic freedom, his position with regard to those charges is understandable. Even the rhetoric of the Regents' statement comes closer to reality when one considers that what the Regents meant by "absolutely free" was true for those areas which they deemed would ultimately contribute to the enlightened harmony and security of the state of Wisconsin. Thus, one might assume that the Regents who signed that document saw little or no contradiction between trying a professor for encouraging strikes, boycotts, or any activity deemed threatening to the harmonious development of the state and announcing the fact that at the great State University of Wisconsin academic freedom flourished. What has been lost over a period of time is a part of the context in which those statements were made. The critical part of the context that explains the paradox is the fact that those men, fresh from the German university experience, automatically assumed definite limitations on their freedom. They in fact saw themselves as servants of the state and the social power that the state wields. The idea that the university is a free marketplace of ideas, where all ideas are equally and fearlessly sifted and winnowed for truth, tends to be a misleading concept which obscures the realities of complex power relationships which exist within and outside of the university. If *all* ideas are not entertained in the university, then the questions are: Which ideas are open for consideration and which are not? Which ideas will be translated into action and which will not? What are the grounds for making these decisions and who decides? Answers to these kinds of questions, though not easily forthcoming, can lead to some sense of the actual boundaries of freedom within the academic community.

Of all Professor Ely's many illustrious students[14] who sent congratulatory messages to their former mentor, only one reflected a degree of concern that he had, perhaps, given up too much. Edward W. Bemis congratulated his former professor for his "glorious victory" but then wrote, "I was sorry only that you seemed to show a vigor of denial as to entertaining a walking delegate or counseling strikers as if either were wrong, instead of under certain circumstances a duty." [15] Before Ely's case was set to rest, Bemis had already been asked to leave his tenured

---

[14] There were many students; to mention just a few: Frederick Jackson Turner, David Kinley, Charles Homer Haskins, Edward A. Ross, John R. Commons, and Albion Small.

[15] As quoted by Hofstadter and Metzger, *The Development of Academic Freedom in the United States*, p. 434.

position at the new University of Chicago. The differences between Ely and Bemis are illuminating. Although both men were liberal reformers, believing in essentially the same kind of solutions for the social problems of their day, they differed in that Bemis saw his role as a professor more in terms of an advocate of what turned out to be unpopular causes, than did his former mentor. Here, again, the problem of the relationship between thought and action is critical. When does a teacher unfit himself as an instructor in a great university? Is it reached when he counsels workers to strike and engage in boycotts or when he counsels politicians to create industrial labor relations' laws which prevent strikes? Or, perhaps the point is reached when he counsels students to strike against the Vietnam War, or when he counsels the military on improving bombing accuracy.

The Bemis case warrants close scrutiny for a number of reasons. First, the case illustrates nicely the problem of relating thought to action, when that action runs against definite power interests. Second, the case is representative of many disputed academic freedom cases in the way in which it reflects the difficulty in objectively determining the reason for dismissal. Third, the case involves the influence of powerful people outside the academic community. Fourth, the case illustrates the pattern of charges, counter-charges, frail human judgments, and conflicts of purpose so characteristic of most academic freedom cases.

Hofstadter has suggested that perhaps Ely won and Bemis lost his case because not only did Ely carry more status and national prestige within the academic community, but Bemis appeared to be up against a more sophisticated and powerful antagonist. In Wisconsin, the charges were made by a relatively unpopular state Superintendent of Public Instruction, while in the Bemis case charges were never stated publicly until after Bemis had been forced to resign. While this hypothesis might be true, it is also clear that Bemis was far more the Ralph Nader type of advocate which led him directly into conflict with powerful interests. For example, shortly before accepting the position at the University of Chicago, he had written a controversial article dealing with the ownership of utilities. In the article, he was not content to discuss the advantage of public ownership of utilities in general terms, as Professor Ely might have done. Rather, he pinpointed the problem in the various Gas Trusts and the exorbitant, unfair rates those private concerns were charging the people in Chicago and other major cities across the nation. It was essentially this kind of activity which led him into serious conflicts at the University of Chicago.

Edward Bemis was hired by President William Rainy Harper as a tenured associate professor to teach in both the university extension division and in Professor Laughlin's department of political economy at the University of Chicago. Bemis took up his duties with the university in the fall of 1892. The doors of the University of Chicago had just opened due to the generous financial support of John D. Rockefeller. Within the year, Bemis had run afoul of significant interests in the Chicago area. Bemis testified that during the summer of 1893 a "prominent officer in the Gas Trust, already controlling the gas supply of over forty cities said to him: Professor Bemis, we can't and don't intend to tolerate your work any longer. It means millions to us. And if we can't convert you we are going to down you." [16] That same summer, the Chicago Gas Trust, then not connected with Standard Oil, refused to grant a customary reduction in gas rates to the university. The connection between this event and Bemis's role at the university, however, is only circumstantial. During the fall term, Bemis's course enrollment at extension began to fall off and three months later, on January 2, 1894, Harper asked Bemis to resign. Bemis refused, and Harper then exerted more pressure until Bemis finally resigned in the summer of 1895. During the year and a half interim, the case received extensive national publicity.

Although Harper and the university insinuated incompetence, they never brought formal public charges against him. Not until the fall of 1895, after Bemis had resigned, were the charges against him even made public. In a lengthy correspondence between Bemis and Ely, it is clear that Bemis had made his case to the press on a number of occasions, while the university, under Harper's direction, had refrained from talking about Bemis's case. This was done in the name, interestingly enough, of protecting the professor against bad publicity. The university strategy to remove Bemis was simply to deny any restriction of freedom of expression and to deny any connection of the case with the "Chicago gas monopoly." When the incompetence charges were finally made, they were based largely on course enrollments in his extension classes. There appeared to have developed a concern for the proper strategy for removing Bemis. In retrospect, Albion Small wrote Harper:

> At this distance it seems . . . clear that the Bemis case would have been bungled if you had given the papers more than you did. Denial that it had any connection with a principle of freedom was enough, and it has been impertinence in the papers to ask for more.[17]

Harper had not bungled the job. Bemis's academic career was "downed." He never seemed to live down the partisan malcontent and incompetence label that became part of his academic reputation. After a short tenure at Kansas State, he and Frank Parsons were dismissed for their "position on economic questions," (1899). Shortly thereafter, he became superintendent of the water department in Cleveland, and later became a member of the

---

[16] *The Literary Digest*, August 31, 1895.
[17] Letter of Albion Small to President Harper, August 27 (undated), From the Small File, University of Chicago Archives.

advisory board of the Valuation Bureau of the Interstate Commerce Commission.

Just why was Professor Bemis asked to resign his position at Chicago? Was he really incompetent? The testimony that Ely and others gave indicates that he was not. Was he too radical? It seems fairly clear that Professor Charles Zeublin and Professor Thorstein Veblen, in the same department, held far more radical views than Professor Bemis. The academic crime Bemis appears to have committed was that he managed to locate, confront, and offend key people who existed as part of the power structure in the Chicago University community. For example, during the height of the conflict over the Pullman Strike, Bemis was invited by Dr. Barrows, a member of the university faculty and pastor of the First Presbyterian Church, to speak to his congregation. On July 15, 1894, Bemis gave a speech at the church in which he criticized both labor and management's involvement in the Pullman Strike. After criticizing labor, he turned his attention to the railroads and argued:

> If the railroads would expect their men to be law-abiding, they must set the example. Let their open violations of the interstate-commerce law, and their relations to corrupt Legislatures and assessors testify as to their part in this regard. I do not attempt to justify the strikers in their boycott of the railroads; but the railroads themselves not long ago placed an offending road under the ban and refused to honor its tickets. Such boycotts on the part of the railroads are no more to be justified than is a boycott of the railroads by the strikers.[18]

President Hughitt of the Chicago and Northwestern Railroad, a member of Dr. Barrow's congregation, engaged Bemis in heated discussion. After this exchange, he registered a complaint about Bemis's speech to key members of the university trustees. In response to the heated debate in Dr. Barrow's church, President Harper wrote Bemis on July 28, 1894.

> Your speech at the First Presbyterian Church has caused me a great deal of annoyance. It is hardly safe for me to venture into any of the Chicago clubs. I am pounced upon from all sides. I propose that during the remainder of your connection with the University you exercise great care in public utterances about questions that are agitating the mind of the people.[19]

Shortly thereafter, on August 6, 1894, J. Lawrence Laughlin, chairman of the department of political economy, (Bemis was shifted from his department to Small's department of sociology) wrote Harper, "I fear the affair

---

[18] Bemis Press Statement, October 9, 1895, Bemis File, Chicago Archives. For many of the insights used here with respect to the Bemis case, the author is indebted to Harold E. Berquist's essay, "The Edward W. Bemis Controversy," 1959.

[19] *Ibid.*

in Dr. Barrow's Church has been a last straw to some good friends of the University, like A. A. Sprague. And in antagonizing President Hughitt he is making very hard the establishment of a great railway interest in the University." [20]

This, indeed, had been the last of a series of straws which offended the "good friends" of the university. While this appears to be the reason for Bemis's dismissal, in the opinions of Laughlin, Small and Harper, the issue was one of incompetence. Bemis was being held to account for his "partisan unscientific methods" of his work.[21] At the following June convocation, President Harper asserted that a professor should not:

> . . . confound personal pleading for scientific thought. Where such con-
> fusion arises the time has come for us to forfeit our positions of officers in
> the University because we have mistaken the purpose for which we were
> appointed and because we have forgotten that to serve the University we
> must employ scientific methods and do scientific work.[22]

The argument that "scientific method" somehow frees one from the prior partisan question of who that approach serves is an argument which consistently reappears in the academic freedom literature of the twentieth century. The presumed neutrality of "scientific" work is, of course, a basic tenet of the scientific credo which undergirds the rationale for academic freedom. It is interesting that the "scientific" argument seems to be used more often in restricting the range of inquiry than in extending it.

Bemis was charged with incompetence and dismissed without a trial or public hearing. In the twentieth century, John Dewey and others in the American Association of University Professors labored long and hard to create institutional practices and procedures which would prevent this occurrence. However, uniform sets of procedures alone cannot protect against unfair dismissal. In the hands of unfair or frightened people, uniform practices can easily be used as an institutional weapon to protect it from charges that it is responding to political and economic influence.

The university is, after all, a political and economic institution, serving very definite political and economic purposes and interests. Repeatedly, however, the rhetoric of academic freedom is used to obscure those purposes and interests. The liberal ideal of a free university where professors are free to pursue *all* forms of knowledge without restraint of the larger society is one such concept. The educational rhetoric often tends to mis-

---

[20] Letter from Laughlin to Harper, August 6, 1894, Laughlin File, Chicago Archives.

[21] It is interesting that Laughlin regretted the fact that Ely was being tried for his beliefs rather than his "partisan unscientific methods of work." See *Ibid*.

[22] The Statement of the President of the University for the Quarter Ending June 30, 1895." *The Quarterly Calendar*, IV, No. 1, (University of Chicago, August 1895), p. 15.

lead those seeking to understand the operations of the university within the educational state. Thus, one might take seriously William Rainy Harper's public educational rhetoric when, in 1895, he said:

> From the beginning of the University, there has never been an occasion for condemning the utterance of any professor upon any subject, nor has any objection been taken to the teachings of a professor, and in reference to the particular teachings of an instructor no interference has ever taken place.[23]

The fact remains, however, that only the year before, in private correspondence, he cautioned Professor Bemis to take "care in public utterances about questions that are agitating the mind of the people." While "sifting and winnowing" may, at times, satisfy one's sense of utopian idealism, it should not be allowed to obscure one's view of the men who run the threshing machine. The following Bemis case documents are relevant for highlighting the many issues that set the realistic boundaries within which the real boundaries of academic freedom may be assessed.

Following the Bemis documents are a series of letters which take one behind the scenes of scientific objectivity and show the direct influence of business on the affairs of the University of Chicago. These letters are samples of different kinds of involvement. First, there is a letter to Rockefeller from Harper, asking advice in hiring a history professor. Second, there is a letter from F. T. Gates, Rockefeller's executive secretary, to Harper, calling his attention to an offensive newspaper account of Professor Albion Small's address to a senior class. This is followed by Rockefeller's letter of inquiry requesting an explanation, which in turn, is followed by Harper's letter accounting for what presumably happened. Lastly, there is a letter from F. T. Gates to Harper, advising him not to write for a particular magazine because of an attack on Standard Oil which evidently appeared in that journal. The direct influence of the financial donor on the academic affairs of the University of Chicago is self-evident.

Hardly had the heated arguments over the limits of freedom at the University of Chicago receded from public view when another firing at a major private university occurred. On November 13, 1900, Edward Ross was forced to resign from Stanford University for taking stands on significant economic and social issues that conflicted with the perceived economic interests of the major contributors of Stanford University. Ross had repeatedly taken public stands on issues involving silver and public regulation of private utilities. The issue, however, that apparently made

---

[23] "The Statement of the President of the University for the Quarter Ending September 30, 1895." *The Quarterly Calendar*, IV, No. 2, (University of Chicago, November 1895), p. 13.

Ross *persona non grata* at Stanford University was the question of the exclusion of Oriental coolie labor. Throughout Professor Ross's personal papers and public utterances runs a distinctive fear of the "yellow peril" rooted in a strong racial bias. These views led him to speak out strongly against the emigration of Japanese and Chinese coolie labor into this country.

The unpopularity of Ross's speeches among the financial interests supporting Stanford University can easily be appreciated when one considers that a fairly large share of the personal railroad fortunes which created and maintained Stanford were themselves created, and indeed, sustained by a large supply of coolie labor. Ross, interestingly enough, was not fired because of his racist views but because his racist views ran counter to the prevailing economic interest of those who governed Stanford University.[24] The limits on freedom for the university professor could be found at precisely those points at which he cut across the limits and was penalized for doing so. Reacting to the Ross firing, Lester Frank Ward perceptively put his finger on the issue when he said:

> They may talk all they please about the freedom of the universities, but there is no freedom, and everybody I know is playing a role to conciliate controlling interests.[25]

Professor Edward Ross' Press Statement Regarding His Forced Resignation from Stanford University, November 13, 1900

At the beginning of last May a representative of organized labor asked Dr. Jordan to be one of the speakers at a mass meeting called to protest against coolie immigration, and to present "the scholar's view." He was unable to attend, but recommended me as a substitute. Accordingly I accepted, and on the evening of May 7th read a twenty-five minute paper from the platform of Metropolitan Hall in San Francisco. My remarks

---

[24] See Edward A. Ross, *Seventy Years of It: An Autobiography*. (New York: Appleton–Century Co., 1936), pp. 64–86. Also see Letter from Ross to Ward, Stanford University, Calif., October 14, 1900; and Ward to Ross, Washington, D. C., October 26, 1900 found in the *American Sociological Review*, Vol. II, 1946, pp. 741–743.

[25] *American Sociological Review*, p. 743.

appeared in part in the San Francisco dailies of May 8th, and in full, on May 19th, in a weekly called "Organized Labor."

I tried to show that, owing to its high, Malthusian birth-rate, the Orient is the land of "cheap men," and that the coolie, though he cannot outdo the American, can underlive him. I took the ground that the high standard of living that restrains multiplication in America will be imperiled if Orientals are allowed to pour into this country in great numbers before they have raised their standard of living and lowered their birth-rate. I argued that the Pacific is the natural frontier of East and West, and that California might easily experience the same terrible famines as India and China if it teemed with the same kind of men. In thus scientifically coordinating the birth-rate with the intensity of the struggle for existence, I struck a new note in the discussion of Oriental immigration, which, to quote one of the newspapers, "made a profound impression."

At Stanford University the professors are appointed from year to year and receive their re-appointment early in May. I did not get mine then, but thought nothing of it until, on May 18th, Dr. Jordan told me that, quite unexpectedly to him, Mrs. Stanford had shown herself greatly displeased with me and had refused to re-appoint me. He had heard from her just after my address on coolie immigration. He had no criticism for me and was profoundly distressed at the idea of dismissing a scientist for utterances within the scientist's own field. He made earnest representations to Mrs. Stanford and on June 2nd, I received my belated re-appointment for 1900–1901. The outlook was such, however, that on June 5th I offered the following resignation:

> Dear Dr. Jordan: I was sorry to learn from you a fortnight ago that Mrs. Stanford does not approve of me as an economist and does not want me to remain here. It was a pleasure, however, to learn at the same time of the unqualified terms in which you had expressed to her your high opinion of my work and your complete confidence in me as a teacher, a scientist and a man.
>
> While I appreciate the steadfast support you have given me, I am unwilling to become a cause of worry to Mrs. Stanford, or of embarrassment to you. I, therefore, beg leave to offer my resignation as professor of sociology, the same to take effect at the close of the academic year, 1900–1901.

When I handed in the above, Dr. Jordan read me a letter which he had just received from Mrs. Stanford, and which had, of course, been written without knowledge of my resignation. In this letter she insisted that my connection with the university end, and directed that I be given my time from January 1st to the end of the academic year.

My resignation was not acted upon at once, and efforts were made by President Jordan and the President of the Board of Trustees to induce Mrs. Stanford to alter her decision. These proved unavailing, and on Monday, November 12th, Dr. Jordan accepted my resignation in the following terms:

> I have waited till now in the hope that circumstances might arise which would lead you to a reconsideration. As this has not been the case, I, therefore, with great reluctance, accept your resignation to take effect at your own convenience. In doing so, I wish to express once more the high esteem in which your work as a student and a teacher, as well as your character as a man, is held by all your colleagues.

My coolie immigration speech is not my sole offense. Last April I complied with an invitation from the Unitarian Church of Oakland to lecture before them on "The Twentieth Century City." I addressed myself almost wholly to questions of city growth and city health and touched only incidentally on the matter of public utilities. I pointed out, however, the drift, both here and abroad, toward the municipal ownership of water and gas works, and predicted that, as regards street railways, American cities would probably pass through a period of municipal ownership and then revert to private ownership under regulation. My remarks were general in character and, of course, I took no stand on local questions. Only months of special investigation could enable me to say whether a particular city like Oakland or San Francisco could better itself by supplying its own water or light. Yet this lecture was objected to.

Last year I spoke three times in public, once before a university extension center on "The British Empire," once before a church on "The Twentieth Century" and once before a mass meeting on coolie immigration. To my utterances on two of these occasions objection has been made. It is plain, therefore, that this is no place for me. I cannot with self-respect decline to speak on topics to which I have given years of investigation. It is my duty as an economist to impart, on occasion, to sober people, and in a scientific spirit, my conclusions on subjects with which I am expert. And if I speak I cannot but take positions which are justified by statistics and by the experience of the old world, such as the municipal ownership of water works or the monopoly profits of street car companies; or by standard economic science such as the relation of the standard of life to the density of population.

I have long been aware that my every appearance in public drew upon me the hostile attention of certain powerful persons and interests in San Francisco and redoubled their efforts to be rid of me. But I had no choice but to go straight ahead. The scientist's business is to know some things clear to the bottom, and if he hides what he knows, he loses his virtue.

I am sorry to go, for I have put too much of my life into this university not to love it. My chief regret in leaving is that I must break the ties that bind me to my colleagues of seven years and must part from my great chief, Dr. Jordan.

Dr. Ely Denies Charges Against Him

*Every Charge against Him False
So He Declares to the Chautauquans.
State Superintendent Wells Pictured in
Peppery Phrase—Every one of His
Allegations Impaled as a Lie—Ely's
Position on Socialism and Anarchy
Fully Defined*

CHAUTAUQUA, N.Y., AUG. 15   In the amphitheater at 11 o'clock yesterday forenoon Dr. Richard T. Ely made to an immense audience what he termed a "personal statement." It was in fact an answer to the published communication of State Superintendent O. E. Wells, of Wisconsin, criticising Dr. Ely's conduct during the printers' strike in the Madison (Wis.), Democrat office more than a year ago, and also his teachings and writings. Profound attention was paid to Dr. Ely.

"A solemn sense of duty," said he, "not merely to myself but to my family, my friends, my opinions and the institutions with which I am connected compels me to overcome my repugnance to a personal declaration touching certain things of which I have been publicly accused. The rising flood of calumny and falsehood, which has spared not even my conduct in my own home, must be met by a clear and explicit statement and an appeal for justice to the fair-minded American public.

"You, my friends, have read with amazement the charges which have been brought against me. It is said that I not only believe in strikes and boycotts, but have justified and encouraged them, having given counsel and assistance to striking printers in the city of Madison, Wis., and having entertained a walking delegate at my house, with whom I was in constant consultation, while he was managing the strike. It is alleged that I demanded that a printing office, which was doing some printing for a society of which I was secretary, should become a union office, that I told one of the proprietors that the most disreputable union printer was preferable to the most upright and skillful non-union man, and that, finally, I withdrew the printing when my demands were not acceded to. It is stated that my opinions, as expressed in my books, are socialistic and anarchistic, affording 'a seeming moral justification to attacks upon life and property, such as the country has become too familiar with.' These are the charges brought against me, and surely they are grave enough. *If true, they, unquestionably, unfit me to occupy a responsible position as an instructor of youth in a great university.*[1]

---

[1] Italicizing added for emphasis.

"Taking up, first, the series of charges brought against my conduct and character, I deny each and every one in each and every particular. I defy the author of these base and cruel calumnies to prove one statement that he has made, and until he does so I shall hold him up to the public as an unmanly and shameless slanderer. I have never, to my knowledge, exchanged a word with a striking printer in Madison; I never entertained a walking delegate at my house; I never, so far as I can recollect, expressed any opinion about any strikes in Madison, except to condemn them. I never demanded of the printers for the society in question that they should make their office a union office, and the bills, in possession of the treasurer of the society shows that they and all the printing there was, including work given after they had won their strike and made their office a non-union office. The short time which I may take does not permit further details, which are of interest and importance. The man who makes these charges against me is well known to his neighbors as a politician of the meaner sort, who, too small to appreciate the most important trust ever committed to him, betrayed it in his insensate love of notoriety. As to my views, I have nothing to retract. I may have modified my opinions, for only fools never change, and as the years have passed I have shared a common fate and become, on the whole, more conservative. But in the main, the views I now hold I have held for years, and they are so clearly expressed in my writings that no honest and intelligent man, who reads my books with care, need misunderstand them.

"The assertion that I favor strikes and boycotts must impress the candid reader of my works as false and malignant. Repeatedly have I pointed to the disastrous nature of the railway strikes in particular, and predicted the failure which we have recently witnessed. When the hard times were coming on, forseeing the probability of industrial troubles, I commended to working men the advice not to strike, pointing out the probability of failure, and urged upon employers a conciliatory policy. This was in an article on The Unemployed, in Harpers' Weekly. In conversation in these grounds, with the distinguished commissioner of labor, Hon. C. D. Wright, he bluntly pronounced the idea that anything I have said or done could have promoted strikes, as 'idiotic.'

"As to trades unions, I have held, and still hold, that their province must be a limited one, and I expect less from them than economists like Prof. Brentano, and the late Thorold Rogers. The old-fashioned, striking trades' union has outlived its time and usefulness. In my last two works, namely Outlines of Economics, and Socialism and Social Reform, I clearly show the limitations of labor organizations.

"But am I not a socialist? On the contrary, I have thought that agriculture offered insuperable obstacles to its proposed organization of industry, and I have maintained that even could socialism be organized and put in operation, it would stop progress and overthrow our civilization.

"But what about anarchy? I was the first writer to examine exhaustively, to expose and to attack unsparingly, anarchy in the United States. This I did in my Labor Movement in America. The propaganda of anarchy is a dire national calamity against which all right minded people should work with all the resources at their command. Especially should the wage earning people shun all connection with it. It is of hell, and its slightest touch brings disaster to them and all others. Plague, pestilence, and famine combined are mild evils compared with wide-spread anarchy. Anything more foreign to my thought and feeling than anarchy I do not know; anything more diametrically opposed to my social philosophy I cannot conceive. In obedience to the laws and constituted authorities of the land lies our only hope of progress.

"But it is alleged my teachings have a pernicious influence on my students, making them socialists and anarchists. I have been teaching for thirteen years and my students are mostly young men; but you know some of them, and more than one has begun to acquire national fame. Who are these dangerous men? Shall I name a few? They are men like Profs. Turner, Haskins, Scott, Blackmar, Ross, Warner, Charles Lee Smith, Bemis, Small, Commons, Powers, Kinley, Gould, Wilson, Dewey, President John Finley; journalists like Edward Ingle, George P. Morris, W. B. Shaw, Robert Finley and Albert Shaw; workers in associated charities and municipal reform, like McDougall, Hubbard, Ayres, and Tolman. A host of others in various walks of life could be named; men who, wherever they are, are faithfully discharging the duties of citizenship, are prominent in all good works, are leaders in their community, who are contributing of their strength and resources to the elevation and advancement of humanity. Of few things will I boast, but my students I will boast. No other flock had fewer black sheep, and of those to whom I have borne the relation of teacher, I will say, like the noble Roman matron: 'These are my jewels.'

"The University of Wisconsin and other American colleges and universities have been assailed in sensational and wild stories which reached their climax in a recently published, and widely circulated book. Others will speak when the time comes, and among them I am confident will be my friend, the honored president of the University of Wisconsin, who is falsely and maliciously accused of having rebuked me for my doctrines. I will simply express the conviction that never heretofore have these institutions of learning done work of such high quality as to scholarship; never before have they exercised such a beneficent influence on the youth of the land, as at present. It is my belief that parents and the general public may safely refuse to heed the noisy talk of alarmists.

"Finally, I have not attempted to nail every lie, nor to refute every insult with which I have been unfairly assailed. It is needless. So far as history may deign to judge the people and events involved in this unpleasant affair, persuaded that it will mete out justice to all concerned, I calmly await its final verdict. Fearlessly I bide my time."

A Department Chairman Fears Prof. Bemis Has Damaged the Railroad Interest in the University

THE UNIVERSITY OF CHICAGO
HYDE PARK

NEWMAN, N.Y.
AUG. 6, 1894

Dear Pres. Harper,

Mr. Ely has stated in Madison that he was offered the position I now hold, but refused it "because the institution was supported in part by a monopolist." Is that true? Judging from what you have told me I supposed he had never had any offer from you, even to Small's chair. I regret that the trustees of the University of Wisconsin are examining Ely merely on the grounds of his beliefs—if that is a correct report. If at all, he should be held to account for partisan unscientific methods of work; if that cannot be shown, there is no case against him.

This recalls Bemis. I fear the affair in Dr. Barrows' church has been a last straw to some good friends of the University, like A. A. Sprague. And in antagonizing Pres. Hughitt, he is making very hard the establishment of a great railway interest in the University. And Bemis is wholly one-sided on this railway question. I have looked into it; but I could do nothing without throwing out all his railway lectures. This was some time ago. At every turn in Chicago, in July, I heard indignant remarks about Bemis, and I had nothing whatever to do in introducing the subject. I know you have done what seemed best to stop him; and Small has told me regretfully how he somewhat spoiled your arrangement; but in my opinion, the duty to the good name of the University now transcends any softheartedness to an individual. I do not now see how we can escape saving ourselves except by letting the public know that he goes because we do not regard him as up to the standard of the University in ability and scientific methods. It would have been better for him to have gone quietly. You probably know he told Small that his hold on the working classes was so strong that the University dare not drop him—or something to that purport. I believe you will find the Extension men of my opinion—certainly Mr. Butler.

At any rate, I see Bemis is no longer in my Department; and I understand that his economic lectures will not be announced next year by the Extension Division. The labor subjects will be covered by Brooks. As regards the money lectures, I have a suggestion. How would it do to tie to us in this way Prof. Kinley, of the University of Illinois. Is it feasible? Could he not be asked to give 6 or 12 lectures on money, appear in our list as an Extension lecturer, and yet hold his position at Champaign? His work is of a radically different kind from Bemis', and yet he was one of Ely's men. You can also get Miller's idea of Kinley. I quite like him; and he would, I think, welcome getting closer to us. His book on the "Independent Treasury" is quite good. This is only a suggestion. If it is worthless, then better no lectures at all on money than those Bemis gives.

I should be very glad to have the sheets giving the courses for "my baby" by the end of the week, so that I can finish my work before I leave here at the end of August. During September I shall be on the go, and unable to work.

I have a translation of about 140 pages to publish in the autumn on the "Indian Currency Question." Have you anything to say against Veblen's contract on the Cohn?

Sincerely yours,

J. LAWRENCE LAUGHLIN

President Harper Requests Prof. Bemis' Resignation

CHICAGO JAN. 2, 1894

My dear Prof. Bemis:

I write you this letter because I think I can state what is in my mind more easily in writing than in conversation. You will remember that I was very anxious to have you take hold of the work with us in the University, and you will recall the battle I had with some of our gentlemen in reference to it, a battle fought and won. I counted upon great results from the Extension work, and I hoped that as time passed there would be opportunities for your doing a larger amount of work in the University Proper. As matters now stand the Extension work has been this year largely a failure so far as you are concerned, and instead of the opportunity becoming better on your part for work in the University Proper, the doors seem to be closing. You will perhaps be surprised, but it is necessary for me to say that it does not seem best for us to look forward to your coming more

definitely into the work of the University Proper. After a long consideration of the matter, and a study of all circumstances; looking at it too from
your point of view and with a view to your interests, I am persuaded that
in the long run you can do in another institution because of the peculiar
circumstances here, a better and more satisfactory work to yourself than
you can do here. I am very sorry to say this, for as I need not assure you,
I am personally very much attached both to you and to Mrs. Bemis. You
are, however, man of the world enough to know that unless one is in the
best environment, he cannot work to the best advantage. You are so well
known and your ability so widely recognized that there will surely be no
difficulty in securing for you a good position, one in which you will be
monarch, and one in which you will be above all things else independent. I
wish to say that I will do all I can, and I think I can do much to help you in
this matter, and I beg you to understand that I have come to this conclusion
after much study and with greatest reluctance. If you will accept this and
allow me to help you, I am sure that we can arrange matters in a first rate
way. The interests of all I think would be conserved if the new arrangement could be made for the year beginning July 1st or Oct. 1st. I shall be
very glad to meet you, not to discuss this, for I think it best to call it
settled, but to discuss the question of your future work, in which I wish to
express the deepest interest. You will, I am confident, distinguish in your
mind between the official act which I am compelled to perform, and the
personal attitude which I wish now and always to assume toward you. I
should be glad to see you at your earliest convenience.

Yours very truly,

W. R. HARPER

Dr. Ely Defends His Former Student, Prof. Bemis

UNIVERSITY OF WISCONSIN
MADISON, WIS., AUGUST 24, 1895

Hamilton W. Mabie Esq.,
Editor of the "Outlook,"
New York City, N.Y.

My Dear Mr. Mabie:

I see that I cannot any longer escape a very disagreeable duty. I have
felt for some time that I ought to write you a letter regarding Professor

Bemis, and the utterances in the last "Outlook" show me that I must tell you at once what I believe about this case, for I feel that you are in great danger of being misled. I will speak about one thing after another, without attempting any very logical arrangements of my thoughts. As I am very busy, I trust you will find this explanation satisfactory.

I will say at once, that it is my firm conviction that Professor Bemis, who is stronger than any man they now have in the department of economics, would be a member of the faculty of the University of Chicago in good standing had he not held the views which he entertains. It is claimed by the University of Chicago that opinions more radical than those of Dr. Bemis's are held by other members of the faculty. I suppose Professor Zeublin is really more radical than Dr. Bemis. I asked some time ago a member of the faculty, how it happened that Zeublin could retain his position? The explanation was, that although Zeublin's views were quite pronounced and probably socialistic, the nature of his work did not bring him into conflict with any great corporations. His work was more general dealing with the literary aspects of social questions very largely, while Dr. Bemis's work has been more special. I believe this is Professor Zeublin's own view. I have no doubt Professor Zeublin is quite as brave as Dr. Bemis, but the nature of his work is such that he does not feel called upon to deal specially with the gas question, street car corporations, etc. Dr. Bemis is not by any means radical, but he happened to take interest in one or two lines of scientific work which appear to be particularly dangerous. You can see how plausible it is to say that other members of the force of the University of Chicago are more radical, but this explanation does not stand the test of any critical examination.

You stated in your editorial a few words in regard to the continuance of Professor Bemis's service by the University of Chicago, which are hardly in keeping with the best university traditions. It appears all right until you look into the facts of the case. Professor Bemis had a permanent engagement at Vanderbilt University. The authorities of that institution wished to retain his service. Professor C. F. Smith, now the head of our Greek department, and others made special efforts to induce him to remain. He was strongly urged to go to Chicago by President Harper and others, and they gave him the most satisfactory assurance that, that would not happen, which has happened. He has their letters still in his possession. He was not engaged merely for University Extension Work, but for inside work also, a fact which the authorities of the University of Chicago did not mention. He had some apprehension himself in regard to University Extension, but he received assurances from President Harper which satisfied him. Now he is dropped and an attempt is made to ruin him by the statement that his work is unsatisfactory. Our Professor C. F. Smith is, however, ready to publish a statement over his own name, speaking of Professor Bemis's work at Vanderbilt University in high terms. Why should a man who succeeded at Vanderbilt become a failure in Chicago? The truth is, that Professor Bemis is far stronger than he ever was before, as a teacher and original student. I never valued him so highly as I do now. I do not mean personally, but as a professor and student of Economics.

It is true that on the popular platform Professor Bemis can attain only a moderate success, but if his work as a popular lecturer was not satisfactory he should have been given inside work. However, when you look into the facts of the case, you find that his success as a University Extension lecturer has been fair. Any one who examines the statistics regarding the courses which Professor Bemis has given and reads letters which have been written from University Extension centers, will be forced to the conclusion that the University of Chicago had no excuse for dropping him, even from the standpoint of his University Extension work alone.

The University of Chicago gives out figures which seem to show that the institution has lost money on his work. First of all, the question must be asked, is a university to be regarded as a money making institution? Apart from that, however, we must remember Professor Bemis's work inside the university, but for that they make no allowance whatever when they say that the university has lost money on his work.

Professor Bemis's strength is in the class room, but in the class room he never had any fair chance at the University of Chicago. If you go to this institution, and mingle freely with the students, you will find that it required something like an act of heroism on their part to attend Professor Bemis's lectures. Professor Laughlin made it known from the start, that Professor Bemis was unwelcome and that students had better leave his course alone. I think it was in his opening lecture that Professor Laughlin made insulting remarks about the work in Political Economy in the Johns Hopkins University, and said that students who came from that institution would not be allowed any credit for what they had done, but that they must begin over again. Professor Porrin now of Alleghany College at Meadville, Pa., went to President Harper and told him he could not take any work in Political Economy. What kind of a chance could a man have who was antagonized from the very start by the head of his department? The organization of the University of Chicago is such that he could have no show at all. . . .

I now come to the part of my letter which I write with the greatest reluctance, because it relates to one, who for years, was my personal friend. Of course you know I refer to President Harper. President Harper, although in many respects estimable, was never a man of a very high moral type. During the three years he has been at the University of Chicago, I think he has been going down the hill morally, and I am not alone in this opinion. He has, I think come to a parting of the ways more than once, and has taken the downward path. He is a man who quibbles and whose statements cannot be taken to cover the whole case. When you wrote to him, of course, he gave you satisfactory answers. Professor Bemis is morally a higher type of a man, and far more ingenuous. President Harper's statements, if brought to Dr. Bemis, appear to be misleading in the light of simple statements and documentary evidence. Harper says that no benefactor of the university has urged the removal of Dr. Bemis, or made statements in regard to the teachings in the University of Chicago. Why should they? You can feel what is in the atmosphere. As Professor Smith says, "You do not need to tell a flock of sheep when a thunder storm is coming, they can feel it and see it."

What happened at Chautauqua last summer, throws a good deal of light on the situation. About the time President Harper and I were there, Professor Bemis had been attacked by a railway president. At that time, also, a fool article in regard to the teachings in American Universities had appeared in many different newspapers as it was a syndicate article. Radical opinions were attributed to the department of sociology of the University of Chicago. President Harper placed all the blame upon Professor Bemis. He was very much annoyed. At that time he had nothing to say about the quality of Dr. Bemis's work, but his annoyance was simply on account of the views which Dr. Bemis held. He wrote him a letter which Dr. Bemis now has, in which he proposed that during the remainder of his (Dr. Bemis's) connection with the University of Chicago, he should exercise great discretion in his public utterances.

Although we have been friends for years, President Harper's conduct towards me last summer was anything but friendly. You remember it was at the time of the trouble in Madison. President Harper never offered me one word of sympathy or encouragement. When I asked him to read over my public statement at Chautauqua, and give me his opinion of it before it was made, he did so with reluctance and impatience. When urged by Mr. Frank Beard now of the Ram's Horn—an honest and fearless man—to exort himself in my behalf, his reply was, "but Dr. Ely's opinions." His solicitude at that time touched merely views held. Moreover I have heard President Harper say, without the slightest reservation, that in the conflict between labor and capital he was on the side of the capitalists every time, because it was from them that the University of Chicago must draw its money. . . .

This brings me in conclusion to your last letter. You seemed to think it strange that I took exception to what you said about my being a radical. I suppose every man is limited by his own occupation. I dare say I cannot understand the position of a journalist, and probably a journalist cannot quite understand the position of a professor. Let me suppose a case, however. Suppose if you should become known as a radical you would lose your position on the "Outlook," and on account of alleged radicalism you could never secure any other position. Would you not under these circumstances feel a little sensitive about the epithet "radical"? You see what it can do in the case of Professor Bemis. I hope I am no coward. With all my faults, I do not think that anyone has ever accused me of cowardice. If I were a radical or a socialist, I trust I should have grace enough to say so, and to take the consequence. What I object to is having a burden which does not properly belong to me placed on me. It seems to me that no one can read my books fairly and call be a radical. I think I am more conservative than those with whom I was compared to my disadvantage in the "Outlook." I bring this up simply because I do not wish to have you think that I was unreasonable, and not because I wish to continue any discussion of this particular case.

Regretting that I did not see you either here or at Colorado Springs, I remain,

Ever faithfully yours,

RICHARD T. ELY

P.S. I find that I have still overlooked one point. Dr. Bemis was a candidate for the chair of Political Economy at Colorado College. When I told President Slocum this summer that the allegation was made that Dr. Bemis was a failure, he replied simply and bluntly, "that is a lie." He said he did not know when any one had been more strongly recommended by those who knew him well; both by associates and former students. I can imagine that President Slocum would not say anything of this kind publicly, but he regards you as so good a friend, that he would say it to you as readily as to me.

Public Charges Are Officially Made after Bemis Leaves the University of Chicago

A Statement by Professors Small and Butler

In view of the desire of the public as manifested in various ways to know the facts in reference to the work of Mr. Bemis as a University Extension Associate Professor in the University of Chicago, and in order to remove certain impressions which his letter of a recent date occasions, we, who have been from the beginning most thoroughly conversant with all the facts, and indeed officially connected with his work, desire to make the following statement:

1. Mr. Bemis' position in the University from the beginning has been that of a University Extension Associate Professor, the understanding being that his work should be largely in this department, since his services were

not needed in the class work of the University proper, in view of the large number of Professors there employed.

2. During the first year ('92–'93) of his connection with the University, he delivered fifteen courses of Extension Lectures. During the second year ('93–'94) he gave seven courses. During the third year ('94–'95) he gave six courses of lectures. It was a striking fact that, except in one instance, Mr. Bemis never returned to an Extension Centre for a second course. In his course given during '94–'95 in Joliet on "Questions of Labor and Social Reform" the attendance at the first lecture was 124; second, 108; third, 76; fourth, 79; fifth, 75, and sixth, 44. The actual earnings of Mr. Bemis in University Extension work during the three years were about $1,000 a year, his salary being $2,500 a year. A portion of this salary, it is true, was paid him for courses offered in the University proper, but he was permitted to offer a larger number of courses in the University than he would otherwise have done, because the administrative officers of the Extension Division were unable to persuade University Extension Centres to avail themselves of his lectures. It should be added that no man who has ever given a dollar to the University has ever directly or indirectly entered objection to the views taught by Mr. Bemis in his lectures; and that so far as the University knows his teachings upon subjects of municipal reform, trusts, etc., are teachings to which the authorities would not think of inter- posing objection.

3. In no discussion of Mr. Bemis' relations to the University, between ourselves as officers of the University, or with the President of the Univer- sity, has the question of Mr. Bemis' views on subjects of Political Economy or Sociology been raised. Mr. Bemis himself acknowledged in our presence early in August (1895) that he was then convinced that no outside pressure had been brought to bear in reference to his resignation.

4. The simple fact is that the University Extension Division, which at present has no regular endowment to pay the salaries of Professors engaged in this particular work, is dependent upon the fees received from the lec- turers for the money with which to pay the salaries of such lecturers. Inasmuch as the officers of the department were unable to make arrange- ments with Extension Centers for Mr. Bemis to lecture before them, it was evident from a business point of view that the work of Mr. Bemis in this Division of the University must cease.

5. The President's letter to Mr. Bemis, in which he expressed cordial good will and appreciation of his ability, represented the feelings of all who were associated with Mr. Bemis at that time. It was, however, the opinion of the Head of the University department in which Mr. Bemis worked, and of the Director of the University Extension Division, as well as of the President, that Mr. Bemis could find a better field for his work in a smaller institution, in which he would be free to confine his teaching to the class

room, and not be dependent upon the general public through University Extension Centres.

6. The letter of President Harper to Mr. Bemis in reference to his remarks in the First Presbyterian Church, was written at a time when the citizens of Chicago were in great anxiety because of the disturbed condition of affairs. It should be noted that President Harper's request that Mr. Bemis should exercise care in his statements, was not made with reference to any utterances which Mr. Bemis was making in University work, or in a University Extension lecture, but in an outside capacity before a promiscuous audience. This was, as already intimated, at a time when agitation of any kind was universally regarded as imprudent. It should also be noted that President Harper did not even then take issue with Mr. Bemis on any "doctrine," but that he requested him to be careful about making untimely and immature statements.

7. Mr. Bemis was more than a year ago given to understand that it seemed desirable, for the reasons recited above, that he should seek another field of usefulness. This intimation was made and was apparently received by him in the kindest spirit, and efforts were made on the part of the University of Chicago to secure him a position better adapted to his abilities. One of several positions might have been secured had not Mr. Bemis himself, by his public attitude, rendered it out of the question that these positions should be offered him. We refer later to influences which may account for the unfortunate light in which Mr. Bemis has allowed his personal affairs to be presented. The whole case is one in which a University instructor is found to be not well adapted to the position which he holds. Such cases frequently arise in universities. In almost any other department of instruction than the one in which Mr. Bemis occupied a position, such a case would attract no general comment, nor would it be regarded as involving injustice to the instructor. It was perhaps not strange that Mr. Bemis' department of teaching, and the fact that the University of Chicago has been generously endowed by private munificence, should occasion the construction which has been put upon this matter. That construction, however, is absolutely without foundation in truth.

8. Mr. Bemis' real complaint was not that he was asked to resign from the University Extension staff, but that he was not transferred to a corresponding position on the staff of instructors inside the University. We state now only our opinion when we say that, so far as we are able to judge, every member of the faculty who is acquainted with Mr. Bemis would endorse the President's conclusion that such transfer would have placed Mr. Bemis in a position which he is not strong enough to fill. Mr. Bemis dissents from this opinion, and has repeatedly urged the head of the department of sociology to recommend his appointment as a member of the sociological staff. The answer had to be made that if the trustees could

appropriate money without limit to the sociological department, work might be assigned to Mr. Bemis which would be important and valuable in itself, but that the money which would be available for some time to come was much more needed for kinds of instruction which he was not competent to give.

Some of the elements which entered into the failure of his extension work would be fatal objections to a university instructor. In attempting to be judicial he succeeded in being only indefinite. Instead of erring by teaching offensive views, the head and front of his offending was that he did not seem to present any distinct views whatever.

9. We have urged President Harper, throughout the campaign of abuse which has been waged during the past summer, not to depart from his purpose of silence respecting the reasons which led him to call for Mr. Bemis' resignation. We knew that President Harper was more considerate of Mr. Bemis than the latter knew how to be for himself. We had and still have the most friendly feelings for our former associate, and agreed with President Harper that the University could afford to suffer rather than cause needless injury to an individual by publication of facts which a discreet person would wish to suppress.

10. We have changed our view of what is just to all interests concerned, because we are obliged to believe that the prominence which this case has attained through the press is not the result of misunderstanding, but that it is the carrying out of a deliberate design to misrepresent the facts. We believe that Mr. Bemis has received advice which has made him the tool of private animosity toward the University, under the mistaken notion that he is vindicating his violated rights. Our reasons for this view are in part as follows:

Soon after Mr. Bemis was informed, more than a year ago, that his services were no longer desired by the University, one of the signers of this paper was notified, by a friend of Mr. Bemis, first by letter and afterward verbally, that "if Professor Bemis is not retained a newspaper agitation will be begun from which the University will not recover in a generation." The reply was that if this was intended as a threat, no more direct means could be taken to hasten the termination of Mr. Bemis' connection with the University. That it was intended as a threat was evident from the response that "the newspapers are all ready to begin the attack if Bemis is sent away, and the University will drop him at its peril."

Both Mr. Bemis and his mentor have refused to act in accordance with the positive testimony of those who knew the facts, and have persisted in misconstruction of indirect evidence to suit their purpose of detraction. We therefore think it our duty to the University to add these things to previous official statements in behalf of the University.

11. To summarize, Mr. Bemis has compelled us to advertise both his incompetency as a University Extension lecturer, and also the opinion of those most closely associated with him that he is not qualified to fill a University position. We wish to make the most emphatic and unreserved assertion which words can convey that the "freedom of teaching" has never been involved in the case. The case of Mr. Bemis would have been precisely the same if his subject had been Sanskrit or Psychology or Mathematics.

12. As final evidence that the University had no quarrel with Mr. Bemis' "doctrines," we add that the University offered to continue to announce Professor Bemis' extension courses in the University lists and to give him all possible assistance to make lecture engagements. Mr. Bemis to retain all the fees, without the customary deduction for office expenses. This offer was to hold good until January 1, 1896, and Mr. Bemis did not decline it until August, 1895. Had he not chosen to represent himself as a martyr, he might have been lecturing today under the auspices of the University, although on his own *financial* responsibility.

ALBION W. SMALL,

Head Professor of Sociology

NATHANIAL BUTLER,

Director, The University Extension Division

The above has my concurrence and approval. I think that this recital of facts will be sufficient to assure all candid persons who have become interested in the case: first, that no principle has been involved about which there was occasion for public solicitude; second, that the University was guarding Professor Bemis' interests in attempting to avoid the necessity of publishing an official judgment about the value of his services.

WILLIAM R. HARPER,

President

Chicago, October 16, 1895

The above statement was prepared and put in type for the purpose of submitting it to the trustees and leaving the question of its publication to their decision. The proofs of the statement were stolen from the University printing office and given to the public. The employee who committed the theft has been discovered and discharged. If it had been decided to publish the statement, the phraseology would probably have been somewhat changed, and certain additions would have been made. The statement, however, as it was published, is correct. Under the circumstances it seems proper to add the following:

1. The statement placed in my mouth: "It is all very well to sympathize with the workingmen, but we get our money from those on the other side, and we cannot afford to offend them." *I absolutely deny*. I have never even entertained the thought implied in the statement. The University has received contributions from hundreds of workingmen. One, however, can feel no sympathy with those agitators who draw lines between the rich and the poor and seek to array them against each other. It is, of course, true that the president of a university could have no wish to offend the patrons of his institution. But the patrons of the University embrace all classes in the community. The issue raised is an entirely false one, and based on charges without the shadow of a foundation.

2. Mr. Bemis, recognizing that there was no longer a work for him to do in ordinary University Extension, proposed that the University pay his salary and allow him to work in the city in connection with the Civic Federation and other public and charity organizations, this work being, as he suggested, University Extension work in a broad sense. To this proposition it was, of course, necessary to reply that it was a valuable work, and he a good man to do it, but that it was a kind of work which the University could not undertake.

3. It is understood that when an instructor withdraws at the request of the University, his case shall, in no instance, be prejudiced before the public. The University will assist him in every possible way. The real facts in the case of Mr. Bemis would, under ordinary circumstances, never have been given to the public. In the convocation statement care was taken to utter no word which would in the slightest degree injure him. His recent publication of abstracts of letters, in which the facts were grossly misrepresented, has made this statement necessary.

4. Once more it is desired to say that neither the expressed nor the *supposed* wishes and views of the patrons of the University have had anything to do with the case in hand. It has been merely a question of finance, in the effort to bring the expenditures of the division of University Extension within its income. There is not an institution of learning in the country in which freedom of teaching is more absolutely untrammeled than in The University of Chicago. The history of the University during its first three years is sufficient guarantee to those who will examine into it that the policy of the Trustees of the University in reference to this whole subject will not be changed.

WILLIAM R. HARPER

October 21

John D. Rockefeller, Jr. Participates in the Selection of a History Professor

AUGUST 25, 1900

Mr. John D. Rockefeller, Jr.,
26 Broadway, New York City.

My Dear Mr. Rockefeller:

We have been hunting for two years to find a professor of History, one who would really take the place of Mr. vonHolst whose work seems to be finished. The unanimous opinion of our gentlemen after this long investigation and search seems to be that Professor Jameson of Brown is the right man. We recognize the fact that his work with undergraduates is not juicy and is not as interesting as it might be made, but I learn that his case is something like that of Mr. Manly in English. As a matter of fact Mr. Manly has shown himself to be an immensely strong man. We could not have found a better man in the country, and his appointment has been justified in the eyes of the entire Faculty. This fact shows that a man who may not succeed in undergraduate work may have been intended for Graduate work. But I am writing to ask you to tell me what you know about Mr. Jameson. No steps have been taken in the matter and we are still free.

Yours very truly,

W. R. HARPER

Rockefeller's Executive Secretary Sends Pres. Harper a News Clipping Regarding Prof. Small's Recent Lecture

DEC. 14, 1903

Dear Dr. Harper:

Please accept thanks for yours of the 11th, with enclosure, which I take pleasure in passing on to Mr. J. D. Rockefeller, Jr.

I enclose a clipping from the New York Sun of this morning. I regret its extreme timeliness, and its lack of truth.

Yours very truly,

F. T. GATES

President W. R. Harper,
University of Chicago
Chicago, Ill.

[The Enclosed Clipping]

DR. SMALL AND DR. HARPER

Prof. Albion Woodbury Small is the head of the department of sociology of the University of Chicago. There is no more earnest or chronic sociologist. If the Chicago reporters have correct ears, he lately addressed these interesting remarks to his senior class:

> The only thing that deserves financial reward is labor. Capital as such deserves none.

Prof. Small consents to receive a handsome salary, the savings from which would be regarded as sufficient or considerable capital by millions of people. Presumably he refuses to save any of this fat stipend. Otherwise he would become a capitalist and cease to deserve his reward.

Besides, he would be a wrongdoer:

> The present legal right that capital enjoys is all wrong. Capital has this legal right simply because our statutes give the right. There is nothing morally right about it.

Dr. Harper's collection of thinkers contributes much to the happiness of the world; and Dr. Small's words are as apples of gold. Still, we must not be selfish. There is a look of vexation on Dr. Harper's bland and ample countenance, at this time of year wearing what he calls "an expectant" expression. The hypnotist of the pocket, the milker of millionaires, the indefatigable treasure seeker, is a little "put-out." At the very moment when Dr. Harper is waiting to hear a check for a million or so sigh softly into his outstretched hat, why must this too earnest sociologist, Small, remind the patron capitalist of the university that capital deserves no financial reward and that its right is all wrong?

Rockefeller Requests Pres. Harper to Investigate Small's Lecture and Pres. Harper Replies

26 Broadway
New York

DECEMBER 26, 1903

Dear Doctor Harper:

There have been reports in the papers of late regarding the utterances of Professor Small in a recent lecture. What, if any, truth is there in these reports? I write only because so much has been made of the matter that it seems desirable for us to know the facts.

Very truly,
JOHN D. ROCKEFELLER, JR.

President William R. Harper
University of Chicago
Chicago, Illinois

DECEMBER 31, 1903

Mr. John D. Rockefeller, Jr.,
26 Broadway, New York City

My dear Mr. Rockefeller:

In reply to your note of December 26th I should like to say that 95 to 98 percent of the statement ascribed to Professor Small was entirely fictitious. I have his assurance to this effect. It was done by a reporter of the Record Herald. The regular reporter was off duty that day and a new man took the matter up. I referred to this in my Convocation statement, which I hope will be in your hands toward the end of the week.

Yours very truly
W. R. HARPER

F. T. Gates (Rockefeller's Executive Sec.) Advises Harper Not to Publish His Article in a Magazine Which Is Hostile to Standard Oil Co.

26 Broadway
New York

NOVEMBER 9, 1904

Dear Dr. Harper:

My thought in writing you on November 2nd was that the articles on "Frenzied Finance" are not a personal attack on Mr. Rockefeller. Indeed, so far as he personally is concerned, the author in one of the articles especially excepts him from having had anything to do with Amalgamated Copper. It is true that the author makes an onslaught upon the Standard Oil Company and develops what he called its "system," but I think any sober minded reader of the magazine will understand the absurdity of his vaporings. In the latest effusion, I understand he goes still further and charges the Standard Oil Company with seeking to elect Parker, and other matters of this sort. The articles started out rather formidably, but they have rapidly degenerated, from page to page and number to number, and have come to be at last entirely contemptible, and, so far as my observation goes, are making the author and the magazine publishing them a byword and a laughing stock.

The thing, therefore, that concerns me solely is the question whether, altogether apart from any real or fancied feeling of Mr. Rockefeller on the subject, you can yourself afford to appear in this magazine.

I strongly suspect that it is this solicitude and no other feeling that Mr. Rockefeller would have in the matter. I will hand the correspondence to Mr. Rockefeller, Jr., as I am about to take my vacation, and he will no doubt make any further observations which he may think wise or called for in the premises.

Yours very truly,

(SIGNED) F. T. GATES

President William R. Harper,
University of Chicago
Chicago, Ill.

P.S. Since writing the above, I have read the correspondence to Mr. J. D. R. Jr., agreeably to your letter of November 5th, including the above letter to you.

I find that Mr. Rockefeller agrees with me in thinking that his father would have no other solicitude in the matter than whether or not you can afford to appear, for your own sake and possibly the sake of the University, in a magazine which has become so completely discredited with discerning men. That, of course, you must decide for yourself.

CHAPTER 2

Codification of Professorial Roles and the Rationale for Academic Freedom

There is, perhaps, no better example of the liberal's position regarding academic freedom in the educational state in America than that taken by John Dewey. In his essay on "Academic Freedom" in 1902, he outlined some basic ideas which he developed more explicitly thirteen years later as the first president and charter member of the American Association of University Professors. During his presidency, he helped write the landmark document of Committee A's Report on Academic Freedom and Academic Tenure. Dewey's influence was effected not only by what he wrote, but through his organizational efforts in the AAUP and through the efforts of his many students, not the least of whom was Sidney Hook. Professor Hook, in turn, continues to play a significant role in defining the meaning and issues involved in the area of freedom to teach and learn in the educational state.

Although Dewey moved to the University of Chicago in 1894 and was on the faculty the year the Bemis case received the widest public press (1894–95), there appears to be no evidence which indicates that Dewey took a stand on the case or recorded an opinion on the matter. One might suspect, however, that Dewey had Bemis in mind, in his 1902 article, when he criticized professors who take their case to the public press. Specifically he criticized the professor who "poses as a martyr to truth when in reality he is a victim of his own lack of mental and moral poise." If it was not the Bemis case he had in mind, one might reasonably assume that he was responding to the criticism sustained by the University of Chicago as a result of the Bemis case when he so forcefully argued that money benefactors were not a threat to academic freedom. The threat to freedom came,

Dewey argued, not from moneyed benefactors as much as it came from professors who abused their privileges. Quoting President Harper's Commencement Address of 1900, as to the nature of these abuses, Dewey went on to say that the "personal elements detract very much from the simplicity and significance of an issue regarding academic freedom." He was convinced that because of these personal abuses, the "university spirit," "the Public press," and the "increased sensitiveness of public opinion," it had become ". . . well-nigh impossible to have raised, in any of the true universities of this country a straight out-and-out issue of academic freedom."

At the very time Dewey was making the case of noninterference on the part of "moneyed benefactors," the major money benefactor of his own university was exerting considerable interference in the internal activities of the academic community.[1] Was Dewey ignorant of these influences, or was he, perhaps, naive with respect to the operation of a university? It might be said, on Dewey's behalf, that the world in which he moved might not have allowed him to see these kinds of constraints at work. This position seems highly unlikely, however, in view of the fact that he was chairman of the department of philosophy, psychology and pedagogy. It seems more likely that Dewey held such a narrow view of what constituted an infringement on academic freedom that he was unlikely to see even the Bemis case as an "out-and-out issue of academic freedom." Dewey's limited perspective could also explain why, in the midst of so many academic freedom cases at the turn of the century, he could not see a "growing danger threatening academic freedom."[2] This circumscribed view, which he expressed in his 1902 article, is consistent with his later position of trying to organize and guide the American Association of University Professors (1915) as a professional agency dedicated more to the codification of standard rules of operation than as an agency dedicated to protect professors from unfair treatment. Speaking to the committee on the organization of the AAUP, he argued that the organization would not be preoccupied with academic freedom cases simply because they did not exist.

> I do not know of any college teacher who does not hold that such infringement, when it occurs, is an attack on the integrity of our calling. But such cases are too rare to even suggest the formation of an association like this. . . . In any case, I am confident that the topic cannot be more than an incident of the activities of the association in developing professional standards.[3]

[1] See the documents in the previous section.

[2] For the many cases at the turn of the century, see Richard Hofstadter and Walter Metzger, *The Development of Academic Freedom in the United States.* (New York: Columbia University Press, 1955). Then compare that with John Dewey's 1902 article on "Academic Freedom."

[3] As quoted in Hofstadter and Metzger, p. 478.

Just a year later, in his "Annual Address of the President,"[4] Dewey expressed surprise at the number of cases the new association was asked to investigate: "The investigations of particular cases were literally thrust upon us."[5] The reputation that Dewey achieved as a fighter for academic freedom, interestingly enough, was also "literally thrust" upon him. In tune with his liberal philosophy, he seemed more interested in organizing a society of "truth-seekers" than one which would fight militantly for the professor's interest.

The grounds upon which Dewey developed his rationale for academic freedom, in his 1902 article, are those which became the standard arguments for academic freedom in the twentieth century. As "truth-seekers," Dewey asserted, one must be free to inquire and within that process of inquiry, one must be objective, using scientific methods in order to achieve disciplined knowledge of the truth which can be acceptable to the public at large. The problems which result, he argued, are twofold: the lack of scientific method within the field itself, and the public's lag in accepting the validity of the newer discipline. Ultimately these problems were solvable. The solution, however, was premised on an enlightenment philosophy of progress in human knowledge.

Prophetically, Dewey pointed to the problem of academic materialism where the quest for money would overcome the quest for truth. He further pointed to the problems of academic bureaucracy and specialization as being dangerous threats to responsible free inquiry. By the middle of the century, these problems became particularly acute.

"The General Report of the Committee on Academic Freedom and Academic Tenure" (1915) reflects the ideas of Dewey and the combined wisdom of Committee A of the AAUP at its origin. Interestingly, neither Dewey's 1902 article nor the general report deal with *Lernfreiheit* in any serious way. As the report clearly states, "It need scarcely be pointed out that the freedom which is the subject of this report is that of the teacher." For the most part, the issue of the freedom to learn has not been addressed. The report further illustrates the basic difficulty in transplanting institutions from one nation to another without changing the basic social class structure along with it. Recall that the German principle of *Lehrfreiheit* was based, fundamentally, on the preferred elite status of both the professor and students which protected the state and the established economic interest from destructive criticism. In a broad sense, the German system was self-monitoring, screening out destructive radicals like Karl Marx from positions of trust within the system. In America, nineteenth-century college trustees tended to view the professor as a teacher of character and, therefore, a shaper of moral habits and behavior, more in a seminary per-

[4] December 31, 1915.
[5] Hofstadter and Metzger, *The Development of Academic Freedom in the United States*, p. 479.

spective. Thus, the personal characteristics of the professors were a central concern to the trustees. However, when the German function of research was introduced, or rather grafted onto the American college, there was a problem. The German rationale for *Lehrfreiheit* rested on assumptions that the results would be the creation of new knowledge. This whole system was premised, in turn, on a social complex which guaranteed that radicals would be prevented from ever gaining control of these educational institutions. In America, neither the professor nor student were the products of such a social complex. It was not enough, then, to convince the general public and the controlling power groups that the older seminary type of college had to change to one which they perceived as a real "university," dedicated to the search for truth as well as the dissemination of knowledge. But the professors had to organize themselves so as not only to protect the process of inquiry from vested interests of a misguided public, but they had to assure the powers that govern that they could and would protect the public from the dangers of irresponsible radical professors. The latter was crucial if professionalization was to receive the necessary support of the power groups who govern the university. Thus, the AAUP developed a code of conduct aimed as much at controlling the professor's behavior as at protecting the professor from irresponsible actions of people who govern the institutions. Under these circumstances, the "professional" role of the professor as a nonpartisan, objective, scientific, neutral truth-seeker was to be taken as convincing assurance by the powers which control the university that they would be protected not only from specific radical professors, but that the very process of scientific inquiry would have a definite conservative influence. The AAUP report clearly emphasized that the search for truth would have a "conservative influence" on society in general. The authors of the report repeatedly reassured the powers that controlled the purse of society that professionalization would facilitate the growth of a "responsible" expertise, responsible, of course, to those who wield power. The "scientific" objectification and neutralization of the role of the university professor in the educational state effectively undercut any serious political radical criticism. Christopher Lasch had part of this in mind when he said:

> . . . Academic freedom presents itself (as we have seen) not as a defense of the necessarily subversive character of good intellectual work, but as a prerequisite for pure research. Moreover, the more intellectual purity identifies itself with 'value-free' investigations, the more it empties itself of political content and the easier it is for public officials to tolerate it. The 'scientific' spirit, spreading from the natural sciences to social studies, tends to drain the latter of their critical potential while at the same time making them ideal instruments of bureaucratic control.[6]

[6] As quoted by Barton J. Bernstein, *Towards a New Past.* (New York: Pantheon Books, 1968), p. 345.

When one combines the scientific objectification with the professional-ization process, the de-fanging of the American professor was virtually complete. Immanuel Kant had suggested that those who wield power had nothing to fear from philosophers because of their inability to organize. In America, they organized to gain a kind of freedom that would reassure those who wield power that they had nothing to fear. From the perspective of those who control society, the American university professor would prove as politically harmless as his elite counterpart in the German university.

Academic Freedom

John Dewey

In discussing the questions summed up in the phrase academic freedom, it is necessary to make a distinction between the university proper and those teaching bodies, called by whatever name, whose primary business is to inculate a fixed set of ideas and facts. The former aims to discover and communicate truth and to make its recipients better judges of truth and more effective in applying it to the affairs of life. The latter have as their aim the perpetuation of a certain way of looking at things current among a given body of persons. Their purpose is to disciple rather than to disci-pline—not indeed at the expense of truth, but in such a way as to conserve what is already regarded as truth by some considerable body of persons. The problem of freedom of inquiry and instruction clearly assumes dif-ferent forms in these two types of institutions. An ecclesiastical, political, or even economic corporation holding certain tenets certainly has a right to support an institution to maintain and propagate its creed. It is a ques-tion not so much of freedom of thought as of ability to secure competent teachers willing to work under such conditions, to pay bills, and to have a constituency from which to draw students. Needless to say, the line between these two types of institutions is not so clear-cut in practice as it is in theory. Many institutions are in a state of transition. Historically, they are bound by ties to some particular body of beliefs, generally to some denominational association. Nominally, they still owe a certain allegiance to a particular body. But they are also assuming many strictly university functions and are thereby accepting obligations to a larger world of schol-arship and of society. In these respects the institution imposes upon its teaching corps not merely a right, but a duty, to maintain in all ways the university ideal of freedom of inquiry and freedom of communication.

But, in other respects, while the historical denominational ties are elongated and attenuated, they still remain; and thru them the instructor is to some extent bound. Implicit, if not explicit, obligations are assumed. In this situation, conflict between the two concerns of the university may arise; and in the confusion of this conflict it is difficult to determine just which way the instructor is morally bound to face. Upon the whole it is clear, however, that the burden falls upon the individual. If he finds that the particular and local attachment is so strong as to limit him in the pursuit of what he regards as essential, there is one liberty which cannot be taken away from him: the liberty of finding a more congenial sphere of work. So far as the institution is frank in acknowledging and maintaining its denominational connections, he cannot throw the burden back upon it. Nevertheless he, and those who are like-minded, have the right to deplore what they consider as a restriction, and to hope and labor for the time when the obligation in behalf of all the truth to society at large shall be felt as more urgent than that of a part of truth to a part of society.

But it cannot be inferred that the problem is a wholly simple one, even within the frankly announced denominational institutions. The line in almost any case is a shifting one. I am told that a certain denominational college permits and encourages a good deal of instruction in anatomy and physiology because there is biblical authority for the statement that the human body is fearfully and wonderfully made, while it looks askance upon the teaching of geology because the recognized doctrine of the latter appears to it to conflict with the plain statements of Genesis. As regards anatomy and physiology, an instructor in such an institution would naturally feel that his indebtedness was to the world of scholarship rather than to his own denomination, and here conflict might possibly arise. Or a teacher of history might find a conflict existing between the supposed interests of his denomination and the historical facts as determined by the best research at his command. Here, again, he would find himself naturally pulled in two different directions. No possible tie to what his own institution specially stands for can impose upon him the obligation to suppress the truth as he sees it. I quote such cases simply to indicate that, while in a general way there is a line of demarcation between the two types of institutions referred to, and consequently the problem of academic freedom does not arise so definitely in one type, yet even in the latter because all things shift, the question, after all, may assert itself.

In the subsequent discussion I shall confine myself exclusively to institutions of the university type. It is clear that in this sphere any attack, or even any restriction, upon academic freedom is directed against the university itself. To investigate truth; critically to verify fact; to reach conclusions by means of the best methods at command, untrammeled by external fear or favor, to communicate this truth to the student; to interpret to him its bearing on the questions he will have to face in life— this is precisely the aim and object of the university. To aim a blow at any one of these operations is to deal a vital wound to the university itself. The university function is the truth-function. At one time it may be more concerned with the tradition or transmission of truth, and at another time with its discovery. Both functions are necessary, and neither can ever be entirely absent. The exact ratio between them depends upon local and temporal considerations rather than upon anything inherent in the university. The one thing that is inherent and essential is the idea of truth.

So clear are these principles that, in the abstract, no theoretical problem can possibly arise. The difficulties arise from two concrete sources. In the first place, there is no gainsaying the fact that some of the studies taught in the university are inherently in a much more scientific condition than others. In the second place, the popular or general recognition of scientific status is much more widespread as regards some subjects than others. Upon the whole, it is practically impossible for any serious question regarding academic freedom to arise in the sphere of mathematics, astronomy, physics, or chemistry. Each of these subjects has now its definite established technique, and its own sphere within which it is supreme. This is so as fact; and it is generally so recognized by all persons of influence in the community. Consequently, there is no leverage from which to direct an attack upon academic freedom in any of these subjects. Such, of course, was not the case a few centuries ago. We know the storm that raged about astronomy. We know that it is only thru great trial and tribulation that the sciences have worked out such a definite body of truth and such definite instrumentalities of inquiry and verification as to give them a position assured from attack.

The biological sciences are clearly in a transitional state. The conception of evolution is a test case. It is safe to say that no university worthy of the name would put any limitation upon instruction in this theory, or upon its use as an agency of research and classification. Very little sympathy could be secured for an attack upon a university for encouraging the use of this theory. Many of the small colleges, however, would be shaken to their foundations by anything that seemed like a public avowal of belief in this doctrine. These facts would seem to mean that the more influential sections of the community upon which the universities properly depend have adjusted themselves to the fact that biology is a science which must be the judge of its own methods of work; that its facts and tests of fact are to be sought within its own scientific operations, and not in any extraneous sources. There are still, however, large portions of society which have not come to recognize that biology is an established science, and which, therefore, cannot concede to it the right to determine belief in regions that conflict with received opinions, and with the emotions that cluster about them.

There is another group of sciences which, from the standpoint of definitive method and a clearly accepted body of verified fact, are more remote from a scientific status. I refer especially to the social and psychological disciplines, and to some phases of linguistic and historical study— those most intimately associated with religious history and literature. Moreover, the public recognition of the scientific status attained lags behind the fact. As compared with mathematics or physics we can employ the term "science" only in a tentative and somewhat prophetic sense— the aspirations, the tendencies, the movement are scientific. But to the public at large the facts and relations with which these topics deal are still almost wholly in the region of opinion, prejudice, and accepted tradition. It has hardly dawned upon the community as a whole that science really has anything to say upon matters in the social and psychological sphere. The general public may be willing enough to admit in the abstract the existence of a science of political economy, sociology, or psychology, but when these dare to emerge from a remote and technical sphere, and pass authoritative judgment upon affairs of daily life—when they come in contact, that is, with the interests of daily life—they meet with little but skepticism or hostility or, what is worse, sensational exploitation.

It is out of these two facts—the backwardness of some of our sciences and failure of the general public to recognize even the amount of advance actually made—that the concrete problems of academic freedom arise. The case may be stated as follows: On behalf of academic freedom it may be urged that the only way in which the more backward subjects can possibly reach anything like the status of mathematics and mechanics is by encouraging to the utmost freedom of investigation, and the publication, oral and printed, of the results of inquiry. It may be urged that the very failure on the part of the public to recognize rightful jurisdiction for scientific methods and results is only the more reason for unusual frankness and fullness of expression. Because the public is so behind the scientific times, it must be brought up. The points of contact, it may be urged, between the social and moral sciences and social needs, are even more numerous and more urgent than in the case of the mathematical and physical sciences. The latter have secured their independence thru a certain abstractness, a certain remoteness from matters of social concern. Political economy, sociology, historical interpretation, psychology in its various possible applications, deal face to face with problems of life, not with problems of technical theory. Hence the right and duty of academic freedom are even greater here than elsewhere.

Per contra, it may be pointed out that, in so far as these subjects have not reached a scientific status, an expression of opinion on the part of a university instructor remains after all nothing but an expression of opinion, and hardly entitled to any more weight than that of any other reasonably intelligent person. It, however, is almost certain to be regarded as an official judgment. It thus commits and possibly compromises the institution to which the instructor belongs. The sphere of ideas which has not yet come under recognized scientific control is, moreover, precisely that which is bound up most closely with deep-rooted prejudice and intense emotional reaction. These, in turn, exist because of habits and modes of life to which the people have accustomed themselves. To attack them is to appear to be hostile to institutions with which the worth of life is bound up.

John Stuart Mill, with characteristic insight, somewhere points out that the German easily tolerates and welcomes all kinds of new ideas and new speculations because they exist in a region apart; they do not affect, excepting indirectly, the practical conduct of life. With the Englishman it is different. He is instinctively uneasy in the presence of a new idea; the wider the scope of the idea, the more readily uneasiness turns to suspicion and hostility. He recognizes that to accept the new idea means a change in the institutions of life. The idea is too serious a matter to be trifled with. The American has certainly inherited enough of the Englishman's sense for the connection of theory and practice to be conservative in the matter of the public broaching (and under modern conditions even classroom discussion is quasi-public) of ideas which lie much beyond the bounds of the domain publicly allotted to science.

Wherever scientific method is only partially attained the danger of undue dogmatism and of partisanship is very great. It is possible to consecrate ideas born of sheer partisanship with the halo of scientifically established belief. It is possible to state what is currently recognized to be scientific truth in such a way as to violate the most sacred beliefs of a large number of our fellow-men. The manner of conveying the truth may cause an irritation quite foreign to its own substance. This is quite likely to be the case whenever the negative rather than the positive aspect is dwelt upon; wherever the discrepancy between the new truth and established institutions is emphasized, rather than the intrinsic significance of the new conception. The outcome is disintegrating instead of constructive; and the methods inevitably breed distrust and antagonism.

One might, for example, be scientifically convinced of the transitional character of the existing capitalistic control of industrial affairs and its reflected influences upon political life; one might be convinced that many and grave evils and injustices are incident to it, and yet never raise the question of academic freedom, altho developing his views with definiteness and explicitness. He might go at the problem in such an objective, historic, and constructive manner as not to excite the prejudices or inflame the passions even of those who thoroly disagreed with him. On the other hand, views at the bottom exactly the same can be stated in such a way as to rasp the feelings of everyone exercising the capitalistic function. What will stand or fall upon its own scientific merits, if presented as a case of objective social evolution, is mixed up with all sorts of extraneous and passion-inflaming factors when set forth as the outcome of the conscious and aggressive selfishness of a class.

As a result of such influences the problem of academic freedom becomes to a very large extent a personal matter. I mean that it is a matter of the scholarship, judgment, and sympathy of the individual in dealing with matters either only just coming within the range of strict scientific treatment, or, even if fairly annexed to the scientific domain, not yet recognized by contemporary public opinion as belonging there. All sorts of difficulties arise when we attempt to lay down any rules for, or pass any judgment upon, the personal aspects of the matter. Such rules are likely to be innocuous truisms. We can insist upon one hand that the individual must be loyal to truth, and that he must have the courage of his convictions; that he must not permit their presumed unpopularity, the possibly unfavorable reaction of their free expression upon his own career, to swerve him from his singleness of devotion to truth. We may dwell upon the dangers of moral cowardice and of turning traitor to the cause in which every scholar is enlisted. We may indicate the necessity of the use of common sense in the expression of views on controverted points, especially points entering into the arena of current religious and political discussion. We may insist that a man needs tact as well as scholarship; or, let us say, sympathy with human interests—since "tact" suggests perhaps too much a kind of juggling diplomacy with the questions at issue.

It is possible to confuse loyalty to truth with self-conceit in the assertion of personal opinion. It is possible to identify courage with bumptiousness. Lack of reverence for the things that mean much to humanity, joined with a craving for public notoriety, may induce a man to pose as a martyr to truth when in reality he is a victim of his own lack of mental and moral poise. President Harper, in a clear and comprehensive discussion in his Convocation Address of December, 1900,[1] points out so clearly the sources of personal failure of this sort that I make no apology for quoting his words:

(1) A professor is guilty of an abuse of privilege who promulgates as truth ideas or opinions which have not been tested scientifically by his colleagues in the same department of research or investigation. (2) A professor abuses his privilege who takes advantage of a classroom exercise to propagate the partisan view of one or another of the political parties. (3) A professor abuses his privilege who in any way seeks to influence his pupils or the public by sensational methods. (4) A professor abuses his

[1] See *University Record*, Vol. 5, p. 377.

privilege of expression of opinion when, altho a student and perhaps an authority in one department or group of departments, he undertakes to speak authoritatively on subjects which have no relationship to the department in which he was appointed to give instruction. (5) A professor abuses his privelege in many cases when, altho shut off in large measure from the world and engaged within a narrow field of investigation, he undertakes to instruct his colleagues or the public concerning matters in the world at large in connection with which he has had little or no experience.

Now, while all university men will doubtless agree with President Harper when he says "freedom of expression must be given to members of the university faculty, even tho it be abused, for the abuse of it is not so great an evil as the restriction of such liberty," yet it is clear that the presence of these personal elements detracts very much from the simplicity and significance of an issue regarding academic freedom. For reasons into which I cannot fully go, I am convinced that it is now well-nigh impossible to have raised, in any of the true universities of this country, a straight out-and-out issue of academic freedom. The constantly increasing momentum of scientific inquiry, the increasing sense of the university spirit binding together into one whole the scattered members of various faculties thruout the country, the increased sensitiveness of public opinion, and the active willingness of a large part of the public press to seize upon and even to exaggerate anything squinting towards an infringement upon the rights of free inquiry and free speech—these reasons, among others, make me dissent most thoroly from the opinion sometimes expressed that there is a growing danger threatening academic freedom.

The exact contrary is, in my judgment, the case as regards academic freedom in the popular sense, that is to say, of dictatorial interferences by moneyed benefactors with special individual utterances.

It does not follow, however, that there is no danger in the present situation. Academic freedom is not exhausted in the right to express opinion. More fundamental is the matter of freedom of work. Subtle and refined danger is always more to be apprehended than a public and obvious one. Encroachments that arise unconsciously out of the impersonal situation are more to be dreaded than those coming from the voluntary action of individuals. Influences that gradually sap and undermine the conditions of free work are more ominous than those which attack the individual in the open. Ability to talk freely is an important thing, but hardly comparable with ability to work freely. Now freedom of work is not a matter which lends itself to sensational newspaper articles. It is an intangible, undefinable affair; something which is in the atmosphere and operates as a continuous and unconscious stimulus. It affects the spirit in which the university as a whole does its work, rather than the overt expressions of any one individual. The influences which help and hinder in this freedom are internal and organic, rather than outward and personal.

Without being a pessimist, I think it behooves the community of university men to be watchful on this side. Upon the whole, we are pretty sure that actual freedom of expression is not going to be interrupted at the behest of any immediate outside influence, even if accompanied with the prospective gift of large sums of money. Things are too far along for that. The man with money hardly dare directly interfere with freedom of inquiry, even if he wished to; and no respectable university administration would have the courage, even if it were willing, to defy the combined condemnation of other universities and of the general public.

None the less the financial factor in the conduct of the modern university is continually growing in importance, and very serious problems arise in adjusting this factor to strict educational ideals. Money is absolutely indispensible as a means. But it is only a means. The danger lies in the difficulty of making money adequate as a means, and yet keeping it in its place—not permitting it to usurp any of the functions of control which belong only to educational purposes. To these, if the university is to be a true university, money and all things connected therewith must be subordinate. But the pressure to get the means is tending to make it an end; and this is academic materialism—the worst foe of freedom of work in its widest sense.

Garfield's conception of the college as a bench with a student at one end and a great teacher at the other, is still a pious topic of after-dinner reminiscence; but it is without bearing in the present situation. The modern university is itself a great economic plant. It needs libraries, museums, and laboratories, numerous, expensive to found and to maintain. It requires a large staff of teachers.

Now the need for money is not in itself external to genuine university concerns; much less antagonistic to them. The university must expand in order to be true to itself, and to expand it must have money. The danger is that means absorb attention and thus possess the value that attaches alone to the ultimate educational end. The public mind gives an importance to the money side of educational institutions which is insensibly modifying the standard of judgment both within and without the college walls. The great event in the history of an institution is now likely to be a big gift, rather than a new investigation or the development of a strong and vigorous teacher. Institutions are ranked by their obvious material prosperity, until the atmosphere of money-getting and money-spending hides from view the interests for the sake of which money alone has a place. The imagination is more or less taken by the thought of this force, vague but potent; the emotions are enkindled by grandiose conceptions of the possibilities latent in money. Unconsciously, without intention, the money argument comes to be an argument out of proportion, out of perspective. It is bound up in so many ways, seen and unseen, with the glory and dignity of the institution that it derives from association an importance to which it has in itself no claim.

This vague potentiality, invading imagination and seducing emotion, checks initiative and limits responsibility. Many an individual who would pursue his straight course of action unhindered by thought of personal harm to himself, is deflected because of fear of injury to the institution to which he belongs. The temptation is attractive just because it does not appeal to the lower and selfish motives of the individual, but comes clothed in the garb of the ideals of an institution. Loyalty to an institution, *esprit de corps*, is strong in the university, as in the army and navy. A vague apprehension of bringing harm upon the body with which one is connected is kept alive by the tendency of the general public to make no distinction between an individual in his personal and his professional capacity. Whatever he says and does is popularly regarded as an official expression of the institution with which he is connected. All this tends to paralyze independence and drive the individual back into a narrower corner of work.

Moreover, a new type of college administration has been called into being by the great expansion on the material side. A ponderous machinery has come into existence for carrying on the multiplicity of business and quasi-business matters without which the modern university would come to a standstill. This machinery tends to come between the individual and the region of moral aims in which he should assert himself. Personality counts for less than the apparatus thru which, it sometimes seems, the individual alone can accomplish anything. Moreover, the minutiae, the routine turning of the machinery, absorb time and energy. Many a modern college man is asking himself where he is to get the leisure and strength to devote himself to his ultimate ends, so much, willy-nilly, has to be spent on the intermediate means. The side-tracking of personal energy into the routine of academic machinery is a serious problem.

All this, while absorbing some of the energy which ought to find outlet in dealing with the larger issues of life, would not be so threatening were it not for its association with the contemporary tendency to specialization. Specialization, in its measure and degree, means withdrawal. It means preoccupation with a comparatively remote field in relatively minute detail. I have no doubt that in the long run the method of specialization will justify itself, not only scientifically, but practically. But value in terms of ultimate results is no reason for disguising the immediate danger to courage, and the freedom that can come only from courage. Teaching, in any case, is something of a protected industry; it is sheltered. The teacher is set somewhat one side from the incidence of the most violent stresses and strains of life. His problems are largely intellectual, not moral; his associates are largely immature. There is always the danger of a teacher's losing something of the virility that comes from having to face and wrestle with economic and political problems on equal terms with competitors. Specialization unfortunately increases these dangers. It leads the individual, if he follows it unreservedly, into bypaths still further off from the highway where men, struggling together, develop strength. The insidious conviction that certain matters of fundamental import to humanity are none of my concern because outside of my *Fach*, is likely to work more harm to genuine freedom of academic work than any fancied dread of interference from a moneyed benefactor.

The expression of the material side of the modern university also carries with it strong tendencies towards centralization. The old-fashioned college faculty was pretty sure to be a thorogoing democracy in its way. Its teachers were selected more often because of their marked individual traits than because of pure scholarship. Each stood his own and for his own. The executive was but *primus inter pares*. It was a question not of organization or administration (or even of execution on any large scale), but rather of person making himself count in contact with person, whether teacher or student. All that is now changed—necessarily so. It requires ability of a very specialized and intensified order to wield the administrative resources of a modern university. The conditions make inevitably for centralization. It is difficult to draw the line between that administrative centralization which is necessary for the economical and efficient use of resources and that moral centralization which restricts initiative and responsibility. Individual participation in legislative authority and position is a guarantee of strong, free, and independent personalities. The old faculty, a genuine republic of letters, is likely to become an oligarchy— more efficient from the standpoint of material results achieved, but of less account in breeding men. This reacts in countless ways upon that freedom of work which is necessary to make the university man a force in the working life of the community. It deprives him of responsibility, and with weakening of responsibility comes loss of initiative.

This is one phase of the matter—fortunately not the whole of it. There has never been a time in the history of the world when the community so recognized its need of expert guidance as to-day. In spite of our intellectual chaos, in spite of the meaningless hullabaloo of opinion kept up so persistently about us by the daily press, there is a very genuine hunger and thirst after light. The man who has the word of wisdom to say is sure of his audience. If he gets his light out from under the bushel, it carries a long way. From this point of view there are strong influences working to free the university spirit, the spirit of inquiry and expression of truth, from its entanglements and concealments. The need being imperative, the stimulus is great. A due degree of courage, a due measure of the spirit of initiative and personal responsibility is the natural response. With the decay of external and merely governmental forms of authority, the demand grows for the authority of wisdom and intelligence. This force is bound to overcome those influences which tend to withdraw and pen the scholar within his own closet.

An immediate resource counteracting the dangers threatening academic freedom, is found also in the growth of intercollegiate sentiment and opinion. No fact is more significant than the growing inclination on the part of scientific associations to assume a right and duty to inquire into what affects the welfare of its own line of inquiry, however and wherever it takes place. This is the growth of the corporate scientific consciousness; the sense of the solidarity of truth. Whatever wounds the body of truth in one of its members attacks the whole organism. It is not chimerical to foresee a time when the consciousness of being a member of an organized society of truth-seekers will solidify and re-enforce otherwise scattered and casual efforts.

Given that individual initiative whose permanent weakening we can scarcely imagine in an Anglo-Saxon community; and two forces, the need of the community for guidance and the sense of membership in the wider university to which every inquirer belongs, will assuredly amply triumph over all dangers attacking academic freedom.

A.A.U.P. General Report of the Committee on Academic Freedom and Academic Tenure

*Presented at the Annual Meeting
of the Association*

DECEMBER 31, 1915

I. GENERAL DECLARATION OF PRINCIPLES

The term "academic freedom" has traditionally had two applications —to the freedom of the teacher and to that of the student, *Lehrfreiheit* and *Lernfreiheit*. It need scarcely be pointed out that the freedom which is the subject of this report is that of the teacher. Academic freedom in this sense comprises three elements: freedom of inquiry and research; freedom of teaching within the university or college; and freedom of extra-mural utterance and action. The first of these is almost everywhere so safeguarded that the dangers of its infringement are slight. It may therefore be disregarded in this report. The second and third phases of academic freedom are closely related, and are often not distinguished. The third, however, has an importance of its own, since of late it has perhaps more frequently been the occasion of difficulties and controversies than has the question of freedom of intra-academic teaching. All five of the cases which have recently been investigated by committees of this Association have involved, at least as one factor, the right of university teachers to express their opinions freely outside the university or to engage in political activities in their capacity as citizens. The general principles which have to do with freedom of teaching in both these senses seem to the committee to be in great part, though not wholly, the same. In this report, therefore, we shall consider the matter primarily with reference to freedom of teaching within the university, and shall assume that what is said thereon is also applicable to the freedom of speech of university teachers outside their institutions, subject to certain qualifications and supplementary considerations which will be pointed out in the course of the report.

An adequate discussion of academic freedom must necessarily consider three matters: (1) the scope and basis of the power exercised by those bodies having ultimate legal authority in academic affairs; (2) the nature of the academic calling; (3) the function of academic institution or university.

1. Basis of academic authority

American institutions of learning are usually controlled by boards of trustees as the ultimate repositories of power. Upon them finally it devolves to determine the measure of academic freedom which is to be realized in the several institutions. It therefore becomes necessary to inquire into the nature of the trust reposed in these boards, and to ascertain to whom the trustees are to be considered accountable.

The simplest case is that of a proprietary school or college designed for the propagation of specific doctrines prescribed by those who have furnished its endowment. It is evident that in such cases the trustees are bound by the deed of gift, and, whatever be their own views, are obligated to carry out the terms of the trust. If a church or religious denomination establishes a college to be governed by a board of trustees, with the express understanding that the college will be used as an instrument of propaganda in the interests of the religious faith professed by the church or denomination creating it, the trustees have a right to demand that everything be subordinated to that end. If, again, as has happened in this country, a wealthy manufacturer establishes a special school in a University in order to teach, among other things, the advantages of a protective tariff, or if, as is also the case, an institution has been endowed for the purpose of propagating the doctrines of socialism, the situation is analogous. All of these are essentially proprietary institutions, in the moral sense. They do not, at least as regards one particular subject, accept the principles of freedom of inquiry, of opinion, and of teaching; and their purpose is not to advance knowledge by the unrestricted research and unfettered discussion of impartial investigators, but rather to subsidize the promotion of the opinions held by the persons, usually not of the scholar's calling, who provide the funds for their maintenance. Concerning the desirability of the existence of such institutions, the committee does not desire to express any opinion. But it is manifestly important that they should not be permitted to sail under false colors. Genuine boldness and thoroughness of inquiry, and freedom of speech, are scarcely reconcilable with the prescribed inculcation of a particular opinion upon a controverted question.

Such institutions are rare, however, and are becoming more rare. We still have, indeed, colleges under denominational auspices; but very few of them impose upon their trustees responsibility for the spread of specific doctrines. They are more and more coming to occupy, with respect to the freedom enjoyed by the members of their teaching bodies, the position of untrammeled institutions of learning, and are differentiated only by the natural influence of their respective historic antecedents and traditions.

Leaving aside, then, the small number of institutions of the proprietary type, what is the nature of the trust reposed in the governing boards of the ordinary institutions of learning? Can colleges and universities that are not strictly bound by their founders to a propagandist duty ever be included in the class of institutions that we have just described as being in a moral sense proprietary? The answer is clear. If the former class of institutions constitute a private or proprietary trust, the latter constitute a public trust. The trustees are trustees for the public. In the case of our state universities this is self-evident. In the case of most of our privately endowed institutions, the situation is really not different. They cannot be permitted to assume the proprietary attitude and privilege, if they are appealing to the general public for support. Trustees of such universities or colleges have no moral right to bind the reason or the conscience of any professor. All claim to such right is waived by the appeal to the general public for contributions and for moral support in the maintenance, not of a propaganda, but of a non-partisan institution of learning. It follows that any university which lays restrictions upon the intellectual freedom of its professors proclaims itself a proprietary institution, and should be so described whenever it makes a general appeal for funds; and the public should be advised that the institution has no claim whatever to general support or regard.

This elementary distinction between a private and a public trust is not yet so universally accepted as it should be in our American institutions. While in many universities and colleges the situation has come to be entirely satisfactory, there are others in which the relation of trustees to professors is apparently still conceived to be analogous to that of a private employer to his employees; in which, therefore, trustees are not regarded as debarred by any moral restrictions, beyond their own sense of expediency, from imposing their personal opinions upon the teaching of the institution, or even from employing the power of dismissal to gratify their private antipathies or resentments. An eminent university president thus described the situation not many years since:

> In the institution of higher education the board of trustees is the body on whose discretion, good feeling, and experience the securing of academic freedom now depends. There are boards which leave nothing to be desired in these respects; but there are also numerous bodies that have everything to learn with regard to academic freedom. These barbarous boards exercise an arbitrary power of dismissal. They exclude from the teachings of the university unpopular or dangerous subjects. In some states they even treat professors' positions as common political spoils; and all too frequently, both in state and endowed institutions, they fail to treat the members of the teaching staff with that high consideration to which their functions entitle them.[1]

It is, then, a prerequisite to a realization of the proper measure of academic freedom in American institutions of learning, that all boards of trustees should undersrtand—as many already do—the full implications of the distinction between private proprietorship and a public trust.

2. The nature of the academic calling

The above-mentioned conception of a university as an ordinary business venture, and of academic teaching as a purely private employment, manifests also a radical failure to apprehend the nature of the social function discharged by the professional scholar. While we should be reluctant to believe that any large number of educated persons suffer from such a misapprehension, it seems desirable at this time to restate clearly the chief reasons, lying in the nature of the university teaching profession, why it is to the public interest that the professorial office should be one both of dignity and of independence.

If education is the corner stone of the structure of society and if progress in scientific knowledge is essential to civilization, few things can be more important than to enhance the dignity of the scholar's profession,

---

[1] From "Academic Freedom," an address delivered before the New York Chapter of the Phi Beta Kappa Society at Cornell University by Charles William Eliot, LL.D., President of Harvard University, May 29, 1907.

with a view to attracting into its ranks men of the highest ability, of sound learning, and of strong and independent character. This is the more essential because the pecuniary emoluments of the profession are not, and doubtless never will be, equal to those open to the more successful members of other professions. It is not, in our opinion, desirable that men should be drawn into this profession by the magnitude of the economic rewards which it offers; but it is for this reason the more needful that men of high gifts and character should be drawn into it by the assurance of an honorable and secure position, and of freedom to perform honestly and according to their own consciences the distinctive and important function which the nature of the profession lays upon them.

That function is to deal at first hand, after prolonged and specialized technical training, with the sources of knowledge; and to impart the results of their own and of their fellow-specialists' investigations and reflection, both to students and to the general public, without fear or favor. The proper discharge of this function requires (among other things) that the university teacher shall be exempt from any pecuniary motive or inducement to hold, or to express, any conclusion which is not the genuine and uncolored product of his own study or that of fellow-specialists. Indeed, the proper fulfilment of the work of the professorate requires that our universities shall be so free that no fair-minded person shall find any excuse for even a suspicion that the utterances of university teachers are shaped or restricted by the judgment, not of professional scholars, but of inexpert and possibly not wholly disinterested persons outside of their ranks. The lay public is under no compulsion to accept or to act upon the opinions of the scientific experts whom, through the universities, it employs. But it is highly needful, in the interest of society at large, that what purport to be the conclusions of men trained for, and dedicated to, the quest for truth, shall in fact be the conclusions of such men, and not echoes of the opinions of the lay public, or of the individuals who endow or manage universities. To the degree that professional scholars, in the formation and promulgation of their opinions, are, or by the character of their tenure appear to be, subject to any motive other than their own scientific conscience and a desire for the respect of their fellow-experts, to that degree the university teaching profession is corrupted; its proper influence upon public opinion is diminished and vitiated; and society at large fails to get from its scholars, in an unadulterated form, the peculiar and necessary service which it is the office of the professional scholar to furnish.

These considerations make still more clear the nature of the relationship between university trustees and members of university faculties. The latter are the appointees, but not in any proper sense the employees, of the former. For, once appointed, the scholar has professional functions to perform in which the appointing authorities have neither the competency nor moral right to intervene. The responsibility of the university teacher is primarily to the public itself, and to the judgment of his own profession; and while, with respect to certain external conditions of his vocation, he accepts a responsibility to the authorities of the institution in which he serves, in the essentials of his professional activity his duty is to the wider public to which the institution itself is morally amenable. So far as the university teacher's independence of thought and utterance is concerned—though not in other regards—the relationship of professor to trustees may be compared to that between judges of the Federal courts and the Executive who appoints them. University teachers should be understood to be, with respect to the conclusions reached and expressed by them, no more subject to the control of the trustees, than are judges subject to the control of the President, with respect to their decisions; while of course, for the same reason, trustees are no more to be held responsible for, or to be presumed to agree with, the opinions or utterances of professors, than the President can be assumed to approve of all the legal reasonings of the courts. A university is a great and indispensable organ of the higher life of a civilized community, in the work of which the trustees hold an essential and highly honorable place, but in which the faculties hold an independent place, with quite equal responsibilities—and in relation to purely scientific and educational questions, and primary responsibility. Misconception or obscurity in this matter has undoubtedly been a source of occasional difficulty in the past, and even in several instances during the current year, however much, in the main, a long tradition of kindly and courteous intercourse between trustees and members of university faculty has kept the question in the background.

3. The function of the academic institution

The importance of academic freedom is most clearly perceived in the light of the purposes for which universities exist. These are three in number:

A. To promote inquiry and advance the sum of human knowledge.
B. To provide general instruction to the students.
C. To develop experts for various branches of the public service.

Let us consider each of these. In the earlier stages of a nation's intellectual development, the chief concern of educational institutions is to train the growing generation and to diffuse the already accepted knowledge. It is only slowly that there comes to be provided in the highest institutions of learning the opportunity for the gradual wresting from nature of her intimate secrets. The modern university is becoming more and more the home of scientific research. There are three fields of human inquiry in which the race is only at the beginning; natural science, social science, and philosophy and religion, dealing with the relations of man to outer nature, to his fellow men, and to the ultimate realities and values. In natural science all that we have learned but serves to make us realize more deeply how much more remains to be discovered. In social science in its largest sense, which is concerned with the relations of men in society and with the conditions of social order and well-being, we have learned only an adumbration of the laws which govern these vastly complex phenomena. Finally, in the spiritual life, and in the interpretation of the general meaning and ends of human existence and its relation to the universe, we are still far from a comprehension of the final truths, and from a universal agreement among all sincere and earnest men. In all of these domains of knowledge, the first condition of progress is complete and unlimited freedom to pursue inquiry and publish its results. Such freedom is the breath in the nostrils of all scientific activity.

The second function—which for a long time was the only function— of the American college or university is to provide instruction for students. It is scarcely open to question that freedom of utterance is as important to the teacher as it is to the investigator. No man can be a successful teacher unless he enjoys the respect of his students, and their confidence in his intellectual integrity. It is clear, however, that this confidence will be impaired if there is suspicion on the part of the student that the teacher is not expressing himself fully or frankly, or that college and university teachers in general are a repressed and intimidated class who dare not speak with that candor and courage which youth always demands in those whom it is to esteem. The average student is a discerning observer, who soon takes the measure of his instructor. It is not only the character of the instruction but also the character of the instructor that counts; and if the student has reason to believe that the instructor is not true to himself, the virtue of the instruction as an educative force is incalculably diminished. There must be in the mind of the teacher no mental reservation. He must give the student the best of what he has and what he is.

The third function of the modern university is to develop experts for the use of the community. If there is one thing that distinguishes the more recent developments of democracy, it is the recognition by legislators of the inherent complexities of economic, social, and political life, and the difficulty of solving problems of technical adjustment without technical knowledge. The recognition of this fact has led to a continually greater demand for the aid of experts in these subjects, to advise both legislators and administrators. The training of such experts has, accordingly, in recent years, become an important part of the work of the universities; and in almost every one of our higher institutions of learning the professors of the economic, social, and political sciences have been drafted to an increasing extent into more or less unofficial participation in the public service.

It is obvious that here again the scholar must be absolutely free not only to pursue his investigations but to declare the results of his researches, no matter where they may lead him or to what extent they may come into conflict with accepted opinion. To be of use to the legislator or the administrator, he must enjoy their complete confidence in the disinterestedness of his conclusions.

It is clear, then, that the university cannot perform its threefold function without accepting and enforcing to the fullest extent the principle of academic freedom. The responsibility of the university as a whole is to the community at large, and any restriction upon the freedom of the instructor is bound to react injuriously upon the efficiency and the *morale* of the institution, and therefore ultimately upon the interests of the community.

The attempted infringements of academic freedom at present are probably not only of less frequency than, but of a different character from, those to be found in former times. In the early period of university development in America the chief menace to academic freedom was ecclesiastical, and the disciplines chiefly affected were philosophy and the natural sciences. In more recent times the danger zone has been shifted to the political and social sciences—though we still have sporadic examples of the former class of cases in some of our smaller institutions. But it is precisely in these provinces of knowledge in which academic freedom is now most likely to be threatened, that the need for it is at the same time most evident. No person of intelligence believes that all of our political problems have been solved, or that the final stage of social evolution has been reached. Grave issues in the adjustment of men's social and economic relations are certain to call for settlement in the years that are to come; and for the right settlement of them mankind will need all the wisdom, all the good will, all the soberness of mind, and all the knowledge drawn from experience, that it can command. Towards this settlement the university has potentially its own very great contribution to make; for if the adjustment reached is to be a wise one, it must take due account of economic science, and be guided by that breadth of historic vision which it should be one of the functions of a university to cultivate. But if the universities are to render any such service towards the right solution of the social problems of the future, it is the first essential that the scholars who carry on the work of universities shall not be in a position of dependence upon the favor of any social class or group, that the disinterestedness and impartiality of their inquiries and their conclusions shall be, so far as is humanly possible, beyond the reach of suspicion.

The special dangers to freedom of teaching in the domain of the social sciences are evidently two. The one which is the more likely to affect the privately endowed colleges and universities is the danger of restrictions upon the expression of opinions which point towards extensive social innovations, or call in question the moral legitimacy of social expediency of economic conditions or commercial practices in which large vested interests are involved. In the political, social, and economic field almost every question, no matter how large and general it at first appears, is more or less affected with private or class interests; and, as the governing body of a university is naturally made up of men who through their standing and ability are personally interested in great private enterprises, the points of possible conflict are numberless. When to this, is added the consideration that benefactors, as well as most of the parents who send their children to privately endowed institutions, themselves belong to the more prosperous and therefore usually to the more conservative classes, it is apparent that, so long as effectual safeguards for academic freedom are not established, there is a real danger that pressures from vested interests may, sometimes deliberately and sometimes unconsciously, sometimes openly and sometimes subtly in obscure ways, be brought to bear upon academic authorities.

On the other hand, in our state universities the danger may be the reverse. Where the university is dependent for funds upon legislative favor, it has sometimes happened that the conduct of the institution has been affected by political considerations; and where there is a definite governmental policy or a strong public feeling on economic, social, or political questions, the menace to academic freedom may consist in the repression of opinions that in the particular political situation are deemed ultra-conservative rather than ultra-radical. The essential point, however, is not so much that the opinion is of one or another shade, as that it differs from the views entertained by the authorities. The question resolves itself into one of departure from accepted standards; whether the departure is in the one direction or the other is immaterial.

This brings us to the most serious difficulty of this problem; namely, the dangers connected with the existence in a democracy of an overwhelming and concentrated public opinion. The tendency of modern democracy is for men to think alike, to feel alike, and to speak alike. Any departure from the conventional standards is apt to be regarded with suspicion. Public opinion is at once the chief safeguard of a democracy, and the chief menace to the real liberty of the individual. It almost seems as if the danger of despotism cannot be wholly averted under any form of government. In a political autocracy there is no effective public opinion, and all are subject to the tyranny of the ruler; in a democracy there is political freedom, but there is likely to be a tyranny of public opinion.

An inviolable refuge from such tyranny should be found in the university. It should be an intellectual experiment station, where new ideas may germinate and where their fruit, though still distasteful to the community as a whole, may be allowed to ripen until finally, perchance, it may become a part of the accepted intellectual food of the nation or of the world. Not less is it a distinctive duty of the university to be the conservator of all genuine elements of value in the past thought and life of mankind which are not in the fashion of the moment. Though it need not be the "home of beaten causes," the university is, indeed, likely always to exercise a certain form of conservative influence. For by its nature it is committed to the principle that knowledge should precede action, to the caution (by no means synonymous with intellectual timidity) which is an essential part of the scientific method, to a sense of the complexity of social problems, to the practice of taking long views into the future, and to a reasonable regard for the teachings of experience. One of its most characteristic functions in a democratic society is to help make public opinion more self-critical and more circumspect, to check the more hasty and unconsidered impulses of popular feeling, to train the democracy to the habit of looking before and after. It is precisely this function of the university which is most injured by any restriction upon academic freedom; and it is precisely those who most value this aspect of the university's work who should most earnestly protest against any such restriction. For the public may respect, and be influenced by, the counsels of prudence and of moderation which are given by men of science, if it believes those counsels to be the disinterested expression of the scientific temper and of unbiased inquiry. It is little likely to respect or heed them if it has reason to believe that they are the expression of the interests, or the timidities, of the limited portion of the community which is in a position to endow institutions of learning, or is most likely to be represented upon their boards of trustees. And a plausible reason for this belief is given the public so long as our universities are not organized in such a way as to make impossible any exercise of pressure upon professorial opinions and utterances by governing boards of laymen.

Since there are no rights without corresponding duties, the considerations heretofore set down with respect to the freedom of the academic teacher entail certain correlative obligations. The claim to freedom of teaching is made in the interest of the integrity and of the progress of scientific inquiry; it is, therefore, only those who carry on their work in the temper of the scientific inquirer who may justly assert this claim. The liberty of the scholar within the university to set forth his conclusions, be they what they may, is conditioned by their being conclusions gained by a scholar's method and held in a scholar's spirit; that is to say, they must be the fruits of competent and patient and sincere inquiry, and they should be set forth with dignity, courtesy, and temperateness of language. The university teacher, in giving instruction upon controversial matters, while he is under no obligation to hide his own opinion under a mountain of equivocal verbiage, should, if he is fit for his position, be a person of a fair and judicial mind; he should, in dealing with such subjects, set forth justly, without suppression or innuendo, the divergent opinions of other investigators; he should cause his students to become familiar with the best published expressions of the great historic types of doctrine upon the questions at issue; and he should, above all, remember that his business is not to provide his students with ready-made conclusions, but to train them to think for themselves, and to provide them access to those materials which they need if they are to think intelligently.

It is, however, for reasons which have already been made evident, inadmissible that the power of determining when departures from the requirements of the scientific spirit and method have occurred, should be vested in bodies not composed of members of the academic profession. Such bodies necessarily lack full competency to judge of those requirements; their intervention can never be exempt from the suspicion that it is dictated by other motives than zeal for the integrity of science; and it is, in any case, unsuitable to the dignity of a great profession that the initial responsibility for the maintenance of its professional standards should not be in the hands of its own members. It follows that university teachers must be prepared to assume this responsibility for themselves. They have hitherto seldom had the opportunity, or perhaps the disposition, to do so. The obligation will doubtless, therefore, seem to many an unwelcome and burdensome one; and for its proper discharge members of the profession will perhaps need to acquire, in a greater measure than they at present possess it, the capacity for impersonal judgment in such cases, and for judicial severity when the occasion requires it. But the responsibility cannot, in this committee's opinion, be rightfully evaded. If this profession should prove itself unwilling to purge its ranks of the incompetent and the unworthy, or to prevent the freedom which it claims in the name of science from being used as a shelter for inefficiency, for superficiality, or for uncritical and intemperate partisanship, it is certain that the task will be performed by others—by others who lack certain essential qualifications for performing it, and whose action is sure to breed suspicions and recurrent controversies deeply injurious to the internal order and the public standing of universities. Your committee has, therefore, in the appended "Practical Proposals" attempted to suggest means by which judicial action by representatives of the profession, with respect to the matters here referred to, may be secured.

There is one case in which the academic teacher is under an obligation to observe certain special restraints—namely, the instruction of immature students. In many of our American colleges, and especially in the first two years of the course, the student's character is not yet fully formed, his mind is still relatively immature. In these circumstances it may reasonably be expected that the instructor will present scientific truth with discretion, that he will introduce the student to new conceptions gradually, with some consideration for the student's preconceptions and traditions, and with due regard to character-building. The teacher ought also to be especially on his guard against taking unfair advantage of the student's immaturity by indoctrinating him with the teacher's own opinions before the student has had an opportunity fairly to examine other opinions upon the matters in question, and before he has sufficient knowledge and ripeness of judgment to be entitled to form any definitive opinion of his own. It is not the least service which a college or university may render to those under its instruction, to habituate them to looking not only patiently but methodically on both sides, before adopting any conclusion upon controverted issues. By these suggestions, however, it need scarcely be said that the committee does not intend to imply that it is not the duty of an academic instructor to give to any students old enough to be in college a genuine intellectual awakening and to arouse in them a keen desire to reach personally verified conclusions upon all questions of general concernment to mankind, or of special significance for their own time. There is much truth in some remarks recently made in this connection by a college president:

> Certain professors have been refused reelection lately, apparently because they set their students to thinking in ways objectionable to the trustees. It would be well if more teachers were dismissed because they fail to stimulate thinking of any kind. We can afford to forgive a college professor what we regard as the occasional error of his doctrine, especially as we may be wrong, provided he is a contagious center of intellectual enthusiasm. It is better for students to think about heresies than not to think at all; better for them to climb new trails, and stumble over error if need be, than to ride forever in upholstered ease in the overcrowded highway. It is a primary duty of a teacher to make a student take an honest account of his stock of ideas, throw out the dead matter, place revised price marks on what is left, and try to fill his empty shelves with new goods.[2]

It is, however, possible and necessary that such intellectual awakening be brought about with patience, considerateness and pedagogical wisdom.

There is one further consideration with regard to the classroom utterances of college and university teachers to which the committee thinks it important to call the attention of members of the profession, and of administrative authorities. Such utterances ought always to be considered privileged communications. Discussions in the class room ought not to be supposed to be utterances for the public at large. They are often designed to provoke opposition or arouse debate. It has, unfortunately, sometimes happened in this country that sensational newspapers have quoted and garbled such remarks. As a matter of common law, it is clear that the utterances of an academic instructor are privileged, and may not be published, in whole or part, without his authorization. But our practice, unfortunately, still differs from that of foreign countries, and no effective check has in this country been put upon such unauthorized and often mis-

[2] President William T. Foster in *The Nation*, November 11, 1915.

leading publication. It is much to be desired that test cases should be made of any infractions of the rule.[3]

In their extra-mural utterances, it is obvious that academic teachers are under a peculiar obligation to avoid hasty or unverified or exaggerated statements, and to refrain from intemperate or sensational modes of expression. But, subject to these restraints, it is not, in this committee's opinion, desirable that scholars should be debarred from giving expression to their judgments upon controversial questions, or that their freedom of speech, outside the university, should be limited to questions falling within their own specialities. It is clearly not proper that they should be prohibited from lending their active support to organized movements which they believe to be in the public interest. And, speaking broadly, it may be said in the words of a non-academic body already once quoted in a publication of this Association, that "it is neither possible nor desirable to deprive a college professor of the political rights vouchsafed to every citizen."

It is, however, a question deserving of consideration by members of this Association, and by university officials, how far academic teachers, at least those dealing with political, economic and social subjects, should be prominent in the management of our great party organizations, or should be candidates for state or national offices of a distinctly political character. It is manifestly desirable that such teachers have minds untrammeled by party loyalties, unexcited by party enthusiasms, and unbiased by personal political ambitions; and that universities should remain uninvolved in party antagonisms. On the other hand, it is equally manifest that the material available for the service of the State would be restricted in a highly undesirable way, if it were understood that no member of the academic profession should ever be called upon to assume the responsibilities of public office. This question may, in the committee's opinion, suitably be made a topic for special discussion at some future meeting of this Association, in order that a practical policy, which shall do justice to the two partially conflicting considerations that bear upon the matter, may be agreed upon.

It is, it will be seen, in no sense the contention of this committee that academic freedom implies that individual teachers should be exempt from all restraints as to the matter or manner of their utterances, either within or without the university. Such restraints as are necessary should in the main, your committee holds, be self-imposed, or enforced by the public

---

[3] The leading case is Abernethy vs. Hutchinson, 3 L.J., Ch. 209. In this case where damages were awarded the court held as follows. "That persons who are admitted as pupils or otherwise to hear these lectures, although they are orally delivered and the parties might go to the extent, if they were able to do so, of putting down the whole by means of shorthand, yet they can do that only for the purpose of their own information and could not publish, for profit, that which they had not obtained the right of selling." (Report of the Wisconsin State Board of Public Affairs, December 1914.)

opinion of the profession. But there may, undoubtedly, arise occasional cases in which the aberrations of individuals may require to be checked by definite disciplinary action. What this report chiefly maintains is that such action can not with safety be taken by bodies not composed of members of the academic profession. Lay governing boards are competent to judge concerning charges of habitual neglect of assigned duties, on the part of individual teachers, and concerning charges of grave moral delinquency. But in matters of opinion, and of the utterance of opinion, such boards can not intervene without destroying, to the extent of their intervention, the essential nature of a university—without converting it from a place dedicated to openness of mind, in which the conclusions expressed are the tested conclusions of trained scholars, into a place barred against the access of new light, and precommitted to the opinions of prejudices of men who have not been set apart or expressly trained for the scholar's duties. It is, in short, not the absolute freedom of utterance of the individual scholar, but the absolute freedom of thought, of inquiry, of discussion and of teaching, of the academic profession, that is asserted by this declaration of principles. It is conceivable that our profession may prove unworthy of its high calling, and unfit to exercise the responsibilities that belong to it. But it will scarcely be said as yet to have given evidence of such unfitness. And the existence of this Association, as it seems to your committee, must be construed as a pledge, not only that the profession will earnestly guard those liberties without which it can not rightly render its distinctive and indispensible service to society, but also that it will with equal earnestness seek to maintain such standards of professional character, and of scientific integrity and competency, as shall make it a fit instrument for that service.

II. PRACTICAL PROPOSALS

As the foregoing declaration implies, the ends to be accomplished are chiefly three:

First: To safeguard freedom of inquiry and of teaching against both covert and overt attacks, by providing suitable judicial bodies, composed of members of the academic profession, which may be called into action before university teachers are dismissed or disciplined, and may determine in what cases the question of academic freedom is actually involved.

Second: By the same means, to protect college executives and governing boards against unjust charges of infringement of academic freedom, or of arbitrary and dictatorial conduct—charges which, when they gain wide currency and belief, are highly detrimental to the good repute and the influence of universities.

Third: To render the profession more attractive to men of high ability and strong personality by insuring the dignity, the independence, and the reasonable security of tenure, of the professorial office.

The measures which it is believed to be necessary for our universities to adopt to realize these ends—measures which have already been adopted in part by some institutions—are four:

A. *Action by Faculty Committees on Reappointments.* Official action relating to reappointments and refusals of reappointment should be taken only with the advice and consent of some board of committee representative of the faculty. Your committee does not desire to make at this time any suggestion as to the manner of selection of such boards.

B. *Definition of Tenure of Office.* In every institution there should be an unequivocal understanding as to the term of each appointment; and the tenure of professorships and associate professorships, and of all positions above the grade of instructor after ten years of service, should be permanent (subject to the provisions hereinafter given for removal upon charges). In those state universities which are legally incapable of making contracts for more than a limited period, the governing boards should announce their policy with respect to the presumption of reappointment in the several classes of position, and such announcements, though not legally enforceable, should be regarded as morally binding. No university teacher of any rank should, except in cases of grave moral delinquency, receive notice of dismissal or of refusal of reappointment, later than three months before the close of any academic year, and in the case of teachers above the grade of instructor, one year's notice should be given.

C. *Formulation of Grounds For Dismissal.* In every institution the grounds which will be regarded as justifying the dismissal of members of the faculty should be formulated with reasonable definiteness; and in the case of institutions which impose upon their faculties doctrinal standards of a sectarian or partisan character, these standards should be clearly defined and the body or individual having authority to interpret them, in case of controversy, should be designated. Your committee does not think it best at this time to attempt to enumerate the legitimate grounds for dismissal, believing it to be preferable that individual insitutions should take the initiative in this.

D. *Judicial Hearings Before Dismissal.* Every university or college teacher should be entitled, before dismissal[4] or demotion, to have the

---

[4] This does not refer to refusals of reappointment at the expiration of the terms of office of teachers below the rank of associate professor. All such questions of reappointment should, as above provided, be acted upon by a faculty committee.

charges against him stated in writing in specific terms and to have a fair trial on those charges before a special or permanent judicial committee chosen by the faculty senate or council, or by the faculty at large. At such trial the teacher accused should have full opportunity to present evidence, and, if the charge is one of professional incompetency, a formal report upon his work should be first made in writing by the teachers of his own department and of cognate departments in the university, and, if the teacher concerned so desire, by a committee of his fellow specialists from other institutions, appointed by some competent authority.

The above declaration of principles and practical proposals are respecfully submitted by your committee to the approval of the Association, with the suggestion that, if approved, they be recommended to the consideration of the faculties, administrative officers, and governing boards of the American universities and colleges.

EDWIN R. A. SELIGMAN, *Chairman*
Columbia University

CHARLES E. BENNETT,
Cornell University

JAMES Q. DEALEY,
Brown University

RICHARD T. ELY,
University of Wisconsin

HENRY W. FARNAM,
Yale University

FRANK A. FETTER,
Princeton University

FRANKLIN H. GIDDINGS,
Columbia University

CHARLES A. KOFOID,
University of California

ARTHUR O. LOVEJOY,
Johns Hopkins University

FREDERICK W. PADELFORD,
University of Washington

ROSCOE POUND,
Harvard University

HOWARD C. WARREN,
Princeton University

ULYSSES G. WEATHERLY,
University of Indiana

At the annual meeting of the American Association of University Professors held in Washington, D.C., on January 1, 1916, it was moved and carried that the report of the Committee on Academic Freedom and Academic Tenure be accepted and approved.

JOHN DEWEY, *President*

A. O. LOVEJOY, *Secretary*

CHAPTER 3

Policing Professors and Students in the Educational State

Freedom for professors in the university was tolerated by the larger society on the grounds that such a freedom was necessary to produce new knowledge. It was further premised on the assumption that the organization of university professors would police their own members, thereby protecting society from the dangers of irrational, unscientific professors and students who abuse their privileges. Although the boundaries of freedom were set essentially by the power complex of the larger corporate state, professional organizations reinforced those boundaries by organizing to discipline themselves in the name of academic freedom.

THE COMMUNIST AND THE PROFESSOR

Sidney Hook tirelessly led the battle to maintain the boundaries of freedom. Through a sequential reading of his essays on academic freedom one can clearly catch the continuity in basic philosophy which has been maintained throughout the discussion of freedom in the educational state for over thirty years. One can also sense in his work the shifts in issues and the testing of the boundaries of freedom by both professors and students.

After receiving his doctorate under John Dewey, Hook studied at Munich, Berlin, and the Marx-Engels Institute in Moscow. By 1932, he openly supported the Communist ticket, and by 1933, when he published *Towards the Understanding of Karl Marx,* he was working as a Communist theoretician attempting to reconcile the works of Dewey and Marx.[1] Hook's revisionism, however, was condemned by Earl Browder and other

[1] See Robert W. Iverson, *The Communists and the Schools.* (New York: Harcourt Brace & Co., 1959), pp. 196–197.

79

Communist party regulars. Publicly expelled from the party, Hook became one of the leading anti-Communist fighters within the liberal leadership in the educational state. By 1939, with John Dewey, George S. Counts, Granville Hicks and others, he formed the Committee for Cultural Freedom. This committee served as a key organization in breaking the Communist control of Local Number 5 of the American Federation of Teachers.[2] By 1940, the most effective opposition to Communist involvement in the schools came not from the reactionary right, but from the liberal left. Locked in bitter battle against Communists, the Committee for Cultural Freedom successfully developed the general procedures and policies which were later employed by Senator Joseph McCarthy and others in ferreting out Communists in the schools. In "Academic Freedom and 'The Trojan Horse' in American Education," (1939) Hook reflected the perspective of the committee when he argued that we must now expose the danger of Communists and fellow-travellers within academia through a concerted effort for public investigations which turns "the searchlights of pitiless publicity and analysis upon it, [so that] we can compel every dark figure lurking in its shadows to emerge into the light, and fight for his ideas in the open." [3]

Here, then, was the threat of the Communist conspiracy and a way of dealing with it: punishment by exposure. Those who belonged to the party were members of a totalitarian conspiracy and, therefore, could not function as "honest teachers or scholars." [4] Hook consistently argued that any Communist party member is a committed agent of a foreign power and, therefore, can be expected to behave dogmatically in the classroom. The Communist automatically violated the basic canon of academic freedom, i.e., the disinterested pursuit of truth. Hook had made the case of guilt by association long before Joseph McCarthy took up the cudgel.[5] In this sense, the roots of the McCarthy era lie embedded as much in the thinking of 1930 liberals as it does in populist reactionaries.[6] It was, in fact, the unholy alliance of the two which later led to the creation of the American Committee for Cultural Freedom in 1951. With Sidney Hook as its first president, the organization became a subsidiary of the CIA sponsored Congress for Cultural Freedom.[7] As an outspoken Cold War warrior, Hook com-

[2] See *Ibid.*

[3] Sidney Hook, "Academic Freedom and 'The Trojan Horse' in American Education," *American Association of University Professors Bulletin*, December 1939, p. 555.

[4] *Ibid.*, p. 552.

[5] For an interesting analysis involving the problems of academic freedom, see Paul Violas, "Fears and Constraints on Academic Freedom of Public School Teachers, 1930–1960," *Educational Theory*, Vol. 21, Winter 1971.

[6] See Michael Paul Rogin, *The Intellectuals and McCarthy*. (Cambridge: M.I.T. Press, 1967).

[7] See Christopher Lasch, "The Cultural Cold War," in Barton J. Bernstein's, *Towards a New Past*. (New York: Pantheon Books, 1968).

plained about "cultural vigilantism," not because there was anything wrong with employing the principle of guilt by association, but because the wrong people were exercising the principle. Hook argued that it was the expert, the professional, who should control the searchlight. In the hands of the professionally uninitiated, like Senator McCarthy, considerable damage might be done to the anti-Communist cause. Hook specifically complained of such harm when McCarthy attacked the Voice of America. Eventually, Hook openly attacked McCarthy for bringing great harm to the nation's "reputation." [8]

While Hook insisted that the final determination of fitness be made by faculty committees, he found that professional ethics, as he defined such ethics, prohibited the teacher from exercising his right against self-incrimination, supposedly guaranteed by the Fifth Amendment.

> It is morally and professionally inadmissible to refuse to answer questions relevant to one's educational fitness and integrity on the ground that a truthful answer would be self-incriminating. Such a refusal should be construed as presumptive evidence of unfitness, final determination to be left to faculty committees elected for that purpose.[9]

Hook thus approved of firing a professor for the exercise of his constitutional rights.

Repeatedly, Hook argued for faculties to organize and police their own ranks and destroy the "enemy within." During the McCarthy era and the Cold War, Hook, through the American Committee for Cultural Freedom exerted considerable influence in shaping the educational state to fit the needs of the military industrial complex. He more than rode the crest of the anti-Communist wave; he was part of it. In his thinking and perspective, one can see the kind of liberal thought which went into the creation of the Cold War and the warfare state which eventually culminated in the Vietnam War.[10]

By mid-century, Hook, along with others, had persuaded the Educational Policies Commission, the National Educational Association, the American Federation of Teachers, and the Association of American University Presidents that membership in the party should constitute prima

---

[8] For the relationship between the CIA and the very significant role the Voice of America played in the maintenance of the Cold War, see Erik Barnouw, *The Image Empire*, Vol. III. (New York: Oxford University Press, 1970). Also see Sidney Hook's letter to the New York Times, May 8, 1953.

[9] As quoted by Iverson, *The Communists and the Schools*, p 341.

[10] In this same sense, William Appleman Williams argues that the Vietnam War was not an accident of history, but rather a culmination of Cold War activities which, in turn, were a culmination of long standing values and attitudes of American liberal leadership. Although one need not be reminded of the role liberal presidents and advisors have played in the Cold War, one ought to reflect on the fact that it was a liberal, Thomas W. Braden, who supervised the CIA's clandestine involvement in various cultural associations in the 1960s which ranged from infiltrating music and art associations to international student associations.

facie evidence for dismissal from teaching. In contrast, the American Association of University Professors rejected the assumption of guilt by association.[11]

In "Academic Integrity and Academic Freedom," Hook further developed his argument against "fellow-travelling professors," as well as those liberals who have gone "soft" on communism. Hook asserted that, "The groves of the academy have become one of the battlefields in the current struggle for freedom." Furthermore, he argued, "muddled thinking" liberals must quit crying "Redbaiter!" every time criticism is leveled against the Communists in academia and get to work to police the academic battlefield. In "Should Communists be Allowed to Teach?" Hook argued that the communist was not a free, objective scholar and, therefore, should not be allowed to teach. In response to Hook's assertions and heated rhetoric, in the same article, which is reprinted in the readings section that follows, Alexander Meiklejohn defended the time-honored notion that a man is innocent until he is proven guilty. He further argued that it is, in fact, a real lack of faith in democracy and freedom that leads men to the tragic position of suppression of freedom in the name of freedom.

POLICING THE STUDENTS

The great tragedy of the Cold War was that truth, freedom and integrity became the first casualties in a long list of casualties which reached down to the very root of all American institutions. The road from Guatemala to the Bay of Pigs, to MyLai, was engineered out of Cold War fears and hatreds and paved with public deception and lies which shattered the credibility of most governmental institutions for many Americans. After the Bay of Pigs, C. Wright Mills spoke for what remained of the American conscience when he said, "I feel a desperate shame for my country." Mills knew that the problem of the use of American power was fundamental, touching the very heart of the philosophy by which much of America had lived in the twentieth century corporate society. The pragmatic liberal philosophy of Dewey and Hook operationalized within a bureaucratic structure, in effect, turned every moral question into a tactical survival problem. Pragmatism, as a philosophy, was admirably suited to facilitating a growing bureaucratic technological state, but tragically ill-suited to address the great moral issues which required limitations on power.[12] Bertrand

---

[11] Not until 1967, in *Keyishian v. Board of Regents*, did the United States Supreme Court squarely face the issue. In that case they declared this practice unconstitutional.

[12] See Clarence J. Karier, "Liberal Ideology and the Quest for Orderly Change," *History of Education Quarterly*, Spring, 1972.

Russell earlier had recognized this tendency in Dewey's philosophy, and by extention in American liberal philosophy in general, when he said,

> His philosophy is a power philosophy, though not, like Nietzsche's, a philosophy of individual power; it is the power of the community that is felt to be valuable. It is this element of social power that seems to me to make the philosophy of instrumentalism attractive to those who are more impressed by our new control over natural forces than by the limitations to which that control is still subject.[13]

Yet, the great problem of the twentieth century was not the freedom to produce new knowledge, but rather the moral issues involved in the corporate collective use of that knowledge. What, then, was the responsibility of the intellectual regarding the use of the knowledge he helped to create? Noam Chomsky asserted that, at a bare minimum, he should, "speak the truth and expose lies." [14] When professors of the stature of Arthur Schlesinger, Jr., Walt Rostow and others worked for the government, they all too often failed to live up to such a bare minimum standard. Instead, they brought an intellectual sophistication to a process of deceit and lying, pragmatically justified in the name of the so-called "national interest." [15] The successful pragmatist judged his own worth on his ability to achieve his ends, and the ultimate end was national survival. Thus, truth was validated by the perceived survival value that ideas exhibited when put to the test of action. Such a validation made truth or falsehood contingent on a win or lose strategy. American pragmatic liberalism, when stripped of its restraining humanitarian ethic and reduced to a cold, hard operationalism, came dangerously close to a Fascist perspective on thought and action. This, it seems, is what Benito Mussolini had in mind when he said,

> The pragmatism of William James was of great use to me in my political career. James taught me that an action should be judged rather by its results than by its doctrinary basis. I learnt of James that faith in action, that ardent will to live and fight, to which Fascism owes a great part of its success. . . .[16]

Action, untroubled by doctrinaire moral principles, judged solely by its success value in terms of production results, marketing results, national interest, personal interest, etc., would gradually become the operational philosophy for many decision makers in the American liberal technological state. When the truth of an idea is determined by the success of the idea in

---

[13] Bertrand Russell, *A History of Western Philosophy*. (New York: Simon and Schuster, 1945), p. 827.

[14] Noam Chomsky, "The Responsibility of Intellectuals," in *The Dissenting Academy*, Theodore Roszak, editor. (New York: Pantheon Books, 1967), p. 256.

[15] Noam Chomsky, *American Power and the New Mandarins*. (New York: Pantheon Books, 1967), p. 325.

[16] As quoted in Ralph Barton Perry, *The Thought and Character of William James*. (Cambridge, Mass.: Harvard Univ. Press, 1948), p. 317.

action and the success or failure of an idea in turn is contingent on power relationships, what emerges is a kind of flexible multiple truth which is validated largely on the basis of who said it and what effect it might have. With this kind of operationalism, truth becomes that which the powers who control the institutions want it to be. As Noam Chomsky pointed out, such criteria is not far from what national socialist Martin Heidegger espoused when he argued that, "Truth is the revelation of that which makes a people certain, clear, and strong in its action and knowledge." [17]

One of the roots of Fascist thought undoubtedly lies in the corruption of intellect where words take on an "Alice in Wonderland" usage. Truth, defined in these terms, can have disastrous consequences. As Bertrand Russell put it:

> The concept of 'truth' as something dependent upon facts largely outside human control has been one of the ways in which philosophy hitherto has inculcated the necessary elements of humility. When this check upon pride is removed, a further step is taken on the road towards a certain kind of madness—the intoxication of power which invaded philosophy with Fichte, and to which modern men, whether philosophers or not, are prone. I am persuaded that this intoxication is the greatest danger of our time, and that any philosophy which, however unintentionally, contributes to it is increasing the danger of vast social disaster.[18]

The philosophy of many liberal professors working for the government, both in and out of the university, was contributing to just such a disaster.

Arguing pragmatically that the "national interest" justifies the means, more and more university professors, such as Sidney Hook and Arthur Schlesinger, Jr., welded their function in education to that of the larger corporate liberal state. The university played an indispensable role in the creation of sophisticated weaponry and trained manpower needed for the push-button, but still very bloody, warfare in Vietnam. Major universities and their professors, under CIA and Pentagon contracts, repeatedly violated the liberal's own definition of disinterested pursuit of knowledge as a prerequisite for academic freedom. While the rhetoric of academic freedom still abounds behind the liberal mask of objectivity and disinterested pursuit of scientific truth, few who have been involved with student demonstrations and the aftermath of repression which has engulfed many universities can take seriously the liberal notion of a free university.

The student protests, from the Dow demonstration of 1968 to the Cambodian strikes and Kent and Jackson State shootings of 1970, represent, to a large extent, the testing of the liberal rhetoric with respect to scientific objectivity and the disinterested pursuit of truth within a pre-

---

[17] Noam Chomsky, "The Responsibility of Intellectuals," *American Power and the New Mandarins.* (New York: Vintage Books, 1969), p. 325.
[18] Russell, *A History of Western Philosophy*, p. 828.

sumed "free" university. Repeatedly, the students challenged the university as a collective entity to take a moral stand, not solely on the creation of new knowledge, but also on the use of that knowledge. And repeatedly, they were told that the university could not take a stand, moral or otherwise, against the hand that fed it. The university might be a critic of society, but only so far as the powers that control tolerate the criticism. Criticism that was tolerated usually carried such adjectives as reasonable, rational, intelligent, constructive; while criticism that was not tolerated was unreasonable, irrational, unintelligent and destructive. The boundaries of freedom clearly fell between these two sets of adjectives. Over and over again, it was pointed out that the university, by its collective action or inaction, was taking a stand on the side of power. The stand was set by the power configuration which, in fact, controlled the universities. While professors could pass resolutions, they usually only passed those resolutions which simply reinforced the boundaries already determined by the power elite. In "Some Thoughts On Intellectuals and the Schools," Noam Chomsky urged teachers to raise the difficult moral questions and take unpopular moral stands. Few professors, however, dared take the socratic course. The hemlock they rightly sensed would be served by their own "professional" societies.

One argument frequently heard in the many debates that surrounded the role of the university professor in protesting the Vietnam War was that as an individual the professor was free to take a stand against the government; but as a member of an academic community, he was not free to commit collectively the university community to a stand against the war. While some argued this point from the standpoint of protecting the academic freedom of those who supported the war, others argued that while professors might have a unique collective freedom to inquire, they do not have a unique collective responsibility with respect to the social uses of knowledge. In this sense, it was clear that the professor was simply a servant of power. The professionalization of the university professor had resulted in the rather strange anomaly of the professor, as a member of the university, being able to stand in judgement of a professor's work, and yet, unable to stand in judgement of the social uses of that same work, especially when that judgement conflicted with public policy. These, then, were the parameters of the professional's role in the educational state. While some called this pragmatic realism, others called it institutional hypocrisy, and still others called it academic prostitution. With the multiplication of American atrocities in Vietnam, the memory of Nuremberg seemed to fade in the afterglow of napalmed children and burning villages.

The crisis in the university, led by a small number of students and still smaller number of faculty, presented a management problem of some proportion. The distinctive danger of a morally conscious university operating in an immoral society was too threatening to be tolerated. In the fall of 1970, President Richard Nixon sent a letter to all university presidents endorsing Sidney Hook's "Plan to Achieve Campus Peace." Once again, for Hook, the "enemy within" had to be ferreted out, and again it would have to be accomplished by the professorial community itself. They had opened the door to "academic vandals" and they now had to find the "moral courage" to uphold the "professional standards of their calling as teachers and seekers of the truth."

Within months, Hook's proposals were initiated. Faculty and student university senates created "professional" codes of conduct for both professors and their students. The grounds for dismissal were established professionally and the faculty and students proceeded to police their own ranks. To insure further that proper policing would take place, further measures were necessary. Through a concerted effort on the part of the federal and state governments, as well as the philanthropic foundations, budgets were slashed, professors and students were fired and expelled, while still others were intimidated.[19] Uniform repressive practices including budget freezes, one-year contracts, the cutting of assistantships, and the elimination of post-doctoral fellowships artificially induced a surplus of teachers and students. While some recognized what was taking place, many viewed these events as a consequence of natural economic and political circumstances unrelated to the question of control and management of the university. Law and order was restored to the university. With that restoration, men of power breathed a sigh of relief. As the boundaries of the campus were once again established, the threat of a university as a critical agent of society had passed.

With that passage had gone also much of the credibility of the liberal's definition of a "free" university based on its own canons of objective scientific inquiry guarded by disciplined professionals. Perhaps the German concept of *Lehrfreiheit* was correct, after all. The university created as an agent of the state could not also serve as a conscience of the state. Within that frame of reference, one can understand why Professor Ely would consider himself unfit as an instructor at a "great" state university if he, in fact, supported strikes and boycotts as an instructor. The German concept of academic freedom had always assumed that those who wield

[19] The University of Illinois, at the Champaign–Urbana campus, the home of the largest AAUP chapter, was one of many institutions that rid itself of its radical professors through various kinds of tenure and procedural devices. For many in the State Legislature, this was not done fast enough. On June 15, 1972, the Illinois House narrowly failed to attach a rider to a bill which would, in effect, have prevented the university from paying the salary of a controversial professor. As the State Representative who introduced the rider put it, "This is a warning to faculty and administrators that the Legislature will not tolerate radicals." *Daily Illini*, June 16, 1972.

power would also determine the parameters of critical inquiry within the university. One suspects that is essentially what Alexander Meiklejohn had in mind when he said, "The purpose of all teaching is to express the cultural authority of the group by which the teaching is given," and that, "teachers and pupils . . . are both agents of the state." [20] Sidney Hook was correct when he labeled this an "illiberal Hegelian notion." It did not carry with it the rather confusing notion of neutrality that engulfs the liberal rationale for scientific inquiry, professionalism and academic freedom within the educational state. Meiklejohn's notion, though "illiberal" in the eyes of Hook, is, it seems, more honest than the liberal's professional rhetoric which obscures the reality of power.

The professionalization of "truth-seekers" was rooted in an elitism of the expert. Such an elite required a free sanctuary in order to carry out in society their assumed function as creators of knowledge. Perhaps the elitist concept upon which the idea of academic freedom was founded and functions should be questioned. The very notion of a privileged sanctuary, which implies that some people within the sanctuary are permitted to think freely, while others outside are not, may inherently conflict with the structure of a free and open society. In a Kantian aristocratic society, where men of wealth and power must protect the creators of knowledge against the irrational masses, such sanctuaries seem appropriate. In a truly free society, however, the boundaries of such sanctuaries might dissolve in the freedom of the larger community, and one of the key arguments for academic freedom, i.e., the need for intellectual sanctuary to produce new knowledge, might disappear. Professional organizations would then be recognized simply as groups of experts serving their own interests. Under such circumstances, the status of the "professional" in the social hierarchy might suffer.

CONFLICTS IN VALUE

In both the German and the liberal American model, the problem of the relationship of the intellectual elite who create knowledge and the power elite who use the knowledge was the same. For the most part, the intellectual's relationship to power has been that of a servant. As such the universities participated in the best and worst events of the century. After Buchenwald, Hiroshima and MyLai, few sensitive observers could find credence in the liberal academic freedom credo which asserted the neutrality of the scientific inquirer and the assumed beneficence of science. On

[20] As quoted by Sidney Hook in "Academic Integrity and Academic Freedom," *Commentary*, October, 1949, p. 335.

the other hand, after the Eichmann trial, few would find the role of the professor as a Hegelian servant of power morally tenable. The moral dilemma of the university professor was and is rooted in the social consequences of the use and abuse of new knowledge.

While many, such as Hermann Hesse, would long for the honesty and intellectual purity of a future Castalia where the search for truth might go unsullied by the practical world of politics and where the aesthetic game of art for art's sake might be played in full fidelity to the life of the mind, Hesse, himself, in the figure of Joseph Knecht would return to the practical world of the teacher. Sensing the danger of the coming storm, he would resign his post as Magister Ludi and give up his pleasure of playing the Glass Bead Game for the more difficult task of transmitting to the children of the world the central value of Castalia; loyalty and love of truth before country or person.

> The mind of man is beneficent and noble when it obeys truth. As soon as it betrays truth, as soon as it ceases to revere truth, as soon as it sells out, it becomes intensely diabolical. . . . The scholar who knowingly speaks, writes, or teaches falsehood, who knowingly supports lies and deceptions, not only violates organic principles. He also, no matter how things may seem at the given moment, does his people a great disservice. He corrupts its air and soil, its food and drink; he poisons its thinking and its laws, and he gives aid and comfort to all the hostile evil forces that threaten the nation with annihilation.[21]

For the most part, the betrayal of the intellectual in the twentieth century has not been a betrayal of country or person, but a betrayal of calling. To be sure, the university has never been a Castalian sanctuary where knowledge of the truth was sought for its own sake, free of political, economic and personal interests and motivations; and yet, the promise of that calling repeatedly aroused the hopes of those who sought a more enlightened civilization. Incorporated in the promise of that calling was the dream that some men, eventually all men, might pursue the truth wherever that might lead. This assumed, on the one hand, that men and their institutions could tolerate such a quest, and on the other, that a profession of "truth-seekers" honestly pursuing such a calling must be prepared to sacrifice self and country during times of plague in the interest of truth. Socrates knew full well that the hemlock was a necessary and essential part of that calling. Only if the intellectual was prepared to sacrifice himself, his wealth and his country in the interest of truth, could he be true to his calling and cease to be a servant of power by becoming a servant of truth.

[21] Hermann Hesse, *Magister Ludi* (The Glass Bead Game). (New York: Bantam Books, 1972), p. 332.

Historically, the university and its cultural humanism was not so much based on a life of sacrifice for truth as it was based on the tradition of the sophists of ancient Greece who sold their culture for a price.[22] In many ways the dilemma of the university professor reflected the problems and issues which surrounded the sophists who Plato complained viewed their culture as a "marketable commodity to be put on sale." This similarity was not accidental. Humanist culture was firmly rooted in the rhetorical tradition of Cicero's and Isocrates's model of the orator.

The arguments over the role of the orator that took place between Isocrates and Plato is instructive. Plato and Aristotle both insisted that truth was to be found in the philosopher's use of logical analysis and not in the orator's use of rhetoric. Rhetoric, it was argued, was only the art of persuasion.[23] To Isocrates, however, rhetoric was, itself, the art of arriving at the truth. Isocrates argued that, other than in the world of men's imagination, there was no haven where the truth might be found in the pure form. He insisted that there existed only one life of action where men loved, hated, lived and died and it was in that world of action, alone, that truth was to be found. The orator, as an active participant fully engaged in the decision-making process, was a midwife to truth. In this one-dimensional, pragmatic world of thought and action the orator could become both a servant of power and a servant of truth.

The educational ideal of the orator embodied what Matthew Arnold called the "best that was thought and said in the past" with the necessary social skills for a life of effective political action. As direct participants in political action, some men such as Cicero, would risk and even lose their lives, while others, such as the courtiers of the Renaissance or the courtiers of the present society, would act out their roles from a somewhat safer position, as advisors to power rather than wielders of power.

The crisis of humanistic culture came in the nineteenth century as Matthew Arnold suggested when men, for economic reasons, could begin to think of culture in democratic rather than aristocratic terms.[24] The humanist tradition had been and still is fundamentally elitist. Based on an economic system of limited wealth, men of this tradition usually assumed that society would inevitably be organized in a hierarchial social system with an aristocracy of power, wealth, virtue and talent. It was both the possibility of a more affluent productive system and an apparent decline in

---

[22] Werner Jaeger, *Paideia: The Ideals of Greek Culture*, Vol. I. (New York: Galaxy Books, 1965), pp. 286–331.

[23] See Aristotle's *Rhetoric*.

[24] See Lionel Trilling, *The Portable Matthew Arnold*. (New York: Viking Press, 1956). Consider his three essays on "Democracy," "Culture and Anarchy," and "Equality."

the vital life signs of classical humanist culture which stimulated Karl Marx to dream his utopian dream of the possibility of an equalitarian society. By the opening decades of the twentieth century in America, the classical tradition had died. However, the notion of the necessity of an aristocratic hierarchial social order did not die with American classicism. It reappeared in the Jeffersonian dream toward which Horace Mann had worked and which Charles W. Eliot and others successfully fashioned into the liberal meritocratic educational state of the twentieth century. The issue of social hierarchy and maldistribution of wealth would be avoided successfully, as Horace Mann in the nineteenth century and most liberals in the twentieth century argued, not by changing the social hierarchy and redistributing the wealth, but by increased productivity which would allow increased consumption by a larger middle class without ever changing the hierarchial social order. At its worst, the meritocratic ideal was a sham that concealed the fact that society was not organized on the basis of merit but on the basis of inherited privilege, wealth and status. At its best, the meritocratic ideal was a society where the reward system would be distributed in an assumed differential heirarchy according to merit. The meritocratic ideal at its best still incorporated a conception of an aristocracy of virtue and talent.

While some men, such as Jose Ortega Y Gasset, would fear the cultural insensitivity of the masses and advocate one kind of elite and Vilfredo Pareto pointed to the effective means of manipulating the masses on the basis of their irrational needs and advocated another, John Dewey and other liberals helped fashion the meritocratic educational system which effectively incorporated some very basic elite assumptions of the humanist tradition. John Dewey and other liberals signed the Humanist Manifesto (1933) as authentic standard-bearers of the humanist tradition.[25] They not only reconstructed the ideal of educational Paideia based on an assumed aristocracy of virtue and talent, they, as had Protagoras, proclaimed "man the measure of all things," and, as had Isocrates, proclaimed that truth is to be found in the world of "action." The issue of the professional liberal expert as an elite, rooted in the concept of meritocracy, would reappear whether one turned to political, educational, economic or social reform throughout the century. Reform from the top down could not result in a more democratic equalitarian society. Those who sought a more equali-tarian society by following the efforts of liberal reformers were doomed to frustration. Those, however, who believed that the "good" society was a meritocratic society with its natural elites would be heartened by the efforts of some liberal reformers to "equalize" opportunity without

[25] This interpretation is, of course, contrary to the position taken by Irving Babbitt, Paul Elmer More and Norman Foerster.

equalizing the system. The very aristocratic role of the intellectual and professional as an expert may in and of itself prevent the emergence of a more equalitarian system. The goal of a free society where all men can realize their creative potential, in the end, may be in very basic conflict with the goals of the humanistic tradition which permeates all institutions of higher learning. The paradox appears, that given this society and the social values which prevail, it may be that only through a cultivation of elite values, which in turn, reinforces the elite nature of the system can the creative potential of anyone be achieved.

The moral tension surrounding the role and function of the university professor is inescapable. As a servant of power or as a servant of truth, he is morally culpable. As a servant of power he has chosen to contribute his life and efforts toward the development of a particular social system. He may, at any time, sacrifice himself, his wealth and/or his country for what he believes it takes to be true to his calling. While he may willingly take the hemlock in the cause of service to truth, he may not hold this value as absolute without peril. He can not escape the social consequences of his search for truth. He may, at times, even find it necessary to compromise his calling to prevent the destruction of humanity. Consider, for example, the hypothetical case which Noam Chomsky raised: What would one say of a scientific "truth-seeker" who, in Hitler's Germany, wished to pursue the hypothesis that usury is a genetically determined tendency among Jews?[26] The virtue of "truth-seeking," blind to social consequences, can quickly become a vice. The search for truth cannot be held as an absolute value in our society without possibly having devastating consequences to large segments of humanity. Responsible for at least the immediate consequences of his inquiry, the sensitive university professor will find his social values, at times, in direct conflict with his value for free and untrammeled inquiry. When that time comes, whether he is a servant of power or a servant of truth, he is condemned to the anguish of choice. In that choice, as Jean Paul Sartre has stated, he chooses himself, and in choosing for himself, he chooses for all mankind.

> When we say that man chooses himself, we do mean that every one of us must choose himself; but by that we also mean that in choosing for himself he chooses for all men. For in effect, of all the actions a man may take in order to create himself as he wills to be, there is not one which is not creative, at the same time, of an image of man such as he believes he ought to be.[27]

[26] See Noam Chomsky, "I. Q. Tests: Building Block for the New Class System," *Ramparts*, Vol. II, No. 1 (July 1972), pp. 24–30.

[27] Excerpt from Jean Paul Sartre, "Portrait of the Antisemite," in Walter Kaufmann, *Existentialism from Dostoevsky to Sartre*. (New York: Meridian Books, 1963), p. 291.

A Summary of Sidney Hook's "Academic Freedom and 'The Trojan Horse' in American Culture"

Clarence J. Karier

In May, 1939, John Dewey, G. S. Counts, Horace Kallen, Sidney Hook and other prominent liberals organized the "Committee for Cultural Freedom" which was instrumental in wresting control of New York's Local No. 5 of the American Federation of Teachers from Communist control. Sidney Hook's "Academic Freedom and 'The Trojan Horse' in American Education" was written in the context of an extended, bruising battle with Communists for control not only of Local No. 5, but for eventual control over the larger association itself. In this article, Hook makes direct reference to the work of the committee. The arguments which Hook began to develop in this essay on the eve of World War II eventually became standard arguments that he and other liberals used throughout the post–World War II Cold War period.

In a democracy, Hook argued, the freedom inherent in the Bill of Rights is extended to all men within the body politic. Significantly, however, he believed there were limits. We should not, he argued, allow those freedoms to be used to conceal the activities of America's totalitarian enemies within American education. The totalitarian whether he be Nazi or Communist, Hook insisted, was a committed agent of a foreign power who inevitably violated what he termed the "ethics and logic of scientific inquiry," and therefore, could not function as an honest teacher and scholar in the American classroom. As Hook put it, "A totalitarian may make an efficient government agent: he can not be an honest teacher or scholar." [1]

There were, however, some differences between the way the Nazis and the Communists functioned in American Education. In general he found the Nazi attempt to influence American higher education "crude and obvious" [2] whereas, the Communist attempts he found "much more numerous and even more devious in their methods of penetration. . . ." [3] While it was difficult enough, Hook contended, to identify card-carrying Communists because so many held secret membership, it was even more difficult to identify the Communist sympathizers or "fellow travellers." Yet, no matter how much the "fellow traveller" disguised himself as a liberal and progressive, he must be publicly exposed as the enemy of freedom and decency who lives within the Trojan Horse, already " . . . drawn

---

[1] Sidney Hook, "Academic Freedom and 'The Trojan Horse' in American Education." *AAUP Bulletin*, p. 552.

[2] *Ibid.*, p. 552.

[3] *Ibid.*, p. 553.

into our temples of learning." [4] This enemy, Hook argued, could be fairly and clearly identified not only by the company he kept but by the causes he espoused. As Hook put it:

> But there is one sure sign by which they can be recognized. Vociferous in their protests against abuses of cultural and academic freedom in this country, and in every other country, which happens at the moment to be at odds with Russia, they noisily acclaim the intellectual and academic terrorism that exists in the Soviet Union as the high water mark of progress. Their strongest fire is directed, at the behest of the Communist Party, against American liberals and educators who are opposed to all forms of totalitarianism.[5]

Hook went on to argue that the fellow traveller in academic circles who secretly carried out the directives of the Communist Party and still disavowed any connection with it, invited public reaction which ultimately would destroy academic freedom for the university professor. The solution, he argued, was not to be found in government repression, but rather by " . . . *public exposure and criticism in the educational and cultural professions themselves.*" [6] Professors must police their own ranks.

In this article, fully a decade before the McCarthy era, Hook articulated certain principles which became commonplace during the Cold War. First the principle of guilt by association was established. The card-carrying Communist was guilty of unscholarly behavior by virtue of the association to which he belonged. Secondly, the fellow traveller was to be judged intellectually dishonest on the basis of a cluster of political and social sympathies he exhibited. Thirdly, both the card-carrying Communist and the fellow traveller were to be handled not by direct repressive government action, but by massive "pitiless publicity" and "public exposure." In this article, Hook delineated some of the essential ingredients of what became the mainstream liberal response to the threat of a Communist conspiracy.

A Summary of Sidney Hook's "Should Communists Be Permitted to Teach?"

Clarence J. Karier

Ten years after Hook laid down his guidelines for managing the threat of Communists in the school and in the midst of the McCarthy era, he once again turned his attention to the question, "Should Communists Be Permitted to Teach?" This article was prompted by the then recent firing

---

[4] *Ibid.*, p. 555.
[5] *Ibid.*, p. 553.
[6] *Ibid.*, p. 555. Italicizing for emphasis is Hook's.

of professors from the University of Washington in Seattle for being members of the Communist party. In this essay, he asserted that the function of the university was to discover, teach and publish the truth. Given this function, he argued, it is imperative to allow professors a wide latitude of freedom. Controversial issues would inevitably emerge, but these issues, he believed, must be weighed and examined objectively by experts within a discipline who are dedicated and loyal to the search for truth. Such experts must engage in "honest presentation" and reasoned investigation. If, in the process of "honestly" searching for the truth, an individual brings down upon his head the charge of being a "communist" or a "fascist," the university, Hook asserted, must steadfastly protect him. The professor who has this special privilege occupies a special position of trust which carries with it a correlative duty which requires that he be steadfastly loyal to the "ethics and logic of scientific inquiry." Hook then turned to the problem of the Communist party member and asked if that professor who knowingly belonged to the party is capable of carrying out his duties as a free, inquiring agent. The answer, from Hook's point of view, was no. He urged the reader to look to the directives of the party and the actual behavior of known Communists within academia. There are, he insisted, no "sleeper or passive members of the party" because party members are required to take a pledge which commits them to the "Leninist" line of the party. They are also under explicit party directive, he asserted, to inject into every class the teachings of Marx and Lenin. They are further instructed to redirect rebellious spirit of youth against the capitalist system with as little exposure to their own position as possible. This directive, Hook concluded, violated the requirement of free, open and honest inquiry. The party, he argued, requires discipline of all its members. Deviation or reflective thought are not permitted. When the party shifts, the party member is required to shift with it, if he wishes to remain within the party. Granville Hicks, Hook pointed out, was forced to resign from the party because he could not agree with the party line.

Hook went on to say that some civil libertarians asserted that a teacher must be judged guilty or innocent on the basis of his or her behavior in the classroom, rather than the political party to which he belongs. Hook rejected this position because first, the only way one could know what a teacher was actually doing in his or her classroom was to set up a spying system within the school to monitor all classes. In a "free" university this was not practically possible without seriously destroying the process of freedom of inquiry. Hook, further surmised that, "It would be very difficult to determine when a teacher was defending a conclusion because he honestly believed it followed from the evidence and when he was carrying out his task as a good soldier in the party cause." [1] Under such

[1] Sidney Hook, "Should Communists Be Permitted to Teach?" *New York Times Magazine*, February 27, 1949.

circumstances, it was practically impossible, Hook believed, to judge a teacher on the basis of his classroom behavior. On the other hand, judgment of innocence or guilt as to violation of the ethic and logic of scientific inquiry and teaching could be rendered, he asserted, on the sole grounds of whether or not one was a member of the Communist party. He explicitly denied this was "guilt by association" on the grounds that the very act of belonging to the party was a violation of academic freedom.[2]

In response to the worry by some that, if the behavior of communists were judged on the basis of party membership, what might be the possible judgment rendered by the teachers in secular schools who were loyal to the Catholic faith? Hook declared this was a "red herring." There was, he believed, no party line imposed on Catholic teachers in the schools by the Catholic Church.

While it was clear to Hook that the Communist should not be allowed to teach, the fellow-traveller presented a more difficult problem. He claimed there are all kinds of "varieties."

> No one is wise enough to pick out the dumb innocent sheep from the cunning and dishonest goats. So long as they are not under the discipline of the Communist Party, they may still be sensitive to the results of honest inquiry.[3]

Indeed, without the "steel core" discipline of the party, they are apt to prove ineffective and "fly off in all directions." In general, however, while Hook asserted that party members should not be allowed to teach, the decision to act and the nature of the action to be taken against fellow-travelling professors should be left up to their colleagues. The professors had the obligation to police their own ranks to protect against fellow-travellers.

Should Communists Be Allowed to Teach?

Yes, says Professor Meiklejohn, who argues that democracy will win in the competition of ideas.

Alexander Meiklejohn

In a recent issue *The New York Times* Magazine published an article by Professor Sidney Hook of New York University in

[2] Some eighteen years later the U.S. Supreme Court in the Keyishian v. Board of Regents Case (1967) rejected this line of argument by asserting that this was, indeed, "guilt by association."
[3] *Ibid.*, p. 28.

which he argued that known Communist party members should not be allowed to teach in American colleges because, as adherents to the party "line," they are not free to seek the truth. Herewith is an article challenging Professor Hook's views, written by Dr. Alexander Meiklejohn, former president of Amherst, teacher, philosopher and author of "Freedom and the College" and other works.

BERKELEY, CALIF.

The president and regents of the University of Washington have dismissed three professors and have placed three others on probation. That statement fails to mention the most significant feature of what has been done. The entire faculty is now on probation. Every scholar, every teacher, is officially notified that if, in his search for the truth, he finds the policies of the American Communist Party to be wise, and acts on that belief, he will be dismissed from the university.

In one of the dismissal cases, the evidence is not clear enough to enable an outsider to measure the validity of the decision. But the other five cases force an issue on which everyone who cares for the integrity and freedom of American scholarship and teaching must take his stand. Cool and careful consideration of that issue should be given by all of us, whether or not we agree with the teachers in question, but especially if we do not agree with them.

The general question in dispute is that of the meaning of academic freedom. But that question has three distinct phases. The first of these has to do with the organization of a university. It asks about the rights and duties of the faculty in relation to the rights and duties of the administration. And the principle at issue corresponds closely to that which, in the Government of the United States, is laid down by the First Amendment to the Constitution. Just as that Amendment declares that "Congress shall make no law abridging the freedom of speech," so, generally, our universities and colleges have adopted a principle which forbids the administration to abridge the intellectual freedom of scholars and teachers. And, at this point, the question is whether or not the president and regents at Washington have violated an agreement, made in good faith, and of vital importance to the work of the university.

The principle of academic freedom was clearly stated by Sidney Hook in *The New York Times* Magazine of Feb. 27, 1949. After noting that "administrators and trustees" are "harried by pressure-groups," Mr. Hook concluded his argument by saying, "In the last analysis, there is no safer repository of the integrity of teaching and scholarship than the dedicated men and women who constitute the faculties of our colleges and universities." On the basis of that conviction, the Association of University Professors has advocated, and most of our universities, including Washington, have adopted, a "tenure system." That system recognizes that legal authority to appoint, promote, and dismiss teachers belongs to the president and regents. But so far as dismissals are concerned, the purpose of the tenure agreement is to set definite limits to the exercise of that authority.

This limitation of their power, governing boards throughout the nation have gladly recognized and accepted. To the Association of University Professors it has seemed so important that violations of it have been held to justify a "blacklisting" of a transgressor institution—a recommendation by the association that scholars and teachers refuse to serve in a university or college which has thus broken down the defenses of free inquiry and belief.

It is essential at this point to note the fact that the fear expressed by the tenure system is a fear of action by the president and regents. Since these officers control the status and the salaries of teachers, it is only through them or by them that effective external pressure can be used to limit faculty freedom. To say, then, as we must, that the explicit purpose of the tenure system is to protect freedom against the president and regents, is not to say that these officials are more evil than others. It says only that they are more powerful than others. Theirs is the power by which, unless it is checked by a tenure system, evil may be done.

Under the excellent code adopted at the University of Washington, it is agreed that, after a trial period in which the university makes sure that a teacher is competent and worthy of confidence, he is given "permanence" of tenure. This means that he is secure from dismissal unless one or more of five carefully specified charges are proved against him. And the crucial feature of this defense of freedom is that the holding of any set of opinions, however unpopular or unconventional, is scrupulously excluded from the list of proper grounds for dismissal. The teacher who has tenure may, therefore, go fearlessly wherever his search for the truth may lead him. And no officer of the university has authority, openly or by indirection, to abridge that freedom.

When, under the Washington code, charges are made against a teacher, it is provided that prosecution and defense shall be heard by a tenure committee of the faculty, which shall judge whether or not the accusations have been established. In the five cases here under discussion, the only charge made was that of present or past membership in the American Communist Party. Specific evidence of acts revealing unfitness or misconduct in university or other activities was deliberately excluded from the prosecution case. And, further, since the alleged fact of party membership was frankly admitted by the defense, the only question at issue was the abstract inquiry whether or not such membership is forbidden under the five provisions of the tenure code.

Upon that issue, the faculty committee decided unanimously that, in the cases of the ex-members of the Communist Party, there were, under the code, no grounds for dismissal. And, by a vote of eight to three, the same conclusion was reached concerning the two men who were still members of the party. In the discussions of the committee, the suggestion was made that the code should be so amended that party membership would give ground for dismissal. But that action was not recommended. In its capacity as the interpreter of the code which now protects academic freedom, the committee, in all five cases, declared the charges to be not supported by the evidence presented.

In response to this judgment upon teachers by their intellectual peers, the regents, on recommendation of the president, dismissed the two party members. And, second, going beyond the recommendation of the president, they placed the three ex-members "on probation" for two years. These actions are clearly a violation of the agreement under which faculty members have accepted or continued service in the university. They deserve the condemnation of everyone who respects the integrity of a covenant, of everyone who values faculty freedom and faculty responsibility for the maintaining of freedom.

The second phase of the general question goes deeper than the forms of university organization. It challenges the wisdom of the tenure code as it now stands. It may be that, though the regents are wrong in procedure, they are right in principle. Here, then, we must ask whether President Allen is justified in saying that a teacher who is "sincere in his belief in communism" cannot "at the same time be a sincere seeker after truth which is the first obligation of the teacher." In a press interview, Mr. Allen is quoted as saying, "I insist that the Communist Party exercises thought control over every one of its members. That's what I object to." Such teachers, he tells us, are "incompetent, intellectually dishonest, and derelict in their duty to find and teach the truth." Can those assertions be verified? If so, then the tenure code should be amended. If not, then the action of the university should be immediately and decisively reversed.

No one can deny that a member of the American Communist Party accepts a "discipline." He follows a party "line." As the policies of the party shift, he shifts with them. That statement is in some measure true of all parties, whose members agree to work together by common tactics toward a common end. But the Communist discipline, it must be added, is unusually rigid and severe. Our question is, then, whether submission to that discipline unfits for university work men who, on grounds of scholarship and character, have been judged by their colleagues to be fitted for it.

For the judging of that issue we must examine the forces by means of which the discipline of the American Communist Party is exercised. It is idle to speak of "thought control" except as we measure the compulsions by which that control is made effective. What, then, are the inducements, the dominations which, by their impact upon the minds of these university teachers, rob them of the scholar's proper objectivity?

So far as inducements are concerned, good measuring of them requires that we place side by side the advantages offered to a scholar by the Communist Party and those offered by the president and regents of a university. On the one hand, as seen in the present case, the administration can break a man's career at one stroke. It has power over every external thing he cares for. It can destroy his means of livelihood, can thwart his deepest inclinations and intentions. For example, in very many of our universities it is today taken for granted that a young scholar who is known to be a Communist has not the slightest chance of a faculty appointment. He is barred from academic work. And, as against this, what has the American Communist Party to offer? Its "inducements" are the torments of suspicion, disrepute, insecurity, personal and family disaster.

Why, then, do men and women of scholarly training and taste choose party membership? Undoubtedly, some of them are hysterically attracted by disrepute and disaster. But, in general, the only explanation which fits the facts is that these scholars are moved by a passionate determination to follow the truth where it seems to lead, no matter what may be the cost to themselves and their families. If anyone wishes to unearth the "inducements" which threaten the integrity of American scholarship he can find far more fruitful lines of inquiry than that taken by the administration of the University of Washington.

But Communist controls, we are told, go far deeper than "inducements." The members of the party, it is said, "take orders from Moscow;" they are subject to "thought control by a foreign power." Now, here again, the fact of rigid party discipline makes these assertions, in some ambiguous sense, true. But, in the sense in which President Allen and his regents interpret them, they are radically false.

Let us assume as valid the statement that, in the American Communist Party "orders" do come from Moscow. But by what power are those orders enforced in the United States? In the Soviet Union, Mr. Stalin and his colleagues can, and do, enforce orders by police and military might. In that nation their control is violent and dictatorial. But by what form of "might" do they control an American teacher in an American university? What can they do to him? At its extreme limit, their only enforcing action is that of dismissal from the party. They can say to him, "You cannot be a member of this party unless you believe our doctrines, unless you conform to our policies." But, under that form of control, a man's acceptance of doctrines and policies is not "required." It is voluntary.

To say that beliefs are required as "conditions of membership" in a party is not to say that the beliefs are required by force, unless it is shown that membership in the party is enforced. If membership is free, then the beliefs are free.

Misled by the hatreds and fears of the cold war, President Allen and his regents are unconsciously tricked by the ambiguities of the words, "control," and "require," and "free," and "objective." The scholars whom they condemn are, so far as the evidence shows, free American citizens. For purposes of social action, they have chosen party affiliation with other men, here and abroad, whose beliefs are akin to their own. In a word, they do not accept Communist beliefs because they are members of the party. They are members of the party because they accept Communist beliefs.

Specific evidence to support the assertion just made was staring President Allen and his regents in the face at the very time when they were abstractly denying that such evidence could exist. Three of the five men whom they condemned as enslaved by party orders had already, by their own free and independent thinking, resigned from the party. How could they have done that if, as charged, they were incapable of free and independent thinking? Slaves do not resign.

At the committee hearings, these men explained, simply and directly, that, under past conditions, they had found the party the most effective available weapon for attack upon evil social forces but that, with changing conditions, the use of that weapon seemed no longer advisable. Shall we say that the decision to be in the party gave evidence of a lack of objectivity while the decision to resign gave evidence of the possession of it? Such a statement would have no meaning except as indicating our own lack of objectivity.

In these three cases, as in the more famous case of Granville Hicks who, some years ago, resigned party membership with a brilliant account of his reasons for doing so, the charge made cannot be sustained. The accusation as it stands means nothing more than that the president and regents are advocating one set of ideas and are banning another. They are attributing to their victims their own intellectual sins. And the tragedy of their action is that it has immeasurably injured the cause which they seek to serve and, correspondingly, has advanced the cause which they are seeking to hold back.

The third phase of our question has to do with the wisdom, the effectiveness, of the educational policy under which teachers have been dismissed or put on probation. And, on this issue, the evidence against the president and regents is clear and decisive. However good their intention, they have made a fatal blunder in teaching method.

As that statement is made, it is taken for granted that the primary task of education in our colleges and universities is the teaching of the theory and practice of intellectual freedom, as the first principle of the democratic way of life. Whatever else our students may do or fail to do, they must learn what freedom is. They must learn to believe in it, to love it, and most important of all, to trust it.

What, then, is this faith in freedom, so far as the conflict of opinions is concerned? With respect to the world-wide controversy now raging between the advocates of the freedom of belief and the advocates of suppression of belief, what is our American doctrine? Simply stated, that doctrine expresses our confidence that whenever, in the field of ideas, the advocates of freedom and the advocates of suppression meet in fair and unabridged discussion, freedom will win. If that were not true, if the intellectual program of democracy could not hold its own in fair debate, then that program itself would require of us its own abandonment. That chance we believers in self-government have determined to take. We have put our faith in democracy.

But the president and regents have, at this point, taken the opposite course. They have gone over to the enemy. They are not willing to give a fair and equal hearing to those who disagree with us. They are convinced that suppression is more effective as an agency of freedom than is freedom itself.

But this procedure violates the one basic principle on which all teaching rests. It is impossible to teach what one does not believe. It is idle to preach what one does not practice. These men who advocate that we do to the Russians what the Russians, if they had the power, would do to us are declaring that the Russians are right and that we are wrong. They practice suppression because they have more faith in the methods of dictatorship than in those of a free self-governing society.

For many years the writer of these words has watched the disastrous educational effects upon student opinion and attitude when suppression has been used, openly or secretly, in our universities and colleges. The outcome is always the same. Dictatorship breeds rebellion and dissatisfaction. High-spirited youth will not stand the double-dealing which prates of academic freedom and muzzles its teachers by putting them "on probation."

If we suggest to these young people that they believe in democracy, then they will insist on knowing what can be said against it as well as what can be said for it. If we ask them to get ready to lay down their lives in conflict against an enemy, they want to know not only how strong or how weak are the military forces of that enemy, but also what he has to say for himself as against what we are saying for ourselves.

Many of the students in our colleges and universities are today driven into an irresponsible radicalism. But that drive does not come from the critics of our American political institutions. It comes chiefly from the irresponsible defenders of those institutions—the men who make a mockery of freedom by using in its service the forces of suppression.

Underlying and surrounding the Washington controversy is the same controversy as it runs through our national life. The most tragic mistake of the contemporary American mind is its failure to recognize the inherent strength and stability of free institutions when they are true to themselves. Democracy is not a weak and unstable thing which forever needs propping up by the devices of dictatorship. It is the only form of social life and of government which today has assurance of maintaining itself.

As contrasted with it, all governments of suppression are temporary and insecure. The regimes of Hitler and Mussolini flared into strength, and quickly died away. The power of the Soviet Union cannot endure unless that nation can find its way into the practices of political freedom. And all the other dictatorships are falling, and will fall, day by day. Free self-government alone gives promise of permanence and peace. The only real danger which threatens our democracy is that lack of faith which leads us into the devices and follies of suppression.

A Summary of Sidney Hook's "Academic Integrity and Academic Freedom: How to Deal with the Fellow-travelling Professor"

Clarence J. Karier

In this essay, Hook further developed his anti-Communist position. He provided a lengthy analysis of the nature of the fellow-traveller in American universities and colleges; analyzed the reasons why they behaved as they did; examined their sources of strengths and weaknesses; and then went on to make recommendations as to how they ought to be handled. While he assumed the card-carrying-Communist should not be allowed to teach, the fellow-traveller presented a different situation as far as Hook was concerned. The fellow-traveller was not a Communist (or at least it could not be proved). He was, however, a Communist sympathizer who could be found repeatedly supporting causes which supported the Soviet Union and the international Communist conspiracy as Hook saw it working its way out in America.

Although he cited no statistics, Hook argued that,

> Statistical studies show that to this day members of the professoriat constitute the strongest and most influential group of communist fellow-travellers in the United States.[1]

[1] Sidney Hook, "Academic Integrity and Academic Freedom: How to Deal with the Fellow-Travelling Professor," *Commentary*, 8, October 1949, p. 330.

He believed this resulted, in part, from the success of the Popular Front during the depression years and the work of the party to align itself with liberal causes for its own political purposes. The Communist sympathizer, Hook asserted, was often very effective in channeling youthful rebellion; this was the case not only because Communists actively championed liberal causes, but because they were in general more willing to spend the time and effort with students in order to have an impact. They could thus be seen as effectively "softening" students for participation in the Communist movement.

The fellow-traveller, Hook also argued, is likely to be a competent scholar in his field. Outside of his field, however, he loses all sense of objectivity and rational argument. Intellectual integrity, Hook noted, is lost as the fellow-traveller becomes embroiled in social political issues. As he does so he can repeatedly be found vigorously arguing for the civil rights of Communists, but not Fascists or Ku Klux Klanners. This, he believed, resulted from their basic one-sided and distorted vision. That distorted view which avoids and ignores Communist failings also arises, in part, from the tendency of these people to associate the Communist movement on the liberal left and as an "integral element in the wider movement of progress and enlightenment." This, of course, Hook asserted, is "nonsense." The fellow-traveller, he concluded, is often simply a politically unsophisticated dupe of the hard-core card-carrying-Communist.

What, then, should be done? Rejecting such administrative measures as loyalty oaths and the New York State Feinberg Law, Hook went on to argue, first, that the case of the fellow-traveller was not so much an issue of political subversion as it was a problem of "professional misconduct." Under the circumstances, it was necessary for faculties to police their own ranks. Sanctions, he urged, must be brought by faculty committees against faculty who go beyond their limited areas of expertise. Secondly, he recommended that courses on communism be developed in every university not only to enlighten the students, but also the fellow-travelling faculty about the enemy within.

In Part III of his article, Hook turned directly to Alexander Meiklejohn's article (*New York Times*, March 27, 1949) and argued that Meiklejohn held a naive notion of the role of a Communist teacher. He asserted that Meiklejohn fails to deal with party directives, party discipline and foolishly overestimates the freedom and the willingness of the Communists to inquire objectively and openly. In quoting Meiklejohn as saying, "If membership is free, then the beliefs are free," Hook correctly pointed out that the latter phrase does not logically follow from the former. Interestingly, at this point, he turned the question around and argued that just because membership is free, the beliefs held by members of the party are not held as free. As he said:

Lenin made this crystal-clear even before the October Revolution. He reversed Dr. Meiklejohn's argument and with better justification. *Just because* membership is voluntary, those who join the Communist Party must accept its intellectual discipline; they are not free to think and write as they please.[2]

Hook, then, characterized the party member as a *totally* committed agent and therefore, by definition, an unfree scholar.[3]

In Part IV of his essay, he proceeded to call forth a militant defense of academic liberty through a hard-hitting, tough intellectual attack on what he characterized as the "fuzzy thinking" of the fellow-traveller. The fellow-traveller must be exposed as a "political hypocrite" and his "credentials to competent scholarship openly questioned by his peers." The fellow-traveller, he believed, is guilty of "treason to *academic* integrity":

> What crucially defines the treason to *academic* integrity on the part of these non-party scholars I have described is not even their violations of the canons of inquiry, which may only be occasional. It is their defense of, or silent acquiescence in, the use of police methods against their colleagues abroad—and what police methods!—to suppress ideas in any field not countenanced by party dogma, and their direct and indirect support in this country of a movement which whenever it comes to power aims to destroy every vestige of academic freedom.[4]

To Hook, the "groves of the academy" had become the "battlefield in the current struggle for freedom whose outcome will determine the pattern of culture for centuries to come." [5] Faculty, he contended, must be prepared to police their own ranks.

The Real Crisis on the Campus: An Interview with Sidney Hook

A Noted Educator Sounds a Warning—Exclusive Interview

Assaults . . . sit-ins . . . arson . . . arms-carrying students: Are the days of the American campus as it once existed numbered? What happens to academic freedom if student disorders continue?

---

[2] *Ibid.*, p. 337.

[3] While one might argue, as Hook did at times, the historic impact the party had on controlling beliefs, it is clear that logically, it does not necessarily follow as Meiklejohn suggested that because one freely joined the party he necessarily holds his beliefs freely. Neither does the inverse of that proposition, which Hook appeared to espouse, hold to be logically true; namely, that because one volunteered to be a Communist party member his beliefs were necessarily unfree. At this point, neither Meiklejohn nor Hook had the force of logic on their side.

[4] *Ibid.*, p. 338–339.

[5] *Ibid.*, p. 339.

Editors of "U.S. News & World Report" interviewed one of America's best-known philosophers, Prof. Sidney Hook, for answers to these and other questions now stirring nationwide concern.

Q. Dr. Hook, have campus disorders brought universities to a turning point in their history?

A. Yes. Recent events on American campuses have precipitated a genuine crisis in higher education. Because of events at Harvard, Cornell and other institutions, it is no exaggeration to say that American higher education is confronted with the most fundamental challenge to its basic principles in history. And by its basic principles, here, I mean the principles of academic freedom.

After all, the demand on the part of students to determine not only the nature of the curriculum but who is to teach them, and who is to be hired and fired, implies an abandonment of the traditions of academic freedom.

Q. Just how do you define academic freedom?

A. It is the freedom of professionally qualified individuals to inquire, to discover, to publish and teach the truth as they see it, independently of any controls except the standards by which conclusions or truths are established in their discipline.

Therefore, the principles of academic freedom require that, once a teacher is certified by his peers as professionally competent, there should be no interference with his right to reach and teach any conclusions in the field in which he is an expert. This principle obviously no longer applies with respect to black studies, because it is quite clear that, if black students disagree with the position of the teacher, they have the right to veto him. They have already moved in that direction in several institutions.

A year ago at Cornell, black students invaded the office of the chairman of the department of economics and demanded an apology, and later dismissal, of a lecturer because he expressed conclusions about Africa of which they disapproved. At UCLA [University of California at Los Angeles], a course in race was canceled at their demand.

Now, if this right to determine the nature of a black-studies curriculum and to select its teachers is given to black students, the natural thing will be to give white students the same right. Otherwise, it's an expression of racism. Otherwise, the implication would be: "Well, black studies are so unimportant, one can let black students determine what they want to be taught. But where white students are concerned, one must recognize traditional standards." This would be not only absurd but invidious.

If the practice is legitimate with respect to black students, why not for white students?

This demand is already part of the program of the Students for a Democratic Society. A few years ago it issued literature demanding that students have equal rights with the faculty in determining what should be taught and who is to teach it. Later on, in some places, it contended that students should have preponderant power.

Now that Harvard has recognized the principle that students can determine the content and personnel of instruction, the demand is sure to be made by white students in various fields. Only a few days ago, at the University of Colorado, an assembly of students passed a resolution condemning a professor of anthropology for having published an article on the American Indian which they regarded as racist. They rebuked him. Some demanded his dismissal.

It is quite clear that the epoch-making decision Harvard took will bring in its wake a demand by white students to control *their* curriculum and teachers.

However, this is only the beginning. What happens next will parallel what has happened with respect to black studies. The control of black studies today in most institutions is in the hands of black nationalists who are committed to separatism. They denounce people like Roy Wilkins, A. Philip Randolph and Bayard Rustin. In controlling what should be studied, they explicitly say that the curriculum must be organized in such a way as to reinforce the truth of black nationalism.

In other words, black studies have been politicized. Partly by threats and partly by actual coercion, in various places where black studies are being taught and controlled by black students we find only one point of view expressed.

This was already prefigured at a meeting at Yale University in May, 1968, when Ron Karenga and Nathan Hare [black militants] indicated that "genuine" black studies must be organized and taught by blacks—and only by blacks committed to the ideals of black nationalism. This is equivalent to saying that if there are Jewish studies on campus, they must be taught only by Zionists and not by any other Jews or by gentiles.

Now, when white students take over and demand the same rights, the SDS or the Peace and Freedom Party will demonstrate—as they already have in some places—against some teacher of economics or history or anthropology or even some scientist on the ground that his conclusions, in their exalted wisdom, are "imperialist" or "class-biased." They will then demand he be dismissed.

This will definitely spell the end of academic freedom. If the faculties of this country do not organize themselves now to resist this mass assault against the principles of academic freedom, the end result will be the politicalization of the American university in the style of the universities of Asia and South America, many of which have been politicalized to a point where little study actually takes place.

Its not accidental that when South American and Asian students want a thorough education in any particular field they go to other countries. What they can get at their own institutions is a political education—and a partisan one at that.

Maybe something can be said for the politicalization of universities in authoritarian countries where there is little opportunity for political opposition. But in our own country, where opportunities abound for the expression of differing political points of view, to make the university a political instrument is educational genocide.

What I am saying is that the tendency legitimized by Harvard and by Cornell may result in a continuous purge of universities by students who have become politicalized. Even the high schools are becoming affected.

At the moment we hear a great deal from "revolutionary" or "left" students. But before long there will be a reaction to these students, and we will hear demands for politicalization from the "right." This backlash may be even more severe than the threat from the so-called "left."

Q. Does this point to civil strife—even gun battles—ahead on the campus between competing factions?

A. I am not convinced that there will be civil war on the campuses. The failure of the educational authorities to implement their own rules will probably lead the civil authorities to step in. If universities refuse to govern themselves, the government will have to take over. It cannot permit assault, arson, possible loss of life merely because administrators—and the faculties— are cowardly.

The betrayal by the faculties, particularly at Cornell, of the principles of liberalism is what is so significant. It goes to the very heart of our agony, of our tragedy. The faculty at Cornell originally repudiated the capitulation of its dean and president in the face of armed threat, and upheld the earlier decision made by a regularly constituted committee of faculty and students to censure certain students for violent acts.

They then reversed themselves. In what did this betrayal consist? In the fact that these faculty members subordinated the processes of deliberation and justice to an opportunistic decision designed to get them off the hook.

Now, the essence of liberal civilization is the belief in due process. It is belief in the importance of rational consideration and evaluation of evidence in the hope of reaching a just conclusion. We have always taught that the process by which we reach conclusions is much more important than any specific conclusion—just as in science, the method is more reliable than any particular conclusion, because the method of science is self-corrective. We have always held that although man may be wrong in his belief, so long as the rational process is not tampered with, so long as the evidence is not "cooked," so long as there is honest inquiry, in time he will reach truth.

Similarly, for the administration of justice: We have believed that once we follow due process, we can correct any inequity that develops. The alternative are mob rule and lynch law.

But the Cornell faculty abandoned the process by which its own committee reached a conclusion. On a Monday, it sustained its committee; on a Wednesday it reversed—on the very same evidence.

Secondly, what is unforgivable in the action of the Cornell faculty is the reason it reversed itself—and yielded to force. It acted in panic, out of sheer fear of the consequence of adhering to its own principles.

Finally, what kind of example did this yielding to the threat of terror set their students? These men are supposed to represent the rational life and its integrities. Instead they sacrificed principle for safety. What kind of example was this to set their fellow citizens who subsidize education, pay them their salaries because they look to the university as the center of courageous objectivity—only to witness the faculty panic in cowardly folly?

This bodes ill for the future of higher education. It will contribute to a growing discontent on the part of citizens with universities and faculty members. It will intensify anti-intellectualism in the country. Already too many bills to curb campus disruption have been introduced in State legislatures.

Q. Does academic freedom extend to students?

A. When we talk about "academic freedom for students," the problem is to give it some acceptable meaning. It could mean the right to go to school or not to go to school, which they have; the right to go to one college or another college, depending upon their interests; or the right to choose one course of study rather than another within any particular college. By and large, students have this right.

Academic freedom could also mean the right to question, to dissent, to develop points of view of their own. And, by and large, I should say that students in this country are freer with respect to the right to dissent than they ever have been in the history of the country. They're freer here than they are in most other countries.

Recall the students who wrote and produced "MacBird." That was a play in which the President of the United States was accused of complicity in a conspiracy to assassinate his predecessor. Now, there isn't a single country in the world where students would have been permitted to publish or produce a play of this sort. And yet, on American campuses they have complete freedom to do so.

However, "academic freedom for students" might be defined as freedom to acquire an education. To this freedom there may be great obstacles: prejudice, poverty, absence of educational facilities. Their removal is the task of all citizens of a democratic community.

Traditionally, we have looked to the university as the source of non-partisan authority—as an institution that studies and illumines problems and proposed solutions, but does not enlist itself in behalf of any partisan outcome. If it becomes a partisan political institution, it cannot escape political retaliation when it backs political proposals rejected by the community.

Q. Is "nonviolence" an excuse for such actions?

A. The forcible occupation of a building is a lawless action, and is always accompanied by the threat of violence. It really is immaterial whether the violence is actual or whether the violence is threatened. At Harvard, the spectacle of deans being carried out on the shoulders of students as though they were so many sacks of potatoes was grim evidence of violence. At other places, like San Francisco State, much worse has occurred—arson, bombing, maiming for life.

Q. Have faculties in many places aided disorders?

A. The truth is that the faculty has the power to curb and to prevent student violence and the attendant outrages against academic freedom.

The faculties have more power over educational curriculum and, ultimately, over discipline than any other group on the campus. But the faculties of this country, by and large, have been loath to exercise it. Notice how few the expulsions have been for actions far worse than actions in the past that brought expulsions for offending students.

At the University of California at Berkeley, the faculty voted down motions that condemned the forcible occupation of Sproul Hall. Therefore, students elsewhere were encouraged to emulate this lawlessness.

At Columbia, the faculties have, in effect, amnestied the students for actions that were criminal in character.

Now it is obvious—especially after what has happened at Cornell—that the faculties, by and large, have been trying to buy peace by capitulating to threats of violence and to the forces of unreason. They will discover that the logic of appeasement is the same in education as it is in politics: It only whets the appetite of the students to make more and more unreasonable demands.

If Harvard is the "Munich" of American education, Cornell is its "Pearl Harbor."

Of course, what I'm saying is not true for all members of the faculty. I must confess, however, to intense disappointment with my colleagues, since I believe in the principle of faculty control. I had hoped that faculties would have more gumption and guts than they have displayed in many institutions, and especially in Harvard and Cornell.

At the turn of the century, there was an English lecturer who, having visited the American universities, returned to England with the observation that there were three sexes in America: men, women and college professors. He obviously meant to call attention to the absence of simple moral courage on the part of the faculties.

I had assumed that this failing—if it ever existed—had been overcome. Alas, there is heart-sickening evidence that many faculties are more interested in buying peace at any price than in defending academic freedom.

The great irony is that American faculties often condemned German faculties that refused to stand up to those who trampled on academic freedom when resistance might have meant the loss of their lives and those of their families. But, in the United States—confronted with a threat that doesn't begin to compare in seriousness with the threat of totalitarians— faculty members have yielded in the hope that, if they gave the students what they demanded, the students would be "reasonable." They only get kicked harder.

"THE WORST EXCESSES"

Q. Is the present structure of the university as an institution outmoded —especially the large, so-called "multiversities"?

A. What has happened has happened not only at large universities but at small. Look what occurred at Swarthmore, a small college where the president died of a heart attack in the midst of student turmoil. Look what happened at Oberlin, where students got out of hand and violated the procedures established by faculty-student committees.

No. It is interesting to observe that the worst excesses have occurred at the most liberal universities, large or small. This is overlooked by some people in positions of political authority whose academic qualifications are rather dubious.

For example, here is Robert Finch, our Secretary of Health, Education and Welfare, who maintained that many universities have brought troubles on themselves because of rigid administrative procedures and outmoded attitudes and because they pay too little attention to students.

This is true of some institutions, but is it the cause of student disorders? If Secretary Finch were right, the worst disorders and excesses would have occurred at the most authoritarian universities. But this is not the case. Secretary Finch is talking through his hat.

The truth is that at Harvard, Cornell, San Francisco State the administrations were very much concerned with students. There existed committees on which faculty and students were represented. Yet it was there that the students were guilty of some of the worst excesses. At Columbia the situation worsened after vast reforms. At Cornell, it was a faculty-student committee that decided, horror of horrors, that three Negro students were to be censured—*censured!* Some punishment! Yet the result was a resort to arms.

Secretary Finch's remarks imply that because none is free from fault, all are equally guilty—that student violence can be equated with administrative ineptitude.

Now that the season for political silliness is over, we are in for its educational variant.

In New York City, Mayor John V. Lindsay has denounced student violence in the high schools and has vowed that he would prevent it. Hurrah for him! But it is the same Mayor Lindsay who in a speech at Princeton University two years ago hailed the "Berkeley rebels," at the University of California, as providing a pattern for the rest of the students in the country to emulate. They have.

Whoever wrote that speech for Mayor Lindsay was actually putting words in his mouth to encourage students to do precisely the things that they're doing today—in high schools, too—which he is deploring. What makes Mayor Lindsay an authority on the colleges?

Scientists often rush in to talk about these matters as if they wish to illustrate that there is no transference of training from one field to another. A famous biologist and Nobel Prize winner at Harvard claims that, if adults would be aroused about social and political affairs, then youth would not be aroused. This is demonstrably false. After all, adults today are more aroused about social and political affairs than they ever have been in the past, but students are not less violent but more.

Secondly, he fails to explain why, in the past, when adults were not aroused, youth was apathetic. Aging scientists, their creative work behind them, like aging business tycoons become "elder statesmen"—and with the same qualifications.

The trouble with such "statesmen" is that they don't bring to the consideration of social and political affairs the same conscientiousness, the background of knowledge, and sense for logical form and evidence that is second nature to them when they are in the laboratory.

But not only scientists wander afield. Take a theologian like Robert McAfee Brown of Stanford, who maintains that, in the name of human freedom, academic freedom should be sacrificed. He seems unaware of the fact that academic freedom is a human freedom, too. Robespierre might have spoken in the vein that Dr. Brown did when the French Revolutionary terrorist decreed the guillotining of Condorcet [progressive philosopher], for Robespierre identified human freedom with "the health of the Revolution."

One would have expected a theologian with insight to have recognized that academic freedom is so fundamental because the real problem is the conflict of freedoms. The reason we've stressed academic freedom is that we believe that the knowledge, the detachment, the objectivity which flows from academic freedom helps us expand other human freedoms as well as resolve the conflicts among them more readily.

HOW AMERICA HAS CHANGED

Or take those who in discussing student violence always refer to the violence of the American Revolution to prove how authentically American violence is. Someone should tell them we've already won the American Revolution—that we already had our Boston Tea Party. And we had them because at the time there did not exist the political institutions by which we could settle grievances peacefully.

Today we have them. We can settle our political differences through the ballot rather than through riots. And what nonsense to hear otherwise intelligent men cite approvingly Rap Brown's discovery that "violence is as American as cherry pie"—as if that made violence or everything American as good as cherry pie. Lynching is American, too. But does that make it good?

Examine remarks like those made by John D. Rockefeller III who, in a recent speech, called down blessings upon the young because of their concern with social and political affairs. I don't know where John D. Rockefeller III gets his information about what's happening on American campuses. Whoever supplies it to him obviously can't distinguish between intellectual dissent and the exercise of violence.

The Nazi students in the '30s were also "concerned" with social and political matters when they trampled on the rights of Jewish and socialist professors. But anybody who merely or mainly praised them for their "concern" at that time would either have been considered a Nazi sympathizer or a political cretin. And to find somebody today who praises violent disrupters because they're "concerned" with social and political issues, who doesn't understand that their violent methods are far more important than any "concern" they are showing, seems to me to be irresponsible—to put it very mildly—because it encourages violence by the "concerned."

Q. What about the claim of the "New Left" philosopher Herbert Marcuse that authority in today's society is so diffuse and so powerful that peaceful methods won't work?

A. No Marcuse is simply muddle-headed. What he is saying is this: Democracy has failed because people choose things of which Marcuse disapproves. He is a Prussian type who believes that we should force people to be free, force them to love each other. Marcuse has publicly declared that he would rather that Negroes didn't have the right to vote than choose wrongly by voting like white workers for the values of a consumer society. Credit where credit is due! He certainly has the courage of his confusions.

For Marcuse, error has no rights. This goes back to Augustine's dictum. Those who believe they have the absolute truth, you see, don't accept the experimental methods of democracy, which is skeptical of absolute truth. The "right to be wrong" is not only necessary in order to be a person; it sometimes is necessary in order to reach the truth. In science, we make progress by eliminating errors. Very often the hypothesis which is refuted furthers our knowledge.

"DEMONSTRABLE NONSENSE"

Q. What about statements that we should listen to the students—that they are trying to tell us something?

A. Of course, we should listen to students—and the truth is that we have been listening to students. But the best way to communicate what one wants is through words, arguments, programs—forms of demonstration that are reasoned and reasonable.

A blow never communicates when we reach for understanding. Power may come out of a gun barrel—not insight or truth. Those who say students are merely "trying to communicate" are unaware of the fact that they have communicated quite well. But some students' conception of whether they're listened to is simply whether faculties will yield to any demands they make.

When students say that they want to determine the nature of the curriculum and have the right to hire and fire professors, we understand very well what they are saying. What they are saying is demonstrable nonsense, because to make such a demand is to equate experience and inexperience, maturity and immaturity, knowledge and ignorance.

If a student wants to learn medicine to be a doctor, the fact that he wants to learn indicates that he hasn't got the authority to determine what he should study in order to become a good doctor. There is an authoritative, as distinct from an authoritarian, aspect to the teaching relationship which flows from the superior knowledge, the tested methods, the objective evidence which the teacher relies on. This is true if you consider the student as an apprentice teacher—or assume even that every student some day will be a professor, which is a very large assumption. After all, in what field does the apprentice have the same authority as his teacher to determine what he should learn in order to become a master journeyman?

What the students are trying to communicate when they make these demands is something which is absurd on its face, and even more absurd upon analysis. But, having communicated this and having failed to convince any reasonable person that this is desirable, they then resort to occupation of buildings, to assault, to the language and violence of the gutter. If their argument wasn't persuasive before they used violence, what makes it more persuasive—the violence? Is might going to determine not only what is right, but what is true? This goes beyond the Orwellian world of 1984.

The issue is not the ideals mouthed in the easy rhetoric of the students, but the means they use to achieve these ideals.

As John Dewey [educator and philosopher] pointed out, "Anybody can proclaim high and mighty ideals, but the world that comes into existence is a consequence only of the means used to achieve these ideals." When black students and SDS radicals use the same methods Nazi students employed to destroy the Weimar Republic and trample into the dust traditional ideals of academic freedom, then no matter how different their rhetoric may be, fundamentally both are enemies of the rational process and of those values of civilization which have developed over the centuries against the forces of obscurantism and barbarism.

WHY STUDENTS ARE DELUDED

Q. Are students especially honest and moral people rebelling against dishonest and immoral elders?

A. This view that the students are suffering from an excess of virtue, whereas their elders are intellectually dishonest, is a lot of horsefeathers. The truth is that the students are completely unhistorical. They have no perspective upon events. They do not compare the situation today with what it was like in the past. They expect overnight transformations which in the nature of the case can't take place if one understands history and the elements of human psychology.

In my own lifetime, I have seen changes in the position of the Negro and in the position of the worker which I would have regarded as almost fantastic in the 1920s. Because there are still abuses, discrimination, problems created in virtue of past progress, doesn't mean that the progress made in 30 or 40 years is minimal or immaterial. After all, our judgment of a situation should rest on whether it is growing better or growing worse— not whether it is absolutely good or absolutely bad.

These students who claim that they are opposed to hypocrisy because they demand all injustices to be abolished overnight probably would denounce those who wrote the Declaration of Independence as hypocrites. Why? Because slavery existed at the time.

Now, would you call those who wrote the Declaration of Independence hypocrites when they proclaimed all men were born free and equal at a time when some had slaves? No. The significant thing is that this principle was enunciated—at a time when all other countries of the world accepted the practices of elite rule and leadership. The new principle had a powerful role in the ultimate abolition of slavery.

Those who think like unhypocritical students would have rejected not only the Declaration of Independence but the Magna Charta, which is regarded as the charter of English liberties.

If one reads the Magna Charta, he finds explicit discrimination against Jews and against women. The students would say this makes it a hypocritical document. But anybody with a knowledge of history and context, and with common sense, would say that the Magna Charta recognized principles that were new at their time—that became the basis for expanding liberties in England, even though they were wrung from King John by barons for their own interest.

You see, the student radicals pass judgment on social and political affairs as if they were born yesterday. In effect, they are saying that they can understand social and political affairs because they are "sincere." But it is not sincerity, it's foolishness to overlook the fact that you cannot escape history. And the history of the United States has been a history of slavery, of the Civil War, of Reconstruction. It has also been a history of fanaticism—for example, of people who, thinking like these students, prevented the adoption of Lincoln's proposal for the liberation of slaves by purchase as an alternative to the Civil War and its more horrible and continuing costs.

Politics is usually the choice of the lesser evil. Those who glorify the students because they are not hypocrites are actually saying it is hypocritical to choose the lesser evil. But why? Lesser evil, in a sense, may be the greater good. There is no sane political alternative to the policy of the lesser evil.

Q. Are many Americans tending to look on student rebels as being somehow pure and innocent? Is a kind of youth worship causing some to condone student violence?

A. There is a large measure of truth in this. There are people who seem to believe that youth can do no wrong—perhaps because they hope thereby to recapture their own youth. Foolish parents coddle their darling young rebels in a vain hope to keep them from flying the nest.

In my experience, there is nothing intrinsically wise about age. There is nothing intrinsically virtuous about the young. What is more important than youth or age is intelligence—intelligence tested by experience.

After all, it was the young Nazi who burned books, marched into battle, constituted the elite of the SA and SS [Brown Shirts and Black Shirts].

Lewis Feuer's masterly book on "The Conflict of Generations" proves that most youth movements have aided reaction. And the Fascist hymn, "Giovinezza"—or "Youth"—is a very good illustration of the fact that the glorification of youth can blossom into a glorification of cruelty and arrogance.

This, I think, is profoundly true today, especially in the United States. Those who uncritically identify with the young overlook its callowness, its insensitiveness. They tend to become apologists for brutality and terror.

"BATTLE IS NOT YET LOST"

Q. Is there a possibility that many professors, rather than continuing to teach in situations like those at Cornell or Harvard, will become discouraged and leave the teaching field and go to other fields, such as foundations?

A. There is no doubt that many people will leave the academy rather than teach under existing conditions.

But I think they would do better to stay and fight. The battle is going against us, but it is not yet lost. I still have faith that, if we keep on fighting, our colleagues will rally to us. That is why we have organized University Centers for Rational Alternatives and are soliciting support from all who wish to defend the free university.

If our faith is a vain hope, then we have to go down fighting. For freedom and self-respect are nonnegotiable.

Some Thoughts on Intellectuals and the Schools

Noam Chomsky

In happier times, I would have liked to approach the topic of this symposium in a rather technical and professional way, asking how students might best be exposed to the leading ideas and the most stimulating and penetrating thought in the fields that particularly interest me, how they might be helped to experience the pleasures of discovery and of deepening insight and be given an opportunity to make their own individual contribution to contemporary culture. At this particular historical moment, however, there are other, more pressing matters.

As I write, the radio is bringing the first reports of the bombings of Hanoi and Haiphong. In itself, this is no atrocity by contemporary standards—surely no atrocity, for example, as compared with the American assault on the rural population of South Vietnam for the past year. But the symbolism of this act casts its shadow over any critique of American institutions. When the bombings of North Vietnam began, Jean Lacauture commented aptly that these acts, and the documents produced to justify them, simply reveal that the American leaders regard themselves as having the right to strike where and when they wish. They reveal, in effect, that these leaders regard the world as an American preserve, to be governed and organized in accordance with superior American wisdom and to be controlled, if necessary, by American power. At this moment of national disgrace, as American technology is running amuck in Southeast Asia, a discussion of American schools can hardly avoid noting the fact that these schools are the first training ground for the troops that will enforce the muted, unending terror of the status quo in the coming years of a projected American century for the technicians who will be developing the means for extension of American power; for the intellectuals who can be counted on, in significant measure, to provide the ideological justification for this particular form of barbarism and to decry the irresponsibility and lack of sophistication of those who will find all of this intolerable and revolting.

Thirty years ago, Franz Borkenau concluded a brilliant study of the crushing of the popular revolution in Spain with this comment: "In this tremendous contrast with previous revolutions one fact is reflected. Before these latter years, counter-revolution usually depended upon the support of reactionary powers, which were technically and intellectually inferior to the forces of revolution. This has changed with the advent of fascism. Now, every revolution is likely to meet the attack of the most modern, most efficient, most ruthless machinery yet in existence. It means that the age of revolutions free to evolve according to their own laws is over."[1]

It would have taken a fair amount of foresight, at this time, to realize that the prediction would be proved accurate, with substitution of "liberal imperialism" for "fascism," and that the United States would, in a generation, be employing the most efficient and most ruthless machinery in existence to ensure that revolutionary movements will not evolve according to their own laws, to guarantee that its own particular concept of civilization and justice and order will prevail. And it would have required considerable insight, in the late 1930's, to realize that before too long a reformist American administration with a "welfare state" domestic orientation would be doing its utmost to prove the correctness of Marx's grim observation about this concept of civilization and justice and order: "The civilization and justice of bourgeois order comes out in its lurid light whenever the slaves and drudges of that order rise against their masters; then this civilization and justice stand forth as undisguised savagery and lawless revenge."

[1] Franz Borkenau, *The Spanish Cockpit* (1938; reprinted Ann Arbor, University of Michigan Press, 1963), pp. 288–89.

It is conceivable that American actions in Vietnam are simply a single outburst of criminal insanity, of no general or long-range significance except to the miserable inhabitants of that tortured land. It is difficult, however, to put much credence in this possibility. In half a dozen Latin American countries there are guerrilla movements that are approaching the early stages of the second Vietnamese war, and the American reaction is, apparently, comparable. That is, American arms are used to attack guerrilla forces and to "dry up the sea in which they swim," in the Maoist terminology affected by the military; and American "advisers" guide and train the troops which, as Latin American liberals observe, are needed only to occupy their own country in the interests of domestic ruling classes and Northern capital. In these countries it has not yet become necessary, as in Vietnam, to convert the fact of Communist involvement into the myth of Communist aggression in justification of open United States control of the counterrevolutionary forces, nor has the time yet arrived for application of the full arsenal of terror in support of the regime selected as most favorable to American interests. But it seems that this next step is fully expected. In *Le Nouvel Observateur*, the peasant organizer Francisco Julião was recently quoted as certain of United States intervention when rebellion breaks out in the Brazilian Northeast Provinces. Others, less well known, have expressed themselves similarly. There is little basis, in history or logic, for supposing them to be wrong—little basis, that is, apart from the kind of sentimentality that sees the United States, alone among nations, as a selfless (if rather oafish) public benefactor, devoted only to projects of "international good will," though frequently blundering in an excess of warmhearted generosity. One should no doubt take seriously the insistence of administration spokesmen that one purpose of the present violence is to prove that wars of national liberation cannot succeed; to demonstrate, that is, in the clearest and most explicit terms, that any revolutionary movement that we—unilaterally, as in Vietnam—designate as illegitimate will face the most efficient and ruthless machinery that can be developed by modern technology.

In minor ways, world opinion can serve as some kind of brake on full-scale utilization of the technology of terror and destruction. There has, as yet, been no use of nuclear weapons in Vietnam; and although rural populations are considered fair game for any sort of military attack, urban areas, where the butchery would be more evident to the outside world, are still relatively immune. Similarly, the use of gas attacks and chemical warfare has been extended only slowly, as habituation permits each gradual increment to pass unnoticed.[2] But ultimately, the only effective brake can

[2] This essay was written in June 1966; it now goes to press again in May 1968. On the use of gas in Vietnam, see Seymour Hersh, "Poison Gas in Vietnam," *New York Review of Books*, May 9, 1968. On current plans for chemical warfare, *Science*, May 24, 1968, contains the following note (p. 863):

be popular revulsion on a mass scale in the United States itself. Consequently, the level of culture that can be achieved in the United States is a life-and-death matter for large masses of suffering humanity. This too is a fact that must color any discussion of contemporary American institutions.

It is easy to be carried away by the sheer horror of what the daily press reveals and to lose sight of the fact that this is merely the brutal exterior of a deeper crime, of commitment to a social order that guarantees endless suffering and humiliation and denial of elementary human rights. It is tragic that the United States should have become, in Toynbee's words, "the leader of a world-wide anti-revolutionary movement in defense of vested interests." For American intellectuals and for the schools, there is no more vital issue than this indescribable tragedy.

No one would seriously propose that the schools attempt to deal directly with such contemporary events as the American attack on the rural population of Vietnam or the backgrounds in recent history for the atrocities that are detailed in the mass media. No sane person would have expected the schools in France, for example, to explore the character of and justification for the Algerian war, or the schools in Russia to have dealt honestly with the crushing of the Hungarian revolution, or the

---

Expanded Chemical Warfare: The Air Force has told Congress that it will spend $70.8 million on 10 million gallons of chemicals used for Vietnam defoliation and crop-killing in the fiscal year beginning 1 July, a $24.9 million increase over this year's figure. Next year's expanded efforts are in line with the continuing increase in the U.S. chemical warfare program in Vietnam. In the first 9 months of 1967, 843,606 acres in Vietnam were drenched with defoliants and 121,400 acres with crop-killing chemicals, a figure which slightly exceeded the totals for the whole of 1966.

In its issue of May 10, 1968, *Science* carries a letter by Thomas O. Perry of the Harvard University Forest, who comments as follows on chemical warfare (p. 601):

The DOD can raise the red herring of "long-term" effects, but there can be no doubt about the short-term effects: 2,4-D and 2,4,5-T kill the green vegetation. When followed by fire bombs, the dead foliage and twigs burn, as they did on some 100,000 acres (about 40,000 hectares) in the "Iron Triangle" last spring.

Through the simple process of starvation, a land without green foliage will quickly become a land without insects, without birds, without animal life of any form. News photographs and on-the-spot descriptions indicate that some areas have been sprayed repeatedly to assure a complete kill of the vegetation. There can be no doubt that the DOD is, in the short run, going beyond mere genocide to biocide. It commandeered the entire U.S. production of 2,4,5-T for 1967 and 1968 [some 13 to 14 million pounds (6.36 million kilos) according to U.S. Tariff Commission reports]. If one combines this with the other chemicals the DOD concedes it is using, there is a sufficient amount to kill 97 percent of the aboveground vegetation on over 10 million acres of land (about 4 million hectares)—an area so big that it would require over 60 years for a man to walk on each acre.

The long-term effects of spraying such an area may be imponderable, but the short-term effects of using these chemicals are certain: a lot of leaves, trees, rice plants, and other vegetation are dead or dying; and a lot of insects, birds, animals, and a few humans have either migrated or died of starvation. The North Vietnamese are fortunate—they have only bombs to contend with.

schools in Italy to have analyzed the invasion of Ethiopia in an objective way, or the schools in England to have exposed the contemporary suppression of Irish nationalism. But it is perhaps not ridiculous to propose that the schools might direct themselves to something more abstract, to an attempt to offer students some means for defending themselves from the onslaught of the massive government propaganda apparatus, from the natural bias of the mass media, and—to turn specifically to our present topic—from the equally natural tendency of significant segments of the American intellectual community to offer their allegiance, not to truth and justice, but to power and the effective exercise of power.

It is frightening to observe the comparative indifference of American intellectuals to the immediate actions of their government and its long-range policies, and their frequent willingness—often eagerness—to play a role in implementing these policies. This is not the place to illustrate in detail; in any event, I do not command the rhetoric to speak, in the only accurate and appropriate terms, of the actual conduct of the war and the way it has been tolerated at home. But more superficial examples make the point well enough.

Only marginal groups of American academics have reacted to the fact that while the United States stands in the way of the only sort of meaningful negotiations, namely, negotiations among indigenous South Vietnamese political forces to the exclusion of the foreign invaders from the United States and Korea, and (on a vastly different scale) from North Vietnam, it nevertheless is able to persist in its pretense of interest in a "negotiated settlement" with no outcry of protest against this farce. When Secretary Rusk openly admits that we cannot accept the North Vietnamese proposals of April 1965 because they require that the Saigon government be supplanted by a broad, national democratic coalition representing existing political forces in the country, there is no public denunciation of the cynicism of the position he upholds. When the press reports that the electoral law commission in South Vietnam faces the "awesome task" of running "honest elections" while making sure that the Communists do not win and that no Communists or "neutralists whose actions are advantageous to the Communists" appear on the ballot, there is little editorial comment, few letters to the editor, no general dismay. There is little point in multiplying examples. One can only be appalled at the willingness of American intellectuals, who, after all, have access to the facts, to tolerate or even approve of this deceitfulness and hypocrisy. Instead of shocked denunciations, we hear and read mock-serious discussions of the rationality of the American attempt to drive the North Vietnamese by force towards the negotiations that they had been demanding; of the sincere American desire to permit the South Vietnamese people to elect freely the government of their choice (now that the domestic opposition has been crushed and all Communist and neutralist candidates excluded); of the "great complexity" of international affairs (which, strangely, did not seem to justify Russian domination of East Europe or the Japanese attempt to impose a new order in Asia); of the judicious restraint of the administration, presumably, in refraining from genocide at a single stroke; and so on. Or what is worse, we read of the "bedrock vital interest of the United States" in demonstrating that its military power, once committed for whatever reason, cannot be forced to withdraw—a viewpoint which, had it been accepted by the world's second superpower as well, would have brought the history of Western civilization to a close in 1962, and which, if consistently pursued, must lead either to a Pax Americana or to a devastating world conflict.

Traditionally, the role of the intellectual, or at least his self-image, has been that of a dispassionate critic. Insofar as that role has been lost, the relation of the schools to intellectuals should, in fact, be one of self-defense. This is a matter that should be seriously considered. It is, to be sure, ridiculous to propose that the schools, in any country, deal objectively with contemporary history—they cannot sufficiently free themselves from the pressures of ideology for that. But it is not necessarily absurd to suppose that in Western democracies, at least, it should be possible to study in a fairly objective way the national scandals of the past. It might be possible in the United States to study, let us say, the American occupation of the Philippines, leaving implicit its message for the present. Suppose that high school students were exposed to the best of current American scholarship, for example, George Taylor's recent study for the Council on Foreign Relations, *The Philippines and the United States*. Here they would learn how, half a century after the bloody suppression of the native independence movement at a cost of well over 100,000 lives in the years 1898–1900, the country achieved nominal independence and the surface forms of democracy. They would also learn that the United States is guaranteed long-term military bases and unparalleled economic privileges; that for three fourths of the population, living standards have not risen since the Spanish occupation; that 70 percent of the population is estimated to have tuberculosis; that profits flowing to the United States have exceeded new investment in each postwar year; that the democratic forms give a new legitimacy to an old elite, allied now to American interests. They would read that "Colonial policy had tended to consolidate the power of an oligarchy that profited . . . from the free trade relationship and would be likely to respect, after independence, the rights and privileges of Americans"; that economically, "the contrast between the small upper class and the rest of the population . . . [is] . . . one of the most extreme in Asia"; that the consequences of American colonial policy were "that little was done to improve the lot of the average Filipino and that the Philippine economy was tied to the American to the advantage of the few"; and so on. They would then read the book's final recommendation, that we go on with our good work: "In spite of our many shortcomings, the record shows that we are more than equal to the task." It is at least possible that to a young mind, still uncontaminated by cant and sophistry, such a study can teach a revealing lesson, not only about what American dominance is likely to mean concretely, in the Third World, but also about the way in which American intellectuals are likely to interpret this impact.

In general, the history of imperialism and of imperialist apologia, particularly as seen from the point of view of those at the wrong end of the guns, should be a central part of any civilized curriculum. But there are other aspects to a program of intellectual self-defense that should not be overlooked. In an age of science and technology, it is inevitable that their prestige will be employed as an ideological instrument—specifically, that the social and behavioral sciences will in various ways be made to serve in defense of national policy or as a mask for special interest. It is not merely that intellectuals are strongly tempted, in a society that offers them prestige and affluence, to take what is now called a "pragmatic attitude" (in a perverse sense of "pragmatism" which is, sad to say, not without some historical justification, as shown in the Dewey–Bourne interchange during the First World War . . .), that is, an attitude that one must "accept," not critically analyze or struggle to change, the existing distribution of power, domestic or international, and the political realities that flow from it, and must work only for "slow measures of improvement" in a technological, piecemeal manner. It is not merely that having taken this position (conceivably with some justification, at a particular historical moment), one is strongly tempted to provide it with an ideological justification of a very general sort. Rather, what we must also expect is that political elites will use the terminology of the social and behavioral sciences to protect their actions from critical analysis—the nonspecialist does not, after all, presume to tell physicists and engineers how to build an atomic reactor. And for any particular action, experts can certainly be found in the universities who will solemnly testify as to its appropriateness and realism. This is not a matter of speculation; thus we already find, in congressional testimony, the proposal by a leading political scientist that we try to impose mass starvation on a quarter of the human race, if their government does not accept our dictates. And it is commonly argued that the free-floating intellectual, who is now outdated, has no business questioning the conclusions of the professional expert, equipped with the tools of modern science.

This situation again carries a lesson for the schools, one to which teachers in particular should be quite sensitive, bombarded as they have been in recent years by authoritative conclusions about what has been "demonstrated" with regard to human learning, language, and so on. The social and behavioral sciences should be seriously studied not only for their intrinsic interest, but so that the student can be made quite aware of exactly how little they have to say about the problems of man and society that really matter. They should, furthermore, be studied in the context of the physical sciences, so that the student can be brought to appreciate clearly the limits of their intellectual content. This can be an important way to protect a student from the propaganda of the future, and to put him in a position to comprehend the true nature of the means that are sure to be used to conceal the real significance of domestic or international policy.

Suppose, however, that contrary to all present indications, the United States will stop short of using its awesome resources of violence and devastation to impose its passionately held ideology and its approved form of social organization on large areas of the world. Suppose, that is, that American policy ceases to be dominated by the principles that were crudely outlined by President Truman almost twenty years ago, when he suggested in a famous and important speech that the basic freedom is freedom of enterprise, and that the whole world should adopt the American system which could survive in America only if it became a world system. . . . It would nevertheless remain true that the level of culture that can be achieved in the United States is a matter of overwhelming importance for the rest of the world. If we want to be truly utopian, we may consider the possibility that American resources might be used to alleviate the terrorism that seems to be an inevitable correlate of modernization, if we can judge from past and present history. We can conceive of the possibility that the schools, or the intellectuals, might pay serious attention to questions that have been posed for centuries, that they might ask whether society must, indeed, be a Hobbesian *bellum omnium contra omnes*, and might inquire into the contemporary meaning of Rousseau's protest that it is contrary to natural right that "a handful of men be glutted with superfluities while the starving multitude lacks necessities." They might raise the moral issue faced, or avoided, by one who enjoys his wealth and privilege undisturbed by the knowledge that half of the children born in Nicaragua will not reach five years of age, or that only a few miles away there is unspeakable poverty, brutal suppression of human rights, and almost no hope for the future; and they might raise the intellectual issue of how this can be changed. They might ask, with Keynes, how long we must continue to "exalt some of the most distasteful of human qualities into the position of the highest virtues," setting up, "avarice and usury and precaution . . . [as] . . . our gods," and pretending to ourselves that "fair is foul and foul is fair, for foul is useful and fair is not." If American intellectuals will be preoccupied with such questions as these, they can have an invaluable civilizing influence on society and on the schools. If, as is more likely, they regard them with disdain as mere sentimental nonsense, then our children will have to look elsewhere for enlightenment and guidance.

Text of a Letter from Richard Nixon to Educators and College and University Presidents and Trustees

The enclosed article by Dr. Sidney Hook is among the most cogent and compelling documents I have read on the question of campus violence. I commend it to your consideration, for I know that you share my deep interest in resolving the crucial problems which our colleges and universities are facing at this time.

The heart of the matter—and of Dr. Hook's thesis—is that the primary responsibility for maintaining a climate of free discussion and inquiry on the college campus rests with the academic community itself. As I said in my news conference in California in July, I hold this same point of view.

Thus it is with concern that I have noted—as did Dr. Hook—the growing tendency of college administrators to place the primary blame for campus violence and disruption on the failure of government to solve all our major problems at home and abroad. I recognize that many deeply concerned students and faculty members disagree with governmental positions at the national, state and local level, but while government can and must accept and carry out its responsibilities in connection with policies which may be unpopular on college and university campuses, there can be no substitute for the acceptance of responsibility for order and discipline on campuses by college administrators and college faculty.

The university is a precious national asset, a place in American society where the rule of reason and not the rule of force must prevail. Those who cannot accept that rule of reason, those who resort to the rule of force, have no place on a college campus. Only when college administrators, faculties and students accept and act on these premises will all of our universities again be able to go about the vital and important work of preserving and expanding our cultural heritage and training the future leaders of America.

I would appreciate receiving the benefit of your views on this vitally important subject.

With my best wishes,

Sincerely,

/s/ RICHARD NIXON

A Summary of Sidney Hook's
"A Plan to Achieve Campus Peace"

Clarence J. Karier

In this article, Hook analyzed the problem of the anti-Vietnam War protests on American campuses and concluded that what was happening was a "betrayal of the primary commitment of the university to the quest for truth and integrity, in learning, and teaching." The problem on campus, he argued, was neither controversy nor academic unrest, but academic disruption and violence. This, he asserted, results from a faulty educational philosophy as well as a loss of nerve on the part of both faculty and administrators. This faulty philosophy, he believed, was reflected in the proposition expressed by leading university administrators that campus peace could only be obtained "when the major social and foreign policy problems of our society" were solved. One administrator, he said, went so far as to claim the problem resulted from the distance separating the American dream from the American reality. Aside from the immediate consequences of political polarization and alienation of the campus from the democratic community and the resulting academic genocide, Hook asked what is wrong with the above proposition. First, he argued, there will always be a disparity between the American dream and reality, just as there will always be social and foreign policy problems. Secondly, he said that such a position perverts the function of a university from that of *study* to that of providing an agenda of action which carries set political consequences. Third, he surmised such a position implies rule by an elite minority, contrary to the basic democratic process. Professors and students who "threaten or even condone violence," Hook believed, demonstrate their contempt for the democratic process. Suppose, he said, the trade unionist or farmers of the nation were to threaten violence unless their interest and views were honored? Lastly, he argued, that the university is not a homogeneous community and those who, in fact, do advocate violence on campus are, in their effectiveness, way out of proportion to their numbers. A small conspiratorial group has learned to manipulate the mass media and the administration and faculty for their own purposes. Under such circumstances, academic freedom has been eroded because faculty have "lacked the moral courage to uphold the professional standards of their calling as teachers and seekers of the truth."

What, then, he asked, is to be done? In brief, he suggested the following steps:

1. Convoke an assembly of constituent bodies of the university community of faculty, students and administrators in order to establish principles

and rules which can serve as guidelines to acceptable dissent on campus.

2. Set up a faculty-student discipline committee to hear cases involving faculty-student infractions of the rules.

3. All violators of rules should be swiftly punished.

4. Faculty-student marshalls equipped with cameras should be used as a first line of defense against forcible disruption.

5. If the demonstration proceeds to disrupt normal university activity, a court injunction ought to be obtained.

6. If and when a court injunction is disregarded, legal proceedings by civil authorities ought to be implemented immediately.

7. If, however, faculty-student violence proceeds to escalate, police power ought to be employed along with faculty-student marshalls.

8. If the scale of violence continues to increase, then as a last resort, the university ought to be closed and legal civil action as well as university sanction ought to be applied to the guilty.[1]

---

[1] Interestingly enough, within a matter of months after this article, with President Nixon's cover letter, reached the hands of administrators and trustees of American universities, the steps which Hook recommended were implemented on many university campuses.

CHAPTER 4

Rationalizing the Meritocratic State: The Idea of Progress and the Educational State

The eighteenth-century enlightenment ideology espoused by Condorcet, Diderot, Jefferson and Madison included education as a key to national progress and the perfectibility of man. Progressive developments in scientific knowledge, they thought, would break the chains of ignorance and superstition which enslaves and ensnares men to support evil social systems. The rational man would thus stand free and tall. Since evil was caused by ignorance, and education could banish ignorance, mass compulsory education of an enlightened humanity could be expected to banish evil, while it set men free. Jefferson, then, preached his "crusade against ignorance" to overcome every form of social evil in order to progressively improve human nature and the social order. The ideology of the enlightenment, thus carried with it a strong argument for universal schooling.

While some assumed that those who would know the good would be more apt to do the good, others settled for the notion that a knowledgeable humanity might function more out of an ethic of enlightened self-interest. In either case, talent and virtue were intimately related. Jefferson believed in a natural aristocracy of talent and virtue. A really good educational system, he believed, would be a meritocratic system which rewarded both. Proposing a rigorous evaluation procedure, he would "rake from the rubbish annually" in order to insure that only the best would go on to higher education at public expense.[1]

[1] See Thomas Jefferson's, "Bill for the More General Diffusion of Knowledge."

The good society, for most sons of the enlightenment, was the meritocratic ideal where men took up their positions in life not because of special
privilege resulting from wealth, caste, status, or power, but because of
natural talent and virtue. The various inequalities which resulted from
caste, class, and privilege had to be overcome in order to allow the true
natural talents of men to emerge. All men, however, were not viewed as
equal in talent. According to Antoine-Nicolas De Condorcet,

> We, therefore, need to show that these three sorts of real inequality
> [wealth, status and education] must constantly diminish without however
> disappearing altogether; for they are the result of natural and necessary
> causes which it would be foolish and dangerous to wish to eradicate. . . .[2]

Few held the notion that "all men are created equal" in any absolute
sense, except in the eyes of God or the law. The revolution of the rights
of men was to be directed against those ancient artificial barriers which
prevented the full development of mankind. Such a millennium, some
believed, was not far off. As Saint-Simon said in 1814,

> The golden age is not behind us, but in front of us. It is the perfection of
> social order. Our fathers have not seen it; our children will arrive there
> one day, and it is for us to clear the way for them.[3]

Less than a century later, Edward Bellamy, in *Looking Backward*
(1887), echoed similar sentiments as he spoke for many liberal progressive
reformers.

> The Golden Age lies before us and not behind us, and is not far away. Our
> children will surely see it, and we, too, who are already men and women,
> if we deserve it by our faith and by our works.[4]

The enlightenment dream became the American dream. Those who
were worthy by their "faith" and their "works" might participate as
children of a dream in ushering in the new meritocratic social order.
Through their efforts to perfect social scientific knowledge and to apply
that knowledge to our social institutions, educational reformers would
participate in the fashioning of that utopian ideal. If the advancement in
the physical sciences meant an increase in the power of men to control
and predict physical phenomena, any comparable progress in our knowledge of human behavior might, when applied, usher in an equal advance

---

[2] Antoine-Nicolas De Condorcet, *Sketch for a Historical Picture of the Progress
of the Human Mind*, trans. by June Barroclough. (New York: The Noonday Press,
1955), p. 179.

[3] Quoted in J. B. Bury, *The Idea of Progress*. (New York: Dover Publications,
Inc., 1955), p. 282.

[4] Edward Bellamy, *Looking Backward*. (New York: The New American Library,
1963), p. 222. It should be noted that Bellamy touched a significant segment of the
reformist idealism of his day. Within three years of the publication of his book, 162
Bellamy clubs were organized in 27 states to spread his message. See Merle Curti, *The
Growth of American Thought*. (New York: Harper and Row, 1964), p. 610.

in our control and prediction of human behavior. Helvetius, the philosopher of enlightenment environments, suggested that: "To guide the motions of the human puppet it is necessary to know the wires by which he is moved. . . ." [5]

With a similar perspective in mind, Auguste Comte, in his *Positive Philosophy*, predicted that in the scientific society of tomorrow, a universal system of positive education would teach men to know and do their duty in such a way as to diminish, if not eliminate, conflict between individuals. The masses were to be educated to know and want the good and to develop those proper social attitudes so necessary to fit into the social occupational structure of the evolving educational state. Thus, the enlightenment dream included more than the mere identification and development of natural talent. That dream also included the process of shaping the proper social attitudes so that the individual might fit more easily into the organic whole of society. This perspective was, perhaps, best reflected by Edward Ross when he suggested that to educate is ". . . to collect little plastic lumps of human dough from private households and shape them on the social kneadingboard. . . ." [6]

A considerable number of new social scientists who applied their intellectual efforts to help organize the educational state in twentieth-century America ideologically were sons of the enlightenment. In general, they thought of science as the process of classifying and ordering phenomena along the lines laid down by Auguste Comte in his *Positive Philosophy*. In applying this philosophy, they usually saw themselves cultivating both a science and profession of education in the overall national interest. Deeply involved in the overall problems of industrialization, immigration and urbanization in the opening decades of the century, these men helped shape the compulsory educational state.

The idea of using compulsory schooling to solve social problems was not, of course, new. Horace Mann's argument for the common school as a "balance wheel of the social machinery" reflected an earlier thrust. Now, however, at the dawn of the twentieth century, with waves of immigrants from southeastern Europe flooding the centers of American culture[7] and

[5] Mordecai Grossman, *The Philosophy of Helvetius*. (New York: Bureau of Publications, Teachers College, Columbia University, 1926), p. 78.

[6] Edward A. Ross, *Social Control*. (New York: Macmillan Company, 1906), p. 168. For an extended analysis of both Edward A. Ross and Charles H. Cooley's social philosophy, see: Paul Violas, *Roots of Crisis: American Education in the Twentieth Century*, Chapter 3. (Chicago: Rand McNally and Co., 1973).

[7] The total number of immigrants not only increased from 3.7 million in the period 1891–1900, to 8.8 million in the period 1901–1910, but the percentage coming from northern Europe declined from 44.6 percent in the former period, to 21.7 percent in the later period, while the percentage of immigrants coming from southeastern Europe increased from 51.9 percent to 70.8 percent for the same period. See R. Freeman Butts and Lawrence A. Cremin, *A History of Education in American Culture*. (New York: Holt, Rinehart & Winston, 1953), p. 308.

with the industrial and urban need for standardized consumers and producers,[8] came the acute need to create an educational system which would
classify, standardize, socialize and Americanize youth on a massive scale.
This was to be done in the interest of national progress.

To many Americans who listened to the debates over evolution in the
closing decades of the nineteenth century, the enlightenment idea of progress and Darwinian evolution seemed to blend together logically. Herbert
Spencer helped when he said, "To be a good animal is the first requisite
to success in life and to be a nation of good animals is the first condition
of national prosperity." [9] The idea of evolution cast in the American
model of progress made sense to those who were nurtured on the belief
that this land and its people had a "manifest destiny" which included not
only such weighty responsibilities as assuming the "white man's burden"
but also the more awesome, messianic challenge of making the "world
safe for democracy."

National pride mixed easily with Anglo-Saxon racism under the rubric
of cultural evolution. American racism rested on the assumed superiority
of that special racial mix fortuitously drawn from northern and western
Europe. Those who saw themselves as members of the superior race
usually looked with fear and uncertainty on the new immigrants. If evolution was to continue along the enlightenment lines of perfectibility of man,
indeed, if the progress of the American nation was to continue, the problem
of dysgenics would have to be overcome. Race degeneration was the
shadow which stalked, and at times, mocked the troubled race superiority
image of the American. Darwin pointed to the problem when he said:

> Thus the weak members of civilized societies propagate their kind. No
> one who has attended to the breeding of domestic animals will doubt that
> this must be highly injurious to the race of man.[10]

Americans also knew that "good" breeding counts and that the future
progress of their nation would depend, in part, not only on creating the
social environment which encourages the fit to reproduce, but also in
creating those laws and institutions which, in effect, would prevent the
degenerates of the culture from reproducing. Both eugenics and euthenics
were propelled by the enlightenment quest for the perfectibility of man
and society in the context of a social and intellectual climate dominated by
Darwinian evolution. While America has had a long history of eugenics
advocates, some of the key leaders of the testing movement which emerged

[8] See Robert H. Wiebe, *The Search for Order, 1877–1920.* (New York: Hill and
Wang, 1967).

[9] As quoted in the *Proceedings of the First National Conference on Race Betterment.* (Battle Creek, Mich.: Race Betterment Foundation, Jan. 8, 1914).

[10] Charles Darwin, *The Descent of Man and Selection in Relation to Sex*, Second
edition revised. (New York: D. Appleton Company, 1922), p. 136.

at the beginning of the century were also the strongest advocates for eugenics control. In the twentieth century the eugenics and testing movements often came together in the same people under the name of "scientific" psychology and for one cause or the other received foundation support.

One such leader of the eugenics movement in America was Charles Benedict Davenport who, having seriously studied Galton and Pearson, sought to persuade the new Carnegie Institution of Washington to support a biological experiment station with himself as director. In 1904, he became director of such a station at Cold Spring Harbor on Long Island. As his interest in experiments in animal breeding began to wane, he used his influence as secretary of the Committee on Eugenics of the American Breeders Association to interest others in the study of human heredity. Supported by the donations of Mrs. E. H. Harriman, Davenport founded the Eugenics Record Office in 1910, and by 1918 the Carnegie Institution of Washington assumed control. The work of the Record Office was facilitated by the work of various committees: the Committee on Inheritance of Mental Traits included Robert M. Yerkes and Edward L. Thorndike; the Committee on Heredity of Deaf-mutism included Alexander Graham Bell; while the Committee on Sterilization included H. H. Laughlin; and Committee on the Heredity of the Feeble Minded included, among others, H. H. Goddard.

These committees took the lead in identifying those who carried defective germ plasm and in disseminating the propaganda which became necessary to pass sterilization laws. For example, it was Laughlin's "Committee to Study and Report on the Best Practical Means of Cutting off the Defective Germ-Plasm in the American Population," which reported that "society must look upon germ-plasm as belonging to society and not solely to the individual who carries it." [11] Laughlin found that approximately 10 percent of the American population carried bad seed and called for sterilization as a solution. More precisely, he defined these people as "feebleminded, insane, criminalistic (including the delinquent and wayward), epileptic, inebriate, diseased, blind, deaf, deformed and dependent (including orphans, ne'er-do-wells, the homeless, tramps and paupers)." [12] For one proposed segregation and sterilization program, see Figure 1. Social character, from murder to prostitution, was associated with intelligence and the nature of one's germ plasm. The first sterilization law was passed in Indiana in 1907, followed in quick succession by 15 other states. In Wisconsin, such progressives as Edward A. Ross and Charles R. Van Hise, president of the University of Wisconsin, took strong public stands

[11] As quoted in Mark H. Haller, *Eugenics.* (New Brunswick, N.J.: Rutgers University Press, 1963), p. 133.
[12] *Ibid.,* p. 133.

Effectiveness of the program depends upon:—

1. The length of time required to send to State institutions—regardless of length of commitments—all of the breeding stock of the varieties sought to eliminate.

2. The sterilization upon release from State custody of all individuals of such varieties possessing reproductive potentialities.

The following table shows the reasonable expectation of the approximate working out of this program—if consistently followed—for eliminating the defective and anti-social varieties from the American population, under the following specific conditions:—

1. That the varieties (*i.e.*, the breeding stock of defectives, including both affected and unaffected individuals of all ages) sought to exterminate now (1915) constitutes 10% of the population.

2. That those portions of the defective varieties permitted to reproduce, increase at a rate equal to that of the general population, plus 5% each half decade.

3. That the group of State institutions for the socially inadequate, whose inmates by actual count constituted in 1890, .590%; in 1900, .807%; and in 1910, .914% of the total population, provide for and receive inmates at a rate equal to that of the increase of the general population, plus 5% each half decade.

4. That the inmates of institutions continue to be drawn from the two sexes and from each age group in even proportions to the total numbers of individuals of the corresponding sex and age group in the total population of the varieties sought to eliminate.

5. That the average "institution generation" (*i.e.*, average period of commitment) be 5 years.

6. That the Federal Government co-operate with the States to the extent of prohibiting the landing of foreigners of potential parenthood of innate traits lower than the lowest of the better 90% of the blood already established here, *i.e.*, belonging to the

132

2 Per cent of total population constituting the varieties sought to eliminate	1.32	.18	1.54	2.77	3.88	4.88	5.77	6.57	7.28	7.91	8.46	8.94	9.35	9.70	10.00
3 Per cent of total population in institutions	1.588	1.512	1.1440	1.371	1.306	1.244	1.185	1.126	1.072	1.021	.972	.926	.882	.840	.800
4 Probable total population of the U. S.		275,000,000		241,000,000		210,000,000		181,000,000		155,000,000		131,000,000		110,000,000	
5 Probable total numbers in the varieties sought to eliminate if program is carried out		495,000		6,675,700		10,248,000		11,891,700		12,260,500		11,711,400		10,670,000	
6 Total number of inmates in institutions called for by proposed program		4,158,000		3,304,110		2,612,400		2,038,060		1,582,550		1,213,060		924,000	
7 Number of sterilization operations required per year per 100,000 population	158.8	151.2	144.0	137.1	130.6	124.4	118.5	112.6	107.2	102.1	97.2	92.6	88.2	84.0	80.0
8 Probable total number of sterilizing operations required per year for the entire population		415,500		330,170		260,400		203,806		158,255		121,306		92,400	

TABLE 1.

Figure 1. *Rate of Efficiency of the Proposed Segregation and Sterilization Program.* From *Proceedings of the First National Conference on Race Betterment*, Januaray 8–12, 1914, Battle Creek, Michigan. Published by the Race Betterment Foundation, p. 479.

supporting the passage of sterilization laws. America pioneered in the sterilization of mental and social defectives twenty years ahead of other nations.[13]

Between 1907 and 1928, twenty-one states practiced eugenic sterilization involving over 8,500 people. California, under the influence of the Human Betterment Foundation which counted Lewis M. Terman and David Starr Jordan as its leading members, accounted for 6,200 sterilizations. California's sterilization law was based on race purity as well as criminology. Those who were "morally and sexually depraved" could be sterilized. Throughout the sterilization movement in America ran a *zeitgeist* reflecting the temper of pious reformers calling for clean living, temperance, fresh air schools as well as sterilization. (See Figures 2, 3, and 4.) The use of sterilization for punishment rather than race improvement reached the point where laws were introduced which called for sterilization for chicken stealing, car theft, and prostitution.[14]

At the turn of the century, America was so thoroughly a racist nation that the following eulogy, supposedly honoring Frederick Douglas, could pass unchallenged.

> Amid the universal commendation of Frederick Douglas as a colored man, who, against the greatest difficulties and in the most unfavorable circumstances, achieved well-deserved distinction, it might not be unreasonable perhaps, to intimate that his white blood may have had something to do with the remarkable energy he displayed and the superior intelligence he manifested. Indeed, it might not be altogether unreasonable to ask whether with more white blood, he would have been an even better and greater man than he was, and whether the fact that he had any black blood at all may not have cost the world a genius, and be, in consequence, a cause for lamentation instead of a source of lyrical enthusiasm over African possibilities.[15]

The superiority of the Anglo-Saxon Nordic race over the Alpine, Mediterranean, Negroid races repeatedly reappears in the literature of the social and educational reformers of the first three decades of the century.

[13] See H. H. Laughlin, *Eugenical Sterilization in the United States*. (Psychopathic Laboratory of the Municipal Court of Chicago, Illinois, December 1922).

[14] State authority is still being used to sterilize people. On March 4, 1971, a bill was introduced into the Illinois Legislature which required sterilization of a mother who had two or more children while on welfare roles before that mother could draw further support. The argument, however, is no longer based on racial purity or punishment, but more on the economic burden to society. While the constitutionality of pauper sterilization might be questionable, the right of the state to sterilize for eugenics purposes was settled in the Buck v. Bell case when Justice Holmes argued: "The principle that sustains compulsory vaccination is broad enough to cover the cutting of the Fallopian tubes . . . three generations of imbeciles are enough." As quoted in Haller, *Eugenics*, p. 129

[15] New York *Times* Editorial, February 27, 1895, p. 4, Col. 6. The author is indebted to Chris Shay for calling his attention to this quote.

The Race Betterment Movement Aims

To Create a New and Superior Race thru EUTHENICS, or Personal and Public Hygiene and EUGENICS, or Race Hygeine.

A thoroughgoing application of PUBLIC AND PERSONAL HYGIENE will save our nation annually:

1,000,000 premature deaths.

2,000,000 lives rendered perpetually useless by sickness.

200,000 infant lives (two-thirds of the baby crop)

The science of EUGENICS intelligently and universally applied would in a few centuries practically

WIPE OUT

Idiocy   Insanity   Imbecility   Epilepsy

and a score of other hereditary disorders, and create a race of HUMAN THOROUGHBREDS such as the world has never seen.

Figure 2. From *Official Proceedings of the Second National Conference on Race Betterment*, August 4–8, 1915, Battle Creek, Michigan. Published by the Race Betterment Foundation, p. 147.

Methods of Race Betterment

Simple and Natural Habits of Life.

Out-of-Door Life Day and Night, Fresh-Air Schools, Playgrounds, Out-of-Door Gymnasiums, etc.

Total Abstinence from the Use of Alcohol and Other Drugs.

Eugenic Marriages.

Medical Certificates before Marriage.

Health Inspection of Schools.

Periodical Medical Examinations.

Vigorous Campaign of Education in Health and Eugenics.

Eugenic Registry.

Sterilization or Isolation of Defectives.

Figure 3. From *Official Proceedings of the Second National Conference on Race Betterment*, August 4–8, 1915, Battle Creek, Michigan. Published by the Race Betterment Foundation, p. 160.

Evidences of Race Degeneracy

Increase of Degenerative Diseases - - - -

- Cancer
- Insanity
- Diseases of Heart and Blood Vessels
- Diseases of Kidneys
- Most Chronic Diseases
- Diabetes

Increase of Defectives

- Idiots
- Imbeciles
- Morons
- Criminals
- Inebriates
- Paupers

Diminishing Individual Longevity

Diminished Birth Rate

Disappearance, Complete or Partial, of Various Bodily Organs - - - -

According to Wiedersheim there are more than two hundred such changes in the structures of the body

Figure 4. From *Official Proceedings of the Second National Conference on Race Betterment*, August 4–8, 1915, Battle Creek, Michigan. Published by the Race Betterment Foundation, p. 150.

America was profoundly a racist nation, as were many of its educational psychologists. Not yet a generation away from black slavery and Indian genocide, the Anglo-Saxon American faced the massive immigration from Southern and Eastern Europe with fear and dread. Over and over again, these fears found expression in the arguments for intelligence testing, tracking in schools, eugenic laws, Americanization programs, guidance programs, and, finally, in immigration restriction. Leadership for most of these movements came from the ranks of the liberal progressives who saw themselves as committed to the intelligent, orderly reform of society.

Many educators like David Starr Jordan (chancellor at Stanford), A. Lawrence Lowell (president of Harvard), Leon C. Marshall (dean at the University of Chicago), John R. Commons and Edward Ross (professors at the University of Wisconsin) served on the national Committee of the Immigration Restriction League and actively lobbied for discriminatory immigration restrictions against Southern and Eastern Europeans. Other educators with similar views, such as Lewis M. Terman, H. H. Goddard, Frank Freeman, Edward L. Thorndike and C. C. Brigham, lent their efforts to rationalize efficiently and to standardize the educational system along the lines of what they viewed as the emerging social order. That order was hierarchial and stratified.

MERITOCRACY: THE DREAM AND THE REALITY

The hierarchial social class system was effectively maintained then as it is today, not so much by the sheer force of power and violence, but by the ideological beliefs of people within that system. There is, perhaps, no stronger social class stabilizer, if not tranquilizer, within a hierarchially ordered social class system than the belief, on the part of the lower class, that their place in life is really not arbitrarily determined by privilege, status, wealth and power, but is a consequence of merit, fairly derived. This idea is fundamental to the maintenance of the basically class-structured "meritocratic" educational state in twentieth-century America. If enough men believed that the system was based on merit and that all who participated had an "equal opportunity" to demonstrate their merit, and thus determine their social and economic position, then the system might, indeed, be judged fair.[16]

[16] Samuel Bowles and Herbert Gintis in "I.Q. in the U.S. Class Structure," *Social Policy*, January–February, 1973, make a persuasive case that, while I.Q. and cognitive tested skills do not apparently cause hierarchial social stratification, they do serve to legitimatize the hierarchial division of labor. For an interesting analysis of the way lower class children lose their dignity and self esteem as they get caught in the double bind of the meritocratic system see: Sennett and Cobb, *The Hidden Injuries of Class*.

Real equal opportunity is, of course, difficult to approximate and ultimately may be impossible to achieve in a hierarchially ordered social system. The idea of equal opportunity has served as a credibility valve, if not a safety valve, which maintains the social class system under the mantle of meritocracy. To believe such a system fair, one must assume equal opportunity or something which people can believe approximates that condition. In a society like that in the United States, with its hierarchial social-economic structure where the rich have superior health and educational care and the poor have inferior health and educational care, one realizes rather quickly that equal opportunity is not only difficult to approximate but ultimately impossible to achieve without a social revolution. Such a realization fundamentally throws into question the fairness of the system. Many of the arguments for equal opportunity in the twentieth century often appeared as rhetorical devices to appease the oppressed and, thereby, protect the established social system. Indeed, the more heated debates involving equal opportunity as well as the extension of opportunity usually occurred at just those times when the credibility of the meritocracy was rigorously being challenged by minority groups.

Although the educational state in the twentieth century became the mirror image of the hierarchial social order, there were some in the nineteenth century who held out hope for a more egalitarian system. Recognizing the consequences of inequality of wealth, Robert Dale Owen advocated state boarding schools.

> Respect ought to be paid, and will always be paid, to virtue and to talent; but it ought not to be paid to riches, or withheld from poverty. Yet if the children from these state schools are to go every evening, the one to his wealthy parent's soft carpeted drawing room, and the other to its poor father's or widowed mother's comfortless cabin, will they return the next day as friends and equals? He knows little of human nature who thinks they will.[17]

Owen knew that before one could develop equal educational opportunity, one had to lessen the impact of inequalities of wealth and privilege on the lives of the young. Ignoring this crucial point, some forty years later, Lester Frank Ward, the father of the "American concept of the planned society," [18] argued that the evils of social class hierarchy could be overcome by developing a universal state system of publicly supported day schools.

> Universal education is the power, which is destined to overthrow every species of hierarchy. It is destined to remove all artificial inequality and

[17] Robert Dale Owen, *The Working Man's Advocate*, Vol. I. (New York: April 24, 1830), p. 4.
[18] Ralph Henry Gabriel, *The Course of American Democratic Thought*. (New York: The Ronald Press Co., 1956), p. 215.

leave the natural inequalities to find their true level. With the artificial inequalities of caste, rank, title, blood, birth, race, color, sex, etc., will fall nearly all the oppression, abuse, prejudice, enmity, and injustice, that humanity is now subject to.[19]

Universal education was the path which could usher in the true meritocracy which would reflect only natural inequalities. In true enlightenment fashion, Ward saw ignorance as a cause of evil which might be banished by schooling. Under the circumstances, the state had a right to protect itself and its people through the development of compulsory schooling. He further argued that if the state could compel a man to join the army and invade a foreign country, why was it not reasonable to assume that it could compel him to attend school? Ward argued,

It [the state] may therefore compel the most unwilling, even where his unwillingness grows out of principle or religious scruple, to go into the army and invade a foreign country. Why then may it not compel him also to send his children to the public school or to go himself?[20]

Ward insisted that "the interests of society are paramount." [21] In the cause of progress and the cultivation of a true meritocracy, he further insisted that the ignorant must not be allowed to remain in their ignorance but must be coerced if necessary to become enlightened.

But the task of education is a positive task. It must be forced upon an unwilling people. No laissez-faire policy will do. To wait for the ignorant to demand it before giving it to them is like waiting till you have learned to swim before venturing into the water.[22]

While Ward believed the old social class hierarchy might disappear in his new meritocracy, one senses that a new hierarchy based on native talent would emerge. Progressive increase in knowledge on the part of all classes was dependent, he believed, on a kind of knowledge not readily grasped by all people. As he said:

And this substantial knowledge which alone is capable of promoting great progressive schemes and work vast social ameliorations is of the kind which does not come by experience, by spontaneous effort, by impulse, ambition and avarice; it is of the kind which comes only by study, by calm reflection, by assiduous labor. It is of the kind which the young and the ignorant would never choose, which the wild natural spirit of man never loves. It is the kind which must be enforced by regulations, established by law, maintained by custom. Those who know its value must compel its acceptance by those who do not. Wisdom, not years is the

[19] Lester Frank Ward, "Education," unpublished manuscript dated 1871–1873, p. 132. Special Collections Div. of Brown University, Providence, R. I. The author is indebted to Adelia Peters for calling his attention to this manuscript.
[20] *Ibid.*, p. 342.
[21] *Ibid.,* p 624.
[22] *Ibid.,* p. 312.

true maturity. The wise of the state are the parents of the ignorant. As the parent compels the attendance of his unwilling son at school, so the consolidated wisdom of the state must obligate the benighted citizen to do what is for the interest of the state and of morality, as well in matters of education as in matters of civil rights.[23]

In Ward's true meritocracy, there would still be the struggle between the wise and the ignorant with the resulting need for compulsion. It would still be necessary, as Rousseau put it in the *Social Contract*, to "force men to be free" or, as Ward put it, to "force men to be educated." This, again, was the faith of the enlightenment. Since evil was a product of ignorance and schooling was the instrument by which ignorance might be eliminated, the state had the right, indeed, the duty to protect itself and its citizens from evil by instituting compulsory public schooling. Compulsory schooling, compulsory military training and compulsory public health care emerged on the basis of similar arguments.

Ward's blueprint for the coming educational state in America carried with it not only the justification for compulsory schooling and the functional role of the knowledgeable expert, but also the utopian vision where all social institutions within the educational state might be used to cultivate and extend the "native power" of all members of the community. The day would come, he believed, when "the reign of hierarchy will be at an end, and that of equality will be inaugurated." [24] When that day dawned, Ward argued, "The false arbitrary value now set upon individuals will disappear and their true intrinsic value will take its place." Men and women, alike, will be judged and find their place in life on the basis of true intrinsic value.

> The true value of a new born infant lies, not in the social position of its parents or ancestors. It is not even measured by what it actually will do during its life. It lies in what it might do under proper circumstances; in its naked capacity for acquiring the ability to do when subjected to conditions favorable for the development of that native power. This is the true standard for the determination of real worth of a human being.[25]

When he turned from his ideal society to his real society he asked:

> What are we lauding? What are we rewarding? What are we condemning and punishing? I will tell you. We are lauding circumstance. We are rewarding wealth. We are condemning the unfortunate victims of social imperfection. We are punishing wretched beings for being what we have made them.[26]

---

23 *Ibid.*, p. 647.
24 *Ibid.*, p. 148.
25 *Ibid.*, p. 149.
26 *Ibid.*, p. 149.

The way out of his malaise was to construct a kind of educational state where natural merit could be rewarded. Such a system, he believed, would recognize "the average natural equality of all men, not only in rights but in capabilities, and propose to insure to each the opportunity of placing himself in the highest sphere for which nature has qualified him to move." [27] Although Ward did believe in what he called the "average natural equality" of all men, he did not believe in the absolute equality of all men when it came to capabilities. He did argue, however, that the differences among men are not as great as most suspect. While he insisted that his ideal social system would do away with all kinds of artificial hierarchy based on caste, title, race, sex, wealth, and power, his meritocracy would still have a natural hierarchy based on true talent.

> On the ruins of our present false and fictitious hierarchy will be built a system of true and natural hierarchy in which each will be satisfied to occupy the place to which nature assigned him and none will be able by means of deception, false appearances, wealth or power, to receive the advantages of a higher place.[28]

The educational state in America should, he argued, be a meritocratic state where the child's true worth was to be seen in terms of what he might become if only "circumstances permitted."

While Ward made a strong case for a utopian future, he also made an equally strong case for using the educational power of the state for direct social control. Predating the efficiency and social control language of Cubberly, Terman, and Thorndike by some three decades, Ward argued, as early as 1871–73, that

> Every child born into the world should be looked upon by society as so much raw material to be manufactured. Its quality is to be tested. It is the business of society as an intelligent economist to make the most of it.[29]

Ward delineated what was to become the hope and the ideal of much of the reform-minded educational philosophy of the twentieth century. The school was to be the vehicle through which nature's raw material was to be processed, and out of which men and women might find their true station in life. Ward's meritocracy would not only sift and winnow what nature had wrought, but would "manufacture" a better man. Perceptively, Ward saw that, if universal schooling was both to sort for natural talent and, at the same time, to "manufacture" better people, the first step would

[27] *Ibid.*, p. 152.
[28] *Ibid.*, p. 200.
[29] *Ibid.*, p. 151.

be to develop a universal testing and evaluation system. As he put it, "The process of universal education is that of first assaying the whole and rejecting only so much as shall, after thorough testing, prove worthless." [30] The testing and evaluation program was the crucial vehicle through which the organization of the educational state could be organized, shaped and directed.

Crucial, also, was the utopian vision of an open meritocratic society where all would receive their just rewards on the basis of "true" natural talent. Again and again, one finds this utopian assumption reflected in the testing literature of the twentieth century. Few, however, held Ward's utopian ideal image of the "good" society. More were willing to accept the social system as they saw it. For most, their "good" society was the existing hierarchial and socially stratified system. Repeatedly, throughout the twentieth century the testers tested and measured the consequences of social conditioning and social repression, and insisted they had accurately measured natural talent and virtue. So it was that Richard Herrnstein, just one hundred years after Ward, argued in his essay "IQ," that the "experts in the field" have concluded that genetic factors account for 80 percent of one's IQ, while environment constitutes 20 percent. As this society equalises environment, he then concluded ". . . the closer will human society approach a virtual caste system." [31] Rather than rallying against such a system, he suggested Americans should be preparing themselves to accept such a system. Herrnstein measured the consequences of social conditioning and repression and mistakenly assumed he had measured native talent.

> Greater wealth, health, freedom, fairness, and educational opportunity are not going to give us the equalitarian society of our philosophical heritage. It will instead give us a society sharply graduated, with ever greater innate separation between the top and the bottom, and ever more uniformity within families as far as inherited abilities are concerned. Naturally we find this vista appalling, for we have been raised to think of social equality as our goal. The vista reminds us of the world we had hoped to leave behind—aristocracies, privileged classes, unfair advantages and disadvantages of birth. But it is different, for the privileged classes of the past were probably not much superior biologically to the downtrodden, which is why revolutions had a fair chance of success. By removing arbitrary barriers between classes, society has encouraged the creation of biological barriers. When people can freely take their natural level in society, the upper classes will, virtually by definition, have greater capacity than the lower.[32]

[30] *Ibid.*, p. 15.
[31] Richard Herrnstein, "I.Q.," *Atlantic Monthly*, September, 1971, p. 64.
[32] *Ibid.*, p. 64.

From the perspective of Herrnstein's Harvard Yard, apparently, "society had removed the arbitrary barriers between classes," and natural talent was now presumedly freely surfacing, thus accounting for the social class system which existed. The educational state in America had been developing toward Herrnstein's conception of meritocracy for half a century.[33] Accordingly, Herrnstein remarked that "The data on IQ and social class differences show that we have been living with an inherited stratification of our society for some time." [34] Unlike Ward's ideal meritocracy which supposedly rejected "caste, class, race, wealth and power bias" of his world, Herrnstein's ideal meritocracy clearly mirrored as well as justified the existing social class system. One hundred years after Ward called for the development of the compulsory educational state to overcome arbitrary social class privilege, Herrnstein was asserting that society had just about arrived at a real meritocratic state. By conveniently ignoring the factors of privilege, wealth, power, status, and race through which his society functioned, Herrnstein's ideal meritocracy became the real meritocracy. Under such circumstances, he could conclude that unfortunately one's quest for merit led not to a lessening of social hierarchy, but towards a greater hierarchy.

For the children of the privileged, the American dream was a success; for the children of the repressed, the American dream had become a nightmare of futility and hopelessness. Ward's utopian dream had vanished. In its place had emerged a class system which professed to reward the meritorious through a "scientific" and "professional" testing system objectively determined. Herrnstein's conclusions about the meritocracy of the present and future were drawn from the experience of over half a century of testing within the educational state. That Herrnstein came out essentially where the testing movement began was not surprising, however. He, as Binet, Terman, Goddard, Thorndike, Yerkes, and others before him, had tested the results of the socialization process and ascribed their findings to natural talents. The creation of the education state was, in the end, not a way out of Ward's soulful plea that ". . . we are punishing wretched beings for being what we have made them."

---

[33] Herrnstein's ideas, in one sense, appear incredibly naive, while, in another sense, incredibly devastating when leveled against the lower classes. His belief that somehow past revolutions were successful because the lower classes were once more intelligent is nothing short of absurd. By simply ignoring the question of which classes produced leaders for revolutions in the past, as well as ignoring the use of mass communication and efficient police state tactics in putting down revolutionary groups in the modern totalitarian society, he speciously blames the failures of lower-class rebellion on a shortage of intelligence.

[34] Herrnstein, "I.Q.," p. 64.

Education (1871-1873)

Lester Frank Ward

The very cases which are used to prove the natural superiority of the learned over the unlearned, become, when rationally regarded, the best arguments in support of the view that the average native capacity for knowledge is equal for all classes of society. The multiplied instances which have been placed on record and are so frequently referred to, of person's rising from lower to higher ranks through their own merits; through energy, perseverence, will-power, and other qualities which have enabled them to overcome the great obstacles which are admitted to have stood in their way, leave the thinking mind to wonder how many more, perhaps equally endowed have struggled against obstacles only a little more insurmountable and failed, or who having equal or even less obstacles, have failed, because they lacked one of the qualities which, though wholly unnecessary to usefulness, was necessary to break through the barriers which shut them out of the field of usefulness.

Those who have succeeded have perhaps only just succeeded. Many of them attribute all their success to some slight timely event which chanced to lift them above the clouds of obscurity. "There is a tide in human life which taken at the flood leads on to fortune." But how few get into its auspicious current! How few take it at the flood! Most human beings are like mariners on an unknown sea. If there are favorable currents they know not where. If by chance they fall into one it is their good fortune; if they strike adverse currents it is their misfortune.

Education is the exploration of this unknown sea and the establishment of accurate charts for its navigation. As society is now constituted everything is left to chance. Life is a general scramble after success. Those who attain to it are lionized as great geniuses and superhuman beings, while in nine out of every ten cases it is due to pure fortuity. For every natural genius who succeeds there are nine who have either never tried or who have tried and failed. This is an exceedingly low estimate. These two classes are again very disproportionate. The great bulk of those at and below mediocrity are there because they have never tried to rise above it, and most of these have not only never tried but never thought of such a thing.

The chances are thus a hundred to one that the individual really most gifted by nature belonging to each age lives and dies in obscurity, and the

For calling his attention to this manuscript, the author is indebted to Adelia Peters of Bowling Green University.

one which each age honors as its *chief d'oeuvre* is only one of the productions of that age slightly above the average and highly favored by circumstance. How do we know that had all had equal opportunities the Newtons, Humboldts and Franklins might not have been each many times eclipsed in their own ages and countries? The doctrine of average natural equality points indeniably to such a result. And how much would society have gained if such had been the case! How much greater would have been its material advancement! Yet the eclipsing of Newtons and Humboldts would have been as nothing compared with the multiplication of them, which on mathematical principles the extension of equal opportunities to all would have produced. If from the few dozens who in their day possessed such opportunities one or two such minds were revealed, how many should we not be justified in believing to have contemporaneously existed unrevealed among the millions who possessed no opportunities? And how many times would this number be itself multiplied to represent the perhaps somewhat less magnificent but scarcely less valuable auxiliaries who must have risen to promote and extend all the various branches and departments of human industry and usefulness!

Universal education is the power which is destined to overthrow every species of hierarchy. It is destined to remove all artificial inequality and leave the natural inequalities to find their true level. With the artificial inequalities of caste, rank, title, blood, birth, race, color, sex, etc., will fall nearly all the oppression, abuse, prejudice, enmity and injustice that humanity is now subject to. It is true there will still be room for passion to rage and strife to continue, but it will be between equals, it will be between individuals, it will be isolated and sporadic; not, as now, general, organized, systematic. This is not the place, however, to point out the prospective results of universal education. I reserve that subject for another place. I am specially interested now in showing the possibility and propriety of such a scheme.

The time has come for dropping the qualitative distinction of men. The term "better" as applied to human beings is growing obsolete. When we say that one man is "better" than another, that a white man is "better" than a negro, that a noble is "better than a peasant, we use the term in a special sense. What is that sense? It does not relate to moral quality, nor to any other of the qualities to which the adjective "good" is applicable. The idea is special and peculiar. And though special it is extremely vague and undefinable. If you ask a man how he is better than another he will be unable to tell you. He will indicate without a direct answer that *cela va sans dire*. If it be a nobleman who predicates his superiority of a mechanic, when asked in what respect he makes this claim, he will specify, if he deign to answer at all, his high birth, his superior wealth, his more liberal education. Yet these are not his real grounds, for he would consider himself just as much better than any other mechanic, though in point of birth, of education, nay of wealth even, he be his equal. Thus this alleged superiority, whether it be of rank or nationality or social position, always eludes definition. No matter how superior the one who claims it may in point of fact be, in certain respects, to the one of whom it is claimed, and no matter how inferior he may and generally is in many other perhaps equally important respects, the least attempt as a rational analysis of his claim at once reveals the fact that none of these qualities, nor all of them combined, amounts to a definition or have any special bearing upon the pretention itself. It is something else or it is nothing. A further insight shows us that this alleged quality is a subjective without being an objective one; in other words it is a pure assumption on the part of the party asserting it and has no existence in fact. That it is believed in by the assumed inferior party does not at all disprove this. He believes what he is taught respecting his relations to his fellow men as respecting his relations to deity, without questioning it, regarding it all in the same light, as a divine revelation, to question which, is to blaspheme. And the party making the assumption is also sincere, and believes in his superiority without any disposition to investigate the title.

He has received it as an inheritance from his ancestors, back of whose right he is as careful not to trace its descent as he is not to trace that of his lauded estate; intuitively realizing perhaps, what is the truth, that neither had its origin in justice. And thus, the world goes on believing in imaginary inequalities and setting up unreal distinctions to the infinite prejudice of its real interest and the most fatal consequences for the supposed inferior classes. This vast system of self imposed misery must be charged up against man's ignorant reason, whose subtle reasonings have spun the threat and woven the web into a snare for his own feet; to brush away which entangling webs I propose the *education of reason.*

When I say that all men are created equal, I do not of course mean equal in all respects, neither do I mean equal in one particular respect (that of right), as the phrase is used to imply in the American charter of rights. I mean simply that the average native intellect of all classes of society is equal; that out of a hundred peasants there will be the same quantity of natural intellectual forces developed as out of a hundred nobles; that mechanics know as much by nature as lawyers, that the privileged classes possess no natural title to their privileges; that subject classes are not naturally subject but artificially, that if the learned were unlearned they would present no superiority over those who are unlearned; that if the unlearned were learned they would be the equals of the now learned.

If these propositions are not strictly and universally true, it cannot now be authoritatively asserted; if there are whole classes who in fact would upon trial prove exceptions we are in no position to determine which ones they are. We have no right to pass an *a priori* judgment upon any class until they have enjoyed the benefit of a full and fair trial. Such judgments might have done in the days of scholastic reasoning, they will not satisfy the reasoning of this age. If certain degraded classes, as the agricultural laborers of Ireland, for example, appear to form an obvious exception, it will be formed due to hereditary subjection and only demands that the trial will be extended longer and the results patiently awaited. Time is required for such vast experiments.

Respecting other races than the Caucasian, though the superficial mind would be quick to deny their equality with that race, yet it is of these that we are least of all qualified to judge. It must not be forgotten that intellect may develop itself in a vast number of ways. The Chinese may be less brilliant but he may be more precise and persevering. The African is probably less energetic and less intellectual, but he may prove more artistic, more imaginative. Beneath the tawny exterior of the Malaysian or the American who shall say what germs of genius a few centuries of civilization and education may reveal? When Humboldts and Goethes spring from the barbarian hordes of Attila, Alaric and Hendric, we need not be surprised at any transformation which culture shall work out in raw humanity.

But if we were to confine ourselves to the territorial limits usually assigned to civilization and enlightenment, the field would still be ample. That which I would insist upon would be that universal education should form a necessary constituent element of civilization. What is civilization? Is it not the exaltation of mind? the supremacy of intellect? the dominion of intelligence? And what lifts the civilization of the last three centuries into such a bold relief above that of preceding ages? Is it not knowledge? Is it not the fruitful marriage of science with genius, of truth with intellect? Yet immense and marvelous as has been this movement, it has all been done by the merest fraction of mankind, by those (as I have shown) whom fortune and circumstance have chanced to favor, by the rare few, who, in the varied vicissitudes of life's stern experience have been jostled into positions from which they could not avoid seeing and realizing the necessity of investigation and study. Remove these and the somewhat larger but yet comparatively insignificant number whom the imperfect systems of eduction which have been established have fitted for civilization, and what remains? I answer, and without disrespect or exaggeration—a barbarian horde, spreading out over all Europe and America, an uncivilized mass of humanity, swarming in the lowest precincts of great cities, laboring (for barbarians work) in the great workshops of the grasping manufacturers, organized by the belligerent governments of the world into the mercenary soldiery of immense standing armies, and even, spreading out far into the rural districts where they are everywhere to be found, leading a sort of Arcadian, almost vegetable existence cultivating the soil, it is true, in their rude unscientific way, and therefore in a certain economic sense useful, speaking a sort of jargon or *patois* corruption of the language of their respective countries, and representing every stage of illiteracy and ignorance from the inability to tell their right hand from their left, to the bare capability of writing their names. Shall we call these people civilized because the same country or even city in which they subsist can boast of scholars and statesmen, because those countries possess railroad and telegraph communications and postal systems; because those cities support libraries and art galleries and institutions of learning? (Dispel the illusion.) Eradicate the false idea that to live in a civilized country is to be civilized, that the culture of a few will answer for the masses. Recognize that civilization is a personal, not a national or territorial condition.

The perfection of the means of communication is making the enlightened part of mankind stand aghast at the frequent and horrid pictures of crime which daily crowd the telegraphic wires. The unreasoning portion imagine they see a dreadful degeneracy in the human race, while in truth we only as yet partially see the human race as it is and always has been. But we should draw from it the weighty lesson that a large part of that race, though in the niches of a giddy civilization, are still in truth savages, crushing each other's skulls and ripping open each other's entrails at slight bursts of uncontrolled passion. But I am asked if education will diminish or prevent these crimes. I venture to answer yes, it will render them impossible. But it must be remembered that by education I mean something more than the mere smattering which is generally doled out now. Those who will follow me through will comprehend me in this by the time they have finished the perusal of this volume. But as it is I appeal to statistics, I summon the imperfect statistics which we have and I demand complete and accurate statistics in future. If attainable I undertake to prove by them that the immense majority of these crimes are the direct and legitimate fruit of ignorance.

It will be a long time before it will be possible to obtain statistics at all adequate to the development of the causes and the laws of crime. It is one of those unfortunate facts which necessitarians are accustomed, and justly, to set over against optimistic theories, that human nature and the universe are so constituted that a limited knowledge of many things is calculated to establish convictions the reverse of those which would result from thorough knowledge, the reverse of reality. Decision from complete statistics often reverses that of meager ones. The case of crime is evidently one of such cases. And it is because only the crimes of the most notable persons are at first known, and persons are as a rule notable in proportion as they are intelligent.

To read the history of the world one would be led to suppose that the only murders, suicides, assassinations and outrages that were committed among the ancients were confined to the imperial courts and the opulent and influential classes, to Brutuses, Catos, Cleopatras, Lucretias, Neros, and Constantines. Coming further down we begin to hear of crimes among citizens belonging to the upper classes of society. Then comes the printing press which removes the veil from a stratum still lower, the middle classes, and there we see it going on on a still greater scale than before. And now last of all the telegraph has commenced its mighty work of garnering facts, and as it slowly lays bare the condition of the lower strata and reveals the vast carnival of horrors that is being celebrated among the unlettered millions it is no wonder the blood of enlightened humanity curdles at the contemplation of the scene. And what are we to conclude? That the human animal has always and in all countries been engaged in this rivalry of animal passion, in this contest for supremacy, for possession in this (permit me the expression) struggle for existence. History is but the embryo of that greater science, statistics. Through them alone can we discover the laws of crime, and until we know its laws we can never hope to effect its systematic suppression. We have I think by this time, however, gone far enough to lay down one, probably the chief, fundamental law, viz: that crime is in the inverse proportion to intelligence or in the direct proportion to ignorance. This law is one which is easy of application, and points unmistakably to universal education as the antidote to crime.

These are a few of the stupendous problems which are destined to be solved by universal education. The human race under its all-pervading influence will be clothed with an entirely new character. The reign of hierarchy will be at an end, and that of equality will be inaugurated. The false arbitrary value now set upon individuals will disappear and their true intrinsic value will take its place. The true value of a new-born infant lies, not in the social position of its parents or ancestors. It is not even measured by what it actually will do during its life. It lies in what it might do under proper circumstances; in its naked capacity for acquiring the ability to do, when subjected to conditions favorable for the development of that native power. This is the true standard for the determination of the real worth of a human being. And measured by this standard how infinitely harsh and unjust fall the needs of praise now lavished upon men! What are we lauding? What are we rewarding? What are we condemning and punishing? I will tell you. We are lauding circumstance. We are rewarding wealth. We are condemning the unfortunate victims of social imperfection. We are punishing wretched beings for being what we have made them. It has been a reproach of the theology now passing off the stage of civilization, that it makes the Creator to punish his own creatures. This is the crime of society itself, for which there is not one extenuating circumstance. To it the injunction justly and forcibly applies: "Physician heal thyself."

Measured by the standard above set up this praise bestowed upon the statesman, the discoverer, the genius, the artist, should have been given to obscure peasants, rough mariners, "greasy mechanics" and menial servants. There might have been twenty Napoleons among the private soldiers of his army. A hundred Washingtons might have been developed from the raw materials of the Thirteen Colonies. At every street corner we meet heros, noblemen, reformers and discoverers. Only they do not know it and of course no one else can. Nature cannot be relied upon for the development of the capacity of individuals. It may and does sometimes do this, but it is only sporadic and accidental. It should be made systematic and certain. This is the work only of education.

Every child born into the world should be looked upon by society as so much raw material to be manufactured. Its quality is to be tested. It is the business of society as an intelligent economist to make the very most of it. To do this its actual quality or capacity for usefulness must be definitely and accurately determined. The present process consists in throwing out as dross nine tenths of all the material obtained, with no other test than that this quantity comes from certain alleged ignoble sources rendered so by arbitrary decisions. The process of universal education is that of first assaying the whole and rejecting only so much as shall, after thorough testing, prove worthless. This latter process promises, if the above proportions are correctly stated, to obtain just ten times the amount of the pure metal.

In other words it recognizes the average natural equality of all men, not only in rights but in capabilities, and proposes to insure to each the opportunity of placing himself in the highest sphere for which nature has qualified him to move. It gives the same importance to every human being. It reaches out and takes in the great proletariat and lifts it up to a level with highest stratum of existing society. The idea to my mind is immense. No longer to see the machinery of civilization circumscribed to the limits of small arbitrarily determined fraction. No longer to behold wily demogogues leading the illiterate masses. No longer to contemplate the latter, buried in superstition and error, perpetuating, by their own voluntary acts, their own degradation and slavery. Emancipate the mind first, and the body will disenthrall itself.

To the question then "who shall be educated?" I unhesitatingly answer, *everybody*. I see no distinction which it is either reasonable, just or safe to make between sane human beings. All the distinctions ever yet made are totally arbitrary and irrational. Wherever it is supposed that a natural reason does exist, it is because those who think so are incapable of seeing the true and ultimate effect of education. All such cases involve either untenable paralogisms or shallow sophisms, or else they rise from a general misapprehension and shortsighted ignorance of human character and human destiny. With distinctions of rank or birth or nationality I am done. Such considerations are wholly arbitrary and artificial and offer nothing upon which the rational mind can lay hold. There are however a

few specious grounds of objection to universal education. I shall endeavor
to analyze these with a view to the detection of their invalidity.

The first that occurs to me is of a general character and while it does
not discriminate at all between individuals or classes it bases itself upon the
assumption that the duties of society are such that it is necessary that there
should exist grades of people corresponding to them. It is asserted that inasmuch as all duties are necessary to be performed and as there is great
variety in the nature and character of them, so should there be a corresponding variety in the individuals upon whom their performance devolves.
The lowest menial service, the most degrading, the most disagreeable and
disgusting labor and the most tedious and exhaustive toil, are all necessary
to keep the great social factory in operation, as well as the more liberal
and congenial pursuits. Nay further, this same great object requires the
employment of millions of people upon the most mechanical operations
which become physically a sort of second nature and call for no degree
of intelligence above the most ordinary conceptions of surrounding circumstances. And it is inquired, as I must confess with some apparent force,
of what use could it be to educate such persons? To reply to this objection I feel that I just anticipate a portion of a future chapter. If society is
to remain the great tread-mill that it now is, I certainly can see no use in
the education of the animals employed to work it. If manual labor is
always to be regarded a degradation as it now is, of course there should be
degraded persons to perform it. But this is just what universal education
proposes to change, what it will and must change. Although its tendency
will necessarily be to diminish the amount of manual and increase the
amount of mechanical labor; to make the natural forces do more and more
of the mechanical labor and thus enable man to do more and more of the
mental labor. Still it seems as if the time can never come when there will
not be required a very large amount of manual labor calling only for that
species of mental effort which becomes nearly or quite wholly involuntary
by the force of habit. The introduction of machinery in fact lends rather
to the production of increased results, to the accomplishment of a greater
amount with the same labor than to the diminution of labor itself. The
most mechanical and monotonous of all labor is that in connection with
machinery. What could be more purely automatic and habitual than the
duties of a nail maker as he sits all day in the same position and does nothing
but perpetually turn his hand half over and back while the complicated
machinery performs its ceaseless work. This labor is far more unintellec-
tual, far more tedious than the old fashioned way of forging nails upon
an anvil. The work which machinery has accomplished here is not to throw
men out of employ and perform their duty for them, but to enable them
by its aid to make fifty or a hundred nails in the time before required to
make one. While I cannot doubt that even this species of labor will one

day be performed by an extension of the machinery, still this will only relieve these men to enable them to perform other equally monotonous duties. No. There is a great mistake made as to the effect of practical science upon manual labor. Its tendency is to multiply products not to dispense with labor. The great mass must always labor. They must expect to perform labor which does not call out their intellectual faculties. And I sometimes think that this, instead of being a misfortune is indeed the greatest blessing. The time is coming when it will no longer be a disgrace to labor, when every order of intellect will perform mechanical operations, when the mechanic and the farmer will be cultivated men, when labor will be recreation instead of drudgery, when at the lathe and the plow will be digested and organized the ideas which will be received from the library and the lecture hall, when mind and body will share alike the waking hours, when the hands and the head will neither be over-tasked neither neglected.

But I am encroaching upon the field of a later investigation. I will let this suffice for all the cases coming within this objection. Even menial service will come within their scope. For all the menial service which is now imposed upon servants because the employers regard it humiliating will, under the universal sentiment of equality which equal education will inspire be performed by themselves, while all that has a rational cause for its performance by others, will stand upon a level with all work, equally honorable and respectable.

It may be said that I presuppose a revolution in society, and that my answer to this objection is not applicable to things as they now are. I admit this and yet I insist that the social state to which I do apply it is such only as much result from the very operation of universal education. It is because I see that this measure, if adopted and continued a few generations, must revolutionize the present society and destroy the false prejudice which now stigmatizes labor, that I demand a trial of it on a grand scale, I do not deny the legitimacy of the objection, but deploring the state of things which render it legitimate, I would destroy the grounds of the objection and the objection itself must fall with them. Another objection relates to the female sex. It is said that universal education must comprehend both sexes. Shall then women receive the same education as men? Now I am aware that such a question in very recent times is somewhat timidly asked. It is a question which never has been much discussed. And the reason is that it will not bear discussion. The least discussion to the natural mind, amounts to solution. Such questions are like some liquid chemical mixtures which so long as kept perfectly quiet remain undissolved and cloudy, but the least agitation of which results in immediate solution rendering the liquid transparent. There are many questions which remain thus clouded before the minds of men but which need but a slight agitation to solve them into transparency. The equality of the two sexes as regards their title to the advantages of civilization is such a question. That the male sex practically does deny this equality to the female is apparent to every ordinary observer. The ground of this denial it would not do to seek. I hope to show in another place that this ground is none other than that of the superior physical force of the male sex, which is no logical reason at all because the humanitarian principle of justice is wanting and we are thrown back upon blind physical law. And it is precisely because there is no *just* reason for this social phenomenon that it requires so little agitation to expose its fallacy. The only thing that perpetuates it in an age which professes the dominion of justice is the prevalent superstition that whatever exists is of divine appointment. If men could be made to see that such customs are not sacred but the mere products of cold physical laws, operating spontaneously and uncontrolled by reason, they would no more allow them to be perpetuated than they would hesitate to cut down the weeds in their gardens on the ground that they were there by divine appointment.

As to the education of women there is but one thing to be ascertained. This is whether women have minds. The true educationalist knows no sex any more than he knows rank, color or stature. He sees only mind. This is his material. Mind is one thing. It may vary in minor characteristics but it is one in essence. It has neither sex nor color, neither local limits nor degrees of dignity. It is a force and is useful only when cultivated and guided. But these are the objects of education. Demonstrate that education is advantageous to male persons and you have proved that it is equally so to females. Show that men have a right to knowledge and you have shown that women have the same right. Establish the fact that society is benefited by the education of one sex, class or individual, and you have established that it will be as much more benefited by the education of both sexes, all classes and every individual. It is impossible to secure too much education. It is impossible to subordinate nature and society too much to the dominance of mind. Progress, civilization, human happiness, everything worth anything have ever been in exact proportion to the supremacy of the intellectual over the physical. We should trust this unwarying index and proceed to carry on the work till a state of the most perfect attainable knowledge shall usher in a state of the most perfect attainable happiness.

That there is a difference in the stamp and mould, in the shading and structures of the male and female mind is only an additional reason why it should be developed equally in both sexes. Those qualities which are termed feminine are as useful in their place as those termed masculine. Both alike require cultivation to render them elements of safety. Both must be educated before they can be understood. It requires culture in both before the good can be distinguished from the bad ones, before the former can be suitably developed and the latter eliminated.

Humanity, as now constituted, consists of a vast complex mass of natural and acquired qualities. These are all indiscriminately and undistinguishably mingled together. No one can tell which are natural and which derivative, which beneficial and which injurious. Many of the so-called virile qualities are little less than foul excrescences, while some of the effeminate ones are really beautiful and pure. Education like a great fan will winnow out the chaff from this composite mass and preserving the wheat will purify humanity.

I might refer to the position of woman as the natural and necessary guardian of childhood and hence the true educator of the young of both sexes, the one of whom a thousand juvenile and yet often profound inquiries are every day addressed in the nursery, now alas too often destined to remain unanswered, or what is worse falsely or erroneously answered, by an ignorant mother; when if a ripened scholarship and a broad mental culture could have met these interrogations with clear, correct and copious explanations, years of study might be spared and errors of a lifetime averted.

Everybody knows how the task of learning is seasoned by the spice of interest. When a child asks a question it is because it desires to know the truth respecting that about which it inquires. Thus learned are so deeply impressed upon the mind that they are rarely ever effaced. If instead of repressing this inquisitiveness as an ignorant mother is compelled to do, and as it is far better that she should do, it could be encouraged and, attracted to useful subjects, the rising generation might find itself fairly launched upon the sea of knowledge, before the period of mental application should arrive, ready and eager to make the voyage of education, now so tedious to many, because inspired by inculcations of a wise but loved mother with a reverence for truth and a zeal for the acquisition of knowledge. If instead of fretfully hushing them as the ignorant mother, meaningless prattle of children, and instead of soothing their greedy minds with fairy tales, and strange impossible stories which fill them with credulity and superstition, the nursery could be made, unbeknown to them, a real school, a perpetual kindergarten, for filling their young and anxious minds with the most useful truths within their comprehension, there is no estimating the influence of such a system upon the condition of society. But no such thing can be expected while woman remains uneducated. With her education the world will gradually approach it. The young will come forth to meet life, eager to taste the good things promised them in their infancy, when their future paths were made pleasant by foretastes from a mother's lips. In such anticipation the anxious mind is never disappointed in its passage over the rich fields of literature and science.

I might also refer to the still more fundamental consideration that the mental qualities are inherited from both parents and that by leaving one sex uncultivated one half of the benefit flowing from this source is lost. It is a subject of common remark that the descendants of great men are rarely above mediocrity, often far below it. That much of this is to be attributed to the vanity of such people who imagine that because their fathers were great they must be so also, and disdain the labor which can alone confer true greatness, but may there not be a still deeper reason in many or perhaps *all* such cases, in the circumstance that she of whom these children are as much the descendants as they are of their father was neither great by nature nor by culture, but only an ordinary or perhaps quite an inferior person? It is from among such, unfortunately, that even the most brilliant of men are compelled, at this time, to select their companions. The number of really educated women is so small that even if always united to great men, the latter, as we now are in the habit of conferring that title, would not be supplied in the proportion of one to ten. But such a rare coincidence is next to impossible. The artificial barrrier which society has erected between the sexes is so high that the best in these two separated spheres rarely find each other. Besides it is not mental adaptation that usually determines such unions.

Where it is not a low physical attraction it is usually some emotional one, which, however pure and worthy, is little influenced by any speculations regarding the desired intellectual qualities of offspring. People rush together like chemical substances on the establishment of the proper conditions and reason and calculation have little to say. But nature is not so kind as to transmit only the qualities of the superior party; as to leave out of the product of such unions all that is low and groveling and inspire it only with that which is lofty and aspiring. No indeed! It is just as apt to do the reverse. It usually perpetuates all the qualities, either combined or distributed through the different individuals which may be born of the pair. Sometimes, it is true, the character of one only of the parents seems to largely predominate, the causes of which are still very obscure; but it may be regarded certain that whatever may determine nature in the transmission of qualities, it is not our notion of what it ought to do, or any human speculation upon what would most closely conform to our conceptions of utility, nay, it is not, we may safely say, any moral consideration whatever, but merely the blind necessity which the superior physical power of the generative organs of the one or the other for transmitting qualities, occasions. It is scarcely to be hoped, and I doubt whether it should be, that this state of things will ever be changed. Love always will, and I think always should, be the leading passion in marriage. Marriage is essentially a love affair, and any social convention which shall subordinate the natural to any other cause of union will tend to demoralize humanity. The attempts to make royal or noble birth or wealth, the ruling passion in determining marriages has I am sure had this tendency, and, superior as I should regard the consideration of intellectual adaptation I should be loth to trust it. All such attempts are but so much social patchwork at the expense of the natural sentiments. The only true way to meet this crying evil is to elevate the female intellect, to develop the feminine talents, to exalt the whole femininity, in short, to educate woman. If we look at the question in a purely utilitarian aspect, and consider only the happiness of the race, nay, if we consider the happiness of men alone, every principle of reason and common sense would dictate the equal education of both sexes. It is only thus that they can be companions of each other. What companionship can an illiterate woman afford to a cultivated man? Yet such is the condition of society today, and such will always be the nature of humanity, that notwithstanding such bald incongruities, such unions are far from uncommon. The opposite sometimes but rarely occurs. The result is that woman ceases to be a companion and becomes a servant. I had almost said, owing to man-made laws, a slave. Therefore if society knew its own interests, if men themselves knew their own interests, woman would be at once admitted to the same privileges of education with man.

The peculiar fitness which woman seems by nature to possess for teaching the youth, constitutes an additional demand for equal education. In the lower branches of instruction this natural fitness has been practically recognized and woman has already been intrusted with the most unpleasant and laborious part of human education, often unfortunately to the whole of it. Not to speak of the unfairness and ungallantry of this, since woman only seems too glad to be permitted to do even this much, though she can confessedly do it so much better than man, it is a narrow impolitic system. If woman can teach children and rudimentary principles better than men, she can certainly teach adults and advanced principles as well. Trial would probably prove that her superiority to man as an instructor is not limited by the age of the pupil or the degree of the study. But it may be said, that woman is intellectually inferior to man and incompetent to comprehend much less to impart the truths of advanced science. The abstract truth of this assumption is only to be tested by trial. I am inclined on purely a priori grounds to suppose that the female intellect is, in its mere quantity or strength, somewhat below the male. I judge from her position in society, which is certainly less adapted to develop it than that of man. It is a scientific anthropological question and must be settled as are all scientific questions by experimental demonstration. If this shall prove woman even considerably below man in average intellectual vigor, it will only show that inheritance has not wholly neutralized the natural tendency of activity of the sexes. But I desire to protest, in the absence of any such demonstration, against such an assumption on the part of them. Besides being unchivalrous and ungenerous it is selfish and egotistical. As long as the higher schools, colleges and universities are closed to women and they have never been allowed to compare their powers of acquirement with those of their brothers, I can scarcely imagine a greater indignity which could be offered them by the latter than to taunt them with an inferiority which they are forbidden to disprove. It indicates a lower degree of moral development which borders closely upon actual barbarism. So far as woman has been allowed to go in the acquisition of knowledge she has always proved her entire equality with the other sex and almost every report of school commissioners and superintendents of education delights to officially testify to this fact. Nay, there have actually sprung up in the most recent times a very few actual colleges with substantially the same *curriculum* as that adopted by such institutions for men, and the world has yet to learn that the female students in these have proved inadequate to meet it. That a few may prove deficient is no more than can be said of male students between individuals of whom there indeed seems to be the same degrees of capacity as between males and females or between individual females, so far as aptitude and faculty for theoretical learning are concerned. Of course no one can be compelled to go beyond his powers. There are hundreds of male students as every professor knows, who go through the curriculum without really comprehending the half of what they have to study. No one hopes that it would be otherwise with women. Still even these cannot help gathering some crumbs of knowledge, and if it were no more than to know that such sciences exist, it would be well worth all the time devoted to it. But as a general thing it is not because the subjects are so obstruce that they are not comprehended by any but superior minds. It is far more commonly because they are so miserably taught, both by the text book and by the teacher. In both these respects radical reform is needed, and perhaps the establishment of female professorships in the colleges may be one step in the right direction. Lastly I repeat, in this connection the observation previously made, that those truths which are the most useful and most fundamental are not, except in a few cases, the most difficult to acquire. Those branches of education which are now deemed too high even for the universities to deal with except in a merely nominal way, and which are in truth the most fundamental and beneficial to be known, are not at all difficult of comprehension, and could be easily acquired by any student of ordinary natural powers. They possess moreover a certain internal charm which, by keeping up the interest carries the mind unconsciously up to the keenest point of perception, thus rendering easy an amount of thinking which some of the present common school branches, from their natural dryness, could never call forth. Here as everywhere the great law of attraction asserts its irresistable sway.

I have thus intentionally dwelt somewhat at length upon this flimsy and puerile objection to universal education, not because I felt its weight in reason, but in fact, not because I deemed it worthy in itself of refutation, but because I realize that it constitutes one of those wide-spread and deep-seated prejudices which have come down to us from a barbarous antiquity and which in actual practice hang like dark clouds over the progress of humanity. The education of woman! This immense subject has so long weighed upon me that I am happy to seize an opportunity even thus incidentally and briefly to raise my voice in its earnest advocacy. I am tired of this one-sided civilization, of this half-built society, of this false chivalry, this mock-modesty, this pretended regard which one sex assumes for the other, while loads of putrid prejudice hang upon a woman's neck. Away with it all and let the broad shield of equality be the protecting reign of humanity!

CHAPTER 5

Testing, Predicting, Sorting and Tracking

From the very start, standardized tests were seen by those who created them as modeled on the then existing social order. According to Alfred Binet:

> An individual is normal when he is able to conduct himself in life without need of the guardianship of another, and is able to perform work sufficiently renumerative to supply his personal needs, and finally when his intelligence does not exclude him from the social rank of his parents. As a result of this, an attorney's son who is reduced by his intelligence to the condition of a menial employee is a moron; likewise the son of a master mason, who remains a servant at thirty years is a moron; likewise a peasant, normal in ordinary surroundings of the fields, may be considered a moron in the city.[1]

Most testers such as Binet, Terman, Thorndike, Jensen, and Herrnstein recognized that social class differences would not only influence the performance of any individual on a test, but that these differences were the very basis of the tests themselves. These same men usually accepted the social class system as given, and then proceeded to argue that the social class differences add validity to their observations. Thus, Francis Galton postulated in *Hereditary Genius* that the physical superiority of the English leaders proved the heritability of genius because the gifted leaders were "massive, vigorous, capable-looking animals." On the other hand, Ward asserted that "it would be more nearly true to say that they are superior because they are where they are."[2] Receiving the blessings of a

---

[1] Alfred Binet and T. H. Simon, *The Development of Intelligence in Children.* (Baltimore: Williams and Wilkins Co., 1916), p. 266.

[2] As quoted by Thomas F. Gossett, *Race: The History of an Idea in America.* (New York: Schocken Books, 1968), p. 162.

privileged environment Ward reasoned that genius could be expected to be physically superior. Galton, Binet and Thorndike, however, interpreted the physical superiority of the social elites as proof of genetic superiority. At this crucial point, each not only accepted, but in his own way tacitly justified, the existing social order. One can sense this when Binet said:

> Our personal investigations, as well as those of many others, have demonstrated that children of the poorer class are shorter, weigh less, have smaller heads and slighter muscular force, than a child of the upper class; they less often reach the high school; they are more often behind in their studies. Here is a collection of inferiorities which are slight, because they are only appreciated when large numbers are considered, but they are undeniable. Some probably are acquired and result from unavoidable and accessory circumstances; others are congenital.[3]

Binet, Terman, Thorndike, Jensen and Herrnstein's observations of the social order repeatedly confirmed, in their minds, the validity of their tests. The rich were obviously brighter than the poor, just as they were also physically superior to the poor. Ideologically in tune with their social order, the successful tester in America created tests which reflected that social order and the values implicit in that order.

Most testers in America were fully conscious of this social class connection and often saw themselves as guardians of the social class system. The important thing, however, was the maintenance and development of what H. H. Goddard viewed as an "aristocracy in democracy." In such a social system, the natural aristocracy would rule through the leadership of the people. In *Human Efficiency and Levels of Intelligence*, Goddard argued that:

> The disturbing fear is that the masses—the seventy million or even the eighty-six million—will take matters into their own hands. The fact is, matters are already in their hands and have been since the adoption of the Constitution. But it is equally true that the eighty-six million are in the hands of the fourteen million or the four million. Provided always that the four million apply their very superior intelligence to the practical problem of social welfare and efficiency.[4]

Goddard, as did Herrnstein fifty-one years after him, assumed a positive correlation of social class and native intelligence. He expressed the need not only for the intelligent to rule the ignorant masses, but also the need to educate the masses so that they would accept intelligent leadership. Part of that acceptance would depend on the organization and use of tests in the schools themselves. The test questions were written and rewritten by professional educators who held definite attitudes toward the rich, the

---

[3] Binet and Simon, p. 318.
[4] H. H. Goddard, *Human Efficiency and Levels of Intelligence*. (Princeton: Princeton University Press, 1920), p. 97.

poor, the well-washed middle class, and the ill-kept immigrant child. The scores that the test yielded would not only predict academic success in a school which reflected these values, but also success in society which reflected those social class values. The child, then, needed guidance toward his proper role in society. Terman correlated IQ and occupational levels as he perceived those levels.

> At every step in the child's progress the school should take account of his vocational possibilities. Preliminary investigations indicate that an I.Q. below 70 rarely permits anything better than unskilled labor; that the range from 70 to 80 is pre-eminently that of semi-skilled labor, from 80 to 100 that of the skilled or ordinary clerical labor, from 100 to 110 or 115 that of the semi-professional pursuits; and that above all these are the grades of intelligence which permit one to enter the professions or the larger fields of business. Intelligence tests can tell us whether a child's native brightness corresponds more nearly to the median of (1) the professional classes, (2) those in the semi-professional pursuits, (3) ordinary skilled workers, (4) semi-skilled workers, or (5) unskilled laborers. This information will be a great value in planning the education of a particular child and also in planning the differentiated curriculum here recommended.[5]

The test, originally based on skills appropriate for varying occupational classes and eventually standardized on the basis of class, now were used to design a curriculum appropriate for that class and to guide and channel the child toward that occupation which his assumed "native brightness" fits him. The schools would now "assay" the raw material and put him through a manufacturing process which would teach him to accept the social inequalities with the least possible friction. As Frank N. Freeman, from the University of Chicago, argued,

> It is the business of the school to help the child to acquire such an attitude toward the inequalities of life, whether in accomplishment or in reward, that he may adjust himself to its conditions with the least possible friction.[6]

Freeman clearly saw the function of public education as helping the child adjust to the real world of "inequalities of life." The individual "must not think of education as a personal privilege" but must realize its function to fit him into a community. As he put it:

> The real difficulty with this whole line of argument is that it assumes that education is a gift by the state to the individual for the benefit of the individual. The only valid conception of public education is that it is for the purpose of fitting the individual to take his place in the life of the community.[7]

[5] Lewis M. Terman, *Intelligence Tests and School Reorganization.* (New York: World Book, 1923), pp. 27–28.

[6] Frank N. Freeman, "Sorting the Students," *Educational Review*, November 1924, p. 170.

[7] *Ibid.*, p. 171.

Arguments of men like Terman, Freeman and Thorndike helped bring the ability-tracking curricular model into the public school. The children were to be homogeneously grouped according to native ability and then educated accordingly.

Included in Freeman's argument, however, was a social class disclaimer. If the tracking system was based on wealth, or birth or some other external circumstances, he argued, it would be undemocratic. On the other hand, if it was based "upon the inherent capacity of the individual, it is just and in conformity to the demands of public welfare." [8] As long as Freeman could believe that the tests really measured intrinsic capacity and not social privilege, he could maintain his utopian meritocratic view of the system. This belief in the tests was important for educators who wished to avoid the social consequences of their activities in testing and tracking in the schools.

Terman, like Freeman, had come so thoroughly to believe in the idea that IQ was a measure for innate ability that he could see nothing questionable in his own study of gifted children. He found:

> More than 50 percent of our group have sprung from the top 4 percent or 5 percent of the vocational hierarchy. The professional and semi-professional classes together account for more than 80 percent. The unskilled labor classes furnish but a paltry 1 percent or 2 percent.[9]

If one believes, as Terman and Herrnstein seemed to believe, that the social class system had sorted out the best, then these findings are acceptable. Terman argued that it is far more important to cultivate societies' intellectual elites than to become overly concerned with the dullards. He advocated a three track system supplemented by a special track for the gifted and a special track for the intellectually disadvantaged, all of which, interestingly enough, corresponded to the five classes of occupations into which he saw the child channeled.[10]

The test discriminated against members of the lower class—Southern Europeans and Blacks—indirectly by what they seemed to leave out, but more directly by what they included; for example: On a Stanford-Binet (1960 revision),[11] a six-year-old child is presented with a series of pictures which clearly reflect the facial features of a person of Anglo-Saxon, Black, and southern European descent. The child is then asked the question, "Which is prettier?" and must select the Nordic Anglo-Saxon type to be correct. If, however, the child is Black, or Mexican American or of Southern European descent, has looked at himself in a mirror and has a

8 *Ibid.*, p. 172.

9 Lewis M. Terman, "The Conservation of Talent," *School and Society*, March 29, 1924, Vol. XIX, No. 483, p. 363.

10 *Ibid.*, p. 364.

11 It should be noted here that this is the latest revision of the Stanford-Binet Intelligence Test. The Houghton Mifflin Company which controls copyright on the test does not permit reproduction of the pictures referred to.

reasonably healthy respect for himself, he will pick the wrong answer. Worse, yet is the child who recognizes what a "repressive society" calls the "right" answer and has been socialized enough to sacrifice his self-identity for a higher score. Neither Blacks nor southern Europeans were beautiful according to the authors of the Stanford-Binet; but then, there was no beauty recognized in these people when Goddard, Laughlin, Terman,[12] Thorndike and Garrett called for the sterilization of the "socially inadequate," the discriminatory closing of immigration, the tracking organization of the American school or, for that matter, defined their place in the meritocracy.

Mental Levels and Democracy

H. H. Goddard

The discoveries that each individual has his mental level which, once established, he cannot exceed and that the level of the average person is probably between thirteen and fourteen years, explain a great many things not previously understood, but also raise some questions that are at first sight, somewhat disturbing.

One of these questions is: What about democracy, can we hope to have a successful democracy where the average mentality is thirteen? The question is an interesting one and suggests many other questions upon which the doctrine of mental levels can certainly throw much light. Democracy of course means the people rule, as contrasted with aristocracy which means literally, "the best" rule. We would probably all agree that we ought to be ruled by the best, but unfortunately, that term *best* is one of those indefinite terms which must be limited before we can discuss it. It might mean best in physical strength, or best in knowledge, or best in intelligence, or best in administrative powers, or best in any one of the many other things. Now democracy is not opposed to a rule by the best. The essential point of democracy is that every citizen shall have a chance to say whom he thinks is the best. "Governments obtain their just powers from the consent of the governed."

[12] Of this group, only Terman seemingly wavered from the original position. When he wrote his autobiography in 1932 he had stated his belief, "That the major differences between children of high and low IQ and the major differences in the intelligence test-scores of certain races, as Negroes and whites will never be fully accounted for on the environmental hypothesis." By 1951, he penciled in around that statement, "I am less sure of this now," and in 1955, again another note said, "I'm still less sure." See Ernest R. Hilgard, "Lewis Madison Terman," *American Journal of Psychology*, 1957.

In the case of the aristocracies of the past, a few people have said, "We are the best, therefore we will rule," and best has often meant best in physical strength. Had those rulers been best in every sense, the probabilities are that democracy would never have arisen, but because they were often not wise, not humane, not considerate of the welfare and happiness of the masses, those masses gradually developed the idea that they wanted to have something to say as to who was best.

Now it is a question of whether a people whose average intelligence is that of a thirteen year old child can make a sufficiently wise choice of rulers to insure the success of a democracy or as it would often be put, can children of thirteen govern themselves? The fact that we here in the United States have done it for a hundred and forty years is of course an all sufficient answer, unless new conditions are arising which will make the methods of the past, prove a failure in the future.

Let us not at the outset, commit the fallacy of the average. The average only means that there are about as many of lower intelligence as of higher. We have seen that while the average is perhaps thirteen to fourteen years and there are twenty-five million people of this intelligence and forty-five million still lower, there are also thirty million above the average and four and one-half million of *very superior intelligence*. Obviously there are enough people of high intelligence to guide the Ship of State, if they are put in command.

The disturbing fear is that the masses—the seventy million or even the eighty-six million—will take matters into their own hands. The fact is, matters are already in their hands and have been since the adoption of the Constitution. But it is equally true that the eighty-six million are in the hands of the fourteen million or of the four million. Provided always that the four million apply their very superior intelligence to the practical problem of social welfare and efficiency.

Lower intelligence will invariably and inevitably seek and follow the advice of higher intelligence so long as it has confidence in the individuals having the higher intelligence. That is a proposition so invariable as to be recognized as a law of human nature.

The crux of the matter however, lies in the word *confidence*. Here is the root of our social troubles and here is found the explanation of everything from local labor troubles to Bolshevism. Intelligence has made the fundamental error of assuming that it alone is sufficient to inspire confidence. A little thought shows that this is a blunder almost worthy to be called stupid. Intelligence can only inspire confidence when it is appreciated. And how can unintelligence comprehend intelligence? There is an old Persian proverb which says, "The wise man can understand the foolish because he has been foolish; but the foolish cannot comprehend the wise because he has never been wise."

The one source and efficient cause of confidence of lower intelligence for the higher is what we call the human quality. The poet says of the great Agassiz, "His magic was not far to seek—he was so human." It is the man whose activities show that he cares for the welfare and the happiness of those of less intelligence, that has their confidence, their vote and their obedience.

The inmates of the Vineland Training School, imbeciles and morons, did not elect Superintendent Johnstone and his associates to rule over them; *but they would do so if given a chance because they know that the one purpose of that group of officials is to make the children happy.*

Whenever the four million choose to devote their superior intelligence to understanding the lower mental levels and to the problem of the comfort and happiness of the other ninety-six million, they will be elected the rulers of the realm and then will come perfect government—Aristocracy *in* Democracy.

We may suggest in passing, one reform not inconsistent with the above view. While we all believe in democracy, we may nevertheless admit that we have been too free with the franchise and it would seem a self-evident fact that the feeble-minded should not be allowed to take part in civic affairs; should not be allowed to vote. It goes without saying that they cannot vote intelligently, they are so easily led that they constitute the venial vote and one imbecile who knows nothing of civic matters can annul the vote of the most intelligent citizen.

Before passing to a discussion of education according to mental levels, we may perhaps be permitted to apply the principle to another problem that looms up rather large at the present time, namely, socialism and especially its extreme form of Bolshevism. Most of the arguments used by the more intelligent members of these groups are fallacious because they ignore the mental levels. These men in their ultra altruistic and humane attitude, their desire to be fair to the workman, maintain that the great inequalities in social life are wrong and unjust. For example, here is a man who says, "I am wearing $12.00 shoes, there is a laborer who is wearing $3.00 shoes; why should I spend $12.00 while he can only afford $3.00? I live in a home that is artistically decorated, carpets, high-priced furniture, expensive pictures and other luxuries; there is a laborer that lives in a hovel with no carpets, no pictures and the coarsest kind of furniture. It is not right, it is unjust." And so in his enthusiasm for the supposed just treatment of the workman, this gentleman who has been converted to socialism will go on pointing out the inequalities which he considers unjust. As we have said, the argument is fallacious. It assumes that that laborer is on the same mental level with the man who is defending him. It assumes that if you were to change places with the laborer, he would be vastly happier than he is now, that he could live in your house with its artistic decorations and its fine furniture and pictures and appreciate and enjoy those things. Or if it is admitted that this particular laborer could not enjoy it, your gentleman socialist is apt to fall back upon the argument that it is due to the fact that he has not been brought up right, his environment has been poor and so he is accustomed to such conditions and could not enjoy anything better. Therefore we should take the children and educate them to these ideals.

Now the fact is, *that workman* may have a ten year intelligence while you have a twenty. To demand for him such a home as you enjoy is as absurd as it would be to insist that every laborer should receive a graduate fellowship. How can there be such a thing as social equality with this wide range of mental capacity? The different levels of intelligence have different interests and require different treatment to make them happy, and we are committing a serious fallacy when we argue that because we enjoy such things, everybody else could enjoy them and therefore ought to have them.

As for an equal distribution of the wealth of the world that is equally absurd. The man of intelligence has spent his money wisely, has saved until he has enough to provide for his needs in case of sickness, while the man of low intelligence, no matter how much money he would have earned, would have spent much of it foolishly and would never have anything ahead. It is said that during the past year, the coal miners in certain parts of the country have earned more money than the operators and yet today when the mines shut down for a time, those people are the first to suffer. They did not save anything, although their whole life has taught them that mining is an irregular thing and that when they were having plenty of work they should save against the days when they do not have work.

Socialism is a beautiful theory but the facts must be faced. One of the facts is that people differ in mentality and that *each mentality requires its own kind of life for its success and happiness*. There are undoubtedly, a great many abuses; there are a great many ways in which intelligent men, men of means, might alleviate some of the conditions of the poor, but here again, the only way it can be done is by recognizing the mentality of the poor and treating them in accordance with that mentality. For example, if we discover a man with fifteen year intelligence who on account of misfortune, bad luck or something else, is down and cannot get a start, then we may profitably give that man as much as he needs to put him on his feet again, knowing that once that is done he will succeed. Here is another man whose outward circumstances look much like the former but when we examine him we find he has a ten year mentality. To give that man money is a mistake for he has not intelligence enough to use the money when he gets it; though you gave him a thousand dollars today he would be poor tomorrow.

All this has been said often. These facts are appreciated. But it is not so fully appreciated that the cause is to be found in the fixed character of mental levels. In our ignorance we have said let us give these people one more chance—always one more chance.

Much money has been wasted and is continually being wasted by would-be philanthropists who give liberally for alleviating conditions that are to them intolerable. They admit the money is being wasted. They do not understand that it is being wasted because the people who receive it, have not sufficient intelligence to appreciate it and to use it wisely. Moreover, it is a positive fact that many of these people are better contented in their present surroundings than in any that the philanthropists can provide for them. They are like Huckleberry Finn who was most unhappy when dressed up and living in a comfortable room at Aunt Polly's and having good food and everything that Aunt Polly thought ought to make him happy. He stood it for a few days and then he ran away and went back in his hogshead with his old rags on, and getting his food wherever he could pick it up.

Aunt Polly's efforts were wasted because she did not appreciate the mental level of Huckleberry Finn.

We must now consider what is the wise procedure with the various low levels of intelligence. As we stated in an earlier lecture, all work looking to the eventual control of this problem of social efficiency as conditioned by mental levels, must begin with the children. When children enter school their mental level should be determined. Several groups will be found. At the top are those who are exceptionally intelligent, well endowed, who test considerably above their age. This group subdivides into two: first, those who are truly gifted children and second, those whose brilliancy is coupled with nervousness. The superior mentality of the truly gifted will mark them throughout life. They should have the broadest and best education that it is possible to give, not necessarily hurried through the grades at the most rapid rate but while advancing somewhat faster than the average child, they should be given a broader experience. There should be opportunities for them to do many things, in each year, that the average child has not time to do.

The nervously brilliant group is a very important one. It contains those children who are brilliant in school, but whose brilliancy is evidently due to a very high-strung nervous system. It is a case of the well-known but little understood relationship between genius and insanity. While these children may probably not be called insane they are nevertheless in a stage of nervous instability which, while it happens to make them keen, acute and quick, and they give the appearance of brilliancy; on the other hand, it is an exceedingly dangerous situation since experience has taught that a little pushing or overwork may very easily throw them over definitely on the insane side. These children should be treated with the very greatest care.

A second group comprises the moderately bright children, a little above average and yet not enough to be considered especially precocious. They should however, have their condition taken into account and they should not be compelled to drudge along with the average child.

Then comes the *average child* for whom our school systems at present are made, and the only group whom they adequately serve. The question as to whether the training that we are giving this group in the public schools is the best that can be devised is not for us to discuss here.

Our next group is the backward. Those children who are not quite up to age, who have considerable difficulty in getting along with their work and yet who do get along after a fashion. This group should be carefully watched from the start and eventually they will differentiate again into two divisions, possibly three. Perhaps some of them may later on catch up with the average child. Some of them will go through their whole educational career with the same slowness, nevertheless they will get through. There are still others, who while only a little backward at this first examination, later on will show that they are actually feeble-minded children.

Finally there is the group of definitely feeble-minded. In many cases it will not be possible, at this time, to predict just what their final mental level will be. This group will ultimately divide into several grades according to their mental level. There will be the morons with their three or four subdivisions, that is to say, those who have a mentality of eight, those of nine, or ten or eleven, perhaps of twelve. Then come the imbeciles with their mentality of seven and six and five; and each of these should receive special training and treatment.

Suggestions for the Introduction of a Mental Test Program

Lewis M. Terman

WHAT PUPILS SHALL BE TESTED?

The answer is, all. If only selected children are tested, many of the cases most in need of adjustment will be overlooked. The purpose of the tests is to tell us what we do not already know, and it would be a mistake to test only those pupils who are recognized as obviously below or above average. Some of the biggest surprises are encountered in testing those who have been looked upon as close to average in ability. Universal testing is fully warranted, whether considered from the point of view of money cost or labor cost. If we can afford to spend $50 to $100 a year for a child's instruction for ten or twelve years, we can surely afford to spend 6 to 10 cents for a test whose results may affect the child's entire educational career. The labor cost is too small to be counted an obstacle, now that satisfactory group tests are available. If the results are properly used, the cost is a negative quantity, for in the long run labor is saved.

CHOICE OF TESTS

New intelligence tests have recently appeared in such numbers that the average teacher or school administrator is likely to experience a feeling of helplessness in trying to decide regarding their relative merits. However, the number of tests which are really anything like satisfactory from both the scientific and practical point of view is small. It is not within the scope of this report to recommend particular tests, but the following general statements may be made:

1. At present three separate group scales are required in testing Grades 1 to 12: one for Grades 1 to 3, another from Grade 3 or 4 to Grade 8 or 9, and a third from Grade 7 or 8 to Grade 12.
2. Those who are not thoroughly familiar with the merits of the different tests available for each of these levels should seek the help of some one who knows. The director of educational research in almost any city of considerable size is ordinarily in a position to give unprejudiced and expert advice.
3. Brief tests requiring ten or twenty minutes, even when they show a fairly high correlation with more thorough intelligence scales, are too unreliable to be depended upon for the measurement of individual pupils. The saving in time and cost is too small to justify the risk of doing injustice in a considerable percentage of cases by the use of erroneous scores.
4. The group tests devised for grades below the fourth are much less satisfactory than tests for Grades 4 to 12. When "primary" tests are used, they need to be checked up by a large amount of individual testing. This is especially important in the first grade. When possible, individual rather than group tests should be given throughout the first three grades.
5. Pupils of any grade who test extremely high or extremely low, and pupils whose group test score disagrees materially with school performance, should be given an individual test.

WHO SHALL GIVE AND SCORE THE TESTS?

Group tests may be given by the school psychologist (or director of research), the principal, or the teachers themselves. Although the procedure for many of the tests is simple enough to be mastered readily by any teacher, it is on the whole more satisfactory to have all tests given by trained and experienced examiners. When no experienced examiner is available, the teacher should not hesitate to undertake the work herself. Binet testing is of course more difficult, and to do it as it ought to be done requires considerable training. However, countless teachers and principals have attained a fair mastery of the Binet method entirely by their own efforts. Many cities are solving this problem by giving training courses in Binet procedure to selected groups of teachers.

The scoring of group tests may be done by the teachers, provided it is carefully supervised. Scoring done without adequate supervision is certain to contain a large percentage of errors. Additions to secure total score should always be performed twice, preferably by different persons. Copying and transcription of scores should also be verified.

WHO SHALL HAVE ACCESS TO THE SCORES?

Not the public, certainly, and ordinarily not the pupils. In rare cases one may be warranted in letting a particular pupil know his score, but in the long run it is probably wiser never to do so. The child who is inquisitive may simply be told that he has done "well" or "pretty well," etc. If this rule is ever broken, it should be in the case of pupils in the upper grades or high school who test high but lack self-confidence or do not apply themselves diligently.

Nor should the scores ordinarily be given to parents. To keep them from the teachers would be, in the opinion of the writer, to carry secrecy too far. It is always necessary, however, to instruct teachers in the significance of scores and to caution them severely against the evils of making unguarded remarks about the intelligence of this or that child. It is extremely important that every one who uses scores in mental ability tests should have some definite knowledge of and a wholesome respect for their probable errors. Special instruction of this point should be given.

THE USE OF SUPPLEMENTARY DATA

The test score, instead of being considered infallible, should be taken as the point of departure for further study of the pupil. Educational tests should be used and data should be secured on health, interests, habits, and attitude toward school work. Before the tests are given, ratings should be made of each pupil on quality of school work, intelligence, industry, social adaptability, etc. These may be made on a five-point or seven-point scale. The comparison of such ratings with test results will prove of surpassing interest. One pupil tests lower than he was rated, another higher. Why the discrepancy? In trying to find an answer to such questions the teacher will come to understand her pupils as she never did before.

THE ACCOMPLISHMENT RATIO

In this connection use should be made of the Accomplishment Ratio (AR) as worked out by Dr. Franzen . . . ; that is, the ratio secured by dividing accomplishment age by mental age. At present the value of this device is limited somewhat by the lack of reliable age norms for the various educational tests. When this want has been supplied, as it doubtless will be soon, the AR may become as well known as the IQ. In judging a child's educational performance we need to know how well he is living up to his mental possibilities. The AR tells us this. It is the main function of the teacher to keep the AR from dropping below 100; that is, to keep the accomplishment level for each child up to the standard for that child's mental age.

Where only grade standards are available for an educational test, these may be converted into approximate age standards by use of . . . [a table] showing the mental ages which normally correspond to each grade. For example, since the median mental age (also median age) corresponding to Grade 3 is nine years, a child who earns a third-grade score in a given educational test may be said to have an accomplishment age of nine years for that school subject. If the child's mental age is ten years, the AR is $9 \div 10$, or 90. If the score on the educational test is somewhere between the norms for two grades, the corresponding accomplishment age is arrived at by interpolation.

As Franzen has shown, an ideal method of school marking would be to give the child his AR in each subject. It is obvious that the usual method of marking by A, B, C, D, E (or 1, 2, 3, 4, 5) does not tell the pupil whether he is doing as well as he could be expected to do, ability considered.

USING THE TEST RESULTS

The purpose of intelligence tests in the schools is to make a difference in the educational treatment of pupils, not to furnish amusement to the teacher or to gratify an idle curiosity. Unless the results are to be used, the tests had better not be given. On the other hand, immediate wholesale regrading is not always advisable. Reorganization should take place gradually. The opposition sometimes encountered here and there in putting over a testing program in a city usually melts away under the favorable influence of a successful experiment with the tests in one or two schools.

. . . Specific uses . . . may be made of mental test results. . . . The present writer would urge the widespread trial of the multiple-track plan, adapted according to size of city and according to other circumstances. Merely to give a small proportion of children an extra promotion, while this is well worth while, is to be satisfied with too little. More radical measures must be adopted to reduce sufficiently the mental age range in the instruction groups.

PUPIL GUIDANCE

The use of the tests in educational and vocational guidance is hardly less important than their use in re-grouping. In fact, the two uses are bound up together. At present vocational guidance is too largely an end process, an afterthought. To be of most value it should be preceded by years of educational guidance. At every step in the child's progress the school should take account of his vocational possibilities. Preliminary investigations indicate that an IQ below 70 rarely permits anything better than unskilled labor; that the range from 70 to 80 is preeminently that of semi-skilled labor, from 80 to 100 that of the skilled or ordinary clerical labor, from 100 to 110 or 115 that of the semi-professional pursuits; and that above all these are the grades of intelligence which permit one to enter the professions or the larger fields of business. Intelligence tests can tell us whether a child's native brightness corresponds more nearly to the median of (1) the professional classes, (2) those in the semi-professional pursuits, (3) ordinary skilled workers, (4) semi-skilled workers, or (5) unskilled laborers. This information will be of great value in planning the education of a particular child and also in planning the differentiated curriculum here recommended. It will be understood that such figures can only be used as a rough guide, especially since the IQ is not a perfectly accurate measure of intelligence.

THE DISCOVERY AND CULTIVATION OF TALENT

The average school devotes more time and effort to its dullards than to its children of superior ability. The latter are expected to take care of themselves. As a matter of fact, many of them are not discovered. Yet it may be of greater value to society to discover a single gifted child and aid in his proper development than to train a thousand dullards to the limit of their educability or to prevent the birth of a thousand feeble-minded. Investigations show that the brightest children, those who have IQ's above 130 or 140, are usually located from one to three grades below that which corresponds to their mental age. They are not encouraged to live up to their possibilities. Their school work is so easy for them that their wills are in danger of becoming flabby from lack of exertion. How can character develop normally in a child who, during all the years when character is being molded, never meets a task that calls forth his best effort? The school's first task is to find its gifted children and to set them tasks more commensurate with their ability.

In 1921 a survey of gifted children in California was begun under the auspices of Stanford University. It is the purpose of the research, which was financed by a substantial grant from the Commonwealth Fund, of New York City, to locate 1000 of the brightest children in the public schools of the state, to secure a large amount of psychological, educational, and physical data concerning them, and to follow their careers as far into adult life as possible. This is the first research of its kind ever undertaken, but there is reason to hope that such studies will become less rare.

Sorting the Students

Frank N. Freeman

(This is a timely and judicious discussion of the reasons for and against the growing practice of grouping students according to ability and achievement tests. The author, a member of the faculty of the School of Education, University of Chicago, represents the new type of school Missourian who must be shown.)

The fundamental basis for the practice of homogeneous grouping is the psychological fact of extreme differences in the capacity of children to do school work. Every test that has been given in recent years, whether it is an educational test or a special capacity test or a general intelligence test, shows that these differences exist.

There is some disposition to question the acceptance of the findings of tests on their face value. It is believed by some that the differences which appear to be revealed by the tests are not real differences. They may be due to inequalities of early training and they may be amenable to the influence of the school; or if the differences are real they do not materially affect the acquisition of skill and knowledge.

The belief that differences in capacity are illusory is without foundation in fact. This does not mean that we can always determine with precision what the individual's capacity is. An intelilgence test is only a somewhat better measure than is the accomplishment of the student in his school work. The verdict which they give must be taken as provisional, and must be subject to revision as the pupil's accomplishment rises above or falls below the prediction which is based upon the test. This is only to say that our measure of capacity is not a perfect one. It does not imply that the differences in capacity do not exist and are not large in extent. Wherever freedom of opportunity and proper stimulus to accomplishment are given, differences in achievement manifest themselves which are as marked as the differences in the test scores.

An obstacle to the acceptance of ability grouping lies in the confusion between the development of the individual as measured by an absolute standard and as measured by a comparison with others. This confusion creates the bugbear of educational determinism. We are told that classification into ability groups determines the limits of development of the individual. Ability grouping involves no implication regarding the limits of development of either the bright child or the dull child. It may go as far as human nature will allow and the ingenuity and skill of the teacher can contrive. All that grouping implies is that, under the conditions of training, whether they be good or bad, the development of one individual will go beyond that of another. As our methods of education improve, the possibilities of development of all children at all levels will be extended. But the gain from improved methods will correspond with the capacity which each individual had to start with.

While it is true that differential treatment does not imply that any definite limits are set to mental development, there may be some danger that it will encourage in the mind of both pupil and teacher an attitude which overemphasizes possession of ability as distinguished from expenditure of effort. The teacher may suppose that because pupils are properly classified learning will take care of itself. The pupils, particularly in the upper divisions, may be inclined to think that because they possess the necessary ability the mere possession of ability is all that is required to accomplish the work set before them. Ability is never a substitute for work. The pupil, no matter how bright he is, needs to take time and pains to work out his problems and to master details. There is a vast difference between potential intelligence and trained or seasoned intelligence. If classification leads either the teacher or the pupil to minimize the importance of careful training and of serious work, due emphasis must be laid upon these necessities.

Another objection to homogeneous grouping is that it causes the child to feel that he is branded and that this produces a consciousness of inferiority which is neither wholesome nor necessary. It is probably true that, because of its definiteness, an intelligence test score makes distinctions a little clearer than they would otherwise be. It may also be true that classification into ability groups make distinctions more obvious. Let it be noted, however, that neither the test nor the classification creates distinctions. Distinctions have always existed and there seems no immediate prospect that they will be done away with. A much more harmful mode of recognizing distinctions than homogeneous grouping has existed for generations in the school. Failure of promotion is a more serious form of branding than is classification in a low ability group. It can hardly be regarded as kind to allow the child to undertake work which we know he cannot accomplish and then to make his failure in the work conspicuous by forcing him to fall behind his companions. It is much better to attempt to measure his ability and to set him at the work in which he can succeed.

We must not forget that the school is not the only place where distinctions are evident. I may be conscious of the fact that my neighbor has a better house than mine; that he drives a Cadillac while I drive a Ford; that he wears better clothes; that he receives promotion in his profession or his business more rapidly than I do; that his name appears in Who's Who while mine does not; that he has more fame and more prosperity than I have. I may even suffer the pain of losing my position or of being forced to accept a considerably poorer one than I had expected.

All of these facts constitute an aspect of life to which one must adjust oneself. Perhaps there will come a time when there are no distinctions in the rewards of life, but there will never come a time when there are no distinctions between the accomplishments of different individuals. It is the business of the school to help the child to acquire such an attitude toward the inequalities of life, whether in accomplishment or in reward, that he may adjust himself to its conditions with the least possible friction.

Probably this can be accomplished best by leading the child to think more about achievement than about reward. He must learn to estimate the kind of achievement which he is most likely to be able to make and to select the kind of work in which he can achieve the most. One of the chief conditions of satisfaction is attainment in work which is suited to one's powers and is an expression of one's interests. The individual who must perform work which is beneath his capacity, on the one hand, or beyond his capacity, on the other, lacks the fundamental condition for satisfaction in work. It is therefore of the greatest benefit to the individual that he be given the work which is well adjusted to his power. The school is not responsible for the world's system of rewards. It may perhaps somewhat modify the emphasis upon the reward as distinguished from the accomplishment, but it must also train the child to adjust himself to the conditions of life as they exist.

Counterbalancing the possible disadvantage from the student's recognition that he is in a low section, or that he is in a high section, and his consequent depression or elation, is the relief from unduly marked contrasts which arise when pupils of widely different capacities are in the same class. If slow pupils are in a class with others whose ability is of the same order, they are not subject to the discouraging comparison between their own attainments and those of gifted pupils. On the other hand, if the bright pupils are in classes which are composed of others of similar ability they do not have the opportunity to shine so brightly by contrast with dull companions. They are brought into keener competition and are forced to exert themselves in order to show superiority. On the whole, then, homogeneous grouping provides rather less cause for discouragement and for undue elation, due to the contrast with the attainments of one's companions, than does mixed grouping.

More important and vital than the adjustment of a pupil's rank is the adjustment of the requirements so that he does not find it impossible or unduly difficult to meet them, on the one hand, and that, on the other hand, it is necessary to put forth effort in order to come up to them. If the requirements are adjusted to suit the average child, the slow student cannot hope to meet them satisfactorily. He is therefore given no adequate stimulus to work. The bright student can meet the average requirements with little expenditure of effort and he is not likely to be stimulated to exert himself to his full capacity.

We have thus far been considering the psychological aspects of ability grouping. It has also been widely discussed from the point of view of general sociological considerations. Homogeneous grouping has been criticized as being undemocratic. This criticism seems to be based on several grounds. In the first place, democracy is interpreted in a general way as meaning equality. Classification recognized that there is inequality and it is therefore a subversion of democracy. From this point of view democracy means that every child must have precisely the same education. The dull child has a right to a particular quality or kind of education as much as the bright child. He is therefore robbed of his birthright if he is not given precisely the same training.

The assumption underlying this train of thought is, of course, false. The only equality which exists is an equality in the right to opportunity, and opportunity is conditioned by the individual's own nature. Furthermore, it would not even be an advantage to give the dull pupil the same kind of training that is suited to the gifted pupil. The only opportunity this gives him is the opportunity to fail. The only way in which the dull pupil could be given training suited to his capacity and equal to that of the gifted pupil would be to limit the gifted pupil to training far below his capacity. This would be a serious violation of the rights of the gifted pupil.

The real difficulty with this whole line of argument is that it assumes that education is a gift by the state to the individual for the benefit of the individual. The only valid conception of public education is that it is for the purpose of fitting the individual to take his place in the life of the community. The community needs the services of every person in it and it needs the best services of which each individual is capable. It is a loss to the community as well as to the individual if a highly endowed person receives a meager education.

If it is objected that this theory of education is not the one to which the individual subscribes in seeking an education, then it is the fault of the school and of the college that it does not train the individual in the proper conception of his duties to society. He must not think of education as a personal privilege. No public education can be justified on this ground. If public education in general, then, cannot be justified on this ground, the detailed organization of the school must be based upon the broader conception of its function.

The justification of a differentiation in the training given to different individuals depends upon the basis upon which the differentiation is made. If it is based upon birth or wealth or some other circumstance external to the person himself, it is undemocratic and out of harmony with the purposes of public education. If it is based upon the inherent capacity of the individual, it is just and in conformity to the demands of public welfare.

The argument for democracy is sometimes urged in a somewhat more specific form. The school is considered as a training ground for the exercise of the rights and duties of the citizen, particularly for voting and for holding office. The function of the school is sometimes described as training leaders and this description is objected to on the ground that the people must be left to select their own leaders. If differential education is taken as a preparatory stage in the formation of a privileged group of either voters or office-holders, the objection is a vital one. The right to vote and the right to hold office cannot, in my judgment, be based upon differences in intelligence, above the level of the feeble-minded, or on differences in schooling. The citizen in casting his vote is giving expression in part to his personal interest in the conduct of the government, and we have not reached the point, and probably shall not reach the point, when we can assume that one citizen may be trusted with the right to express the interest of another in the fundamental exercise of the franchise. If anybody regards such a practice as a legitimate offshoot of differential training, let us make it perfectly clear that it has no such implication. Every citizen will do his own voting and select his own leaders. Any departure from this practice is in reality an abandonment of democracy.

The next question to be raised is whether one can teach more effectively with mixed classes or with classes which are grouped into those of nearly equal ability. The fundamental advantage of homogeneous grouping from the point of view of methods of instruction is implied in what has already been said in discussing the psychological aspects of the case. It is obviously difficult to set standards for attainment and require the individual pupils to meet those standards when the abilities of individuals differ widely. If one sets the pace to suit the bright pupils the duller ones hopelessly flounder. If one sets it to suit the dull ones, the bright ones are bored. If the bright pupils recite or lead in the discussion, the discussion moves too rapidly or goes over the heads of the slower ones. There is no possible way of overcoming this difficulty. The remedy is obvious.

While the above argument seems to be incontrovertible, the objection is frequently made to homogeneous grouping that the dull pupils lack the stimulus of the bright ones. It is sometimes asserted also that mixed grouping is good because it gives the bright pupils an opportunity to exercise leadership. On the other hand, it is argued that homogeneous grouping is ineffective because it does not really separate the bright pupils from the dull ones. This brings into contrast two opposing objections, both of which cannot be sound. It is asserted, on the one hand, that, in homogeneous grouping, classes are too homogeneous, and it is argued, on the other hand that they are not homogeneous enough. They are not homogeneous enough because the classification does not succeed in distinguishing with sufficient accuracy between the capacities of the individuals in the various groups. Members of the lower group are really equal in capacity to members of the upper groups and vice versa.

It is clear that both of these opposite criticisms cannot be well founded. As a matter of fact, they may be taken to neutralize each other. The truth is that there is a considerable diversity in the ability of pupils in homogeneous groups. There is enough diversity to provide variety in the contributions which are made to the class by the individual students and to give opportunity for the better students of the group to exercise leadership. There is not as great diversity, however, as there is in mixed groups. To assert that we do not succeed in forming groups of more nearly equal ability by our methods of classification is to fly in the face of well attested facts.

There are a number of problems which arise in the administration of homogeneous grouping. Probably the final solution of these problems has not been reached, but if the procedure is sound from the point of view of psychology, of general policy, and of the technique of instruction, a way will be found to carry it out. In the meantime some of the problems may be mentioned.

The first problem grows out of the type of modification to be made in the work of a course to suit it to the various groups. The two general contrasted types of modification are variation in the rate of mastery, on the one hand, and variation in the character of the content on the other hand. The latter variation may consist in enrichment for the upper group and a reduction to minimum essentials for the lower group. The preference of educators in recent years has inclined them toward enrichment. Their practice, however, has been prevailingly of the sort which varies the rate of mastery. It should be pointed out that variation in the rate of mastery may provide enrichment by bringing the students more quickly to advanced courses.

Whichever modification is made, an administrative problem is raised which concerns the disposition of the students in advanced courses. This disposition is easier to adjust if the chief variation has been in the rate of mastery. Students can then be allowed to take advanced courses when they have completed the requirements of the introductory courses. They may be thought of as arriving at the same point at different speeds and as therefore roughly equally well qualified, so far as their preparatory study is concerned, to pursue advanced work. If the chief difference, however, consists in enrichment or in reduction to minimum essentials, it is obvious that the one group is much better prepared for advanced work than is the other group.

Even under a variation in speed, there will be administrative difficulties with the time schedule. If the difference in speed between the slow group and the rapid group can be measured in units of one semester or one quarter, the difficulty is not serious. If, however, the differences are less than these, it would seem necessary to organize groups in the advanced class to which individuals from the corresponding groups in the introductory class shall be promoted.

One possible solution, of course, is to allow only pupils of the middle or upper group to take advanced courses. While this restriction may not be desirable for courses of the second level, it probably is desirable for courses beyond the second level. This assumes that the more advanced courses require a higher degree of ability than the introductory courses, and this assumption seems to be borne out by the fact that the better students, in general, are found to be the ones who pursue the advanced courses in any subject.

Another administrative difficulty concerns marking. Shall the students in the various groups be marked with reference to a standard which is common to all or shall the students in each group be marked with reference to a standard which is set up for that one group? The answer to this question depends upon the use which is to be made of the marks. If they are used to determine promotion in the school and advancement to other institutions, such, for example, as is represented by certification for college, then the marks should be based upon a common standard. If, on the contrary, the marks are used chiefly to indicate the relative achievement of the students in the class and to stimulate them to serious effort, then it would seem that the marks given to each group should be based upon a standard adjusted to that group. This would mean that about the same proportion in each of the groups should receive high marks or low marks.

The latter method is, on the whole, the better one from the point of view of the psychological effect of marking. It is probable that the administrative use of the marks may be adjusted by basing promotion and other similar administrative acts upon a combination of the student's marks and of this membership in the group. Thus, for example, it might be the policy of a high school to recommend no students for college who have habitually occupied a lower group.

Another administrative problem has already been touched upon but may be mentioned more explicitly. The more advanced classes in any subject always contain smaller numbers than the introductory classes. While there may be a sufficient number to permit grouping in the earlier classes there may not be a sufficient number in the upper classes. Are then, the pupils from different groups to be thrown together in the advanced classes? Probably the solution of this problem is to exclude members of the lowest group from advanced classes unless they give some special evidence of ability to do the work successfully. This is not a provision which will be difficult of administration since, as has already been remarked, the lower grade pupils usually fall out of themselves.

An administrative question of somewhat less fundamental character relates to the arrangement of the program. It is desirable that various sections of a class come at the same period in order that transfer from one section to another may readily be made without disrupting a student's program. This, of course, can only be done in the case of a large department in which there are at least two or three teachers. In a small department the various sections must meet at different hours and transfer is rendered more difficult. In such cases particular care must be taken in making the original classification so that as few transfers as possible may be necessary.

Homogeneous grouping, of course, is only possible in schools which are large enough to provide at least fifty students in introductory classes. If three groups are to be formed, the number must be still larger. In small departments, even in a large high school, furthermore, homogeneous grouping cannot be carried out. In such cases one must use the methods of individual attention, elastic assignment or some form of individual instruction as a substitute for homogeneous grouping. Our main problem however, is to discuss the advantages of homogeneous grouping in cases in which it can be applied rather than to discuss substitutes for it.

A final administrative difficulty which may be mentioned is certification of students to college or to any higher institution. If the upper group is allowed to complete the work of a course in less than the standard time, the students of this group may meet with difficulty in being certified for college unless they take enough additional courses to make up the total number of units which are required. It is understood here that the unit is defined in terms of the time spent upon a given course. It may be necessary during a period of adjustment for the bright pupils who do more than the standard amount of work in a given time to take more than the minimum number of courses. It is probable, however, that the colleges will ultimately recognize the superior ability of these students and will give them credit for the amount of work done rather than for the amount of time spent in doing it.

CONCLUSION

While there are considerations against homogeneous grouping as well as for it, the arguments against it are for the most part based either upon denial of well-established psychological facts, upon general social considerations which fail to recognize the facts of human nature and of society, or the nature of public education, or upon questions of administrative detail which it will be possible ultimately to work out if the fundamental principle is sound. The arguments for homogeneous grouping are supported, furthermore, by the favorable testimony of those who have tried it. They find the advantages which are claimed for it to be substantial and the objections which are made against it to be largely illusory when applied to the test of practice.

The Conservation of Talent

Lewis M. Terman

As a great psychologist once observed, civilization advances on two legs—invention and imitation. There are those who show the way and those who follow. Imitation is easy; it takes the creative thinker to set new advances, whether in mechanics, science, commerce, literature, art or religion. A nation's intellectual assets are, therefore, the most precious it will ever have, and the principle of conservation will here find its most useful application.

Now there is reason for believing that a considerable part of the world's talent fails of fruition. That "genius will out" is but a dangerous half-truth, or less. Cattell has shown that Massachusetts in proportion to population produces 84 times as many men of science as Mississippi. That scientific ability is 84 times as prevalent in the germ plasm of Massachusetts as in the germ plasm of Mississippi seems entirely unreasonable. We prefer to believe that educational opportunity has helped to determine the relative output.

A research now in progress on the mental development of 300 of the most eminent men and women of the last few centuries reveals the fact that many of these geniuses owed their greatest opportunities to happy chance. Newton could never have made his scientific and mathematical discoveries without a university education, and he owed his opportunity to enter Cambridge to the chance visit of an uncle. Liebig, the founder of psysiological chemistry, was early withdrawn from school and apprenticed to a pharmacist. There, in a shed behind the apothecary's shop, he began the chemical experiments that later brought him his chance to enter a university. One wonders whether those experiments in chemistry would have been undertaken had he been apprenticed to a shoemaker or tailor instead of to a man who dealt in chemicals. So many instances of this kind have been uncovered as to raise the question whether in the case of many potential geniuses the happy accident may not have failed to happen. The phrase "unsung Miltons" is more than a poetic figure. Certainly it is true that children of superior ability are not always recognized in the schools. The defective child attracts attention by his inability to do the work and by his maladjustment to school discipline. The gifted child is likely to be submerged with the masses because of his very adaptability to the school environment.

Another circumstance that has blocked the educational progress of gifted children is the superstition given currency by Lombroso and others, that intellectual precocity is pathological; that bright children are prone to die young, become insane, or develop post-adolescent stupidity. So thoroughly has this superstition become imbedded in popular thought that even prominent educators are likely to assume that the child of high intelligence quotient must, *ipso facto*, be anaemic, nervous, conceited, eccentric, non-social, and a stranger to play.

So often had I seen this view expressed in perfectly good print that for a time I was myself inclined to suppose it must be true. Then followed a decade of experimental work in which I tested large numbers of children and studied their personal characteristics in the light of their intelligence quotients. It did not take long to discover that the facts were not in line with traditional theory. My subjects of high IQ simply did not answer to the book descriptions of typical Wunderkinder. As a rule they were physically well developed, active in play, normal in their social adjustments, and mentally well balanced. Such was the evidence from more than a hundred cases that we had studied before 1921.

The data, however, were hardly adequate to warrant conclusions. It could be argued that our subjects were too few, that they were not typical, and that our objective measurements were not sufficiently extensive.

Fortunately, a searching investigation of the entire problem was made possible by two grants from the Commonwealth Fund of New York City, supplemented by appropriations from Stanford University. The purpose of the investigation was to locate 1,000 representative gifted children, to secure for each a large amount of objective data along anthropometric, medical, educational, social and psychological lines, and then to follow the later histories of those children as far as possible into adult life.

The subjects have been located. Nearly 100 pages of data, mostly of test nature, have been collected for each. Follow-up work is under way. A brief statement of some of the results to date may be of interest.

1. *Locating the subjects.* Six field assistants devoted an entire school year to the search in Los Angeles, San Francisco, Oakland and the other Bay cities. Nearly a quarter of a million school children were sifted. First, each teacher was asked to name the brightest child in her room, the second brightest, and, in addition, the youngest. These nominees were then given a National intelligence test, and all who scored high in the National were given a Stanford–Binet. Only those who earned an IQ of 140 or higher were included in the study.

As this standard is not reached by more than 4 or 5 pupils in a thousand, it might be supposed that with three nominations from each class-room of 30 or 40 pupils no gifted children would have been missed. However, check-up of the method of search indicated that between 10 percent, and 20 percent, had been overlooked. There were cases in which the brightest pupil in an entire school of 500 was not named even as second brightest in his class of 35. Nevertheless, with a loss of less than 20 percent, our subjects may be considered as reasonably representative of their kind. Whatever is true of them will be true, in general, of children having IQ's between 140 and 200.

2. *Sex-frequency.* The first thing we note here is that the number of boys and girls in the gifted group is nearly equal. There is a slight excess of boys—about 20 percent—but on the other hand the three highest cases are girls. Mental tests are beginning to render the old question of sex difference in intelligence about as obsolete as the question whether the earth is round or flat.

3. *Health and physical traits.* Our data include, for each subject, 34 anthropometric measurements (made with the assistance of Professor Bird T. Baldwin), a one-hour medical examination by a trained specialist in children's diseases, and extensive information furnished by parents and teachers. Not all these data have been worked up, but the main facts are unmistakable. At all ages these children are taller, heavier, better nourished and physically stronger than unselected children. They were above normal weight at birth, and showed noticeable prococity in walking, talking and dentition. They are freer from organic diseases and have a clearer disease history than the average child. Nervousness, stuttering, chorea, habit spasms, and other neurotic symptoms occur with no more than normal frequency. Their sleep records at the different ages are from 30 to 60 minutes a day above the norms for 3,000 unselected children. They come from families with less than average infant mortality and of more than average longevity.

4. *Educational progress.* The typical gifted child enters school at 6¼ years and enrolls in the high first grade, although some enroll at once in the second or third grade. The average progress quotient for our entire group is about 114, which means that the typical gifted child is accelerated 14 percent of his age beyond the normal. In mental age, however, he is 48 percent beyond the normal. The difference between 48 percent and 14 percent is 34 percent; so the typical gifted child is under-promoted to the extent of one third of his age. Whether this retardation is warranted is a hotly debated question. The opponents of rapid progress have rested their case on two arguments: (1) That skipping grades means permanent gaps leading to weak work later on; (2) that rapid promotion jeopardizes the child's social development.

I think the first of these arguments has been answered for good and all by our extensive achievement tests covering all the important subject-matter of grades 2 to 8. The average educational quotients in the different school subjects and at the different ages ranged from 130 to 145. The average of the averages is above 135. That is, the typical gifted child *has already mastered the subject-matter 35 percent beyond the norm for his age.* As we have seen, he is actually accelerated only 14 percent. The difference between 35 percent and 14 percent is 21 percent. Therefore, the typical gifted child is being held 21 per cent of his age below the level to which he has already mastered his work. I think this is a rather momentous fact.

As to the alleged social injury from rapid promotion, I am convinced that this danger is more imaginary than real. The injury done by having a child study and recite a few hours each day with children who are a few years older; but of his own mental level, is probably very slight when compared with the intellectual and moral injury which is wrought by keeping him always at tasks too easy to command his serious efforts.

Another fact brought out by the achievement tests is that the mental development of the gifted child is not often markedly one-sided. Generally speaking, however, the gifted child does his best work in the difficult subjects where success depends most upon the higher thought processes. In all-round information the 8-year-old gifted child is on a level with the average child of 12.

These results have not been attained by the use of hot house methods. Not more than a handful of our cases have been subjected to such treatment. The majority of the parents have either kept hands off, or have tried to hold the child to a slower developmental pace.

In the main, our subjects have educated themselves. They have made astonishing progress in learning because of their intellectual initiative and insatiable curiosity. Forty-five percent of them learned to read before starting to school, for the most part without instruction; 20 percent read before 5; 5 percent before 4; and in 9 cases before 3. Many of them develop strange affinities for such impossible books as dictionaries, atlases and encyclopedias!

5. *Social development.* The wide-spread belief that gifted children are likely to be socially queer, sissified and ignorant of play was considered important enough to justify extensive investigation by the test method. Time is not available for a description of the tests used, and I shall have to ask you to believe me when I say that their validity and reliability have been statistically established. One of these test batteries had to do with interest in, and knowledge of, plays, games and amusements. By first standardizing this test on about 800 unselected children, age and sex norms were established for play information, for the maturity of play life, and for the masculinity or femininity of play interests. In comparison with these norms the scores of our gifted group showed a large excess of play information, noticeable excess maturity of play interests, and normal masculinity indices. That gifted boys tend to be more effeminate in their play interests than unselected boys of the same age appears to have no foundation in fact.

Another test, involving a modification of the Jung–Kent–Rosanoff word association method, measured the relative strength of interests in intellectual, social and activity fields. Its purpose was to determine whether in the gifted child intellectual interests have been developed at the expense of social and active tendencies. The results of this test show that the usual fears along this line have little if any foundation.

Ratings of the children by parents and teachers on such traits as conceit, social adaptability, popularity and leadership, fully confirm the test scores. There are gifted children who are eccentric, socially defective and unpopular; but the proportion of such cases is apparently even less than among children in general.

6. *Character traits.* One of the most significant batteries of tests used was designed to measure certain traits of moral character likely to be associated with delinquency and incorrigibility. It yields objective scores on honesty of report, honesty in following instructions when there is temptation to cheat, tendency to overestimate one's knowledge or ability, moral judgment, and interest in types of reading and activity common among delinquents. By comparing the scores of (1) a large number of reform school inmates, (2) 300 exceptionally "good" public-school boys, (3) 300 exceptionally "bad" public-school boys, and (4) several hundred unselected school children, the value of the test has been sufficiently established. The fact that concerns us here is that in the traits measured by this test our gifted children rank high. As compared with unselected children, they are more conscientious, less boastful and less absorbed in questionable interests. Ratings by teachers and parents on these and other moral traits confirm the test scores. The conclusion is that here as elsewhere gifted children are superior to the common run.

7. *Heredity.* Children of so many superiorities could hardly have acquired them all through environmental influences. Nor have they, for their heredity, too, is demonstrably superior. More than 50 percent of our group have sprung from the top 4 percent or 5 percent of the vocational hierarchy. The professional and semi-professional classes together account for more than 80 percent. The unskilled labor classes furnish but a paltry 1 percent or 2 percent. One fourth of our children have at least one parent who is a college graduate. The average schooling for parents is about 12 grades completed as compared with 6 for the general population.

The list of eminent relatives reads like a roster of American genius. For example, 23 percent of the members of the Hall of Fame are known to have relatives in our gifted group, and the number of high officials, generals, statesmen, writers and other notables is astonishing. One boy of 180 IQ has 34 known relatives listed either in *Who's Who* or Appleton's *Cyclopaedia of American Biography.*

In this connection two facts of serious portent should be mentioned. (1) The racial stocks most prolific of gifted children are those from northern and western Europe, and the Jewish. The least prolific are the Mediterranean races, the Mexicans and the Negroes. (2) The fecundity of the family stocks from which our gifted children come appears to be definitely on the wane. This is an example of the differential birth rate which is rapidly becoming evident in all civilized countries. It has been figured that if the present differential birth rate continues, 1,000 Harvard graduates will at the end of 200 years have but 50 descendants, while in the same period 1,000 South Italians will have multiplied to 100,000.

The differential birth rate is doubtless a social rather than a biological phenomenon, and it is one that threatens the very existence of civilization. In the face of this threat the importance of discovering, conserving and making the most of our resources of genius is self-evident. Yet the pedagogy of gifted children is the "Darkest Africa" of education. We have been too much swayed by the all-American feeling for the fellow at the foot. We have too long taken as our motto the adage that "if we look out for the hindmost the foremost will look out for himself."

I have emphasized the desirability of more rapid advancement of the bright child. This is important. But grade skipping is far from an ideal or complete solution of the problem. The real need is for a *differentiation of curriculum and of methods* such as will give to every child the type of educational diet from which he can derive the maximum nourishment.

No one would claim that in the education of gifted children we are yet in sight of any such goal. Nevertheless, interesting and promising experiments are under way. I predict that within a decade or two something like the three-track plan of Oakland, Berkeley and Detroit, supplemented by opportunity classes for the defectives and for the very gifted, will become the standard. Then, for the first time, will children above or below the average have what every child is entitled to: the opportunity to make the most of whatever ability he possesses. I have no patience with those who condemn this plan as undemocratic. The abandonment of the single-track, pre-high-school curriculum is in fact the first necessary step toward educational democracy. The single-track is a straight jacket which dwarfs the mental development of the inferior as well as the gifted. The educational sentimentalists who defend it, who fear mental tests and ignore or deny individual differences, are of a class with those who stake their life on a coue formula, fear doctors and deny the actuality of disease.

CHAPTER 6

|| IQ, Dysgenics and Racism

Although Lester Frank Ward was interested in the elimination of the artificial barriers such as caste and race, which would obstruct the free development of natural talent in his meritocratic state, he did not believe in the equality of the races. He was convinced, as many of his liberal followers, that while the black race may be superior in feelings and sentiment, they were inferior to the white race in cognitive abilities. Ward, in *Pure Sociology*, suggested that the black man who rapes a white woman does so not only out of lust, but out of an almost unconscious desire "to raise his race to a little higher level." Combining a bit of male chauvinism with his racism, Ward asserted that it is more permissible for a male of a superior race to have sexual relations with a female of an inferior race than it is for a male of an inferior race to have sexual relations with a female of a superior race, because in the first instance it would be a matter of "leveling up" while in the latter case it would be a matter of "leveling down." [1]

While Ward tended to blend all Europeans into the intellectually favored race as opposed to blacks, yellows, and reds, Terman was more discriminating. Just as he believed in the genetic superiority of the professional classes, so too, he believed in the racial superiority of the northern and western Europeans and Jewish groups over the Negro and southern European. He, like other liberals—such as David Starr Jordan, Edward Ross, and later William Shockley—were vitally concerned with the prob-

---

[1] Lester F. Ward, *Pure Sociology*. (New York: Macmillan Co., 1903), p. 359–360. I am indebted to Stephen Yulish for calling my attention to the racial views of Lester F. Ward. Ward's racist views were very much like William Shockley's, who, in a packed auditorium at Stanford University, invited black students to participate in a "scientific" experiment that would test his hypothesis, "that for each one per cent of Caucasian ancestry, average IQ of American black populations goes up approximately one IQ point." *The Stanford Observer*, "Genetics and Intelligence," February 1973, p. 8.

lem of the differential birth rate and the danger of genetic pollution, "that threatens the very existence of civilization." As Terman said:

(1) The racial stocks most prolific of gifted children are those from northern and western Europe, and the Jewish. The least prolific are the Mediterranean races, the Mexicans and the Negroes. (2) The fecundity of the family stocks from which our gifted children come appears to be definitely on the wane. This is an example of the differential birth rate which is rapidly becoming evident in all civilized countries. It has been figured that if the present differential birth rate continues, 1,000 Harvard graduates will at the end of 200 years have but 50 descendants, while in the same period 1,000 South Italians will have multiplied to 100,000.[2]

Under these circumstances, Terman advocated immigration restriction, various eugenics and sterilization measures and massive testing of children so that the gifted could be identified and specially educated.

In, "Were We Born That Way?" Terman argued in 1922, as Herrnstein was to assert in "IQ" in 1971, that the social class occupational system was based on IQ.[3] The arguments used by both are instructive. First, the test questions were created on the basis of behaviors, generally appropriate to certain occupations which were hierarchically arranged according to the social class system. The tests were thus initially developed and standardized on the basis of occupation and social class. Both Terman and Herrnstein then found the median IQ of unskilled workers lower than the median IQ of skilled workers, and concluded that IQ affects one's occupation and social standing. The circularity of the argument is completed in such a way that the beliefs necessary to perpetuate the notion of an educational meritocratic state are maintained. If one takes the argument the other way and suggests that the complicated socialization process involved in social class determines IQ, questions of equity and social justice immediately come to mind. Neither Terman nor Herrnstein seemed to have confronted this problem.

The racist bias of Terman's thought runs through his "scientific" testing.[4] Similarly, his contempt for the lower classes pervades his "science." Terman viewed the bottom 20 percent of the IQ-social class scale as a liability for a democratic society. Like many other liberals,[5] he saw his professional role as an expert, guiding the irrational, ignorant masses to make the most of their limited abilities. In his opinion of the lower class, Terman had this to say:

[2] Lewis M. Terman, "The Conservation of Talent," *School and Society*, March 29, 1924, Vol. XIX, No. 483, p. 363.
[3] See and compare Richard Herrnstein, "I.Q.," *Atlantic Monthly*, Sept. 1971, pp. 50–53, with Lewis M. Terman, "Were We Born That Way?" *World's Work*, 1922, pp. 657–59.
[4] See Terman, "Were We Born That Way?" *World's Work*, 44, 1922, p. 655.
[5] Lewis Terman considered himself a New Deal liberal, just as Arthur Jensen and Richard Herrnstein also considered themselves liberal.

On questions of larger social and national policy they vote blindly or as directed by political bosses. They are democracy's ballast, not always useless but always a potential liability. How to make the most of their limited abilities, both for their own welfare and that of society; how to lead them without making them helpless victims of oppression; are perennial questions in any democracy.[6]

Terman and H. H. Goddard were both concerned with "aristocracy in democracy." The "scientific" tests that they helped to create and the "professional" testing movement that they led, repeatedly confirmed and reinforced their racist and social class beliefs, in large part, because they were created out of those beliefs. Goddard, Terman, Yerkes, Brigham, and Thorndike—all eminent leaders in the testing movement—were expressed racists.[7] Terman believed the American black was vastly inferior to the white man and the mulatto had enough white blood to increase his intelligence to a "mid-position between pure negro and pure white." [8]

C. C. Brigham, in *A Study of American Intelligence*,[9] also concluded that the Nordic race, from which older American stock was drawn, was superior; while the immigrant who came from the Alpine and Mediterranean race was inferior to the Nordic race, but yet, far superior to the Negro. The Negro represented the very bottom of the genetic pool.[10] The fear of polluting that pool with inferior blood, through racial mixture, plagued the racial superiority image of Brigham and others throughout the century. Brigham said:

> We must face a possibility of racial admixture here that is infinitely worse than that faced by any European country today, for we are incorporating the negro into our racial stock, while all of Europe is comparatively free from this taint.[11]

Just as Brigham feared the taint of inferior blood on the American nation, so did Terman, Ellwood Cubberly, and Edward Ross. These distinguished Stanford professors all could agree with their former university president, David Starr Jordan, when he argued:

> The original framework of our nation has been weakened and blurred by racial dilution. The loose adulation of the Nordic races now current, how-

[6] Terman, "Were We Born That Way?" p. 654.

[7] The term "racist" is being used here to mean one who believes in the genetic superiority of one race over another, and that some kind of social action or inaction ought to occur as a result of that alleged superiority or inferiority.

[8] Terman, "Were We Born That Way?" p. 655.

[9] It should be noted that after he published this work, Brigham began to have second thoughts about the "empirical" basis which undergirded his racism. He later repudiated this work, much to the chagrin of men like Thorndike and Terman.

[10] Just to make no mistake about who was thought to be really inferior throughout Brigham's work, Nordic, Alpine, and Mediterranean races are capitalized, while Negro is not.

[11] C. C. Brigham, *A Study of American Intelligence*. (Princeton: Princeton University Press, 1923), p. 209.

ever exaggerated, is based on a primal and vital fact. In history and temper ours is a Nordic nation. Its freedom was won and its integrity maintained by Nordic methods and those races or members of races who have not valued freedom and order are politically and socially a burden on our progress.[12]

The superiority of the Nordic stock, throughout American history, had been clearly demonstrated. "Can we," he asked, "share freedom safely with peoples who do not want it and whose highest aim is merely to vegetate?"[13] His answer was an emphatic, No! He concluded that the gates of Ellis Island and San Francisco must be closed to inferior people. Immigration restriction, though helpful as a temporary device, was not a final solution, nor was the possible extermination of a race. Ultimately, the solution rested in selective breeding. Jordan argued:

> We would not smother nor exterminate races or nations to save food, but we cannot yet feed them all, and the time has come to consider improving the breed by selection. To this end, much serious thought of serious people must be given while in no sense can the present statute of 1924 [immigration restriction] be regarded as final and conclusive.[14]

Forty-seven years later, a Nobel Prize laureate, William Shockley, also from Stanford University, stepped to the speakers' rostrum at the American Psychological Association and pointed once again to the problem of racial pollution, and once again, rejected Hitler's solution for dysgenics and proposed instead a voluntary sterilization bonus plan which would be made available to all welfare recipients. The plan he proposed would permit the state to pay $1,000, for every IQ point below 100, if the welfare recipient voluntarily submitted himself or herself to a government sterilization operation. Thus, he argued, both the dysgenic problem and the welfare problem would be solved within a generation.[15] William Shockley's solution was not far removed from either that which David Starr Jordan had espoused earlier or that which Edward L. Thorndike had advocated. As Thorndike wrote in his last major work, *Human Nature and the Social Order*, in 1940:

> By selective breeding supported by a suitable environment we can have a world in which all men will equal the top ten percent of present men. One sure service of the able and the good is to beget and rear offspring. One sure service (almost the only one) which the inferior and vicious can perform is to prevent their genes from survival.[16]

[12] David Starr Jordan, "Closed Doors or the Melting Pot," *The American Hebrew*, September 26, 1924, p. 538.

[13] *Ibid.*, p. 592.

[14] *Ibid.*, p. 592.

[15] See this volume. p. 407. Also see William Shockley, "Dysgenics—A Social Problem Reality Evaded by Illusion of Infinite Plasticity of Human Intelligence?" *Phi Delta Kappan*, I–291.5, March 1972.

[16] Edward L. Thorndike, *Human Nature and the Social Order*. (New York: Macmillan Co., 1940), p. 957.

To Thorndike, the genetic inferior were the poor. They were also the vicious. The assumption that the more talented are more virtuous as well as more wealthy is an assumption which lies at the base of much school practice in the educational state. In many ways, Thorndike made explicit what others had merely assumed. Well within that enlightenment ideology which assumed a very strong relationship between talent and virtue, Thorndike argued that, "To him that hath a superior intellect is given also on the average a superior character." [17] His empirical, "scientific" study of human behavior led him to conclude that, "The abler persons in the world in the long run are the more clean, decent, just, and kind." Further-more, he argued that it has paid the masses to be ruled by intelligence, because such men are by and large of superior justice and goodwill.[18]

Thorndike was, perhaps, the most influential shaper of the meritocratic educational state in the first half of the century. For almost half a century, Thorndike held sway at Columbia University, during which time he taught thousands of teachers and administrators, published 50 books and 450 monographs and articles. His massive three-volume work entitled, *Educational Psychology* (1913), set the tone of educational psychology for almost the next two decades. From his pen flowed a prodigious number of educational maxims; psychological laws; textbooks and scales of achievement for elementary, secondary and college courses in varied fields; dictionaries for elementary and secondary schools; and teachers' manuals. He not only told the teachers what to teach and how to teach it, he also told them how to evaluate their work. Because he wrote so many of the texts and tests used in elementary and secondary schools, his impact on American educational practice was immediate and extended.

Thorndike believed in the genetic superiority of the white race over the black race, just as he firmly believed that the "good" society was ultimately a society ruled by the talented, morally righteous and wealthy. Wealth, character and intelligence were positively correlated. Thorndike, like Ward, was a son of the enlightenment who believed in the progress of humanity through the manipulation and reform of one's social institution. Thorndike carried the idea of social melioration and the perfectibility of mankind to one of its possible conclusions, eugenics.

Ward's belief in the future development of a scientific society where men would collectively control the course of their future destiny had led him, in 1891, also to espouse eugenics. As Ward said:

> It is the right and the duty of an energetic and virile race of men to seize upon every great principle that can be made subservient to its true

---

[17] Edward L. Thorndike, "Intelligence and Its Uses," *Harpers*, January 1920, p. 233.
[18] *Ibid.*, p. 235.

advancement, and undeterred by any false ideas of its sanctity or inviola-
bility, fearlessly to apply it. Natural selection is the chief agent in the
transformation of species and the evolution of life. Artificial selection has
given to man the most that he possesses of value in the organic products
of the earth. May not men and women be selected as well as sheep and
horses? From the great stirp of humanity with all its multiplied ancestral
plasm—some very poor, some mediocre, some merely indifferent, a goodly
number ranging from middling to fair, only a comparative few very good,
with an occasional crystal of the first water—from all this, why may we
not learn to select on some broad and comprehensive plan with a view to
a general building up and rounding out of the race of human beings? At
least we should by a rigid selection stamp out of the future all the wholly
unworthy elements. Public sentiment should be created in this direction,
and when the day comes that society shall be as profoundly shocked at
the crime of perpetuating the least taint of hereditary disease, insanity, or
other serious defect, as it now is at the comparatively harmless crime of
incest, the way to practical and successful stirpiculture will have already
been found.[19]

Ward, however, shifted his position on eugenics over the next two
decades. By 1906, before the American Sociological Society, he was
arguing against the idea of improving society by way of eugenics. Shortly
before his death in 1913, he made the distinction between what he considered positive and negative eugenics. Positive eugenics, he believed, was
the social process by which the superior are to be encouraged to reproduce;
while negative eugenics was that social process which prevented the mental
and physical defectives from reproducing their defects.[20] While he had
no quarrel with negative eugenics, he objected to positive eugenics as
national policy on a number of grounds. First, he argued that, while he
agreed with the ultimate end of the eugenicists—the perfectibility of the
race; he differed on method. His objection to positive eugenics was that
it inevitably put someone in a master position over the normal man. Man,
he believed, was master over the animal world and over his own defectives;
and therefore, eugenics was permissible in those areas. But, he argued,
"normal people are their own masters." At this point, he eulogized nature
and argued almost in a modified Spencerian way that nature should be
allowed to take its course. Besides, he further asserted, men have "brains
enough," what they now need is knowledge.

Edward L. Thorndike, on the other hand, believed that the great progress of civilization has been made through the investigations and discoveries of great geniuses. His ideological perspective of the "good"
society was, like Herrnstein's, essentially hierarchial and socially stratified.

[19] Lester Frank Ward, *Glimpses of the Cosmos*, Vol. IV, 1891, p. 295. Reprinted
in 1913 and 1918 by G. P. Putnam's Sons, New York.
[20] See Lester F. Ward, "Eugenics, Euthenics and Eudemics," *The American
Journal of Sociology*, Vol. XVIII, No. 6, May 1913, p. 738.

MARTIN KALLIKAK

He dallied with a feeble-minded tavern girl

He married a worthy Quakeress

She bore a son known as "Old Horror" who had ten children

She bore seven upright worthy children

From "Old Horror's" ten children came hundreds of the lowest types of human beings

From these seven worthy children came hundreds of the highest types of human beings

Figure 1. The Influence of Heredity Is Demonstrated by the "Good" and the "Bad Kallikaks. From Henry E. Garrett, *General Psychology*. (New York: American Book Co., 1955), p. 65.

While Ward insisted that society was governed more by privilege of wealth and status than native talent, Thorndike argued that, in fact, the unequal distribution of wealth, privilege and status which existed was a consequence of the superior innate talent and abilities of the upper classes.

The association of wealth, intelligence and moral character continued to appear in psychology textbooks. Henry E. Garrett, a former student and fellow colleague with whom Thorndike was associated, continued to project the story of Martin Kallikak in terms of good and bad in his textbook on *General Psychology* as late at 1955. Just in case someone might miss the point, the children of the feebleminded tavern girl were pictured as having horns, while the "highest types of human beings" were portrayed as solid Puritan types. (See Figure 1.)

Were We Born That Way?

*Or Can We Help It? Is Heredity or Environment
the Power that Moulds Us? What Science Now
Knows About Intellectual Differences, and
Their Significance*

Lewis M. Terman

The most characteristic thing about our political philosophy of the last two centuries is the increased respect this period accords to the common man. Nowhere has this philosophy more completely ruled the day than in America. Although there have been and are eddies in the main current of belief, every one of our political institutions professes as its cardinal function that of helping to guarantee to every individual equal opportunity and equal rights with every other. This ideal is the democrat's religion, and who of us is not, in this sense, a democrat?

However, this political philosophy, which every true American accepts, has been interpreted by many as resting on the assumption that there are no inborn differences of intellectual or other mental functions. Generally speaking, the average person in America is likely to believe that the larger differences he sees among those about him are the product of environment; that the successful business man differs from the unskilled laborer chiefly in his opportunity and his luck; that the difference between the college graduate and the illiterate is entirely a matter of education; that the races of men the world over differ only as their opportunities to acquire the arts of civilization have differed.

Of course we have always recognized the existence of idiots and geniuses, but we have regarded these as belonging to distinct species, separated by an impassable gulf from the intermediate-lying normals, who, as far as native endowment is concerned, are supposed to constitute a perfectly undifferentiated mass. Many believe that some such assumption is a necessary presupposition of democracy.

To those who hold this view the findings of individual psychology in the last decade have come as a rude shock. Let us review a few of the facts which have been brought to light and consider their bearing upon social, economic and educational theory. We are not likely to jettison the American ideal of democracy, so it behooves us to reconcile it with the demonstrable facts of psychological and biological science.

"Individual psychology" has achieved its greatest successes in the field of intelligence testing. Indeed, the developments of the last two decades in this line constitute the most notable event in the history of modern psychology. The guiding genius was the great French psychologist, Alfred Binet, although Galton, Cattell, and a few others had broken ground before him. The Binet–Simon tests were the first really successful scale for measuring intelligence. Published less than a decade and a half ago, these tests have in various revised forms come into general use throughout the civilized world. In America, especially, improved types of intelligence tests have been developed which permit the wholesale examination of subjects in groups. Some of these "group tests" are interesting examples of American inventive ingenuity. It was the group method that made it possible to test the intelligence of nearly two million soldiers in our draft army and that now makes it possible to grade and classify every year millions of children in our public schools.

Intelligence tests are based upon the principle of sampling. Just as the value of a mountain of ore can be appraised by assaying a few pocketfuls of material, so it is possible to appraise one's intelligence by sinking shafts at a few critical points and analyzing the samples thus secured. The more varied the range of mental functions tested, the more valid the test. Standard intelligence scales include tests of memory, language comprehension, orientation in time and space, eye-hand coordinations, ability to find likenesses and differences between familiar objects, arithmetical reasoning, resourcefulness and ingenuity, speed, and richness of mental associations, the capacity to generalize from particulars, etc.

Inspection of an intelligence scale gives no idea of the amount of work that has gone into its making. The several tests have not been thought out casually and thrown together. The methods used are empirical, inductive, and quantitative. A large number of drag-net tests are first devised for extensive sampling of mental processes. These are then given to numerous subjects and the responses are minutely analyzed. Test elements which do not help to differentiate subjects of known superiority from subjects of known inferiority are eliminated. The elements retained are weighted and combined so as to permit the reckoning of a composite score. Reliability coefficients are computed, the probable error of a score is established, and the correlation of the test with various kinds of outside criteria is ascertained. It is then known how far the test may be relied upon and for what purposes its use is justified.

No intelligence scale at present can be regarded as satisfactorily accurate. What they do seems wonderful only by contrast with the methods they have replaced. The psychologist himself is keenly aware of their imperfections because he has figured these in terms of reliability coefficients and probable errors. He appreciates the vitiating effects of inequalities of schooling, language handicaps, specialized practice, variations in test procedure, emotional attitude of the subject, etc. At the same time he knows that our everyday intuitional methods of judging intelligence are subject to errors far more serious. He therefore uses the best tests available, imperfect as they are, and labors to make them a more satisfactory instrument for his purpose.

Superficially regarded, intelligence tests are likely to appear trivial. Their significance becomes evident only when a subject's responses are compared with norms, or standards. The task of the psychologist is like that of the paleontologist. The latter, through his acquaintance with comparative norms, is able to reconstruct the physical features of a prehistoric man with nothing to guide him but a few fragments of bone which most of us would not recognize as belonging to human remains. So it is with mental tests. Responses which signify nothing to the uninitiated are readily interpreted by the psychologist as characteristic of intellectual brilliance, dullness, moronity, imbecility, etc. The most convenient and widely used comparative standard of intellectual ability is the average test performance of normal unselected children of the different ages. This is where we get the term "mental age," which means simply the intelligence level which has been reached by the average child who is any given number of years old.

THE INTELLIGENCE QUOTIENT, OR "IQ"

Mental age takes on a very special significance when it is considered in relation to the subject's life age. From this comparison is derived the "intelligence quotient" (IQ), which is simply the ratio of mental age to life age. If a child of ten years has a mental age of eight, his IQ is 80. (It is customary to omit the decimal.) The ten-year-old with a mental age of twelve has an IQ of 120. In calculating the IQ of an adult subject life age above fifteen or sixteen is disregarded, for, strange to say, intellectual ability seems to improve little if at all after that age.

The IQ's of idiots are below 25 or 30, those of imbeciles range from the borderline of idiocy to about 50, and those of morons from the borderline of imbecility to 70 or 75. IQ's of 80 or 85 signify moderate dullness, the average child tests at 100, and anything above 100 indicates superiority. About one child in fifty tests as high as 130, and about one in two hundred and fifty as high as 140. IQ's as high as 190 are on record.

The IQ is therefore a "brightness index," and as such it is very service-able even if far from accurate. Its significance lies in the fact that it has a marked tendency to remain constant, thus affording a rough basis for pre-dicting a child's later development. Children do not test at 50 today and 100 tomorrow. The average change is not much more than five points, even over a period of years. The six-year-old who tests at four, IQ 67, will probably at the age of twelve test not far from eight, or at the age of fifteen not far from ten. Moreover, since there is little mental growth after the age of fifteen, it can be predicted, within fairly well known limits of error, that this hypothetical subject will probably as an adult have a mental age not very far from ten years. In a certain proportion of cases the forecast is not borne out.

Psychology, like meteorology, lacks much of being an exact science. However, it is well known that weather prophecy has in a few decades advanced from the joke stage and become a national institution. It is not so well known that long-range prophecy of mental growth is now more dependable than short-range prophecy of weather changes.

The IQ is not chiefly a product of formal instruction. Schooling doubtless affects it to some extent; how much, psychologists are not agreed. The writer can find little evidence that *ordinary* inequalities of home environment and school training, such inequalities, for example, as obtain in the average small city of California, invalidate the IQ very materially. Twice he has supervised experiments designed to ascertain how much a child's IQ could be improved by intensive training. The results in both cases were almost entirely negative. The special classes for back-ward children in the public schools are such an experiment on an enormous scale. No other pupils in our public schools are taught in such small groups or by such able teachers. But rarely do the IQ's of children given these special advantages show significant improvement. Generally speak-ing, once feeble-minded, always feeble-minded; once dull, always dull. The stories of dullards who became geniuses are not based on mental test evidence. When they are not merely old wives' tales, they can readily be accounted for by the fact that the narrow curriculum of the old-time school often failed to interest the child of specialized ability or exceptional originality.

If dullards remain dull, it is probably no less true that bright children remain bright. The writer has followed the development of a considerable number of gifted children for five to ten years. Thus far not one of them has developed symptoms of that dread condition of "post adolescent stupidity" which psychologists used to think was the almost certain fate of the intellectually precocious.

As an exact unit of measure the IQ is anything but satisfactory. Compared to units of measure used by the physicist, for example, it is grossly inaccurate and clumsy. It does seem, however, to be founded on more than the accidental influences of environment and to reflect, in some degree, the quality of native endowment. When our intelligence scales have become more accurate and the laws governing IQ changes have been more definitely established it will then be possible to say that there is nothing about an individual as important as his IQ, except possibly his morals; that the greatest educational problem is to determine the kind of education best suited to each IQ level; that the first concern of a nation should be the average IQ of its citizens, and the eugenic and dysgenic influences which are capable of raising or lowering that level; that the great test problem of democracy is how to adjust itself to the large IQ differences which can be demonstrated to exist among the members of any race or nationality group.

MENTAL HEREDITY

Intelligence is chiefly a matter of native endowment. It depends upon physical and chemical properties of the cerebral cortex which, like other physical traits, are subject to the laws of heredity. In fact, the mathematical coefficient of family resemblances in mental traits, particularly intelligence, has been found to be almost exactly the same as for such physical traits as height, weight, cephalic index, etc. Measurement of twin pairs shows the excess of resemblance for such pairs, as compared with ordinary brother-brother or sister-sister pairs, to be as great for mental as for physical traits. The attempts to explain familiar resemblances on any other hypothesis than that of heredity have not been successful. All the available facts that science has to offer support the Galtonian theory that mental abilities are chiefly a matter of original endowment. Even the most extreme advocates of "free will" do not believe that the feeble-minded could successfully will to become intelligent, the tone-deaf to become musical, or the psychopathic to became stable. The researches of many men, from Galton to Davenport and Goddard, have proved that one family may be characterized by musical genius, another by mathematical genius, another by insanity, another by feeble-mindedness, and so on.

SOCIAL AND OCCUPATIONAL STRATIFICATION

The exact laws which govern the transmission of mental traits have not been determined. It is not surprising, however, that intelligence tests have shown the members of the socially successful classes to have, on the average, better endowment than those of inferior social status. Children of the professional classes have an average IQ of about 115 as compared with about 85 for children of unskilled laborers and 100 for the children of all classes taken together. It will be understood, of course, that we are speaking of averages and that there are many exceptions to the rule. The intellectual spread of any social or occupational class is very wide and greatly overlaps the spread of any other class. The intellectual gap between the average lawyer or minister and the average unskilled laborer is nearly as great as that which separates the borderline defective from the strictly average person. These are differences which the highest arts of pedogogy are powerless to neutralize. One of the really significant discoveries of modern psychology is that when individuals of differing degrees of ability are subjected to the same training the original differences are more likely to be accentuated than to disappear. Equalization of educational opportunity does not equalize the educational product.

Children with an IQ of 140 or more are decidedly gifted. Not more than four children in a thousand taken at random qualify in this class. They are our intellectual elite, the nation's finest asset. The writer is collecting extensive psychological data on a thousand such children in California, sifted by an impartial method from a school population of a quarter-million. It is a matter of profound significance that nearly 50 percent of these gifted children belong to the professional classes. Half our genius comes from the top 4 or 5 percent of the population. The professional and semi-professional classes together furnish 85 percent of it. The three remaining classes (skilled-, semi-skilled-, and unskilled-labor groups) furnish together the remaining 15 percent. It is to the highest 25 percent of our population, and more especially to the top 5 percent, that we must look for the production of leaders who will advance science, art, government, education, and social welfare generally. Obviously, therefore, our civilization of a thousand or ten thousand years hence will depend largely upon the relative fertility of our low-grade and high-grade stocks.

Under the primitive economic conditions which prevailed in our relatively new and unformed civilization up to fifty or a hundred years ago, superior ability was more evenly distributed through the population than it is today. As the industrial and social situation becomes more complicated, there is a marked tendency, in any country which tries to give equal opportunity to all, for each individual to gravitate to the social or occupational level which corresponds to his native capacity. The more democratic the country, the more clearly this intellectual stratification tends to appear. In many parts of America it is well advanced. It is least noticeable among the newly arrived immigrants of an oppressed race. Freed from oppression these also rapidly form into a social hierarchy based largely upon native capacity, the intelligent, the average, and the incompetent finding their own levels.

THE BIRTH-RATE DIFFERENTIAL

Until recently there had not been, at least for hundreds of years, any marked tendency in the civilized countries for one class to produce more rapidly than another. For centuries the average mental endowment of the European and American peoples had held its own. But within the last fifty years a change of sinister portent has taken place. Intellectually superior families are no longer reproducing as rapidly as formerly. Their birth rate is already far below that of the socially incompetent. The average feeble-minded individual leaves two or three times as many offspring as the average college graduate. This biological cataclysm, silent but none the less fateful, is rapidly spreading to all civilized countries. If the differential character of our birth rate continues, the day is not many centuries removed when the only surviving stock will be that descended from the least desirable of our present-day population. Granted that this stratum may have considerable potentialities which have not been developed, the prospect at best is not alluring. As a nation we are faced by no other issue of comparable importance. It is a question of national survival or national decay. Unconscious of the danger that impends we haggle over matters of governmental policy that are infinitesimally trivial in comparison with the problem of differential fecundity. The situation will not be fully grasped until we have come to think more in terms of individual differences and intelligence quotients.

The usual legal measures designed to prevent the reproduction of the unfit are interesting embodiments of our eugenic ideals, but they have so far contributed nothing to race improvement. Reduction of the number of defectives is only a minor aspect of the larger problem of eugenics. It is raising or lowering the average level for the entire population that counts in the long run. Elimination of all the feeble-minded would not raise the average level of intelligence to more than a barely noticeable extent, but a birth rate unfavorably differential according to intelligence will inevitably reduce the average level and render the appearance of geniuses far less frequent. In fact, for reasons which are well known to statisticians but which we can not here set forth, even a moderate lowering of the average reduces the frequency of high grade genius very greatly.

AVERAGE INTELLIGENCE

How intelligent is the average adult in the United States? That his intelligence is lower than most persons would estimate it to be is certain. That it is as low as certain army mental test data have led some to believe is by no means demonstrated. It is true that the most reliable tested soldier group yielded an average mental age 13.4 years, but we can not be certain that this group was representative of the entire draft army, or if it was, that the draft army was representative of our entire male population. More than two-thirds of the nearly ten million registrants were granted exemption, and it is probable that a disproportionate number of these belonged to the professional, semi-professional and skilled labor groups. Allowing for this factor, the average mental age of the population might reach as high as that of an eighth-grade pupil. That it would go much higher than this is very doubtful.

In other words half our adults have no more intellectual acumen than the average pupil in the eighth grade. Probably a quarter have less than the average pupil of the seventh grade. The least intelligent 15 or 20 percent of our population would probably be incapable of mastering, after any amount of instruction, the more difficult portions of the typical eighth grade text in arithmetic, of making any progress in algebra, of getting much sense out of a moderately difficult prose selection, or of understanding the underlying principles of tariff, taxation, bond transactions, or banking. On questions of larger social and national policy they vote blindly or as directed by political bosses. They are democracy's ballast, not always useless but always a potential liability. How to make the most of their limited abilities, both for their own welfare and that of society; how to lead them without making them helpless victims of oppression; are perennial questions in any democracy.

THE CONSERVATION OF TALENT

But instead of worrying over-much about the number of dull people in the world it would be better to concern ourselves more about conserving and developing the vast amount of superior talent that is now wasted.

Granted that only 50 or 60 percent of our children have ability to graduate from an average high school, this is still at least five times as many as actually do complete a high-school course. Probably five times as many have the ability to graduate from college as we are now graduating. Large numbers of highly gifted children are not recognized by their teachers as such. The brightest child in a certain school of five hundred pupils, as shown by mental test, was not named by his teacher as the "brightest," "second brightest," or "third brightest" in his classroom.

The theory that "genius will out" is but a dangerous half truth. There is reason to believe that a good fraction of our intellectual talent is wasted. There are thousands of individuals whom a better education or a wiser guidance would have enabled to make a far bigger and better contribution to civilization than they are making. It has always been so. The biographies of eminent men and women record with disturbing frequency the accidental nature of the circumstances which have often given the genius his chance. But for the fact that Newton's uncle, a graduate of Cambridge, one day found his youthful nephew lying under a hedge engaged in the solution of a difficult mathematical problem, it is doubtful whether this most gifted genius of English science would ever have had a university training. Without it even the giant intellect of Newton could not have formulated the law of gravitation, invented differential calculus, or demonstrated the refrangibility of light rays. One may be very sure that in case of many a gifted youth the "happy accident" fails to happen, and that "mute inglorious Miltons" are more than a poetic figure. The greatest problem of conservation relates not to forests or mines, but to the discovery, encouragement, and proper utilization of human talent. In this process discovery is the necessary first step, and this consideration alone would justify the expense and labor of giving every year an intelligence test to every one of our twenty million school children.

RACIAL DIFFERENCES IN INTELLIGENCE

Do races differ in intelligence? A nation which draws its constituents from all corners of the earth and prides itself on being the melting pot of peoples can not safely ignore this question. It is axiomatic that what comes out of the melting pot depends on what goes into it. A decade ago the majority of anthropologists and psychologists flouted the idea that there are any considerable differences in the native mental capacities of races or nationality groups. Today we have overwhelming evidence that they were mistaken. Army mental tests have shown that not more than 15 percent of American negroes equal or exceed in intelligence the average of our white population, and the the intelligence of the average negro is vastly inferior to that of the average white man. The available data indicate that the average mulatto occupies about a mid-position between pure negro and pure white. The intelligence of the American Indian has also been over-rated, for mental tests indicate that it is not greatly superior to that of the average negro. Our Mexican population, which is largely of Indian extraction, makes little if any better showing. The immigrants who have recently come to us in such large numbers from Southern and Southeastern Europe are distinctly inferior mentally to the Nordic and Alpine strains we have received from Scandinavia, Germany, Great Britain, and France. The samplings we have received do not, of course, afford convincing proof that the Mediterranean race, as a race is inferior. It is quite possible, for example, that our Nordic immigrants have been drawn chiefly from the middle and upper social classes, and our Mediterranean immigrants from the lower social strata. It is well recognized that immigration is often differential with respect to social and economic classes. However this may be, we owe it to the future of our civilization to set a minimum mental standard for our immigrants from every source. The literacy qualification is not without value, but it should be replaced by a more reliable measure of intellectual ability. No nation can afford to overlook the danger that the average quality of its germ plasm may gradually deteriorate as a result of unrestricted immigration.

In this connection it is interesting to note that intelligence tests of Chinese and Japanese in California indicate that these races are approximately the equals of Europeans in mental ability. Unselected Chinese children in San Francisco test almost as high as unselected California white children and enormously higher than the children of our Portuguese and South Italian immigrants. An extensive study of the mental traits of California Japanese children is now under way.

THE INTELLIGENCE OF WOMEN

Mental tests have at last vindicated woman's claim to intellectual equality with man. As far as the *average* ability of the sexes is concerned the question has received a final answer. Among psychologists the issue is as dead as the ancient feud as to the shape of the earth. Two questions, however, have not yet been satisfactorily answered: (1) Granted that women are the equals of men in *general* intelligence, are there nevertheless sex differences in *special* intellectual functions or in emotional and volitional traits? (2) Granted that the *average* intelligence of the sexes is about the same, is it true, as some believe, that the *variability* of the male is greater? If so, this would fully account for the higher incidence of genius among men. On the whole the evidence available to date rather favors this view. At the same time, we can not be sure that the apparent infrequency of genius among women may not be accounted for by lack of opportunity or by a certain weakness of the woman's competitive instinct or "will to power."

A Study of American Intelligence

C. C. Brigham

Our study of the army tests of foreign born individuals has pointed at every step to the conclusions that the average intelligence of our immigrants is declining. This deterioration in the intellectual level of immigrants has been found to be due to two causes. The migrations of the Alpine and Mediterranean races have increased to such an extent in the last thirty or forty years that this blood now constitutes 70 percent or 75 percent of the total immigration. The representatives of the Alpine and Mediterranean races in our immigration are intellectually inferior to the representatives of the Nordic race which formerly made up about 50 percent of our immigration. In addition, we find that we are getting progressively lower and lower types from each nativity group or race.

In the light of our findings in Section IV and IX, it is possible to redraw our curve representing increase of intelligence score with increasing years of residence and to represent it truly as in Figure 1, which shows the decline of intelligence with each succeeding period of immigration.

It is also possible to make a picture of the elements now entering into American intelligence. At one extreme we have the distribution of the Nordic race group. At the other extreme we have the American negro. Between the Nordic and the negro, but closer to the negro than to the Nordic, we find the Alpine and Mediterranean types. These distributions we have projected together in Figure 2.

Throughout this study all measurements have been made in terms of averages and variability about the average. In interpreting averages, we must never forget that they stand for an entire distribution. Careless thinkers are prone to select one or two striking examples of ability from a particular group, and then rest confidently in the belief that they have overthrown an argument based on the total distribution of ability. The Fourth of July orator can convincingly raise the popular belief in the intellectual level of Poland by shouting the name of Kosciusko from a high platform, but he can not alter the distribution of the intelligence of the Polish immigrant. All countries send men of exceptional ability to America, but the point is that some send fewer than others.

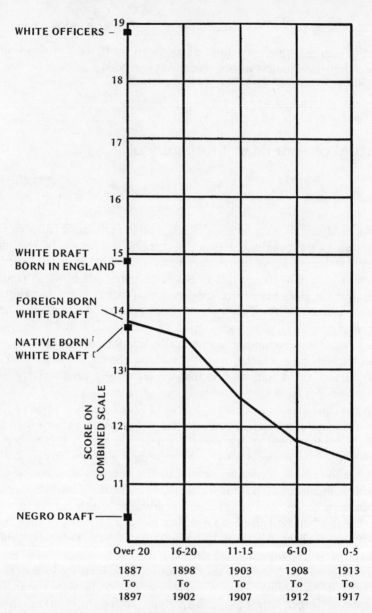

Figure 1. The Decline of Intelligence with Each Succeeding Period of Immigration. The apparent increase of intelligence with increasing length of residence . . . has been proved to be a progressive decrease in the intellectual level of immigrants coming to this country in each succeeding five-year period since 1902. The evidence indicates that the immigrants prior to 1902 were intellectually equal to the native born white draft. The army sample of "native born" includes, besides native born of native parentage, the native born of foreign or mixed parentage. It is perhaps possible that the native born of native parentage might have tested higher than 13.77. The position of the white draft born in England is shown above. Although the true position of the native born American may be a matter of speculation, there is no doubt that the more recent immigrants are intellectually closer to the negro than to the native born white sample.

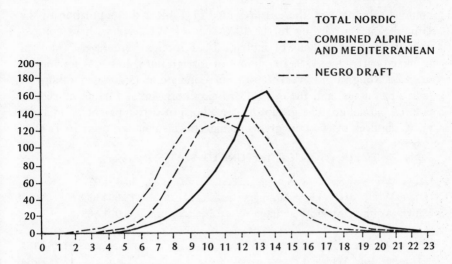

Figure 2. The Constituent Elements of American Intelligence. The distributions of the intelligence scores of the entire Nordic group, the combined Mediterranean and Alpine groups, and the negro draft. The process of racial intermixture cannot result in anything but an average of these elements, with the resulting deterioration of American intelligence. About 85 percent of the Nordic group exceed the average negro. About 75 percent of the Nordic group exceed the Alpine and Mediterranean. About 35 percent of the Alpine and Mediterranean groups are below the average negro.

Our distribution curve of intelligence includes ability as well as defect. The English speaking Nordic group, for instance, averages 13.84, and furnishes at one extreme about 40 men in 1,000 who are above the average white officer, while at the other extreme, the group furnishes about 8 in 1,000 who are below an estimated "mental age" of eight. A distribution further down the scale contributes more to the lower orders of intelligence. The distribution of the intelligence scores of the negro draft, for instance, indicates that they contribute only 4 in 1,000 above the average white officer, while they give us 100 in 1,000 below the approximate "mental age" of eight. The Alpine and Mediterranean races give us only 5 or 10 in 1,000 above the average ability of the white officer, and about 40 in 1,000 below the "mental age" of eight. About 350 in 1,000 of the Alpine and Mediterranean types are below the average negro.

The intellectual characteristics of the immigration to the United States as measured by the samples in the draft have been reported in this study, first by country of birth, and second by race. Parallel with the measurements of intelligence, the figures on immigration have been presented. To complete the picture, there is presented in Table 1 the population of the United States according to the 1920 census.[1] We have with us approximately 15 7/10 millions of individuals of foreign parentage, 7 millions of mixed parentage, 13 7/10 millions of foreign born, and 10½ millions of negroes. Roughly, in every 100 of our population, 55 are native born of native parentage, and the other 45 foreign born, or of foreign, mixed, or colored parentage. The group of native born of native parentage includes many children of the immigrants coming to this country prior to 1890.

Table 1.   POPULATION OF THE UNITED STATES IN 1920

Native White of Native Parentage		58,421,957
Native White of Foreign Parentage		15,694,539
Native White of Mixed Parentage		6,991,665
Total Native White		81,108,161
Foreign Born White		13,712,754
Negro		10,463,131
Indian		244,437
Chinese		61,639
Japanese		111,010
All others:		
	Filipinos	5,603
	Hindus	2,507
	Koreans	1,224
	Hawaiians	110
	Malays	19
	Siamese	17
	Samoans	6
	Maoris	2
Total all others		9,488
Total Population		105,710,620

NOTE: Clinton Stoddard Burr in *America's Race Heritage* (New York: The National Historical Society, 1922, p. 327) estimates that in 1920 there were 44,689,278 descendents of the old Colonial white stock.

[1] Too much reliance can not be placed on the census returns for the foreign born white population. The 1910 census shows the foreign born white population at 13,345,545, while the 1920 census shows that population at 13,712,754, which gives a net increase of 367,209. On the other hand, the figures of the Commissioner General of Immigration show by actual count at the ports 5,725,811 aliens admitted and 2,146,994 aliens departed, leaving a net increase of 3,578,817 for the same period covered by the two censuses (1910 and 1920). Inasmuch as the enumerators could not have missed three million, they are probably counted among the native white.

Our immigration figures show a very decided shift from the Nordic in favor of the Alpine. The immigration between 1820 and 1890 probably never contained more than 50 percent or 60 percent Nordic blood, and prior to 1820 there was very little immigration. The earliest settlers were almost pure Nordic types, and we may assume the existence by 1820 of a race as predominantly Nordic as that of England. This recent change was, of course, reflected in the cross section of the foreign born population taken at 1910, and which constitutes the basis of our present immigration act restricting immigration to 3 percent of the nationals then resident here. A rough estimate of the racial composition of the quotas from various countries admissible under the new law shows about 35 percent Nordic blood, 45 percent Alpine blood and 20 percent Mediterranean blood in the annual stream of approximately 1/3 of a million that may enter.

There can be no doubt that recent history has shown a movement of inferior people or inferior representatives of peoples to this country. Few people realize the magnitude of this movement or the speed with which it has taken place. Since 1901, less than a single generation, it may be estimated that about 10,000,000 Alpine and Mediterranean types have come to this country. Allowing for the return of 1/3 or 3/8 of these, and using our army estimates of intellectual ability, this would give us over 2,000,000 immigrants below the average negro.

We may consider that the population of the United States is made up of four racial elements, the Nordic, Alpine, and Mediterranean races of Europe, and the negro. If these four types blend in the future into one general American type, then it is a foregone conclusion that this future blended American will be less intelligent than the present native born American, for the general results of the admixture of higher and lower orders of intelligence must inevitably be a mean between the two.

If we turn to the history of races, we find that as a general rule where two races have been in contact they have intermingled, and a cross between the two has resulted. Europe shows many examples of areas where the anthropological characteristics of one race shade over into those of another race where the two have intermixed, and, indeed, in countries such as France and Switzerland it is only in areas that are geographically or economically isolated that one finds types that are relatively pure. The Mongol–Tatar element in Russia is an integral part of the population. The Mediterranean race throughout the area of its contact with the negro has crossed with him. Some of the Berbers in Northern Africa show negroid characteristics, and in India the Mediterranean race has crossed with the Dravidians and Pre-Dravidian negroids. The population of Sardinia shows a number of negroid characteristics. Turn where we may, history gives us no great exception to the general rule that propinquity leads to opportunity and opportunity to intermixture.

In considering racial crosses, Professor Conklin[2] states that "It is highly probable that while some of these hybrids may show all the bad qualities of both parents, others may show the good qualities of both and indeed in this respect resemble the children in any pure-bred family. But it is practically certain that the general or average results of the crossing of a superior and an inferior race are to strike a balance somewhere between the two. This is no contradiction of the principles of Mendelian inheritance but rather the application of these principles to a general population. The general effect of the hybridization of races can not fail to lead to a lowering of the qualities of the higher race and a raising of the qualities of the lower one."

And as to the possibility of a cross between races in the future, Professor Conklin writes: "Even if we are horrified by the thought, we cannot hide the fact that all present signs point to an intimate commingling of all existing human types within the next five or ten thousand years at most. Unless we can re-establish geographical isolation of races, we cannot prevent their interbreeding. By rigid laws excluding immigrants of other races, such as they have in New Zealand and Australia, it may be possible for a time to maintain the purity of the white race in certain countries, but with constantly increasing intercommunications between all lands and peoples such artificial barriers will probably prove as ineffectual in the long run as the Great Wall of China. The races of the world are not drawing apart but together, and it needs only the vision that will look ahead a few thousand years to see the blending of all racial currents into a common stream."

If we frankly recognize the fact that the crossing of races in juxtaposition has always occurred in the past, what evidence have we that such crosses had untoward consequences? Our own data from the army tests indicate clearly the intellectual superiority of the Nordic race group. This superiority is confirmed by observation of this race in history. The Alpine race, according to our figures, which are supported by historical evidence, seems to be considerably below the Nordic type intellectually. However, our recruits from Germany, which represents a Nordic–Alpine cross, are about the same as those from Holland, Scotland, the United States, Denmark, and Canada, countries which have on the whole a greater proportion of Nordic blood than Germany. Again, the Nordic and Alpine mixture in Switzerland has given a stable people, who have evolved, in spite of linguistic differences, a very advanced form of government. The evidence indicates that the Nordic–Alpine cross, which occurred in Western Europe when the Nordics overwhelmed the Alpines to such an

---

[2] Edwin G. Conklin, *The Direction of Human Evolution.* (New York, 1921), p. 247.

extent that the type was completely submerged and not re-discovered until recently, has not given unfortunate results.

This evidence, however, can not be carried over to indicate that a cross between the Nordic and Alpine Slav would be desirable. The Alpines that our data sample come for the most part from an area peopled largely by a branch of the Alpine race which appeared late and radiated from the Carpathian Mountains. It is probably a different branch of the Alpine race from that which forms the primitive substratum of the present population of Western Europe. Our data on the Alpine Slav show that he is intellectually inferior to the Nordic, and every indication would point to a lowering of the average intelligence of the Nordic if crossed with the Alpine Slav. There can be no objection to the intermixture of races of equal ability, provided the mingling proceeds equally from all sections of the distribution of ability. Our data, however, indicate that the Alpine Slav we have imported and to whom we give preference in our present immigration law is intellectually inferior to the Nordic type.

The Mediterranean race at its northern extension blends with the Alpine very considerably, and to a less extent with the Nordic. At the point of its furthermost western expansion in Europe it has crossed with the primitive types in Ireland. Throughout the area of its southern and eastern expansion it has crossed with negroid types. In this continent, the Mediterranean has crossed with the Amerind and the imported negro very extensively. In general, the Mediterranean race has crossed with primitive race types more completely and promiscuously than either the Alpine or the Nordic, and with most unfortunate results.

We must now frankly admit the undesirable results which would ensue from a cross between the Nordic in this country with the Alpine Slav, with the degenerated hybrid Mediterranean, or with the negro, or from the promiscuous intermingling of all four types. Granted the undesirable results of such an intermingling, is there any evidence showing that such a process is going on? Unfortunately the evidence is undeniable. The 1920 census shows that we have 7,000,000 native born whites of mixed parentage, a fact which indicates clearly the number of crosses between the native born stock and the European importations.

The evidence in regard to the white and negro cross is also indisputable. If we examine the figures showing the proportion of mulattoes to a thousand blacks for each twenty year period from 1850 to 1910, we find that in 1850 there were 126 mulattoes to a thousand blacks, 136 in 1870, 179 in 1890 and 264 in 1910. This intermixture of white and negro has been a natural result of the emancipation of the negro and the breaking down of social barriers against him, mostly in the North and West. In 1850, the free colored population showed 581 mulattoes to a thousand blacks as against 83 in the slave population. At each of the four censuses (1850, 1870, 1890 and 1910) the South, where the social barriers are more rigid than else-where, has returned the smallest proportion of mulattoes to a thousand blacks. The 1910 census showed 201 in the South, 266 in the North and 321 in the West, and the West has returned the highest proportion at each of the censuses except 1850.

We must face a possibility of racial admixture here that is infinitely worse than that faced by any European country to-day, for we are incor-porating the negro into our racial stock, while all of Europe is compara-tively free from this taint. It is true that the rate of increase of the negro in this country by ten year periods since 1800 has decreased rather steadily from about 30 percent to about 11 percent, but this declining rate has given a gross population increase from approximately 1,000,000 to approximately 10,000,000. It is also true that the negro now constitutes only about 10 percent of the total population, where he formerly constituted 18 percent or 19 percent (1790 to 1830), but part of this decrease in percentage of the total population is due to the great influx of immigrants, and we favor in our immigration law those countries 35 percent of whose representatives here are below the average negro. The declining rate of increase in the negro population from 1800 to 1910 would indicate a correspondingly lower rate to be expected in the future. From 1900 to 1920 the negro population increased 18.4 percent, while the native born white of native parents increased 42.6 percent, and the native born white of foreign parents increased 47.6 percent. It is impossible to predict at the present time that the rate of infiltration of white blood into the negro will be checked by the declining rate of increase in the negro blood itself. The essential point is that there are 10,000,000 negroes here now, and that the proportion of mulattoes to a thousand blacks has increased with alarming rapidity since 1850.

According to all evidence available, then, American intelligence is de-clining, and will proceed with an accelerating rate as the racial admixture becomes more and more extensive. The decline of American intelligence will be more rapid than the decline of the intelligence of European national groups, owing to the presence here of the negro. These are the plain, if somewhat ugly, facts that our study shows. The deterioration of American intelligence is not inevitable, however, if public action can be aroused to prevent it. There is no reason why legal steps should not be taken which would insure a continuously progressive upward evolution.

The steps that should be taken to preserve or increase our present in-tellectual capacity must of course be dictated by science and not by political expediency. Immigration should not only be restrictive but highly selective. And the revision of the immigration and naturalization laws will only afford a slight relief from our present difficulty. The really important steps are those looking toward the prevention of the continued propagation of defective strains in the present population. If all immigration were stopped now, the decline of American intelligence would still be inevitable. This is the problem which must be met, and our manner of meeting it will determine the future course of our national life.

Closed Doors or the Melting Pot

The Original Framework of Our Nation Has Been Weakened and Blurred by Racial Dilution

David Starr Jordan

In contemplating the immigration outlook in America, I am first reminded of these words of Voltaire: "Never foretell the future: there has never been any." The most that we can say is that the tide is turning in America, and that the fact concerns the whole world. For the present I may not discuss the rather crude provisions of the present statute, nor its vicious slap at our Asiatic neighbors—part of a veiled scheme to keep an open sore on the Pacific for the sake of local politics.

The racial relations of humanity, with the variant feelings and customs, constitutes a world problem of great complexity, not to be solved off-hand by any act of legislation.

It seems fairly plain that the different types of man have sprung, long ago, from a single stock, and that they have become separated through individual variations by segregation in a world crossed everywhere by barriers of land and water, climate and food. Separation involves in and in-breeding with selection of various sorts in different regions and circumstances. The essence of selection is this: every individual living being,

We present in the above article by Dr. David Starr Jordan a point of view we do not share. Dr. Jordan, however, has always had our highest admiration and a thoughtful expression of his opinion can never be negligible, however distasteful it may be to accept it in toto. We feel that Dr. Jordan has temperately and courteously stated a conviction which runs counter to the very fundamentals of our republic. As Jews we are not guilty of thinking merely as we wish to think when we say that we have made and will always make a worth-while contribution to world civilization. Our best, we like to think, is the very salt of the earth.

The Nordic ideal is blindly egocentric and if persisted in, will create in America a provincialism and self-satisfaction which must prove hurtful in future progress. We are faced with a problem of selective immigration, very true, but as Dr. Jordan himself points out, no race or nation has a monopoly of the best. Let us examine our potential inhabitants as human beings and not as Nordics or Semites. That is not only the way of our great founders but common sense and fair play as well. (The Editors, *The American Hebrew*, 1924) man, animal or plant, has to run the gauntlet of the years (imperfectly described as the struggle for existence) and those who survive leave progeny in general like themselves. As a rule not more than 50 men or women in a hundred leave a permanent line of descent. Those who survive determine the future. Moreover, no man or woman (or dog or cow or cornstalk) ever had an ancestor who died in infancy. Hence the persistence of sound strains.

As a resultant of all this we have the many races and sub-races and variants among men. Some races are on the average superior to others in one or in many regards and within each race are superior strains, such as the Greeks knew as "aristoi" (not "aristocrat"): men and women of wisdom, or insight or virtue or genius or strength above the mass. On the "care and culture" of these, their continuance or persistence, the advance of any race must chiefly depend. The "moron" group, the "slum populations" have, as a rule, no future.

We speak of the "blood" of a race as indicating its qualities of germ plasm and consequent heredity, a matter with which literal "blood" has nothing to do. We say truly that the "blood" of a nation determines its history. In like fashion the history of a nation determines its blood, for the real values of a race are determined by the man who is left for parentage through the vicissitudes of his generation. The racial type of any nation is determined by its own actual parentage. As war, for example, destroys the best, a warlike nation becomes in time a weak one mentally and physically debilitated. Through selective war, killing the bravest and ablest, fell Greece, Rome and Spain and later nations may well profit by their example. With the extirpation of the forceful Roman farmers whole tribes of odds and ends were brought into Italy to do their work. Other nations since have done the same thing.

Guizot once asked of Lowell, "How long will your republic endure?" Lowell answered, "So long as the spirit of the fathers animates the people." "How long will this be?" we may ask. The answer is this. "So long as the blood of the fathers runs in the veins of the people." This statement, true beyond question, must not be interpreted too narrowly, for the point at issue is freedom of soul, not merely English or Nordic blood.

While the makers of our republic were largely of Puritan stock (English dissenters from conventional religious and social standards), their traits of value lay not in tribe nor creed, but in the fact that they were free men in search of freedom, the right to own themselves, to worship for themselves and in their own way to blaze their path toward righteousness. In the words of Senator Bayard, "they were too self-willed and independent to let any one rule over them except themselves." John Hay said: "They looked on no one as above them and on none as inferior; they knew no want they could not themselves satisfy."

Whatever our dissent from their theological narrowness (coming from a Europe far narrower), or of their lack of aesthetic taste (a matter in their day associated with corrupt and vicious royal courts), we should remember that they had the saving grace which means democracy. Were it not for the dominance of this type of men we should never had formed the American republic nor, once established, would it ever have endured. Men like these from all parts of Europe have joined their fortunes with them to work for the same ends. In the life of a nation the vital differences are not matters of education, but of hereditary potentialities.

It is the freeborn and freedom-loving men of Europe, whatever their race, who made, maintained and will sustain, the republic. The prisoners of debt sent over in the Sixteenth Century—though English in blood—have always been a constant burden, and will remain so through the generations, while from every race in Europe and from some in Asia we have received men bound by no external fetters, imperial, military or ecclesiastical.

Among other traits of this original type has been that of self-control. The good citizen thinks before acting and he prefers any and all other methods of reform to that of violence. He does not "stand on his head to think."

In the great waves of immigration of the last forty years we have received millions of people temperamentally unfit for democracy. "Temperamentalism," in fact, has been on the whole the great defect of most alien races. People guided by tradition, superstition, emotion, rather than by intelligence, cannot create nor sustain a democracy. For self-government no political virtue stands higher than self-control. Politically temperamentalism tends to oscillate between anarchy and tyranny. It still oscillates through most of Europe.

Waves of feeling have little constructive power. Under their influence the individual vibrates between Communism and Fascism, alike in the long run. Black shirts or red head in the same direction—and that direction is not towards democracy or freedom. All are foes of Liberty, Freedom, Order, Justice, these are the basal elements of democracy. Justice means individual opportunity and for this freedom and order must exist, and Peace is a necessary condition and result.

The opening of the oceans to transportation has destroyed forever that isolation which is the primary cause of division of men into tribes and races. In the course of history, only migration or conquest could bring diverging races together. Racial friendliness was rarely dreamed of. In the days to come every type of man will find it everywhere. Every caravan passes through our back yard. It is plain, that if the tendency to fusion is carried to its limit, and all barriers are leveled, all men will tend to settle down toward mediocrity. Mediocrity breeds imperialism, for every king or emperor is a creature of a mob. Their banner could not wave without a shouting populace behind. Free men never welcomed a king unless as a refuge from something worse.

We have in America already felt many of the evils of leveling down. We have imported slum population, slum ideas and slum men we cannot separate from the chains they revere.

The original framework of our nation has been weakened and blurred by racial dilution. The loose adulation of the Nordic races now current, however exaggerated, is based on a primal and vital fact. In history and temper, ours is a Nordic nation. Its freedom was won and its integrity maintained by Nordic methods and those races or members of races who have not valued freedom and order are politically and socially a burden on our progress. It is true that the Nordic peoples in general have had "the best chance." They have education, self-government and a large degree of liberty, the only liberty that counts, the freedom to own themselves body and soul; the freedom to seek truth in the world about them. But who gave them this freedom? Did they not take it themselves? Cannot others do the same if freedom they really crave? Can we share freedom safely with peoples who do not want it and whose highest aim is merely to vegetate?

Broadly speaking, the best of any race is superior to the average of any other. Men must be judged as men, not as part of a more or less artificial tribe. There are other races superior in certain ways to our Nordic average, though perhaps not to our ideal best. Music centers outside of English-speaking areas. Art has its birth in Greece, its growth and development in Italy and Holland: lucidity has still its triumph in France and thoroughness in Germany.

The Jew, at his best, has a freedom from illusion which no other race has surpassed. He was the first to recognize the integrity of the universe and its unity. By the best, we do not mean the wealthiest or most conspicuous. The best human stuff is that richest in possibilities.

On the whole, we seem forced to check a current which may overwhelm us. We must fall back a quarter of a century till we know where we stand. This seems a present necessity whatever the future may demand. We must put our house in order before we welcome any more guests to share its hospitality. For after all it is our own house. We who were and are the overflow of all Europe and of parts of Asia and Africa. The natural barriers to distribution have dissolved and great migration of the world is on. It may, in time, overwhelm all nations and all governments. But we need not blindly anticipate it, not even though our closed doors make America comparable to "a land-locked lake," where once flowed a mighty river. We must take counsel of the future, a future by no means simple nor reassuring.

We would not smother nor exterminate races or nations to save food, but we cannot yet feed them all, and the time has come to consider improving the breed by selection. To this end, much serious thought of serious people must be given while in no sense can the present statute of 1924 be regarded as final and conclusive.

Intelligence and Its Uses

Edward L. Thorndike

In the last hundred years the civilized world has learned to trust science to teach it how to make the powers of wind and water, the energy of chemicals, and the vibrations of the ether do man's will and serve his comfort. Physical forces are being conquered by science for man. We may hope that man's own powers of intellect, character, and skill are no less amenable to understanding, control, and direction; and that in the next hundred years the world may improve its use of man-power as it has improved its use of earth-power.

Not only philanthropists and philosophers, but hard-headed, practical men of affairs in business, education, and government, are now looking to psychology, the science of human behavior, to provide principles for human engineering—for the efficient private and public management of man-power or "personnel." For example, the Secretary of War and Adjutant-General McCain, in seeking specialists to help "(1) secure a contented and efficient army by placing each enlisted man where he has the opportunity to make the most of his talent and skill, (2) to commission, assign, and promote officers on merit, and (3) to simplify the procedure of discovering talent and assigning it where most needed,'" intrusted the task to psychologists. The co-operation between psychologists and business men in the organization that resulted (the Committee on Classification of Personnel in the Army) made clear to each group how much it had to learn from the others. And, in general, to-day, science is eager to make use of the practical experience of men and women who succeed in managing human nature; and men of affairs are realizing that the experiments and measurements and formulae of the scientific man may turn out to be the most "practical" things in the world.

As a sample to illustrate both what the scientific study of personnel has done and what it has to do, we may take the problem of intelligence and its uses.

Men talk freely about intelligence, and rank their acquaintances as having very little, little, much, or very much of it. If, however, they try to state just what it is, and how it is to be measured, there is difficulty. One says, "It is thought-power; and it is measured by the person's ability in school and in life." Another retorts, "What is thought-power?" and calls attention to the fact that ability in school and ability in life are different things. Smith declares that "Intelligence is ability to learn," and when asked, "To learn what?" adds, "To learn anything." A teacher present then observes that one of the slowest boys at learning Latin whom he ever knew made record progress in learning to swim, skate, and play ball. Jones, who has turned to the dictionary, says: "This suits me, '*Readiness of comprehension*'! I call a man intelligent who can understand questions—see the point. Give me fifteen minutes' interview with a man and I can give you a measure of his intelligence." Some one at once objects that a man may be slow and incorrect in responding to questions, but quick and sure in locating the trouble with an automobile, or in seeing a bargain, or in sizing up the temper of a mob of strikers.

The facts of every-day life, when inspected critically, indicate that a man has not some one amount of one kind of intelligence, but varying amounts of different intelligence. His ability to think with numbers may be great; his ability to think with words small. He may be a successful student of history and a failure at learning physics. Compare Grant's intelligence in using an army with his intelligence as a business trader. In our ratings of men we unconsciously strike a sort of average of his abilities in learning, thinking, and acting. The source or cause of this average ability is what we really have in mind when we speak of his intelligence.

Numerous scientific investigations of human intellectual abilities confirm and extend this view. No man is equally intelligent for all sorts of problems. Intelligence varies according to the life situations on which it works. A man so feeble-minded in most matters that he is confined in an asylum is found to play a first-rate game of chess. A man who in his day was famous the country over as editor, speaker, and executive never was able to pass freshman mathematics in college. Such extreme cases are, of course, found rarely. There is a general rough correspondence or correlation, such that a man notably intelligent in one respect will usually be above the average in others also. But the correlation is far from perfect. Shakespeare was successful as a business man, and doubtless would have made a good record as a lawyer, farmer, statesman, navigator, or grammarian; but no competent person believes that his intelligence was equally adapted to all these. The general fact may be kept in mind in the form of a diagram like Fig. 1. The continuous line represents the intelligence possessed by individual A, the height of the line representing the amount of intelligence. The dotted line tells the same story for B. The dash line tells

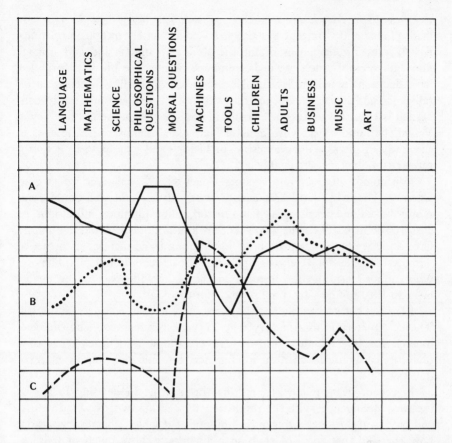

Figure 1. The Shaded Area Represents the Average Intelligence of the Adult American.

the same for C. A is on the average the more intelligent, and C the least; but B surpasses A in several respects, and C surpasses A in two.

A perfect description and measurement of intelligence would involve testing the man's ability to think in all possible lines, just as a perfect description and measurement of the mineral wealth of a state would involve adequate testing for iron, copper, gold, silver, lead, tin, zinc, antimony, petroleum, platinum, tungsten, iridium and the long list of rarer metals.

For ordinary practical purposes, however, it suffices to examine for three "intelligences," which we may call mechanical intelligence, social intelligence, and abstract intelligence. By mechanical intelligence is meant the ability to learn to understand and manage things and mechanisms such as a knife, gun, mowing-machine, automobile, boat, lathe, piece of land, river, or storm. By social intelligence is meant the ability to understand and manage men and women, boys and girls—to act wisely in human relations. By abstract intelligence is meant the ability to understand and manage ideas and symbols, such as words, numbers, chemical or physical formulae, legal decisions, scientific laws and principles, and the like. Mechanical intelligence and social intelligence refer to thought and action directly concerned with actual things and persons in one's hands and before one's eyes. When the mind works with general facts *about* things and people, as in the study of physics and chemistry, or history and sociology, its action is referred to abstract intelligence.

Within any of these intelligences a man displays relatively great consistency. The man who learns carpentering quickly and well could commonly have done nearly as well as a mason, sailor, plumber, millwright, or auto-repair man. The man who succeeds as a politician would commonly have done well as a salesman, hotel clerk, confidence man, or, if provided with certain accessory traits, as a parish priest or school principal. The boy who cannot learn algebra, history, and sciences will probably be unable to learn law, engineering, philosophy, and theology.

Between one and another of the three there is relatively great disparity. The best mechanic in a factory may fail as a foreman for lack of social intelligence. The whole world may revere the abstract intelligence of a philosopher whose mechanical intelligence it would not employ at three dollars a day!

In recent years much progress has been made in devising means to measure intelligence, with the result that we can discover how individuals and races and the sexes differ in the amount of it which characterizes each; how this and that form of training influences it; how much of it is required for success in any given occupation, and how it is related to other desirable qualities, such as mental health, cheerfulness of disposition, leadership, industry, honesty, determination, public spirit, loyalty, and co-operativeness.

The greatest progress has been made in the case of abstract intelligence. If the reader will, without any preparation, turn to the four tests and spend exactly 90 seconds on A, 180 seconds on B, 180 seconds on C, and 480 seconds on D, he will have experienced a fair sample of a measurement of abstract intelligence. If, instead of these four "tests," he had done the ten or twelve of which they are a sample; and if, instead of doing only one form of each, he had done five or six forms on five or six days taken at random so as to represent his average condition of alertness; and if he had been brought up by English-speaking parents with the average opportunity of a child in America to-day—then his score would be an approximate measure of his abstract intelligence. If he had had special opportunities, or previous practice with the tests or others like them, a discount would be necessary before his score would represent his ability. Conversely, if he had had less than ordinary advantages. The score would be only approximate because any limited series of tests can test intelligence only as it operates in certain limited ways with limited problems. If John had devoted his mind chiefly to thinking with words, while James has devoted himself chiefly to thinking with chemical and electrical symbols, John will be overrated and James underrated by the series of four tests in our illustration. Also, if Mary has devoted her mind almost exclusively to one subject, say music, while Jane has devoted hers about equally to a thousand subjects, any dozen short tests are likely to give Jane a better chance than Mary. If the test were, "Choose the thing you know most about and tell what you know about it," Mary would have an unfair advantage. Also, if an individual possesses a very high degree of intelligence, the tests may be too easy and the score may represent the speed with which he can think rather than the total efficiency of his thinking.

Other limitations will occur to the critical reader. The fact remains, however, that, life being as it is, all the limitations do not prevent a well-chosen series of tests, if used with ordinary discretion and interpreted with ordinary common sense, from giving an approximate measure of an individual's abstract intelligence, at least during childhood and youth. Schools find them useful as a means of grading pupils; employment managers find them useful in hiring and placing employees; the army found it profitable so to test nearly two million of its recruits.

TEST A

If the two words of a pair mean the same or nearly the same, write "s" opposite them. If they mean the opposite or nearly the opposite, write "o" opposite.

1	wet—dry.	21	repress—restrain.
2	in—out.	22	bestow—confer.
3	hill—valley.	23	amenable—tractable.
4	allow—permit.	24	avert—prevent.
5	expand—contract.	25	reverence—veneration.
6	class—group.	26	fallacy—verity.
7	former—latter.	27	specific—general.
8	confess—admit.	28	pompous—ostentatious.
9	shy—timid.	29	accumulate—dissipate.
10	delicate—tender.	30	apathy—indifference.
11	extinguish—quench.	31	effeminate—virile.
12	cheerful—melancholy.	32	peculation—embezzlement.
13	accept—reject.	33	benign—genial.
14	concave—convex.	34	acme—climax.
15	lax—strict.	35	largess—donation.
16	assert—maintain.	36	innuendo—insinuation.
17	champion—advocate.	37	vesper—matin.
18	adapt—conform.	38	aphorism—maxim.
19	debase—exalt.	39	abjure—renounce.
20	dissension—harmony.	40	encomium—eulogy.

TEST B

In each of the lines below, the first two words are related to each other in some way. What you are to do in each line is to see what the relation is between the first two words, and underline the word in heavy type that is related in the same way to the third word. Begin with No. 1 and mark as many sets as you can in 180 seconds.

SAMPLES

sky—blue :: grass— **table green warm big**

fish—swims :: man— **paper time walks girls**

day—night :: white— **red black clean pure.**

1 gun—shoots :: knife— **run cuts hat bird.**

2 ear—hear :: eye— **table hand see play.**

3 dress—woman :: feathers— **bird neck feet bill.**

4 handle—hammer :: knob— **key room shut door.**

5 shoe—foot :: hat— **coat nose head collar.**

6 water—drink :: bread— **cake coffee eat pie.**

7 food—man :: gasoline— **gas oil automobile spark.**

8 eat—fat :: starve— **thin food bread thirsty.**

9 man—home :: bird— **fly insect worm nest.**

10 go—come :: sell— **leave buy money papers.**

11 peninsula—land :: bay— **boats pay ocean Massachusetts.**

12 hour—minute :: minute— **man week second short.**

13 abide—depart :: stay— **over home play leave.**

14 January—February :: June— **July May month year.**

15 bold—timid :: advance— **proceed retreat campaign soldier.**

16 above—below :: top— **spin bottom surface side.**

17 lion—animal :: rose— **smell leaf plant thorn.**

18 tiger—carnivorous :: horse— **cow pony buggy herbivorous.**

19 sailor—navy :: soldier— **gun cap hill army.**

20 picture—see :: sound— **noise music hear bark.**

21 success—joy :: failure— **sadness success fail work.**

22 hope—despair :: happiness— **frolic fun joy sadness.**

23 pretty—ugly :: attract— **fine repel nice draw.**

24 pupil—teacher :: child— **parent doll youngster obey.**

25 city—mayor :: army— **navy soldier general private.**

26 establish—begin :: abolish— **slavery wrong abolition end.**

27 December—January :: last— **least worst month first.**

28 giant—dwarf :: large— **big monster queer small.**

29 engine—caboose :: beginning **—commence cabin end train.**

30 dismal—cheerful :: dark— **sad stars night bright.**

31 quarrel—enemy :: agree— **friend disagree agreeable foe.**

32 razor—sharp :: hoe— **bury dull cuts tree.**

33 winter—summer :: cold— **freeze warm wet January.**

34 rudder—ship :: tail— **sail bird dog cat.**

35 granary—wheat :: library— **desk books paper librarian.**

36 tolerate—pain :: welcome— **pleasure unwelcome friends give.**

37 sand—glass :: clay— **stone hay bricks dirt.**

38 moon—earth :: earth— **ground Mars sun sky.**

39 tears—sorrow :: laughter— **joy smile girls grin.**

40 cold—ice :: heat— **lightning warm steam coat.**

TEST C

In lines 1 to 10 draw a fourth figure in each series such that the fourth figure is to the third as the second is to the first, as shown in examples A and B.

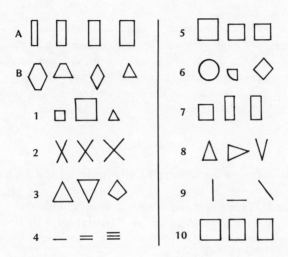

TEST D

On each line write the word or words that make the best meaning. Each sentence completed with entire correctness counts 3. A substantially correct completion will count 1. 2 will be subtracted from your score for each foolish or irrelevant completion of a sentence.

1. A body of_____entirely surrounded by_____is called
   an_____.
2. It is_____that a full-grown man should_____a ghost
   _____he is_____.
3. His friends,_____wished to dissuade him from this undertaking,
   asserted that_____he followed their advice_____would
   withdraw their support.
4. The struggle for_____among the lower_____has
   _____a commonplace of modern scientific thought.
5. Two_____of practical efficiency may be applied to the
   _____of the city: What does it provide for the people and
   what_____it_____the people.
6. And now_____all_____introduction_____
   us go_____at our question.

7. History_____ _____assisted and recorded memory.
8. Ideas distinguish_____from all animals, and all_____
   significant in_____history_____be_____
   back to ideas.
9. We know that power_____purify men in despotic governments, but we talk_____it_____ _____so
   in free_____.
10. The laws of nature are given_____my wishes.
11. Want of uniformity in private law and methods of_____is an
    evil_____minds will_____by different_____.
12. Let the class that_____itself to transportation, for example,
    _____working and the disastrous_____to the rest of
    the_____can scarcely_____imagined.

When an individual is measured by any of the standard tests, he is given a score in such terms as make it convenient to compare him with other individuals and with various requirements. For example, John Smith, aged 15 years, 0 months, may be reported as: "Mental age 12 yr., 0 mo.," or as, "Intelligence quotient (or IQ) 80," or as, "A 7-percentile intelligence," or as, "Int. = − 1.5 S. D." Mental age, 12 yr., 0 mo., means that John did as well in the tests as the average child of 12 years, 0 months. IQ = 80 means that John's mental age as shown by the tests was 80 percent of his chronological age. A 7-percentile intelligence means that 7 percent of the population (white) of age 15 years, 0 months, will do worse than John in the series of tests in question, and 93 percent will do better. Int. = − 1.5 S. D. means that John is below the average for his age to an extent of 1½ times a certain standard amount. Thus, the adult inmates of asylums for the feeble-minded are mostly under 9 years, 0 months, in mental age. Children with IQ's of 60 or below later fill such asylums. An IQ of 100 means average intelligence. Unless he has extraordinary energy and devotion, a boy whose IQ is under 100 will be unable to graduate from a reputable American college. Children selected by competent observers as extremely intelligent will be found to have IQ's from 120 to 160.

Measurements of mechanical intelligence have received much less attention from psychologists and are not yet standardized, but they are under way. Two samples from a set of such tests may be briefly illustrated. The first is a series of dismembered objects to be put together. It begins with something the average child of four can do, such as to put a nut on its bolt, and progresses by graded steps to something which only the 90-pencentile adult can do without special training, such as to put together the pieces of an electric pull-socket, or of a very intricate lock. The second consists of a set of materials out of which the individual tested is told to make something, or to make as many things as he can in an hour, or to make as good a cart, derrick, and boat as he can, or to use the material in some other prescribed way. The merit of the product which he produces is estimated in comparison with certain average performances of 6-year-, 8-year-, and 10-year-olds, and so on, under similar conditions.

Convenient tests of social intelligence are hard to devise. A child's wit in reading facial expression might perhaps be measured by his success in selecting from such photographs as those in Fig. 2 when asked, "Which lady would you ask to help you?" "Which lady is thinking?" "Which lady is worried?" "Which lady is saying 'I will *not*'?" and the like. It is doubtful however, whether pictures can be safely used in place of realities. And for most of the activities of intelligence in response to the behavior of human beings, a genuine situation with real persons is essential. Social intelligence shows itself abundantly in the nursery, on the playground, in barracks and factories and salesroom, but it eludes the formal standardized conditions of the testing laboratory. It requires human beings to respond to, time to adapt its responses, and face, voice, gesture, and mien as tools.

Figure 2.

Whether we consider one of these intelligences or the composite of the three, it appears that each human being is equipped by nature with a certain degree of intelligence, much as he is equipped by nature with a certain strength of body or form of finger-prints. Individuals differ by original nature in intelligence as in stature or eye color or countenance. It is true that good training improves and bad training injures the mind, as it does the body; that nature's gift may be lost by accident or decreased by disease, neglect, and misuse. As things are in America to-day, however, the net effect of these disturbing factors does not greatly disarrange the order or decrease the differences of individuals in respect to intellect. A boy who is the brightest of a thousand at the age of five will usually be in the top fifty of the thousand at the age of ten. The child who is at the lowest of a thousand at ten will almost never rise above the bottom hundred at fifteen. Kelley and others have traced the records of the same children year after year in school and found that in general a child keeps about the same position relative to other children in late as in early years. Terman's measurement of the abstract intelligence of the same children (over a hundred of them) at two periods five years or more apart shows very great constancy. Intelligence grows with general growth from early childhood to adult years, but its growth is in proportion to what it already is. A child holds his place in comparison with other children nearly as closely after five years as after five days.

Because of the recency of the science of mental measurements, we lack tests of the same individual at 16 years of age, 18 years of age, 20, 22, 24, and so on. It may be that certain of the children who seemed essentially dull were only growing slowly; and these may catch up in adult years, and some of the children with high IQs at 10 or 15 may have merely "got their intelligence" early, as some children get their teeth early; these may sink back relatively. It may also be that the new trends of mind due to sex and adult ambitions will act differently on different individuals, stimulating intelligence in different degrees and even subtracting from it in some cases. As a rule, however, those who progress most rapidly go farthest; and those who have the most intelligence are least likely to have it lessened by the distracting force of sex or display or rivalry. Intelligence probably does not fluctuate very much more than fifteen to fifty than from five to fifteen. An individual's intelligence compared with that of other individuals of his age is, within limits, a stable, permanent characteristic of him. It can be at least roughly measured and the measurement used to prophesy and direct his career.

If we take a group of individuals and measure their success in life, as students in school, or as money-makers, or as lawyers, or as carpenters, or as teachers of children, and then measure their intellect by some suitable series of tests and observations, we can determine how closely success in any line goes with the degree of intelligence shown by the test-score.

For example, consider the significance of abstract intelligence for success in schoolwork. If we take a thousand children twelve years old we
may measure the success of each in schoolwork by the grade he has
reached and by the quality of work he is doing in that grade. If we measure
these same children with an adequate series of tests made up of giving the
opposites of words, supplying missing words in sentences, solving practical
problems, following directions, and putting facts in their proper relations,
we have as a result a diagram which shows the *resemblance* or *correlation*
between intelligence score and success in school in the individuals in question. The amount of the resemblance—the closeness of the correlation—is
measured with great exactitude by a *coefficient* of *correlation*, called r, a
number derived by suitable calculation from the thousand pairs of scores.
This number varies from $+ 1.00$, or perfect correlation, to $- 1.00$, perfect
antagonism. Such coefficients of correlation are the shorthand in which
science sums up the extent to which two things go together. The significance of intelligence for success in a given activity of life is measured by
the coefficient of correlation between them.

Scientific investigations of these matters is just beginning; and it is a
matter of great difficulty and expense to measure the intelligence of, say,
a thousand clergymen, and then secure sufficient evidence to rate them
accurately for their success as ministers of the Gospel. Consequently, one
can report no final, perfectly authoritative results in this field. One can
only organize reasonable estimates from the various partial investigations
that have been made. Doing this, I find the following:

Intelligence and success in the elementary schools, $r = + .80$.
Intelligence and success in high-school and colleges in the case of those
    who go, $r = + .60$; but if all were forced to try to do this advanced
    work, the correlation would be $+ .80$ or more.
Intelligence and salary, $r = .35$.
Intelligence and success in athletic sports, $r = + .25$.
Intelligence and character, $r = + .40$ or more.
Intelligence and popularity, $r = + .20$.

Whatever be the eventual exact findings, two sound principles are
illustrated by our provisional list. First, there is always some resemblance;
intellect always counts. Second, the resemblance varies greatly; intellect
counts much more in some lines than in others.

The first fact is in part a consequence of a still broader fact or principle
—namely, that in human nature good traits go together. To him that hath
a superior intellect is given also on the average a superior character; the
quick boy is also in the long run more accurate; the able boy is also more
industrious. There is no principle of compensation whereby a weak intellect is offset by a strong will, a poor memory by good judgment, or a lack
of ambition by an attractive personality. Every pair of such supposed com-

pensating qualities that have been investigated has been found really to show correspondence. Popular opinion has been misled by attending to striking individual cases which attracted attention partly because they were really exceptions to the rule. The rule is that desirable qualities are positively correlated. Intellect is good in and of itself, and also for what it implies about other traits.

The second fact—that intellect varies in utility according to the work to be done—has permitted a very wide diversity in opinions about its utility. Ordinary observation of life is beset by such variety and complexity that persons of generally good judgment can be found who will rate the importance of intellect for success in, say, business, or art, or politics, almost all the way from 0 to 100 percent. Only the painstaking investigation of each such problem can give the correct answer.

The correct answers will put an end to numerous superstitions and fancies about human achievement. About a generation ago America was obsessed by the superstition that money-making had a correlation of from +.80 to +1.00 with general intelligence and good-will, so that to get a representative of the people in Congress, or a trustee for a university, or a vestryman of a church, or a member of a commission on public health or charity or schools or playgrounds, you should look about for a man who had made a great deal of money. To-day the world is being assailed by the much more foolish superstition that money-making is correlated 0 with general intelligence and about −.80 to −1.00 with good-will, the maker of great profits being no more fit intellectually to run his business than his barber is, and being diabolically eager to amass dollars at the cost of misery to anybody who gets in his way and to all innocent bystanders.

Exact and complete knowledge about the correlations of mental traits will be of enormous importance for the utilization of man-power by schools, churches, employers, and the state. When we have such exact knowledge, we shall be able to make up a bill of specifications of the sort of intellect and character required for a certain job, select men efficiently instead of haphazard, and train them according to their individual needs instead of indiscriminately.

The present waste is great, both in efficiency and in happiness. W. P., whose IQ is 83, is being forced through high-school to college by his father. W. P. gets nothing but confusion and misery from his high-school work and is growing a little more inactive, sullen, and idle each year. He wants and has wanted to be a gardener, and could probably succeed and be useful to the world as such. There is not one chance in a hundred that he will graduate from college or get any good from college studies. L. C. was promoted to be foreman of the shop merely because he was the most skilful workman. He possessed very little social intelligence and was unhappy and inefficient in the new job. The management, realizing that it was to blame, continued him at a foreman's salary, but gave him a special mechanical job. P. S., a field salesman of extraordinary success by virtue of his great popularity, energy, and personal tact in face-to-face conferences, was promoted to be in charge of planning sales campaigns and selecting and directing the staff of salesmen. He failed, being only mediocre in general intelligence, and unable to understand the plans of the manufacturing department or teach his subordinates. In selecting these, also, he sometimes mistook "sportiness" for popularity and pleasant manners for real tact.

Knowledge of the correlations of mental traits will also be a protection against many unsound, impracticable theories of business and government. Consider, for example, the correlation between intellect and character. Dickson and Terman found, in the case of little children, that the IQ of abstract intelligence had correlations with the teachers' ratings for persistence, conscientiousness, co-operativeness, industry, courage, dependability, and unselfishness of from $+.30$ to $+.50$, with an average of $+.41$. Chassell has found, in the case of college students, correlations between intelligence and unselfishness, loyalty, justice, courage, self-control, reliability, and activity for social welfare, averaging $+.40$. Woods, rating some six hundred members of European royal families for intellect and for character, finds a correlation of about $+.40$. No impartial student of the matter has found any contrary result. The abler persons in the world in the long run are the more clean, decent, just and kind.

To this feature of human nature which has tied good-will toward men to ability, a large proportion of the blessings which the common man enjoys to-day are due. The brains and ability of the world have been, and still are, working for the profit of others. If Pasteur had been of mean and brutal nature he could have kept his first discoveries as a trade secret, extorted a fortune in fees, and lived in sensuous idleness, leaving the world without his still more important later work. Flexner or Carrel could poison their enemies and rivals except for the tradition of justice and generosity which the positive correlation between intellect and morality has made a part of scientific work, and which their own natures gladly maintain.

The correlation between intellect and character has in fact within a few hundred years produced so strong a body of customs that the world rather expects a gifted man of science to be a public benefactor. It would have been greatly shocked if William James had given up psychology to establish a lucrative organization of spiritualistic mediums over the country, or if the Mayo brothers had retired from medicine to direct a chain of Mayo drug-stores!

The peasants of France did not themselves extort democracy from Louis's autocracy. They were led by intelligent aristocrats. The Russian serfs did not secure their own freedom. Africans did not abolish the slave-trade. In at least three out of four social reforms the reform is initiated and put through largely by leaders from above, men of high intelligence who act, often against their own selfish interests, for the common good. Many men of great intelligence will, of course, be unjust and cruel tyrants; the correlation is .40 or .50, not 1.00; the direction of the world's affairs by men who were guaranteed to be both of great ability and of fine impersonal devotion to the world's welfare, would be best of all. But, in the long run, it has paid the "masses" to be ruled by intelligence. Furthermore, the natural processes which give power to men of ability to gain it and keep it are not, in their results, unmoral. Such men are, by and large, of superior intelligence, and consequently of somewhat superior justice and good-will. They act, in the long run, not against the interest of the world, but for it. What is true in science and government seems to hold good in general for manufacturing, trade, art, law, education, and religion. It seems entirely safe to predict that the world will get better treatment by trusting its fortunes to its 95- or 99-percentile intelligences than it would get by itself. The argument for democracy is not that it gives power to all men without distinction, but that it gives greater freedom for ability and character to attain power.

CHAPTER 7

Toward a Differentiated Curriculum Based on Class, Race and Sex

Reacting negatively to Lester F. Ward's repeated insistence that the intellectual resources of all people have not yet been tapped, Edward L. Thorndike attacked Ward's thought as "intellectual communism." He challenged his opponent to turn to a more realistic, practical view of the curriculum and the educational process. Ward, he said, ought to try to teach six-year olds the same thing in the same way and see the results.[1] Arguing the practical case for individual differences, Thorndike proposed a differentiated curriculum based on tested abilities. In the name of education for individual differences, the child was to be given a curriculum appropriate to his presumed abilities which, in turn, locked him into the social class from which he came. The ideological perspective of the professional "educator" on the social order had a direct bearing on the content, methods and curriculum design in the educational state. One of the great educational myths of the twentieth century has been the belief that a differentiated curriculum based on assumed individual abilities and needs would result in increased choice on the part of the individual. From the very beginning of the century, the differentiated curriculum has served to channel, control and limit the choice of individuals.

One of the great differences between nineteenth- and twentieth-century educational practice lies in the differentiated curriculum of the twentieth century. The differentiated curriculum, created by educational "professionals," objectified the student's abilities and channeled him towards

[1] See Thorndike's review of Ward's *Applied Sociology* in *The Bookman*. Vol. XXIV, Nov. 1906. (New York: Dodd, Mead and Company), pp. 290–294.

an occupation.[2] Repeatedly, Thorndike, Terman, Freeman and others justified the differentiated curriculum on the grounds of (1) making the system more efficient and (2) protecting the child from failure. Blacks and immigrant children were thus protected from failure. Freedom to be successful is, of course, not freedom unless it runs the risk of failure. B. F. Skinner was quite correct when he suggested that the kind of psychology which has dominated the American curriculum in the educational state leads one *Beyond Freedom and Dignity*. It, in fact, does. The current efficiency craze in American education involving behavioral modification techniques, systems analysis, performance-based instruction, accountability, etc., in many ways, is but an extension of the earlier efficiency movement[3] and also involves the same problems of objectification, manipulation, choice and freedom.

Thorndike knew the educational state which he helped create was serving definite class interests. These interests, however, were acceptable because, in his thinking, they represented the best. Thorndike never seemed to lose sight of his ideological model of the "good" society toward which most of his efforts were directed. In *Your City*,[4] he developed a "G" scale, or what he called a "Goodness" scale, for objectively determining the value of the 310 largest cities of the United States. In line with his racial bias he found that, "A high percentage of Negro families is a bad sign. This is true for all groups of cities. In all groups the fewer the Negro families, the better the score of the city in G and P." [5] Other criteria he listed in a later work for determining the "Goodness" of these cities are the following:

1. Percentage of persons eighteen to twenty attending schools.
2. Average wage of workers in factories.
3. Frequency of home ownership (per capita number of homes owned).
4. Per capita support of the Y.M.C.A.
5. Per capita number of automobiles.
6. Per capita circulation of *Better Homes and Gardens, Good House-keeping*, and the *National Geographic*.[6]

[2] For a more complete picture of the social effects of the differentiated curriculum, see Edward Krug, *The Shaping of the American High School*, Volume 2, 1920–1941. (Madison: University of Wisconsin Press, 1972).

[3] For the earlier movement, see Raymond E. Callahan, *Education and the Cult of Efficacy*. (Chicago: University of Chicago Press, 1962).

[4] Edward L. Thorndike, *Your City*. (New York: Harcourt, Brace & Co., 1939).

[5] *Ibid.*, p. 77. G stands for the goodness scale, while P stands for personal qualities.

[6] Edward L. Thorndike, *Human Nature and the Social Order*. (New York: Macmillan Co., 1940), p. 428. This last work by Thorndike, in many ways, suggests approaches to social problems which were later developed by such "think tank" operations as Rand Corporation and Systems Development Corporation.

Thorndike's model of the "good" society reflected the racial and social values of middle America bent on escaping the Black migration to the Northern metropolitan centers by moving to the better homes and gardens of the suburbs after World War II. No doubt his success as an educational leader rested heavily on the fact that his personal values very much coincided with the basic value structure of that well-washed white middle class which dominated the educational state in America.

Unlike Ward, who made an impassioned plea for equality between the sexes, Thorndike believed that men were more variable, and thus, one might find more genius among the male rather than the female of the species. He argued that while, in general, women may be as intelligent as men and can usually profit from similar kinds of education, the variability factor accounts for the disproportionate number of males to be found in graduate work. Women, he believed, are instinctively different from men and that those differences should be taken into account in the guidance and tracking of women through the educational state toward their occupational destiny.

> Two instincts are worthy of special attention. The most striking differences in instinctive equipment consists in the strength of the fighting instinct in the male and of the nursing instinct in the female. No one will doubt that men are more possessed by the instinct to fight, to be the winner in games and serious contests, than are women; nor that women are more possessed than men by the instinct to nurse, to care for and fuss over others, to relieve, comfort and console. And probably no serious student of human nature will doubt that these are matters of original nature. The out-and-out physical fighting for the sake of combat is pre-eminently a male instinct and the resentment at mastery, the zeal to surpass and the general joy at activity in mental as well as physical matters seem to be closely correlated with it. It has been common talk of women's 'dependence.' This is, I am sure, only an awkward name for less resentment at mastery. The actual nursing of the young seems likewise to involve equally unreasoning tenderness to pet, coddle, and 'do for' others. . . . The fighting instinct is in fact the cause of a very large amount of the world's intellectual endeavor. The financier does not think merely for money nor the scientist for truth nor the theologian to save souls. Their intellectual efforts are aimed in great measure to outdo the other man, to subdue nature, to conquer assent. The maternal instinct in its turn is the chief source of woman's superiorities in the moral life. The virtues in which she excels are not so much due to either any general moral superiority or any set of special moral talents as to her original impulses to relieve, comfort and console.[7]

[7] Edward L. Thorndike, *Educational Psychology, Briefer Course.* (New York: Teachers College, Columbia University, 1914), pp. 350–351. This book was designed specifically for teachers.

Since the social demands on women are to serve and the intrinsic nature of women is to "pet, coddle, and 'do for' others;" while the intrinsic nature of man is to compete and overpower; it logically followed, for Thorndike, that men and women ought to receive a partially differentiated curriculum which channels women into those occupations appropriate to their nature such as nursing, teaching and medicine; while men should be channeled into the more competitive world of statesmanship, philosophy and scientific research.[8] The social roles of men and women and virtually every social group were thus rationalized within the educational state in behavioral terms which pointed toward an occupation or a place within the social system.

Just as the social inferiority of immigrants and blacks was reflected in the curriculum content, so too, was the inferior status of women. Much children's literature still reflects a social-psychological profile of women as inferior to men. Here again, is a problem similar to that of IQ and the lower social class. First, the group is classified as having certain characteristics; then they are treated as if they have those characteristics; and, ultimately, they are tested to prove that they, indeed, have those characteristics. Given Thorndike's perceived role for women as a model, it makes sense to look at children's literature. In one study in which 2,760 stories were examined in 134 books, the following ratios were determined:

Boy-centered stories to girl-centered stories — 5:2
Adult male main characters to adult female main characters — 3:1
Male biographies to female biographies — 6:1
Male animal stories to female animal stories — 2:1
Male folk or fantasy stories to female folk or fantasy stories — 4:1[9]

The qualities of ingenuity, creativity, bravery, perseverance, achievement, adventurousness, curiosity, sportsmanship, generativity, autonomy, and self-respect are model behaviors reflected in the literature to which the children are introduced. The odds *against* the female being projected in one of these positive roles is four to one.[10]

The sexist characteristics of the current children's literature are premised on assumptions similar to those which Thorndike and others held with regard to both the place that women ought to hold in society and what they assumed to be her true nature. While the same process

[8] Edward L. Thorndike, *Individuality*. (Boston, New York, and Chicago: Houghton Mifflin Co., 1911), pp. 30–34.
[9] See the pamphlet prepared by A Task Force of the Central New Jersey Chapter of the National Organization for Women, *Dick & Jane as Victims: Sex Stereotyping in Children's Readers*. (Princeton, N.J.: Women on Words and Images, 1972), pp. 6–7.
[10] *Ibid.*, pp. 7–8.

seemed to have occurred for all children, the children of the privileged classes enjoyed the kind of education appropriate for their place in life, and the children of the repressed received the kind of education appropriate for their lesser position in life. The profile of the repressed had behind it, not only the force of empirical evidence, but also the sanction of the "scientific" professional expert who would correct what Thorndike called the pseudo-thinking of the half-educated man.

The world suffered, Thorndike believed, from too many half-educated men. Such men deluded themselves into thinking that they could and should be able to understand their world. The solution was to be found in cultivating a reliance on the professional expert. Thorndike argued: "The cure is twofold, consisting of the displacement of pseudo-thinking by real expertness on the one hand or by intelligent refusal to think on the other." [11] If the common man would only learn intelligently to refuse to think while he accepted the advice of the professional expert, a better-ordered meritocratic society could emerge. Perhaps the fact that his conception of the lower-class poor, the southern European immigrant, the blacks, or women went relatively unchallenged was a testimony to the public's "intelligently refusing to think," and thus accepting the authority of the "scientific" professional expert. On the other hand, it seems more likely that Thorndike's stereotyped profiles of repressed people came so close to the conventional ideology of the rising middle class that most of the assumptions involved in his profiles must have seemed self-evident and, therefore, went unquestioned. Not until that ideology began to shift and some no longer believed in the inherent inferiority of women, blacks or immigrants did both the profile and practice begin to be questioned.

Repeatedly, because of his hierarchial view of the good society and the place of genius in that society, Thorndike called for increasing reliance on the knowledgeable expert for establishment of policy formation within the educational state. Forty years before "think tank" centers, Thorndike was arguing the case of rule by the knowledgeable experts.

> Wherever there is the expert—the man or woman who has mastered the facts and principles on which the best present practice in a certain field is based, and who can adapt this best present practice to special circumstances ingeniously—should we not, in fact, let him do our thinking for us in that field? [12]

A functional rationalization of the student in the educational state depended on the development of a kind of expert professionalism clothed in the rhetoric of science serving what they believed to be the community.

[11] Edward L. Thorndike, "The Psychology of the Half-Educated Man," *Harper's*, April 1920, p. 670.
[12] *Ibid.*

The Psychology of the Half-Educated Man

Edward L. Thorndike

A score of supposedly well-educated men and women were asked to which figure the distance from Petrograd to Vladivostok was nearest— 400 miles, 1,400 miles, 4,000 miles, 14,000 miles. Eight did not answer at all. Two answered 400 miles; two gave other wrong answers. They were asked whether the product of $a + b$ and $a - b$ was $a^2 - 2ab + b^2$, $a^2 - b^2$, $2a - ab + b^2$, or $a(a^2 - b^2)$. Two answered correctly. Eleven did not answer at all. Seven gave wrong answers. They were asked whether the two words in each of these pairs meant nearly the same or nearly the opposite: since—before; bankrupt—solvent; incumbent—obligatory; succinct —concise. Only half had the four correct, and seven made actual errors. These were leading business and professional men and their wives.

The readers of *Harper's Magazine* probably represent the top one or two percent of our population in respect to education, but if they will spend two minutes on these four tasks: Add .07, 7.94, and 1.6; add 1/8 and 5/6; subtract 1.392010 from 7.040201; subtract 4/5 from 9/10, they will show only about half success. One in four of them will not know whether the Ten Commandments are called the decagon or the decalogue or the decament or the decemvirate; or whether light travels in jagged, straight, or wavy lines.

A man need not be ashamed to confess ignorance of such matters, perhaps. One can live happily and usefully not knowing whether Vladivostok is a city, a Bolshevik general, or a college fraternity. For a man to be half-educated in the sense that only a part of him is educated is a relatively innocent defect, provided the man is himself aware of it. When an uneducated part of him needs education he can be aware of the fact and provide for it.

For a man to think his errors are knowledge or to lack all sense of sure distinction between knowledge and ignorance is a more serious matter. One who really thinks that solvent means bankrupt will be misled by his reading of financial items; and a high-school graduate who is sure that $(a + b) \times (a - b) = 2a^2 - ab + b^2$ will probably be willing to be sure that black is white, or that war is profitable, or that all the troubles of the present are due to the Democratic party (or the Republican party, if his predilections direct). Such a man is often only half-educated all over.

In the face of the details and complexities of modern science and technology and art, it is the fate of all to be half-educated in the sense of having large areas of mind uncultivated, many problems answered only by a question mark. And such has always been the fate of the great majority of men.

There is nothing new, and no great public danger in this. We have only in such cases to turn to the doctor, lawyer, engineer, priest, or other specialist who does know. The world has, even in its most successful epochs, got along with its population half-educated, or more truly one-fiftieth educated, in this sense.

In proportion, however, as the man's mind is incompetent all over, in proportion as he has in general only an amateurish semi-knowledge and does not realize its inferiority, there is public danger. Such a man is likely to try (and fail) to understand the specialist instead of obeying him. He does not "know his place" intellectually. He knows enough to criticize and abandon the customs of his fathers, but not enough to preserve their merits or to improve their defective parts. He maintains only a pseudo-independence of mind, being at the mercy of clever charlatans who have an interest in misleading him.

The psychology of such half-educated men and women is perhaps especially instructive at this time, for there are so many of them. There seem to be more than the world has ever had to endure at any one time, though this may be only an appearance. At all events, they represent an intellectual inefficiency and perversion whose cure and prevention are a main part of sound policy in a democracy. And if they have not actually increased in America in the generation past, they have at least not decreased in proportion to the increase in general leisure and the spread of public education. Let us consider, then, this disease of half-education, pseudo-intellect, "fake" thinking.

One of its main features is a belief in magic. Although the great majority of the half-educated would indignantly deny that they believed in alchemy, witchcraft, fairies, or elves, down deep in their make-up there is an active, if unconscious, faith in magic, an expectation that you may with good luck occasionally "beat the game," a willingness to excuse yourself for failure on the ground that "things went against you," a superstition that chance can be induced to favor you this time. A mother says, "I don't see why Mary caught the whooping-cough from Nellie Ames: they were together only a few minutes," meaning that the gods should have been reasonably generous to her and her child. A business man loses ten thousand dollars because of failure to insure his goods and argues: "I ought not to be blamed for that. I had paid insurance a hundred times. Surely I had a right to expect a little luck." A boy thinks that he will pass an examination on a subject in only half of which he is competent. The Germans blame America for disappointing their hopes, instead of blaming themselves for having foolish hopes. The employer thinks that discontent in his factory will blow over, but it doesn't, and a consideration of all the facts would have shown that it couldn't. The labor leader thinks that the A B C's will surely strike in sympathy, though the actual facts, minus luck and fairies, prove conclusively that they probably won't. The communist really looks to some *deus ex machina* to supply new motives to replace the motives of ownership and independence. He is so sure that state ownership of property is desirable that in his heart of hearts he expects some secret powers of the universe to make it succeed, once he gets it started.

Since hardly any one is fully educated, fully rational, entirely sound in his thinking, hardly any one is entirely free from this resort to magic. A most successful man and, as men go, a most acute thinker, explained European history as a result of a progressive movement producing a reaction, which in turn produced a progressive movement, quite as if a progressive movement were a fairy godmother and reaction a wicked ogre of a folk-tale. Some sociologists of the benevolent sort discuss evolution or development or progress in ways that are defensible only if evolution or progress is a tutelary deity holding human welfare up, and even shoving it gently forward, when all other forces would let it slip back.

During the war this subterranean faith in magic played a large part in the universal cursing of the then Kaiser. Men and women reviled him not only because they felt hate, and because it was a cheap and comfortable way of being patriotic, but also probably because they really thought their curses would hurt him and his cause. Ten thousand years ago the best-educated man would rather be soundly beaten or heavily fined than cursed with a proper magical formula; and this fear of the spoken word persists in the half-educated of to-day.

In the present hopes of the manual workers to gain compensation for the discomforts in which the war involved them magic intrudes amusingly. Two out of four employees half regard the employer as a jinn who can command dollars at his own sweet will. If you can cajole or frighten the jinn he will get more dollars for you out of his magic pot. This fantasy has been counteracted not so much by any clear sense of the facts in the case as by the long-established habits of expecting a plumber or brass-worker, or what not, to receive about so much. The war disturbed these habits by its emergency wages, and gave magical fancies their chance.

The fully educated man knows that nothing happens without a natural, matter-of-fact cause, and forms his hopes and fears and acts in harmony with this knowledge. He controls things, other men, and himself by bringing adequate causes into play; leaving no links in the chain to be forged by fairies. If he wins he knows why, and, even in losing, he learns. The half-educated man works in the dark of luck and magic. So even his successes may work for failure, teaching him nothing, or lies.

A second main feature of the half-educated mind is its restriction of thought to self-justification. The really educated man directs his feelings and actions by reason. The half-educated man lets his passions and desires direct his thinking. He thinks chiefly to justify himself in something he wishes or has done. Since he likes to play golf, he thinks how good it is for his health. Since he likes to drive an automobile, he thinks how pleasant it is to go out with all the family. Since he dislikes music, he thinks how much time and money are spent on music that might better be spent in healthy outdoor games. Since he has failed to make money, he considers that money-making is a greedy, materialistic sort of career.

The psychologist calls such thinking in defense of one's selfish interests "rationalizing," though "irrationalizing" would perhaps describe it better. We have some desire or aversion and set our reason at work to defend or "rationalize" it. Led by some motive, we have acted in a certain way and set our thinking to work to defend it, not only to others, but to ourselves. All this may be quite innocent, as in the case of the infant son of William James. The child had played gladly with frogs up to a certain date, and then was seized with a pronounced aversion for them. He would not touch one, and when urged said that he could not take it because it was too heavy! So a woman urged to handle a mouse might think of it as too nasty. So saloon-keepers may quite honestly think prohibition is too great an infringement of personal rights; so the man who is comfortably fixed in the world regards any change in it as too radical.

The fully educated man can and, if he chooses, does think impersonally, being led by the naked facts, regardless of the consequences to his own comfort or self-esteem. His observations and logic are not harnessed to his hopes and fears, but are free to follow the trail of truth wherever it leads. The half-educated man thinks only in self-defense.

There are two ways of achieving a satisfying self-respect in this world. One is to meet the world squarely, conquer its difficulties, make friends with its beneficent forces, meet its requirements so far as you can, and get, so far as the world will give it to you, genuine payment in the blessings of health, work, food, friendship, love, mastery, approval, and pride in what the world thinks of you. The man who does this loses nothing by thinking of things as they are, since it is from things as they are that he wrests durable satisfactions of life. He sees himself as others see him, sees others as they are, and, adapting himself to them and the physical world as best he can, gets what he can. What he does get is genuine. Such a man has at least one element of a real education—he has learned to face the world and win or lose on merit.

The other way is to retreat within your own soul whenever it is convenient, avoiding the world's difficulties, blaming it when its requirements are beyond you, and paying yourself by excuses, hopes, explanations, resignation, and the like if the world does not give you the genuine pleasure, power, and prominence that you crave. If you do not get a job, you tell yourself that you are too independent in spirit. If you fail in courtship, you decide that she was not your real love. If you lack friends, you are consoled by thinking that your individuality is too fine to be appreciated by the common herd. You preserve your self-respect, not by genuine success in the real world, but by retreat to an imaginary world which you construct in such fashion that you can respect yourself. The man who does this may be satisfied, but his wife, if intelligent, cannot be, and he is a nuisance to his neighbors and acquaintances. Such men are found among graduates of colleges, but they are of the half-educated—they have not learned to live and win in the real world.

A third characteristic of the half-educated man is his inability to think a problem through. He is like a chessplayer who fails to consider all the possible replies to his attack, and to consider any one of them more than a few moves ahead. As a merchant, he buys goods that attract him without thinking whether his customers want such goods or ought to want them. As a manufacturer, he hires a beginner for his factory at eight dollars if she will take eight, nine if she asks for nine, ten if she insists on ten, promotes nobody until he is forced to, and then is surprised that there is so bad a spirit in his factory. As a farmer, he works ten hours a day for a dozen cows without ever thinking out whether the cows are supporting him or he is supporting the cows. As a big business director, he votes for bonuses, installs safety devices, hires social workers, and provides amusements, when the real trouble is the petty tyranny of foremen and the brutality of the thugs who are his works-policemen.

One can hardly ride two hours in a trolley-car or train with workingmen without hearing one of them, perhaps in the course of otherwise sagacious remarks, say, "Why shouldn't every working-man receive his fifty dollars a week or his hundred dollars a week?" If you reply, "For the same reason that he can't get fifty eggs a week or fifty quarts of milk a week," he will see no point. If you ask him, "How much is fifty dollars or a hundred dollars multiplied by four hundred million?" he will think you are mildly insane. Since it is easy for him to see where one workman—to wit, himself—could get a hundred dollars a week, and how he could get it without any social or financial miracle, he fails to carry thought on to ask where forty thousand million dollars a week is to come from in the world.

Fully half of our citizens regard it as a mixture of glory and crime that certain men should have great wealth. When they day-dream or read the Sunday supplements they admire the glory. When they read yellow journal editorials or go to the polls they resent the crime. Yet thought pushed just one step further would show that the rich man's crime or glory can be only in how he got wealth or what he does with it.

The educated man may not have thought out any of the matters which I have been mentioning; his mind may not have tackled them at all. If it did tackle them, however, it would fight through to a finish. It would see the issue clear to the end, if it could; and, if it couldn't, it would not claim to have settled the issue. The educated man is full of question marks, but when he does give answers they are bitter-end answers. The half-educated man thinks till he reaches some conclusion that sounds well or otherwise strikes his fancy, and then makes peace with the issue.

We can sum up these three qualities of the half-educated man by a homely analogy. Suppose that a man, who needed to go from New York to Chicago, instead of buying his ticket, finding the train and boarding it, and staying in it till he reached Chicago, should sit in the station hoping that somebody would offer him a private car! Suppose that, having finally bought a ticket to Chicago and boarded the train, he finds that it is the train to Boston, and, instead of realizing his blunder, thinks, "It's good to go by way of Boston, so as to see my mother-in-law!" Suppose that, misled by the look of the station, he gets off at Cleveland, in spite of the fact that he should know that he has ten hours more to travel!

Pseudo-thinking must probably be endured to a considerable extent until a far better human race is bred. Some of it, however, can be cured. The cure is twofold, consisting of the displacement of pseudo-thinking by real expertness on the one hand or by intelligent refusal to think on the other.

Expert thinking cannot be expected of many men outside of a limited field. Within the limits of human capacity we can have as much expert thinking as we will pay for, in time and money. All our medical schools or business schools can be made to teach the best practices in medicine or business, instead of some antiquated, outworn customs, if we will pay the cost. There is the same cure for plumbers or printers or teachers or electrical engineers or salesmen or cooks who now blunder in thinking about their respective problems that there is for children who think that 4×4 is 8, or that $15 \div 1/3$ is 5, or that half of a half of a half is twice as much as a quarter of a quarter of a quarter. In his special field, the size and character of which will vary with his talents, a man may be made a competent thinker. The educated man should be taught to think with approximately 100 per cent efficiency in his share of the world's job.

Outside that field the intelligent procedure for most of us is to refuse to think, spending our energy rather in finding the expert in the case and learning from him. That is what sagacious men already do almost universally in matters like surgery, chemistry, mathematics, or seismology. They are doing it widely in such less recognized fields of expertness as building construction, philanthropy, advertising, and education. They are beginning to do it in fields that not long ago were supposed to be problems anybody could properly think out, such as the selection of one's employees, the choice of occupation for one's children, the planning of a city's government, the tariff, the expenditure of public money, or the regulation of public morals.

Wherever there is the expert—the man or woman who has mastered the facts and principles on which the best present practice in a certain field is based, and who can adapt this best present practice to special circumstances ingeniously—should we not let him be our guide? Should we not, in fact, let him do our thinking for us in that field? Thought is too precious to be wasted in dilettantism; the issues of the twentieth century are too complex and difficult to be played with by amateurs. The general common sense that was admirable for the tasks of the town meeting of our fathers is hopelessly inadequate for the municipal problems of to-day. It is likely to be an easy prey to the selfishness of politicians, the seductiveness of salesmen, and the enthusiasm of fanatics. Our thought, if we trust it too far, will in fact not be our thinking, but only the ready-made conclusions that have been sold to us by somebody. The question is whether we shall buy from somebody who will play on our vanity and prejudices or from a reputable dealer. The educated man should know when not to think, and where to buy the thinking he needs.

Dick & Jane as Victims: Sex Stereotyping in Children's Readers

Women on Words and Images

One of the prime functions of literature and poetry is to make some sense out of the chaos in which human beings live. But readers consistently duck the real issues confronting young lives. Little girls (and boys) seldom have to face grizzly bears or wolves these days. But females frequently have to overcome ridicule and discouragement over gender prejudice. The readers give girls even more to overcome by constantly belittling them.

And what are the subjects so visibly absent from these books?

Challenges and Conflicts. Absent from the readers are fathers and mothers backing their children in their quest for selfhood. Missing are fathers complimenting their daughters on their intelligence and perseverence, rather than their looks. Absent are family moments of mutual appreciation, of love between parents, and non-romantic affection between people. Glossed over are the inner and outer conflicts and moments of indecision that are inevitably part of the human condition. Ignored are one-parent families, adopted children, divorced and/or fighting parents. Missing are *realistic* stories about how to make friends in a new situation. Silent are the readers about the facts that some people remain poor and hungry and that everyone has to cope with aging. Even the wisdom and peace that can come with old age is barely alluded to.

Girls Do Not Excel. Girls are not even shown excelling in school work, something they actually do better than boys. The supposedly fragile male ego is often protected in this way at the expense of girls. The readers present a twisted view that happiness for girls lies chiefly in giving happiness to boys and men. Success, excitement, confidence, and status must be derived from association with the "powerful" sex. Even the real world, prejudiced as it is, allows girls more scope than this. In the readers, girls must take on every trait left over after boys are assigned theirs. Girls are innundated with messages that boys are doers and that girls must stand back passively if they are to remain feminine. Nothing in the readers encourages girls to persevere to complete a lengthy task from beginning to end or to tackle something difficult. Short, mindless tasks like daily domestic work do not lead to future growth or fulfillment.

Boys Are Multidimensional. Boys get a potent message that they are superior human beings above household chores. They learn through countless "rites of passage" stories that they will one day become the sex upon whom the workings of the world depend. No comparable attempt is made to build up the expectations of girls, to create esteem and optimism about their future possibilities. Boys are given a perfectionistic model of the multi-dimensional human being. Not everybody, not even all males, can be superheroes. Ironically, intermixed with the stories of hard work and use of skills are Walter Mitty and dreams-of-glory tales with magical solutions and happy windfalls. To be a boy is to be one of the lucky breed. The readers contain a stronger taboo against boys being dependent (sissies!) at *any* age than they do against *young* girls breaking out of their mold (tomboys) a little bit. Girls must abruptly rout out the so-called masculine component of themselves when they become teenagers, but boys must never give away to the so-called feminine component. This is partly carried out as we noted, by showing boys of all ages alone and away from home, courageously coping with anything that comes along. They never cry; they need no one.

Man over Nature. There are numerous stories about men or boys sub-duing or conquering nature. Little is said about learning to appreciate and protect the natural environment. In a multitude of stories, males bend nature to their wills. Yet it is clear, in this new age of environmental awareness, that men and women will have to learn to live in harmony with nature rather than run roughshod over it. Can our young conquerers be redirected once they gain maturity?

Sexism, No Respecter of Race. Indians are the race we meet most often in these stories and the readers are very ambivalent about them. Now they are courageous, marvelously skilled at meeting the challenges of the wild, and the friend of the white man. Now they are irrational, treacherous, and enemy of the white man. The terms "good Indian" and "bad Indian" are used here exclusively in the sense of what's good or bad for the white settlers, who only once in all these stories go on trial—speaking figuratively—for *their* treatment of the Indians.

But there is no ambiguity about who is the bravest sex of all. Indian males are as achievement-oriented as any palefaced male. The Indian girl, no matter how resourceful or courageous, is no better off than the rest of her sex, and when she is not changed into a shadow for trying to break out of the mold . . . she is subjected to similar subtle propaganda mechanisms that turn her into a domestic, condemned to live in the shadow of other people's lives. Eskimo girls don't fare any better. They are sealed up in their igloos turning hides into clothing, while the men roam the wilds with their reindeer herds or pan for gold.

After an almost total absence of blacks before the mid 1960's, an accelerated effort has been made in primers and pre-primers to integrate the lives of black and white children. They are often seen playing together in their integrated neighborhoods and schools. When blacks play an active role, it is, unsurprisingly, the male who leads; black girls, along with their mothers and white sisters, are used as scenery. Only 9 blacks out of 108 biographical subjects are found in the readers—a shocking fact in the second decade of the Civil Rights Revolution.

Chinese-Americans, though statistically fewer, fare better as a group. They suffer little overt prejudice but the same sex role patterns prevail in their families. In one notable story an old grandmother's precious stone from the old country is saved by a girl so that her *brother* can go to school. As you would expect, traditional sex roles are strongly supported in stories about Mexican-Americans, along with the mystique of *machismo*.

Life in other cultures and/or in other times—Norwegian, Swiss, Hungarian, Russian, Arabian, African, Japanese, Aztec, the Middle Ages, (but notably *not* Jewish life, during Biblical days, the Diaspora, or any other time) are touched on by the readers in some of their infinite varieties. But whatever country or century is being described, when it comes to sex role stereotyping, you'll find tucked away in those faraway places and times the same old sexist plots.[1]

---

[1] As this study was going to print, the reader *I Do, Dare, and Dream*, (ed. John M. Franco et. al, American Book Company, Litton Educational Pub. Inc., 1970) was called to our attention as a good example of the new reader designed for Inner City use. Aside from a story about a Black cowboy, the settings are urban and problems of race and environment are faced with candor and honesty. Photographs of children of many hues are excellent. But the sexism, especially in the pictures, is even worse than in the earlier readers! Overall there are six stories about girls and one biography of a woman, but nineteen stories about boys and four biographies of men. In one story about girls the stress is on a sick Papa; in a second the girl is a hostess for boys; in the third the girl narrator describes a man-run community center; and in the fourth girls babysit and coo over the accomplishments of two little boys. This reader is obviously intended as a boy's book and is a good example of aggravating one wrong in the attempt to correct another.

Subliminal Messages. Dr. Edward Hall, in *The Silent Language*[2] finds that children are indeed assimilating the content and values of their books as they learn to read, without giving it any conscious thought. Watson and Hartley both find that by the age of eight, ninety-nine percent agreement is found among children of both sexes as to which sex does which job, what kind of person a girl or boy should be and what the role limitations and expectations are.[3] School readers must assume their responsibility in directing the subliminal learning process toward more psychological constructive ends.

IMPLICATIONS

There are broad social implications in the use of sex role stereotypes which are seldom considered in connection with the readers.

Children are exposed to conventional sex stereotypes long before they learn to read. The attitudes shown by friends and family, television and books are among the influences which have already begun the process of socialization. School readers have a special place in this process. They convey official approval. In many states, they have to be approved by state officials since they are bought with state money. They are used in state public schools which are attended under state compulsion until a certain age is reached. They are presented to children within a context of authority, in the classroom. Finally, every child must read them. Through the readers, society says, "This is what we would like you to be."

This expectation is presented to children at a time when most of them have not yet attained a critical perspective on themselves and their backgrounds. The official version cannot help but become the norm in childish vision. Dr. Naomi Weisstein in an article entitled "Kinder, Kuche and Kirche as Scientific Law: Psychology Constructs the Female"[4], describes numerous experiments in which both humans and animals, without outside coercion, were forced by the experimenters' expectations alone to behave in prescribed ways even when their natural abilities, desires, and moral standards would have urged otherwise. In the most shocking of these experiments, 62.5 percent of the adult subjects administered what they thought were lethal electric shocks to uncooperative "students" who acted as if they were in great pain as the shocks increased. The bizarre behavior of these subjects was apparently motivated solely by the pressure of the

[2] Greenwich, Connecticut. Fawcett Pub. 1959.

[3] Ruth Hartley, "Sex Role Pressures and the Socialization of the Male Child," *Psycho. Reports* 1959, V.457, p. 268.

Goodwin Watson, "Psychological Aspects of Sex Roles," *Social Psych.: Issues and Insights*, 1966, p. 427.

[4] In *Sisterhood Is Powerful*, ed. Robin Morgan (Vintage, 1970) pp. 205–219.

experimenter's demand for cooperation.[5] If adults are so vulnerable to the power of other people's expectations, how much more vulnerable must young children be!

The pressure of official expectations has a different impact on those children coming from backgrounds which differ sharply from the "approved." They are left with three choices—condemnation of themselves and their families for being atypical or abnormal, a forced conformity to societal norms, or rejection of a society to which they can never fully belong. For these children and for those who realize that the norms are unrealistic and the ideas harmful, exposure to readers can be an introduction to general disaffection with "official" American culture.

Clearly role models of one kind or another must be useful in the process of socialization. For example, Margaret Mead in *Male and Female*,[6] and Eric Erikson in *Childhood and Society*[7] have shown clearly that all societies use role models to encourage self-development of their children as individuals and functioning members of the group. But when the role models remain static while society changes, they lose their value as educational devices and become instead psychological straightjackets which constrict individual development and preparation for life. When the models deliberately build up the self-images of one group at the expense of another, they become viciously repressive. In America such practices are particularly inappropriate to the principles upon which this society supposedly was founded, and to which it still gives at least lip service. If socialization has twin goals, to rear fit individuals as well as individuals who fit, the models presented in school readers can be faulted on both counts.

Psychologists who are women are now beginning to call attention to the great damage done to both men and women by our narrowly defined role models. In a statement to the American Psychological Association in September, 1970, the Association of Women Psychologists said:

> Psychological oppression in the form of sex role socialization clearly conveys to girls from the earliest ages that their nature is to be submissive, servile, and repressed, and their role is to be servant, admirer, sex object and martyr . . . the psychological consequences of goal depression in young women—the negative self-image, emotional dependence, drugged or alcoholic escape—are all too common. In addition, both men and women have come to realize the effects on men of this type of sex role stereotyping, the crippling pressure to compete, to achieve, to produce, to stifle emotion, sensitivity and gentleness, all taking their toll in psychic and physical traumas.[8]

[5] *Ibid.*, p. 216.
[6] Dell, New York, 1949.
[7] Norton, New York, 1950 and 1963.
[8] From printed "Statement, Resolutions, and Motions" presented to the American Psychological Association at its convention in Miami, Florida, September, 1970 by the Association of Women Psychologists.

The practice of separating all people into two arbitrarily defined molds on the basis of sex alone is the Procrustean bed of modern life. Those who do not fit are either stretched out or chopped up. We stretch our sons to fill the ideal dominant male role and fragment our daughters' personalities to make them fit the servile female role. Both processes do violence to the individual. Each damaged person depletes the human resources of the whole society. How many damaged individuals can we afford?

The society into which our children will be expected to fit is very different from that presented by the readers. In a lecture at the Princeton Adult School on October 16, 1970, Dr. Suzanne Keller, a professor of sociology at Princeton University, outlined the rapid changes which are reshaping the roles our daughters can expect to fill as adults.[9] Briefly, they can look forward to biological developments which may make family planning safer and more reliable, giving women much greater control over their own lives. They can also expect population pressures to result in small families. According to present trends, children will be born to younger parents and they will be spaced more closely together, thus giving women several decades of post-parenthood freedom in which to follow their own pursuits.

More women will find themselves on their own, either by choice or through divorce or early widowhood. The *New York Times* of Sunday, January 31, 1971, states that latest census figures show a forty-three percent increase in single adult households in the last ten years. More than half of these are headed by women.[10] Thus more women will be driven into the job market by financial or personal needs. Already forty-eight percent of women between eighteen and sixty-four years of age are working. This percentage increases every year.[11]

The high failure rate of modern marriages, which is now one in four according to *Time*, December 28, 1970,[12] will probably continue or accelerate and will produce a correspondingly expanded search for alternative living patterns, both within the context of marriage and outside it. "The trouble comes from the fact that the institution we call marriage cannot hold two full human beings—it was designed for one and a half . . ." says Cornell Political Scientist Andrew Hacker.[13] Despite our conditioning, fewer and fewer women are accepting this 'half' status.

Whether or not we like these trends, we must prepare our daughters and sons to deal with them. We cannot do this by pretending changes are not happening or that they will go away if we adhere to the ideals of

[9] Unpublished speech entitled, "The Future of the Family."

[10] Sect. 2, p. 56.

[11] *Women at Work*, United States Government Publications, 1969. Analyzed by Dr. Jennifer MacCleod, Princeton Adult School, November 19, 1970.

[12] *Ibid.*, p. 34.

[13] *Ibid.*, p. 35.

some past American Golden Age. That Age was never Golden, and it certainly cannot be recaptured.

The Mother of the Future will be forced to find fulfillment outside traditional motherhood for the greater part of her life. Dependence will no longer be an option for either sex, whether it is financial dependence in the case of Mother, or domestic dependence in the case of Father. Competence will be necessary for both. Men can expect to find women competing with them as equals, and as the laws of probability suggest, it will not be unusual for a man to be surpassed by a woman in fair competition.

As a nation we are developing a greater respect for the rights of minority groups and a recognition of the essentially pluralistic nature of our society. Our children must develop flexibility and tolerance towards other life styles. Publishers of current readers have responded somewhat to this imperative. Readers are now racially integrated in at least a token manner. Some previously pink faces have been literally blacked in, as we discovered in certain instances. More stories are set in urban rather than in rural surroundings. This is only a gesture, but it does represent tacit agreement by publishers with the basic principle that children are influenced psychologically and not just academically by their readers. Publishers, on their own admission, bear a heavy responsibility to refrain from damaging developing people.

However inadvertently damage has been done in the past, publishers can no longer evade responsibility for change. This report makes it clear that readers are potentially and actually very harmful to children and to the general well-being of our society.

The groundwork for a healthy adjustment to social change has to be laid in childhood. Readers are an important part of this groundwork. Changes in role models and the behavior patterns they depict can have a great impact on the changing images children have of themselves. Few but the strong can function under a constant barrage of self-doubt and social disapproval. If we wish our children to avoid the destructive conflicts in social relationships which can be traced to the effects of sex role conditioning with its dehumanizing consequences for men and women alike, then we must begin now to reform the images with which they will form themselves.

RECOMMENDATIONS FOR CHANGE

The authors of this study are convinced that all readers now in use should be revised before going into new printings. In this revision top priority must be given to the eradication of harmful sex stereotypes and to the elimination of all forms of discrimination. We join those educators who have criticized publishers for attempting only token solutions to such problems. Whether readers are in fact necessary in order to teach reading, and whether they do as much harm scholastically as they do socially, are questions beyond the scope of this study. If elementary schools do continue to use readers, then steps must be taken immediately to eradicate the abuses discussed in this report.

One of the reasons often cited for the overwhelming amount of "boys'" to "girls'" material is boys' lack of reading readiness in the primary grades. Boys, we are told, will only read stories about boys, whereas girls will go along with anything. We seriously question this premise. We are convinced that if girls' stories were not so limp, so limited, so downright silly even, boys would cease to discriminate between boys' and girls' stories—there would only be "good" or "bad" stories, (it may be useful to remind ourselves that in adult literature only inferior products are labeled "a woman's book" or "a man's book"). Harriet the Spy, and Pippi Longstocking have no trouble making friends among boys as well as girls. We cannot any longer willingly subscribe to the view that "it's the woman who pays." If boys are to be lured into better performances in the reading program at fixed ages and grades, then other means must be found, and we are sure *can* be found—means which do not demean and diminish the role of women in the world.

Future readers should reflect a sensitivity to the needs and rights of girls and boys without preference or bias. Stories in any given reader should feature girls as well as boys, women as well as men. Half the biographical content should feature women. Outstanding feminist leaders like Susan B. Anthony, Elizabeth Cady Stanton, Emmeline Pankhurst, Sojourner Truth and many other heroines of the fight for women's rights, should appear side by side with male champions of human dignity such as George Washington Carver, Mahatma Gandhi, Benjamin Franklin, Abraham Lincoln, and Martin Luther King. These women form an equally important part of human history. Biographical sections should not be segregated according to sex, nor should adventure sections and similar groupings appear under 'boy' or 'girl' headings. Animal stories should not be used as subtle vehicles for sexist ideas that would be unacceptable in the human family. Future readers should respect the claim of each of us to *all* traits we regard as human, not assign them arbitrarily according to preconceived notions of sex roles. Let the readers man and boy show emotion. Let the reader women and girl demonstrate courage and ambition. Such a reapportionment, however, should not involve any loss of self-regard or blurring of identity for the boys pictured. Future readers should not arbitrarily bar women and girls from the rights, privileges, pursuits, and pleasures granted to men and boys, nor deny them abilities and occupations males have dominated until now. Specifically, there should be girls and mothers solving problems unassisted by boys and fathers; girls earning money and getting recognition in the form of rewards and awards; and mothers and other women functioning in positions of authority, other than the predictable ones of teachers and nurses. Some stories should feature mothers employed outside the home and independent working women. There should be girls operating machinery and constructing things; girls playing with boys on equal terms; girls in strenuous physical situations; girls travelling; girls depicted as taller, wiser, stronger or older than boys—randomly, as in the actual world. Nobody expects readers to conform to strict statistical probability, but blatant bias must be erased.

A temporary moratorium on certain abused stereotypes of females should be declared. We no longer depict Mexicans asleep under sombreros, blacks eating watermelon, or Indians scalping palefaces. The following might also disappear for a while without being missed: mother in her apron; mother baking or offering cookies; girls tirelessly engaged in playing house, dragging dolls or wheeling them in baby carriages, and having tea parties with them; girls wistfully and admiringly watching boys do anything at all. Girls must not be shown exclusively as spectators, but must appear as active participants. Males as perpetual "guests" in the home should also disappear: for example, father reading the newspaper in his armchair while mother serves him, and boys skipping out to play while the women of the house, young and old, clear tables, wash dishes, cook, sweep, wash, mend, iron, work, and work, and work. . . .

We'd like to see males participate in household chores and females in outdoor tasks, just as they often do. Boys might be shown taking music lessons and visiting art museums; girls could rough-house with dogs and boys stroke kittens. Genuine friendships between boys and girls should appear. Women should be seen working and playing together in groups. Girls might occasionally be shown as rough, unpleasing, intractable or rude, just as boys are allowed and even subtly encouraged to be. Finally, childless couples and single-parent families should be shown, unpatronizingly.

There are many possible courses of action for people who will take this study seriously enough to do something about the problem. Parents, teachers, school principals and friends can review books used in classrooms, complain to publishers about offensive stories and illustrations in detail, and try to reach other teachers, principals, school boards and parent teacher associations. They can also carry the campaign as far as official state-wide purchasing and the general public. Pressure groups can coordinate to make an impact on the situation. It is important, however, to understand that sensitivity to sex role stereotyping is a matter of consciousness-raising and can best be done by group discussion and open-ended debate. Opponents of change may need time and patience before they begin to understand.

The subject can be brought up at teachers' meetings and P.T.A. meetings. Programs to air the question can be arranged and suggestions invited on how to deal with it. Teachers can make sure that children using readers are provided with supplementary reading material that will help to counteract the message of the stereotypes. They can guide class discussions upon how the reader world compares with the real world and an ideal world.

Much can be done by small determined groups of like-minded people. Let's do it. We will know that we have succeeded when Dick can speak of his feelings of tenderness without embarrassment and Jane can reveal her career ambitions without shame or guilt.

CHAPTER 8

Immigration Restriction and Americanization

On July 11, 1911, Colonel Theodore Roosevelt wrote to Professor Edward Ross, complimenting his old friend on an article he had written on the "yellow-peril" after his recent trip to China. Roosevelt, like other progressives, was concerned with dysgenics and the maintenance of the genetic superiority of the Anglo-Saxon strain in the American race. A few weeks later, Ross responded to Roosevelt's complimentary letter by pointing out why he had gone to China.

> More than any other, this article represents what I went to China for. I have been anticipating that in a few years an effort will be made to take down the barriers against Oriental immigration as part of a policy of pushing our trade with the Orient. So I busily collected material with the idea of preparing an unanswerable argument against Chinese immigration that should be free from the least taint of race prejudice.[1]

Self-consciously aware of exactly what he was doing, Ross, like so many other progressives, was deeply involved in shaping national policy with respect to immigration restriction. Discriminatory restriction was necessary against Chinese as well as southern Europeans, not only because of race and economics, but because of the difficulty in socializing and Americanizing these groups. As Ross said in another letter:

> I will say that I am in favor of a percentage basis for restricting immigration because it will apply the sharpest restriction to just those strains of the later immigrating which offer the greatest difficulties of Americanization.[2]

The passage of the Immigration Act of 1924, which made permanent the discriminatory immigration restriction against Orientals and southern Europeans, symbolized a victory for many liberal progressives concerned

[1] Letter from Edward Ross to Colonel Roosevelt, August 1, 1911. Edward Ross Collection, Wisconsin Historical Library Archives.
[2] Letter from Edward Ross to Mr. Earl M. Rydell, February 9, 1921. Edward Ross Collection, Wisconsin Historical Library Archives.

with the racial and social stability of the American community. Ross, as many progressives had for two decades before, actively lobbied Congress and the Executive Office to close the gates. The job, however, was only half done. Clearly, the other half of the task was to socialize and Americanize the immigrant and his children properly so that he might be made safe for American democracy. Gregory Mason, after describing what the Rochester, New York, public schools were doing for the foreign-born and their children, said:

> Hypenated citizenship is as dangerous to a republic as a cancer to the human body. Education is the knife to use in cutting out the hyphen, and the public schools of Rochester are a laboratory in which it has been proved that the operation can be done.[3]

Throughout the first half of the century, schools were organized to educate the immigrants away from their un-American traditions, and the children of immigrants away from the ways of their un-American parents, and toward Anglo-Saxon standards. The new conditions in America necessitated state intervention. According to Marion Brown, principal of City Normal School, New Orleans, Louisiana, "Their parents are no longer to be depended upon for safe guidance; hence our American schools must prepare these children for the new conditions." [4] The children were to be shaped to fit into the Anglo-Saxon standard. With that standard went a sense of nationalistic fervor and destiny. Marion Brown spoke for many educators who saw themselves shaping the immigrant's children for the exigency of an emerging *Pax Americana*.

> As Rome brought order, peace, and personal freedom to the various nationalities in her borders, so today must the teacher endeavor for each of the ethical microcosms that we call American children; bring them to the Anglo-Saxon standard, train them to self-control that means freedom, the love of country that foreshadows the brotherhood of man, the developing personality that can take only justice and right as its standard, a consummation possible only thru knowledge of the mazes of inherited tendencies, by sympathy with the soul struggling in shackles of ancestral bondage.[5]

The educational state in America was thus organized to channel millions of youth into what was believed to be their social destiny. The shapers and molders of this assumed meritocratic system ideologically reflected the collective values of the emerging middle class which, itself, had largely been nurtured on liberal enlightenment social philosophy. Racism, sexism, and elitist bias were as much a part of the thinking of the framers of the system of mass schooling as were their beliefs in "professionalism," "scientific" testing, progress, social meliorism, eugenics, and meritocracy.

[3] Gregory Mason, "An Americanization Factory," *The Outlook*, February 23, 1916, p. 448.
[4] Marion Brown, "Is There a Nationality Problem in Our Schools?" *National Education Association Proceedings*, University of Chicago Press, 1900, p. 585.
[5] *Ibid.*, p. 590.

Theodore Roosevelt Compliments Edward Ross on His Latest Work Dealing with the "Yellow-Peril"

The Outlook
287 Fourth Avenue
New York

Office of
Theodore Roosevelt

JULY 11TH 1911

My dear Professor Ross:

I thought your article on China was not only of absorbing interest, but most important. It is a curious thing to see how excellent traits, if carried to an excess, may do real and permanent damage. Thrift, industry and temperance, unguided by ambition and intellect, have reduced the Hindu cultivator to the lowest possible basis, and apparently have done the same thing for the Chinese. How true is the old Greek belief that as regards most matters it is only the middle course that is wise! France is slowly dying because of excessive limitation of population, and China because she will not limit population rationally. There are fewer people of French descent in France today than there were forty years ago, and yet there is more vice and crime, more hideous and villainous degradation of the kind which one would think they would be able to avoid if the problems of over-population did not have to be solved. I need hardly say to you, my dear Professor Ross, that the popular belief that I have advocated enormous families without regard to economic conditions has just about the same foundation as the Wall Street belief to the effect that I pass my time reveling in drink, and am tortured by a wild desire for blood. All that I have ever said was that here in America, if the average family able to have children at all did not have three or four children, the American blood would die out—which is a statement not only of morals but of mathematics.

Do give me a chance to see you sometime. I really look forward to talking with you.

Faithfully yours,
THEODORE ROOSEVELT

Professor Edward A. Ross
Madison, Wisc.

Edward Ross Responds to Theodore Roosevelt's Compliment

AUGUST 1, 1911

My dear Colonel Roosevelt:

I was greatly pleased to receive your kind letter of July 11 about my article on "The Struggle for Existence in China." It is just such approval as yours that I sought to win for I am very eager to impress my interpretation of the Oriental problem upon the great leaders of opinion. More than any other, this article represents what I went to China for. I have been anticipating that in a few years an effort will be made to take down the barriers against Oriental immigration as part of a policy of pushing our trade in the Orient. So I busily collected material with the idea of preparing an unanswerable argument against Chinese immigration that should be free from the least taint of race prejudice.

I greatly regretted missing you when you were in Madison, and keenly appreciate your courtesy to Mrs. Ross.

I expect to be in New York on September 15, and will be happy to call upon you in case you anticipate you will be in town on that date.

In October I am bringing out with the Century Company a book under the title "The Changing Chinese," and I have been intending to see that you get a copy from me as my only way of expressing my appreciation of what you did for my little book "Sin and Society."

Sincerely yours,

EDWARD A. ROSS

A Lobbyist at Work

Prescott Hall

JAN. 16, 1920

Dear Mr. Ross,

We are in process of trying to smoke out possible presidential candidates as to their attitude on immigration, to see if we can prevent the other side from committing theirs in advance, as was the case with Taft and Wilson.

Can't you get somebody to tackle Leuroot for us on this matter. Of course we can't expect anyone to indorse a particular bill, but we want to find out whether he will stand for say as much restriction as would be effected by our numerical bill.

With best regards,

Sincerely,

Prescott Hall

Perhaps you could get Commons to help on this and have Leuroot written to by several persons (or talked with) and transmit us the gist of the result.

Immigration Restriction and Americanization

Edward A. Ross

FEBRUARY 9, 1921

Mr. Earl M. Rydell
St. Peter,
Minnesota

My dear Mr. Rydell:

Replying to your letter, I will say that I am in favor of a percentage basis for restricting immigration because it will apply the sharpest restriction to just those strains of the later immigration which offer the greatest difficulties of Americanization. I object, however, to the percentage being fixed from year to year by a commission. The pressure on this commission would regularly result in the fixing of the highest percentage figure allowed by the act of Congress. I feel that 400,000 a year is as many immigrants as we can properly assimilate under present conditions.

Very sincerely,
EDWARD A. ROSS

Edward A. Ross
LS

An Americanization Factory

*An Account of What the Public Schools of Rochester
Are Doing to Make Americans of Foreigners*

Gregory Mason

The high-ceilinged, square school-room was filled. Every one of the fifty or more seats was occupied. But the pupils were not children. They were men—and one woman—from twenty to fifty years of age, and all were foreigners. There were dark Greeks, and lighter, more voluble Italians; alert, impressionable Russians; attentive but impassive Hungarians;

blond Germans, blonder Scandinavians; and two black Turks, the meekest-looking persons in the room, who shared one text-book and huddled over it in an affectionate embrace. The school-room was in the building of a public school of Rochester, New York. The foreign men and the solitary foreign woman made up the class in citizenship, which is one of the courses for adult foreigners offered by the Rochester Board of Education.

The teacher asked one of the pupils—a German:

"Mr. Kraus, in applying for American citizenship, besides swearing allegiance to the President of the United States, is there any similar duty enjoined upon you?"

"Yes," replied the student, a big raw-boned truck-driver, "I must specially renounce my allegiance to de Kaiser."

"And if, unhappily, the United States went to war with Germany, it would be difficult for you to decide what to do, would it not?" pursued the questioner, while Italians, Russians, Turks, and Hungarians nudged one another.

"Ach no," answered the big blond Saxon. "Certainly I would fight for de President."

This sort of quizzing is making the aliens in Rochester realize that citizenship is not a coat to be put on, worn a while, and lightly tossed away.

This war has awakened Americans to the danger that threatens our country in the existence here of a group of citizens whose allegiance is divided, or at least not thoroughly "Americanized."

During the decade just previous to the beginning of the European war immigrants came into the United States at an average of about a million annually. We took it for granted that they were being assimilated, that they were being rapidly converted into loyal Americans. The war has taught us that they were not.

If we are to remain a Nation, we must have the strength of union. Obviously we must thoroughly Americanize the foreigners already here. And while the flow of immigration is temporarily stopped by the war we must prepare the machinery to Americanize the immigrants who will make up the great stream that can be expected to flow again soon after the end of the war.

Of the males of voting age in the United States, 6,646,817, or more than twenty-five percent, are foreign-born. More than half of these, or 3,612,700, are not citizens of the United States. Certainly there is not pure democracy in a country in which thirteen percent of the males of voting age have no influence in the selection of the Government that rules them!

According to Mr. Richard K. Campbell, United States Commissioner of Naturalization, "under normal conditions a fair estimate of the average annual certificates of citizenship issued in this country is about 100,000."

But, inasmuch as "every certificate issued admits to citizenship, not only the alien to whom it is granted, but also his foreign-born wife and minor children, . . . there would appear to be about 400,000 admitted annually."

It is a mooted question whether we ought to grant citizenship so liberally. Certainly the wisdom of admitting three or four persons to citizenship simply because one has passed the required examinations is open to grave doubt. But, leaving this question aside, it is plainly desirable that men and women who become citizens should become so in fact as well as in name. In other words, the process of Americanization should be thorough. And it is desirable that the foreigners who come here to stay permanently should be helped and encouraged to become American both in name and in sympathies. The smaller the size of the un-American element in our population, the better.

A beginning has been made. Some machinery for making Americans out of foreigners already exists. Young Men's Christian Associations in some cities have opened courses for the education of the immigrant. The Department of Labor of the State of New York issues free "Advice for Immigrants" in useful pamphlet form. Similar leaflets are issued for the benefit of aliens by the Sons of the American Revolution. Several cities have set aside a day to celebrate the attainment of citizenship by alien-born members of their population—an excellent custom, for it makes the foreigner feel that American citizenship means more than the right to vote, and that citizens have duties as well as privileges.

These efforts are well enough in their way, but they do not go far enough. What the immigrant needs to facilitate the process of his assimilation is education. Not only are there in this country about three million foreign-born whites above the age of ten who cannot speak English, but there is a large mass of foreign-born persons who cannot read or write the language of the country of their birth. By the official Census 1,918,825 illiterates of this sort above the age of fourteen entered this country during the first decade of the twentieth century. The State ought to make immigration an asset, not a burden. The natural instrument for the State to use in making good Americans from the raw material that is coming into the country from abroad is the public school.

The public schools of several cities are holding classes for immigrants —New York, Buffalo, Los Angeles, Troy, Boston, and Cleveland, to mention a few of the more prominent ones.

But, so far as I can learn, in all the cities where courses are offered to adult immigrants except one, the initiative came from the Young Men's Christian Association, a civic club, or some other philanthropic enterprise. The one exception is Rochester, New York. In Rochester the immigrant training was begun and carried on by the Board of Education. Instead of placing this work under the department of vocational training, as most cities that have tried to help the adult alien at all have done, Rochester has established a special Department of Immigrant Education.

Rochester's Director of Immigrant Education is Mr. Charles E. Finch. He is a smallish, soft-speaking man with the enthusiasm of an inventor. He is an inventor. He invented a new way of teaching adult foreigners.

About fifty percent of Rochester's population is foreign-born or of pure foreign extraction. For years the public schools of Rochester have given some form of training to immigrants. Of course the teaching of immigrant children is easy enough. They learn English and the customs of America almost as easily as American children do. It is the men and women who come to our shores mature who make up the non-English-speaking, un-American lump that is like a piece of unmixed dough in a loaf of bread. Up to 1908 the few adult foreigners who enrolled in the Rochester schools were taught as if they were children. Their education was of the primer sort—the "I see a lion; do you see a tiger?" variety.

Then Mr. Finch offered his idea. It was simply this: Treat an adult like an adult. The grown-up foreigner is not interested in talking about lions, tigers, and the other phenomena of childhood's primer, rarely seen in American cities. He wants practical knowledge. He is interested in the things around him. He wants to know the names of the familiar objects of factory and city life, he wants to understand the simple customs and laws of his new environment. He wants to be able to read the newspapers. Mr. Finch worked out a course of training for grown-up foreigners which was adopted by the Rochester Board of Education, and later given the sanction of the State Department of Education.

The Rochester system has three aims:

1. To teach prospective Americans to speak, read, and write English.
2. To give them practical information that will make their lives easier and safer.
3. To prepare them for intelligent and patriotic American citizenship, by making them familiar with our laws, customs, ideals, and the fundamental facts of our history.

The foreigners are grouped according to their sex and nationality, and they are classified as "Illiterates," "Educated foreigners," and "Foreigners who speak some English."

The method is entirely practical. The teacher, who speaks only English, communicates with the pupils much as an American landing on a sun-baked isle in the mid-Pacific would communicate with the natives who could speak only an aboriginal tongue. The teacher first tells the class a few fundamental facts about himself, such as his name and the number and street of his dwelling-place, using such simple gestures as are necessary. One after another the students repeat this process. Later each student fills out a leaflet which is given to him, with blank spaces for the inscription of what he has just been learning to say. Here is Lesson 1:

ROCHESTER LEAFLET

Lesson 1

IDENTIFICATION

My name is
I live in Rochester
I live at
I came from
I work at
I go to No.   school
It is on
The school opens at quarter-past seven.
It closes at quarter-past nine.

Note: The teacher should have each student give the above orally, making the statement give the necessary individual information in each case. Later the student should be assisted in copying his own statements into his notebook.

This will serve as an identification page and will teach the student to give information that will often be required.

These "Rochester Leaflets" are used through the whole course, and some of those that accompany the more advanced lessons give the student much practical information, such as the nature of city ordinances which he must observe and the requirements for fire drills in factories.

The student is allowed to learn naturally—that is, he is taught by the use of familiar objects and familiar motions. Learning the words "door" and "window," he is told to "open the door" and "shut the window," and by suiting the action to the word he learns a hundred times more readily than if he were digging into a primer for a description of the antics of a dog giving chase to a cat.

Some of the first lessons naturally involve learning the names of parts of human anatomy, such as "eye," "ear," and "foot." The women are taught the names of household utensils. Everything is dramatized. One of the photographs reproduced with this article [deleted by the editor] shows a class of men learning the rudimentary facts of carpentry. While one of their number pounds a nail with a hammer the teacher writes on the blackboard, "He uses a hammer," and the class chorus it after her. Thus training in reading, writing, and speaking goes on simultaneously, and the study is vitalized by *acting* the particular performance or thing which is being described. In another photograph [photo deleted] we see a class of foreigners producing the drama "Buying a Hat." Two students are acting as salesmen. One of their companions is trying on a hat and is learning to ask for the proper shape, size, color, etc. Another has just bought a hat and is learning to make change in paying for it, while he also learns how to direct the salesman to deliver the purchase at his home.

Much more valuable information is this for the poor foreigner in our cities than statements from primers relating to the characteristics of plants and animals which he may never see. Some of the other practical lessons dramatized for Rochester's foreigners are "Calling on the Doctor," "Mailing a Letter," "Applying for Work," and "Going to the Savings Bank."

The beginner's class in history is taught largely by the calendar. At Thanksgiving time the pupils are told something about the early Pilgrims and the first colonization of the land to which the students are the latest colonists. Washington's Birthday gives an opportunity for a statement of the simple facts about the struggle by which this "Free America" of which the immigrant has heard so much was won from the grip of oppression. Then, in the more advanced classes, the sudden illumination of the school-room by electricity opens the way for a talk about Benjamin Franklin, and likewise in a natural manner the earnest grown-up pupils acquire a good deal of fundamental knowledge of big men and big events in the Nation's past.

Civics is not a formal subject for these aliens; it is a search for knowledge about important facts in their every-day life. The function of the corner policeman as the servant and protector, not the master, of the people is explained. The impinging on the life of the immigrants of city and State ordinances, like fire-escape laws and regulations for the disposal of garbage, provides an opportunity for the clever teacher to make very real to his pupils the "one for all and all for one" idea in American government.

Most important of all to the foreigner and most interesting to the spectator is the class in citizenship. Here, if ever, is practical knowledge. Most of the foreigners in Rochester have come to America with the idea of remaining, and citizenship is the goal of nearly all of them. Without the schools, their only training for the naturalization examinations in many cases would be secured from ward politicians, and would consist of just enough narrow cramming to enable the applicant to win the vote which the politician would then offer to buy from him.

But in Rochester night schools the aliens not only learn the answers to the usual questions of the naturalization courts, but, in addition, the real significance of the attainment of citizenship is drummed into them. The meaning of the words "renounce" and "allegiance" is harped upon, and all the obligations and duties of citizenship, such as jury service and intelligent voting, are fully explained.

The text-book possibilities of the daily newspaper are made the most of at Rochester. This is Mr. Finch's particular hobby, and he sometimes has difficulty in making the teachers under him appreciate the full value of the newspaper. One afternoon, at his invitation, I visited a class made up entirely of Greeks and Italians who were employed as "bus boys" at Rochester's principal hotels. They were writing simple sentences on the blackboard. When Mr. Finch suggested that they try reading a newspaper, the teacher was a bit skeptical.

"I don't think they're far enough along for that yet," she said. "Some of them have been in this country only two months."

But the little man, who looked at the swarthy Latins and Greeks with the affection of a father, was obdurate.

"I'll try them," he remarked, confidently, and handed a newspaper to a young Greek of eighteen who only ten weeks before had left his native Gallipoli to seek his fortune in the great Western country.

The dark-eyed youth glanced over the front page and stopped at a familiar date line.

"Athens, January fift'," he began. "There is good reason to belief that at an early hour Greece will join the Allies despite the antagon—antagonism of the Greek mon—arch to the course," he went on, stumbling at only three words—*believe, antagonism,* and *monarch,* in which he made the *ch* soft. His teacher was astonished. The newspaper was placed in the hands of a stern, gray-eyed son of Piedmont, who read with equal facility a passage relating to a slight fire in a Government building at Washington.

"You see," said Mr. Finch, "what they can do when they're interested."

It is difficult to get teachers intelligent enough to grasp the difference between teaching adult foreigners and teaching children in the grades. Mr. Finch now gives most of his time to training teachers and a course for the instruction of teachers in immigrant education has been put into the curriculum of the State Normal College at the instance of the State.

The Federal Department of Naturalization is now giving valuable aid to the schools in the country that are helping the immigrant. Soon after an alien has come to Rochester he receives a card from the Department of Naturalization urging him to attend school and fit himself for citizenship. Thereupon the school nearest to the home of that immigrant sends him a card, telling him of the free classes for people of his kind and inviting his attendance—but not urging it, for the Rochester school authorities strongly believe that citizenship ought to be assumed with complete volition on the part of the applicant. Then, again, the Federal authorities notify the school officials of the names of the aliens who fail in the examinations for citizenship, with the exact standing each man or woman got in the tests. Thereupon the Rochester Board of Education sends a follow-up card urging the unfortunate candidate to try again. On information received from the courts cards are also sent to those candidates who have met the requirements for citizenship but who have never appeared to claim their reward. Thus the school is a link between the immigrant and the city, the State, and the Nation.

The judges have welcomed the work of the Rochester schools. With the schools helping the immigrant the judges feel that they can fairly be stricter in the examination of candidates for naturalization, and thus the standard of citizenship is raised.

The successful accomplishment of the first step toward citizenship by a group of foreign-born is always made the occasion for public congratulations. Patriotic exercises are held in some hall or school building, and the Superintendent of Schools or some other appropriate official presents each would-be American with a small flag, an emblem of approaching membership in the great National fraternity. In every way possible the neophyte is made to feel the importance, and at the same time the privilege, of the position he is seeking. But the initiate is also made to feel that he is decidedly welcome.

On their part Rochester's foreign-born citizens have signified plainly their appreciation of the service of the schools. The surest way to show appreciation for service of any kind is to use it. The number enrolled in Rochester's classes for grown-up immigrants has steadily increased until this year there are about 2,500 on the lists. The Italians outnumber any other nationality, with Russians—mostly Russian Jews—in second place. Of the total of 2,320 enrolled during the season 1914–1915, there were 983 Italians, 657 Russians and Russian Jews, 159 Austrians, 148 Germans, 102 Poles, and representatives of Holland, Greece, Turkey, Sweden, Hungary, Armenia, Bulgaria, Cuba, Mexico, Brazil, and many other national or racial groups in diminishing numbers. There were 1,804 men, most of them over the age of twenty-one, and 516 women, most of them under that age. More than half of the total, or 1,264, had had no previous education in the United States, and 360 had had no education in their native country, while 810 had been to school only from one to three years in the land of their birth. Not a word of English was known to 622 of them, while 1,108 knew but a few words. Only 536, or less than twenty-five percent, could speak the tongue of their adopted country "quite well," according to the school records.

The only considerable opposition to the dissemination of knowledge among the foreign element has come from some of the powerful members in the various foreign colonies who want to exploit the labor of their countrymen. For instance, the proprietor of an Italian bootblacking "parlor" finds that the boys who are working for three or four dollars a week begin to leave him or demand higher wages as their knowledge of English increases under the tutelage of the night schools.

Some foreigners in the position of this employer of bootblacks and some foreign-born politicians have tried to discourage attendance at the night schools, but in vain. Once they have tasted the waters of the Pierian spring, many of the foreigners feel that they must obey the proverbial injunction to "drink deep." One of the great advantages of the Rochester method is that it is progressive; the schools will take the aliens just as far as they care to go. After completing the special courses open to them some of the immigrants enter the regular grades of the city's high schools. One group even achieved such erudition in English literature as the discussion and dissection of the plays of Ibsen!

Any one who sees what Rochester is doing for the improvement of its alien-born residents comes away with a feeling of wonder that all other American cities and towns have not done likewise. For men may reasonably disagree as to the wisdom of diluting our national stock with foreign blood until it is becoming a saturated solution in which the original Anglo-Saxon strain is fading out; but, granted that ignorant foreigners are to be admitted in great numbers, the necessity of educating and assimilating them as rapidly as possible seems too obvious to need advocacy. If it is wise to force all native-born children to go to school, is it wise to admit hundreds of thousands of illiterate foreigners without providing for their education?

Three things are necessary before there can be adequate provision for the Americanization of our multitude of immigrants. They are:

1. An institution to train teachers for the special work with adult aliens.
2. State aid for the immigrant schools.
3. A compulsory education law for aliens who become permanent residents.

New York has the first, New Jersey the second, and the third is in force in Massachusetts, where there is a law providing that every minor between the ages of sixteen and twenty-one who is unable to pass the examinations of the fourth grade of the public schools in reading, writing, and spelling must attend night school until he is able to meet that test. But in no State are all three of these desiderata found.

It is unfortunate that the sensational German–American propaganda subversive of American laws and neutrality has been necessary to awaken Americans to the danger of having among us a large body of citizens and permanent residents who wear a hyphen. Almost any of the big strikes of the past five years, like the Lawrence strike and the Paterson strike, should have aroused the American public to this danger, for much of the poignancy of these labor disturbances was due to the inability of native American police and populace and foreign-born strikers to understand each other's feelings, or even words. Hyphenated citizenship is as dangerous to a republic as a cancer to the human body. Education is the knife to use in cutting out the hyphen, and the public schools of Rochester are a laboratory in which it has been proved that the operation can be done.

Education of the Immigrant

Joseph H. Wade

There are three types of problems to be met with in the education of the immigrant child—the purely educational, the civic, and the moral.

Many of the children seem to be lawless, but it is not because they are really lawless, but because they do not know what the law is. Also, many of these children are seemingly ungoverned; they are excitable, nervous, and very tenacious of what they consider their rights; but if placed in the class of a good disciplinarian, the children in the C classes are the easiest children in the school.

When large numbers of immigrant children are placed in the same school, they should be segregated if possible, the Jewish children being placed in one C class, and the Italian in another, for they differ radically. The Jewish child is more ambitious than the Italian child for learning. The teacher can get more assistance from the parents of the Jewish child than from the parents of the Italian child. The Jewish children show results in a very short time, but with the Italian children it takes longer.

The second type of problem, the civic, seems very well developed, but we know as teachers that it is not always so. We need the active cooperation, first of all, of the other civic departments; secondly, of the business people of the city; and thirdly, of the general public. What is the use of teaching these children about city ordinances if these children see them violated day after day without any punishment? The only way in which we can train the immigrant child to a realization of what he owes to the city is to make him feel that these laws passed for the good of the city must be obeyed, and that if not obeyed, sooner or later there must come a punishment.

The third type is the moral type. We must put before the children whenever possible that the greatest thing we are doing for them is not in teaching them English or in teaching them how to make a livelihood, but in teaching them to respect their fathers and their mothers, and to have the right kind of reverence for home. We must continually bring this before the immigrant child. The board of education aims to do it by three methods: First, by the evening public school; second, by the parents' meetings; and third, by the public lectures. I find the parents' meetings are probably the most valuable means. We have in our district the Parents' League, which has spread all over the city. During the past two years I have spoken to 22 meetings of Italian parents in English, and I have always been surprised to find how closely the Italians will follow a person who speaks in English, and how seemingly they will understand what he is saying when he is speaking to them of their duties to their children and of their children's duties to them. At these parents' meetings we should always have some speakers who can speak in the language of the parents, and these people should present to them always in the strongest language the highest type of civic duty to the city.

Is There a Nationality Problem in Our Schools?

Marion Brown

The history of a man's childhood is the history of his parents and environment.

Carlyle

For the thousands of children of foreign parentage that now constitute so large a portion of our population the strange environment is so at variance with previous experience and traditions that their parents are no longer to be depended upon for safe guidance; hence our American schools must prepare these children for the new conditions.

A glance at our population shows that every nation under the sun has sent representatives in numbers proportionate to its distance from our shores. In some sections we find colonies have made their home with the avowed object of continuing uninterrupted their national customs or religious practices in this land whose law protects all who do not break their neighbors' heads or too frequently decimate their hen-roosts.

Every town has its German, its Italian, or its Irish colony. In the West there are Scandinavian villages; in the Southwest, perfect reproductions of old Spain.

The census of 1890 reports 32 percent of our entire population of foreign parentage. The native-born white population of native parents has diminished in percentage, swamped by the foreign-born influx. From 1821 to 1890 nearly 15,500,000 of foreign emigrants entered this country. From 1881 to 1890 about one-third of these millions entered our gates. The effect on social conditions and the trend of our national life is as yet discernible on only a few lines.

The vote-necessity of the politician has made the "foreign vote" a factor in practical politics. The voter whose vote has been so openly bid for on no other plea than that of former citizenship in a foreign land must have some acknowledgment of his un-American vote, so he makes a return demand in the name of his foreign nationality, usually on the schools; for there it is only children who are affected; so in one section German, in another French perhaps, must be taught thru the grades, nominally for culture or utilitarian value, in reality for political recognition.

As long as there is unused territory or demand for cheap labor, the children of these people with a different political creed and national ideal will constitute a large part of our public-school attendance.

The census of 1890 shows an enormous proportion of children of foreign parentage, as compared with the number of foreign-born adults. The last report of the United States Commissioners of Education states that, out of our population of nearly 73,000,000, 21,500,000 are of school age, of whom over 15,000,000 are enrolled in schools and 88 percent enrolled in the public schools.

In each nation certain strongly marked characteristics, spiritualized and intensified, seem to constitute the national ideal, typified in the national heroes. Is there an American type? It seems to me that, if we have an ideal, it is the Anglo-Saxon; the Teutonic elements, strong, masterful, land-hungry, self-controlled, imbued with a spirit of independence for all; the modicum of Celtic strain giving a fire and dash that a strenuous pioneer life has developed into push and hustle. In the adult—the law-making, law-abiding citizen, always ready to "pull up stakes" for a better cause, determined that he and his neighbour shall be mentally and morally free agents, unceasingly energetic and progressive till nervous prostration lays him low. The children—keen-eyed, restless, precocious, affectionate, even in play more or less self-controlled, ardent admirers of the "success that succeeds," touchingly eager to leap into the arena of life to become "young Napoleons of finance," youthful Edisons, or George Washingtons.

Today the American of pure Anglo-Saxon descent is rare, probably most numerous in the interior of the region bounded by Mason and Dixon's line, the Gulf of Mexico, and the Mississippi river. Elsewhere "Dutch and Danish, French and Spanish, mingle and vanish, in one grand conglomeration," and of this conglomeration are most of our children. In certain districts a predominating nationality other than English gives a marked tone to the locality, as in the old Spanish, Dutch, or French settlements, or the newer western towns where the Teutonic element predominates. Country populations are more homogeneous than those of the towns, particularly the manufacturing centers. What the larger cities—New York, Chicago, New Orleans—present, the smaller places show in miniature, a mixture socially and ethnologically. In Boston, out of 1,230 boys in the Eliot School, 602 were born in Europe; the parents of 1,117 were born in Europe; only 16 could find that one of their four grandparents was born in America. In the Hancock School, of 2,542 girls over 40 percent were born in foreign countries, and over 38 percent could not speak English when they began school; the fathers of only 98 were born in America. Every nation of Europe was represented, including the Turk. One school in New York city reports 98 percent of its pupils unable to speak English on entering. Some years ago an emigrant ship unloaded 1,100 Italians at a New Orleans wharf; a few days later 250 children from this influx, unable to speak a word of English, were admitted into the nearest public school.

Where there is a predominating nationality, the problems of discipline and teaching are comparatively easy; with several nationalities represented perplexities are unending, and where the nationality mixture in the individual is considerable, the troubles are hydra-headed and Protean. "The boy eternal" is, in certain aspects, the same kind of a problem the world over, but when international complications arise in his individuality, a French grandmother, or Spanish grandfather, or a still more remote English ancestor, or a German forefather, or a canny Scot may speak, in season or out of season, and not always with the tongue of angels.

A schoolroom where the Latin race predominates is always noisier, and more pervaded by a certain indefinable excitability, more subject to unexpected outbursts of feeling, than one where the more phlegmatic Teutonic element prevails. Whether it be heredity or the home influence of parents inheriting the effects of centuries of monarchical rule, there is less inherent capacity for self-restraint, greater difficulty in successful appeal to a desire for self-government—freedom always means license. With these children an autocrat, strong and unshakable in authority, is the most successful disciplinarian; when there is added power to lead to knowledge thru pleasant pathways, there is created an unbounded adoration that means blind obedience—the spirit that made an Austerlitz, but not the spirit that made a Manila Bay. Even here there are definite national differences. The Spanish child evinces a strong dislike to exertion in any form, combined with frequent unreasoning obstinacy and pride. With the taste and talent for expression for which the French nation is justly celebrated there is a quit wit, combined with a curious lack in power of sustained effort, the Romance type being more strongly marked when the descent is traceable to the south of France. When mixed with the firmer English, or its kindred Celt, the Irish, we have a pupil that is the delight of the teacher's heart and dire destruction to "perfect order."

Among the Italian children are found two distinct classes; the children of tradesmen and artisans, a thrifty, law-abiding, and ambitious class; and the children of the slaves of the padrone. Of the latter class our schools get very few, save where there is a well-enforced compulsory law. Ardent lovers of beauty, excellent in form, quick to learn a new tongue, keen at a bargain, loving music and rhythm, passionate, revengeful, proud to shine, easily antagonized, but needing to feel a strong hand at the helm.

The Irish child—warm-hearted, a hard fighter, a good hater, poetic, witty, beguiling of tongue, unsystematic in work, mischievous beyond calculation, but once roused to effort a delight to the teacher; when balanced with the steadier Anglo-Saxon, the best material in our schools; mixed with the German, frequently showing a difficult combination of unexpected fire and unreasoning stubbornness; when mixed with the French, the Celt is the balance-wheel, a capable and interesting type; combined with Italian or Spanish, the traits seldom show the good points of either type.

The various branches of the Teutonic stock show a marked similarity —a steady, quiet, slow to grasp, but tenaciously retentive; tardy in developing, but "the old reliable" when hard work is on hand; a fine illustration of the hare and the tortoise, well controlled at home; and capable of great self-restraint; when mixed with the kindred English, our steadiest and most hopeful material.

Whether due to heredity or environment, the fact yet remains that we may as well make up our minds that certain traditions will have to go when we deal with children of foreign descent. The time-honored rule to close a sentence with the downward inflection receives a death-blow in the clearly pronounced sentences of a child of French extraction; to the end of the chapter there is always a more or less pronounced rising inflection. Most Italian children seem to read with a sing-song—an indication of the rhythm that is their birthright; it is said that the American has little or no rhythm in his soul. Thru dē, dĕ, zē, zĕ, zà, tē, tĕ, dēr the nationality of the struggling reader is betrayed thru the grades till *the* exists in the reader and is a factor in schoolroom utterances, tho play and out-of-school distractions weaken its force. Principals may admonish, supervisors may report, teachers may worry, but from kindergarten to college the scars remain.

At home these children hear a foreign tongue. Untaught therein, they know it only colloquially, soon come to despise it as a useless lingo, and, unless the parental wrath is heavy-handed, at ten or twelve refuse to speak anything but English—that "goes" everywhere. In dealing with these children we find that the parent who can speak American, but is unable to write in any but the native tongue, is, in the estimation of the children, many degrees above the parent who speaks only the native tongue, but considerably below one who is master of both arts. Some time ago a little Italian whose mother spoke no English referred to her as a Dago. Had a schoolmate used the same term to him, war would have been instantly declared. This knowledge on the part of these children of foreign extraction has brought about a feeling that the foreign parent is not as capable of dealing with American conditions as his children, so parental authority has become seriously weakened, and a generation of young foreign "toughs" is growing up.

The children of foreign extraction come from three classes of parents; First, those who were fairly well placed in their own land, but have emigrated only to remain long enough to accumulate a competence. While here they conform to our laws and customs in so far as they consider advisable, but always with a reservation in favor of the fatherland; the mother-tongue is the speech in the home, the children grow up with a divided allegiance and a more or less defective English. A second class have left a land where their fortunes, social or political, were at lowest ebb. They must perforce make America their home; their children have brighter prospects in the new land, for which the parents intend they shall be prepared to the best of the child's ability. A third class are the flotsam and jetsam of society which a paternal government has unloaded on an unsuspecting friend. The product of generations of poor living, of hopeless penury, they have been assisted to relieve a teeming land of their burdensome presence. Mostly unskilled laborers, possessing little energy physical or mental, usually hovering just above or falling back into the tramp or petty criminal class, their children frequently defective physically and morally, they and their children are the greatest problems we have. The descendants of each class have not infrequently married with another nationality, and the mixed descent complicates the problem. The second generation is American-born, but, from the influence of the home, not yet thoroly United States in sentiment. Time alone can tell what the third generation will be. If it takes three generations to make a gentleman, it certainly will take three generations to make an American citizen—I have not said *voter*; that usually takes three years and an accommodating magistrate.

I propound no new proposition; the facts herein stated are well known to this audience; my purpose is to call attention to a phase of child study which my own experience has led me to believe is the masterkey to the labyrinth of many a little soul.

Growing up in probably the most cosmopolitan city in this country, educated in public schools where almost every European nationality had at some time its representatives, the first years of my teaching in a district thoroly foreign in speech and custom, the study of those varied nationalities and their mixtures became a necessity and an interesting investigation; later in the high school the same elements, and consequently similar problems, presented themselves. Now these young people have come into the training school, and again the problem crops up what to do to make them capable in their turn of handling this ever-growing puzzle.

As a people we have solved so many problems that we consider ourselves perfectly capable of settling anything under the sun; and, not satisfied with the economic and political questions thrust upon us by the strangers within our gates, we have taken unto ourselves several millions of new riddles. Today the Normal Department is discussing the training of teachers for the schools of Cuba and Porto Rico; that means, added to the usual child study, the study of a curiously mixed people—the pure Spanish type, the Spanish mixed with Indian, with pure negro, and with every tinge and grade between; the Caucasian enervated by centuries of tropical climate and social dominance, having as its national proverb: "God first, diversion next, and work for donkeys."

Within the opening of this twentieth century the American eagle extends its wings over as great an extent of territory as its Roman prototype. The Roman empire was a collection of national units held together by a strong centralized power; while claiming the privileges of "*Romanus sum*," the individual retained his language and national life untouched by the political rule of the seven-hilled city. With us the aggregation of nationalities is in the community, in the individual, making temperament, that combination of spiritual and mental qualities—character. In youth, and often thruout life, the individual is a ferment of conflicting tendencies, the possibilities for good or evil intensified or counteracted by the ancestral heritage. As Rome brought order, peace, and personal freedom to the various nationalities in her borders, so today must the teacher endeavor for each of the ethical microcosms that we call American children; bring them to the Anglo-Saxon standard, train them to self-control that means freedom, the love of country that foreshadows the brotherhood of man, the developing personality that can take only justice and right as its standard, a consummation possible only thru knowledge of the mazes of inherited tendencies, by sympathy with the soul struggling in shackles of ancestral bondage. And, if the teacher be the inheritor of the nations of the earth—what then?

CHAPTER 9

The Nature-Nurture Debate: Towards a False Consciousness

If one believes that the good society is the meritocratic society and if one becomes accustomed to ignoring certain social injustices and repression and further assumes equal opportunity, it becomes relatively easy to view the existing reward system in the educational state in America as a meritocratic system. If, however, one becomes sensitive to the inequities of this system but still quests for meritocracy, one usually turns his efforts toward the nearly impossible task of equalizing opportunity in an unequal system. This has often been the stance of the fighting liberal or radical, struggling to get some repressed group their share in the system.

If, however, one goes beyond the problem of selecting the right kind of educational rake with which, as Thomas Jefferson said, to "rake from the rubbish annually," and questions the kind of social system that not only produces "rubbish" but leads one to conceive of human beings as "rubbish;" a whole set of disturbing social issues emerge. The part of the philosophy of the enlightenment which viewed man as a product of his social conditioning and called for the application of new knowledge in the interest of the perfectibility of man and his social institutions carried with it a very distinctive objectification and depersonalization which, from the very start, served to destroy the dignity of human beings. Man was not the end, but rather a means for other men's purposes.

Ignoring this perhaps fatal flaw, those who considered themselves elite could view human beings as "rubbish." Others would concern themselves with the kind of social system that they perceived produced the "rubbish." One such example was Lester Frank Ward, when he made his anguished plea: "We are condemning the unfortunate victims of social imperfection. We are punishing wretched beings for being what we have made them."

275

Other heirs of the enlightenment such as Thorndike, Jensen, and Herrn-stein viewed the rubbish as less a consequence of social conditioning and more a consequence of nature. Under these circumstances, genetic manip-ulation was the answer to the problem. While these men might disagree about the cause and about the exact extent to which the social rubbish might be eliminated, most generally agreed to the desirability of eliminat-ing the rubbish in the interest of the progress of humanity toward a more meritocratic order.

Although the nature-nurture paradigm tends to lead one to think in opposites, it is important to recognize that most men who participated in that dialog during the twentieth century have held common assumptions about the nature of the good society. It is also important to recognize that the nature position does not necessarily incline one to support a conserva-tive social philosophy, nor does the nurture position incline one to support a liberal social philosophy. Historically, some of the leading hereditarians, such as Terman and Jensen, have considered themselves liberal, just as some of their leading adversaries such as Walter Lippmann and Jerry Hirsch were also liberal. The myth that the hereditarian position is in-evitably conservative is perpetuated by the false assumption that such a person cannot take remedial social action to correct the defects of nature. What, indeed, might he do? He can, as so many progressive liberal re-formers in the past have done, join the eugenics movement, call for the sterilization of the genetically defective, organize the social institutions so as, in effect, selectively to breed by caste or class, stand guard over the genetic pool through such social legislation as immigrant restriction, and at the same time, call for more effective education in the name of efficiently making the most of what exists.

On the other hand, if one believes that nurture predominantly controls, as did Lester Frank Ward, one might cover the nature side by supporting sterilization of the genetically defective, and then argue for the same educational reform in the interest of both efficiency and equality of op-portunity. The idea that hereditarians are conservative and environmen-talists are liberal thus tends to mislead and interfere with an adequate assessment of the function of educational rhetoric in the twentieth century.

Although the study of the influence of genetics and environment on human behavior is an important study in itself, the findings from these areas of inquiry do not in themselves, incline one to support either a radical or conservative view of the organization of society. There exists no logical connection between either the nature or nurture position and the social organization of society. Nevertheless, evidence from these areas has been used repeatedly as if such evidence necessarily supports one kind of social policy or another.

The nature-nurture argument has surfaced in every decade of the twentieth century. At times, the issue seemed to smolder; while at other apparently more critical times, the issue became one of heated public debate. The nature-nurture argument thus has engaged the conscious attention of thousands of educators and laymen throughout the twentieth century. If, indeed, this paradigm is so misleading, one wonders why this issue appeared so crucial to so many people? In seeking an answer, it might be helpful to look at the broader social context which surrounds the debate and ask the critical question that Russell Marks asks:

> What social difference does it make if one believes that I.Q. is 60 percent genetic and 40 percent environmentally determined or if one believes, like Jensen, it to be 80 percent genetic and 20 percent environmentally determined?[1]

Close scrutiny of the social context of this continuing debate leads one to suspect that while on the surface the discussion seemed to justify a given course of action, at the same time, it more often obscured the more potent reasons for that action. For example, while the hereditarians stressed the genetic defects of southern Europeans and thus justified discriminatory immigration restriction (1924) on hereditarian grounds, their argument, at the same time, obscured the movement of powerful economic and social groups interested in closing the gates for decidedly economic and social reasons.[2] It was in the economic interest of the larger industrialists to close the gates. Major industrial leaders began to think in terms of managing the labor supply rather than in terms of unlimited supply of labor which might lead to social instability in the urban manufacturing centers.

Intense public interest in the nature-nurture question has usually come to symbolize a significant shift in social policy. In this regard, the Terman–Lippmann debates (1922)[3] are instructive. While Terman's hereditarian arguments justified discriminatory immigration restriction, Lippmann did not attack the notion of meritocracy or the notion that people are intellectually different because of inheritance, but he attacked the inadequacy

[1] For many insights involving this controversy, the author is indebted to Russell Marks. See his "Race and Immigration: The Politics of Intelligence Testers." (Unpublished manuscript, 1973). Also see Russell Marks, "Testers, Trackers and Trustees: The Ideology of the Intelligence Testing Movement in America 1900–1954." (Unpublished Ph.D. Dissertation, University of Illinois, 1972).

[2] While most of the Congressional testimony surrounding the immigration restriction law stressed the heredity argument, the larger banking and manufacturing interest represented in the National Civic Federation supported closure on grounds of economic advantage. Many of the arguments used by the liberal-dominated Immigration Restriction League leaned heavily on the need for social harmony and Americanization.

[3] See Walter Lippmann's series of seven articles from *The New Republic*, and Lewis M. Terman, "The Great Conspiracy," from *The New Republic*, all reprinted in the readings section that follows.

of the tests themselves and concluded his remarks with a strong plea for accurate performance-based testing as a useful vehicle in classification of people along the lines of demonstrated merit. As Lippmann put it:

> Instead, therefore of trying to find a test which will with equal success discover artillery officers, Methodist ministers, and branch managers for the rubber business, the psychologists would far better work out special and specific examinations for artillery officers, divinity school candidates and branch managers in the rubber business.[4]

While both Terman and Lippmann considered themselves liberals, each man represented distinctively different rationales for the same meritocratic social ideal. While Terman insisted that IQ and inheritance were the determining factors in placing people in the meritocracy, Lippmann, as so many current liberal educational reformers, begged the prior nature-nurture causal question by arguing for performance-based testing. Lippmann nicely represented that side of the nature-nurture liberal discussants who found their way out of the argument in the 1930s and 1940s by arguing that IQ tests were merely good achievement tests and predictors of possible success in school, if not in society, and should be used accordingly. Lippmann, here, was in line with Allison Davis and others in the 1930s and 1940s who took the next step and used an efficiency argument to call for more effective tests to make more efficient use of the human resources (which by this time included blacks) for the industries of the nation.[5] The broader social policy, with respect to the races, was shifting. Increasingly, segregation was pictured as economically wasteful and contrary to good efficient business practices. It was argued increasingly that all people needed to be integrated into the work force for efficiency sake.[6]

Whether it was Lippmann or the present-day efficiency advocates of performance-based testing, each, in his own way, was part of that ideology of the enlightenment which propounded a kind of objective classification of social occupation performance in the name of efficiently run machines.[7] The liberals who turned to performance-based testing then as now have begged the causal question on why the difference in performance and also failed to give any serious challenge to the differential reward system as it exists. Thus, the system remains effectively intact, well-protected from critical scrutiny.

---

[4] See Lippmann, "A Future For the Tests," *The New Republic*, p. 10; reprinted in the readings section that follows.

[5] See Allison Davis, "Education and the Conservation of Human Resources," *American Association of School Administration*, Washington, D.C., May 1949, pp. 74–83.

[6] For a perceptive analysis of this shift, see Russell Marks, "Race and Immigration: The Politics of Intelligence Testers," reprinted in the reading section that follows.

[7] One is reminded here of Le Mettrie's essay, *L'homme machine*.

A similar phenomena with respect to a major shift in social policy seems to have occurred during the more recent nature-nurture debates surrounding Arthur Jensen's thesis as expressed in 1969 in the *Harvard Educational Review*. Not only have many liberals since taken the "performance testing" way out, the overall argument seems, once again, to have obscured effectively a change in the direction of basic social policy. While the earlier Lippmann–Terman debates tended to obscure the basic economic need for integration of blacks in the work force and the liberal shift from a segregationist to an integrationist position, so, too, did the more recent Jensen–Herrnstein discussion signal a fundamental shift in liberal attitude. That change was toward a withdrawal of white liberal support for black liberation movements.

Arthur Jensen's assertion that intelligence is approximately 80 percent heritable was not born of immaculate conception. Drawing on the experience of 50 years of racial- and class-biased testing, Jensen found that blacks in America were 15 points below the whites, although he noted that in his experience in administering IQ tests to children of impoverished backgrounds, a small bit of "play therapy" usually boosted the IQ score of the youngster from 8 to 10 points. He found the IQ differences in the races significant. In retrospect, it seems incredible that he so easily discounted the cultural bias of the tests and the conditions under which they were administered. What appears more incredible, however, was the ease with which his findings were so readily accepted by so many "professional" educators. Here, Russell Marks' question as to what social difference does 80 percent heritability make, can help.

Jensen's article, "How Much Can We Boost IQ?" appeared in the social context of the initial disappointment of many Great Society's social and educational reform programs. These programs failed, Jensen argued, because they were trying to do the impossible, i.e., raise IQ which was 80 percent genetically determined. To many educators who had failed, for a variety of reasons, to make an educational difference in the lives of ghetto children, Jensen's explanation for their failure was attractive. The heredity argument not only explained their failure, but more importantly, justified it. An explanation for Jensen's almost instant popularity among many liberal educators might also be found in the change of attitude which had occurred among many early supporters of the civil rights movement. For those who believed that the civil rights movement had gone too far and too fast in fanning the economic and social aspirations of the repressed, and, therefore, had to be cooled off, Jensen's argument took on significance. Frightened by the conflict and violence in the burning of cities in the mid-sixties, the organization and development of militant groups, and the "Ocean-Hill Brownsville" experiment, many liberals ceased to give vigorous support to educational programs which effectively raised the aspirations of the repressed minorities. Arthur Jensen's article signaled for many the beginning of the end of the liberal's support of the black liberation movement in the educational state.

The fact that intelligence may be 50 percent heritable or 80 percent heritable does not, in and of itself, lead one to logically come out for one kind of social action or another. Placed in the context in which Jensen used his argument, as well as the broader social movements of the period, the nature-nurture arguments, however, took on profound social importance. To Jensen, most intervention programs, such as Head Start, had failed because they were trying to change the cognitive ability of the child through a process which included a heavy emphasis on cognitive learning. Since the black ghetto child was cognitively inferior due to hereditary factors, he concluded that such programs designed to improve the cognitive ability of these children were thus also doomed to failure.

In true liberal spirit, Jensen then argued that if we study the learning behavior of black children more carefully, we would find that they excel at associative learning tasks. Sympathetic to the Bereiter–Engelman approach, Jensen called for a differentiated curriculum and methodology to capitalize on the presumed talents of the preschool ghetto child. Jensen, here argued as Terman, Thorndike, and other predecessors had, that since the child's abilities are known, a curriculum could be designed to meet his presumed needs most effectively. Once again, the child would be protected from failure. In the name of individual differences, the black ghetto child would be classified and tracked virtually from birth to adulthood, given associative learning tasks which would prepare him to enter the job market on the lower social economic levels. After making a very strong case that occupational hierarchy is related to IQ, that the formal school cultivates the cognitive trait or "G" factor which he found so necessary for entrance into these occupations, and that the "G" factor is heritable and blacks are short of this inheritance, Jensen then called for special education for the ghetto child to cultivate their rote associative learning skill which was necessary for them to become happy workers on the lower level of the job market.

While Jensen suggested that job requirements might be reviewed to allow persons of lower intelligence to occupy positions of somewhat higher social status, he did not fundamentally question or challenge the hierarchial stratified system or the presumed meritocratic principle upon which the system rested. Confronted with the social consequences of a repressive society, Jensen, as so many educational reformers before him, took the traditional way out. Face to face with the children of the oppressed and with the devastating psychological and social consequences of that repression, these reformers would attribute the learning problems to genetic defect and then proceed to "protect the child from failure" by channeling him through a differentiated curriculum which would mark him for his place in life.

Thus, the nature-nurture paradigm appeared in the twentieth century as a kind of false consciousness among educators and laymen alike. First, it was false because while, at times, the argument seemed to explain and justify certain actions, it often obscured the more potent reasons for the action. Secondly, it was false because the argument inclines people to think in polar opposites when, in actuality, few people seriously entertained extreme positions on either heredity or environment; and thirdly, it was false because contrary to conventional wisdom, hereditarians were not necessarily conservative, nor were environmentalists always liberal or did any necessary social action logically follow as so often was implied. Significant education and social policy decisions were thus made for reasons other than those used to justify the choice. In this way the academic community played a significant role in helping to develop the trend of false consciousness which undergirds the thought process of "double think" so necessary to maintain the system.

Andrew Hacker missed an important point when he said:

> The contretemps started a few years ago by Prof. Arthur Jensen is a case in point. Nothing came of it because in this field at least, each researcher's ideology determines his approach to the data.[8]

He was right when he claimed each researcher's ideology determines his approach to the data, and perhaps when he said "nothing came of it," but the important point that he missed was that something came *with* it. Compensatory programs were drastically reduced as liberals withdrew their support of black liberation movements. Jensen's work was profoundly significant, not, perhaps, as a single, direct causal factor, but as part of a syndrome of factors. The significance is to be found not in the persuasiveness of the evidence, but in the reasons why people were persuaded.

A similar analysis, it seems, can be made of Christopher Jenck's more recent work, *Inequality*.[9] Jencks shaped his study toward predetermined ends, not only by the evidence that he selected and left out,[10] but also by the way he handled his data and drew his conclusions.[11] The major thesis

---

[8] Andrew Hacker, "On Original Sin and Conservatives," *The New York Times Magazine*, February 25, 1973, Sec. 6, p. 65.

[9] Christopher Jencks, Marshall Smith, Henry Acland, Mary Jo Bane, David Cohen, Herbert Gintis, Barbara Heyn, Stephen Michelson, *Inequality, A Reassessment of the Effect of Family and Schooling in America*. (New York: Basic Books, 1972).

[10] For evidence on the relationship of family income and schooling which he apparently left out, see Samuel Bowles and Herbert Gintis, "IQ in the U.S. Class Structure." *Social Policy*, January–February, 1973.

[11] The work is flawed at many points, with bad logic as well. For two critical reviews, see Gerald Chasin, "Pull the Ladder Up, Jack—I'm on Board," *The Nation*, Feb. 19, 1973; and Henry M. Levin, "Schooling and Inequality: The Social Science Objectivity Gap," *Saturday Review*, December 1972, Vol. LV, No. 46, pp. 49–51.

that he set out to prove was that inequalities in America are not caused by inequalities in schooling but ultimately result from luck and merit. Merit is cast in terms of job competency or performance. For Jencks, the schools are not vehicles of social mobility. This, indeed, was the end of that enlightenment faith in schooling. The meritocracy, however, still remained well-grounded on Jenck's faith in Horatio Alger stories where one might still achieve mobility because of luck and merit. This conclusion is, indeed, the kind of explanation most sons and daughters of the privileged classes liked to hear. From that perspective, it is always encouraging to know that one had "made it" not because of the superior wealth, privilege and status of·one's parents, but because of his or her own efforts. Jencks' work, however, can be attractive to many liberal social policymakers for more than self-gratification. To whatever extent Jencks' ideas are seriously accepted by the corporate liberal establishment in this country is the same extent to which one can expect the withdrawal of liberal foundational and governmental support of formal education in America. The social implication of Jencks' thesis is not likely to be the equalization of wealth which, in the end, he proposes, but rather the decline in general support for schools. Here, again, the persuasiveness of the evidence is not as significant as the reasons why people are persuaded. Thus, it seems, the recent education dialog does suggest a major shift in social policy as Godfrey Hodgson stated in a recent article:

> . . . liberal education policies of the last few generations . . . and the intellectual assumptions on which they were built, are in bad trouble. They have lost support in the ranks of the social scientists who provided America, from Roosevelt to Johnson, with a major part of its operating ideology.[12]

While one might agree that many older liberal educational policies are in trouble, one might also recognize that a basic shift in liberal social policy has occurred and that present-day social scientists are providing the necessary "operating ideology" for that shift. The role of the social scientist has not changed but his ideology has changed in keeping with the more powerful decision makers in the educational state.

[12] Godfrey Hodgson, "Do Schools Make a Difference?" *The Atlantic*, February 1973, p. 46.

The Mental Age of Americans

Walter Lippmann

A startling bit of news has recently been unearthed and is now being retailed by the credulous to the gullible. "The *average* mental age of Americans," says Mr. Lothrop Stoddard in The Revolt Against Civilization, "is only about fourteen."

Mr. Stoddard did not invent this astonishing conclusion. He found it ready-made in the writings of a number of other writers. They in their turn got the conclusion by misreading the data collected in the army intelligence tests. For the data themselves lead to no such conclusion. It is impossible that they should. It is quite impossible for honest statistics to show that the average adult intelligence of a representative sample of the nation is that of an immature child in that same nation. The average adult intelligence cannot be less than the average adult intelligence, and to anyone who knows what the words "mental age" mean, Mr. Stoddard's remark is precisely as silly as if he had written that the average mile was three quarters of a mile long.

The trouble is that Mr. Stoddard uses the words "mental age" without explaining either to himself or to his readers how the conception of "mental age" is derived. He was in such an enormous hurry to predict the downfall of civilization that he could not pause long enough to straighten out a few simple ideas. The result is that he snatches at a few scarifying statistics and uses them as a base upon which to erect a glittering tower of generalities. For the statement that the average mental age of Americans is only about fourteen is not inaccurate. It is not incorrect. It is nonsense.

Mental age is a yard stick invented by a school of psychologists to measure "intelligence." It is not easy, however, to make a measure of intelligence and the psychologists have never agreed on a definition. This quandary presented itself to Alfred Binet. For years he had tried to reach a definition of intelligence and always he had failed. Finally he gave up the attempt, and started on another tack. He then turned his attention to the practical problem of distinguishing the "backward" child from the "normal" child in the Paris schools. To do this he had to know what was a normal child. Difficult as this promised to be, it was a good deal easier than the attempt to define intelligence. For Binet concluded, quite logically, that the standard of a normal child of any particular age was something or other which an arbitrary percentage of children of that age could do. Binet therefore decided to consider "normal" those abilities which were common to between 65 and 75 percent of the children of a particular age. In deciding on these percentages he thus decided to consider at least twenty-five percent of the children as backward. He might just as easily have fixed a percentage which would have classified ten percent of the children as backward, or fifty percent.

Having fixed a percentage which he would henceforth regard as "normal" he devoted himself to collecting questions, stunts and puzzles of various sorts, hard ones and easy ones. At the end he settled upon fifty-four tests, each of which he guessed and hoped would test some element of intelligence; all of which together would test intelligence as a whole. Binet then gave these tests in Paris to two hundred school children who ranged from three to fifteen years of age. Whenever he found a test that about sixty-five percent of the children of the same age could pass he called that a Binet test of intelligence for that age. Thus a mental age of seven years was the ability to do all the tests which sixty-five to seventy-five percent of a small group of seven-year-old Paris school children had shown themselves able to do.

This was a promising method, but of course the actual tests rested on a very weak foundation indeed. Binet himself died before he could carry his idea much further, and the task of revision and improvement was then transferred to Stanford University. The Binet scale worked badly in California. The same puzzles did not give the same results in California as in Paris. So about 1910 Professor L. M. Terman undertook to revise them. He followed Binet's method. Like Binet he would guess at a stunt which might indicate intelligence, and then try it out on about 2,300 people of various ages, including 1,700 children "in a community of average social status." By editing, rearranging and supplementing the original Binet tests he finally worked out a series of tests for each age which the average child of that age in about one hundred California children could pass.

The puzzles which this average child among a hundred California children of the same age about the year 1913 could answer are the yardstick by which "mental age" is measured in what is known as the Stanford Revision of the Binet–Simon Scale. Each correct answer gives a credit of two months' mental age. So if a child of seven can answer all tests up to the seven-year-old tests perfectly, and cannot answer any of the eight-year-old tests, his total score is seven years. He is said to test "at age," and his "intelligent quotient" or "IQ" is unity or 100 percent. Anybody's IQ can be figured, therefore, by dividing his mental age by his actual age. A child of five who tests at four years' mental age has an IQ of 80 $(4/5 = .80)$. A child of five who tests at six years' mental age has an IQ of 120 $(6/5 = 1.20)$.

The aspect of all this which matters is that "mental age" is simply the average performance with certain rather arbitrary problems. The thing to keep in mind is that all the talk about "a mental age of fourteen" goes back to the performance of eighty-two California school children in 1913–14. Their success and failures on the days they happened to be tested have become embalmed and consecrated as the measure of human intelligence. By means of that measure writers like Mr. Stoddard fix the relative values of all the peoples of the earth and of all social classes within the nations. They don't know they are doing this, however, because Mr. Stoddard at least is quite plainly taking everything at second hand.

However, I am willing for just a moment to grant that Mr. Terman in California has worked out a test for the different ages of a growing child. But I insist that anyone who uses the words "mental age" should remember that Mr. Terman reached his test by seeing what the average child of an age group could do. If his group is too small or is untypical his test is in the same measure inaccurate.

Remembering this, we come to the army tests. Here we are dealing at once with men all of whom are over the age of the mental scale. For the Stanford–Binet scale ends at "sixteen years." It assumes that intelligence stops developing at sixteen and everybody sixteen and over is therefore treated as "adult" or as "superior adult." Now the adult Stanford–Binet tests were "standardized chiefly on the basis of results from 400 adults." (Terman p. 13) "of moderate success and of very limited educational advantages" and also thirty-two high school pupils from sixteen to twenty years of age. Among these adults those who tested close together have the honor of being considered the standard of average adult intelligence.

Before the army tests came along, when anyone talked about the average adult he was talking about a few hundred Californians. The army tested about 1,700,000 adult men. But it did not use the Binet system of scoring by mental ages. It scored by a system of points which we need not stop to describe. Naturally enough everyone interested in mental testing wanted to know whether the army tests agreed in any way with the Stanford–Binet mental age standard. So by another process, which need also not be described, the results of the army tests were translated into Binet terms. The result of this translation is the table which has so badly misled poor Mr. Stoddard. This table showed that the average of the army did not agree at all with the average of Mr. Terman's Californians. There were then two things to do. One was to say that the average intelligence of 1,700,000 men was a more representative average than that of four hundred men. The other was to pin your faith to the four hundred men and insist they gave the true average.

Mr. Stoddard chose the average of four hundred rather than the average of 1,700,000 because he was in such haste to write his own book that he never reached page 785 of Psychological Examining in the United

States Army, the volume of the data edited by Major Yerkes.[1] He would have found there a clear warning against the blunder he was about to commit, the blunder of treating the average of a small number of instances as more valid than the average of a large number.

But instead of pausing to realize that the army tests had knocked the Stanford–Binet measure of adult intelligence into a cocked hat, he wrote his book in the belief that the Stanford measure is as good as it ever was. This is not intelligent. It leads one to suspect that Mr. Stoddard is a propagandist with a tendency to put truth not in the first place but in the second. It leads one to suspect, after such a beginning, that the real promise and value of the investigation which Binet started is in danger of gross perversion by muddleheaded and prejudiced men.

The Mystery of the "A" Men

Walter Lippmann

Because the results are expressed in numbers, it is easy to make the mistake of thinking that the intelligence test is a measure like a foot rule or a pair of scales. It is, of course, a quite different sort of measure. For length and weight are qualities which men have learned how to isolate no matter whether they are found in an army of soldiers, a heap of bricks, or a collection of chlorine molecules. Provided the footrule and the scales agree with the arbitrarily accepted standard foot and standard pound in

[1] "For norms of adult intelligence the results of the Army examinations are undoubtedly the most representative. It is customary to say that the mental age of the average adult is about sixteen years. This figure is based, however, upon examinations of only 62 persons. . . . This group is too small to give very reliable results and is furthermore probably not typical." Psychological Examining in the United States Army, p. 785.

The reader will note that Major Yerkes and his colleagues assert that the Stanford standard of adult intelligence is based on only sixty-two cases. This is a reference to page 49 of Mr. Terman's book on the Stanford Revision of the Binet–Simon Scale. But page 13 of the same book speaks of 400 adults being the basis on which the adult tests were standardized. I have used this larger figure because it is more favorable to the Stanford–Binet scale.

It should also be remarked that the army figures are not the absolute figures but the results of a "sample of the white draft" consisting of nearly 100,000 recruits. In strictest accuracy we ought to say then that the disagreement between army and Stanford–Binet results derives from conclusions drawn from 100,000 cases as against 400.

If these 100,000 recruits are not a fair sample of the nation, as they probably are not, then in addition to saying that the army tests contradict the Stanford–Binet scale, we ought to add that the army tests are themselves no reliable basis for measuring the average American mentality.

the Bureau of Standards at Washington they can be used with confidence. But "intelligence" is not an abstraction like length and weight; it is an exceedingly complicated notion which nobody has as yet succeeded in defining.

When we measure the weight of a schoolchild we mean a very definite thing. We mean that if you put the child on one side of an evenly balanced scale, you will have to put a certain number of standard pounds in the other scale in order to cancel the pull of the child's body towards the centre of the earth. But when you come to measure intelligence you have nothing like this to guide you. You know in a general way that intelligence is the capacity to deal successfully with the problems that confront human beings, but if you try to say what those problems are, or what you mean by "dealing" with them, or by "success," you will soon lose yourself in a fog of controversy. This fundamental difficulty confronts the intelligence tester at all times. The way in which he deals with it is the most important thing to understand about the intelligence tests, for otherwise you are certain to misinterpret the results.

The intelligence tester starts with no clear idea of what intelligence means. He then proceeds by drawing upon his common sense and experience to imagine the different kinds of problems men face which might in a general way be said to call for the exercise of intelligence. But these problems are much too complicated and too vague to be reproduced in the classroom. The intelligence tester cannot confront each child with the thousand and one situations arising in a home, a workshop, a farm, an office or in politics, that call for the exercise of those capacities which in a summary fashion we call intelligence. He proceeds, therefore, to guess at the more abstract mental abilities which come into play again and again. By this rough process the intelligence tester gradually makes up his mind that situations in real life call for memory, definition, ingenuity and so on.

He then invents puzzles which can be employed quickly and with little apparatus, that will according to his best guess test memory, ingenuity, definition and the rest. He gives these puzzles to a mixed group of children and sees how children of different ages answer them. Whenever he finds a puzzle that, say, sixty percent of twelve year old children can do, and twenty percent of the eleven year olds, he adopts that test for the twelve year olds. By a great deal of fitting he gradually works out a series of problems for each age group which sixty percent of his children can pass, twenty percent cannot pass and, say, twenty percent of the children one year younger can also pass. By this method he has arrived under the Stanford–Binet system at a conclusion of this sort. Sixty percent of children twelve years old should be able to define three out of the five words: pity, revenge, charity, envy, justice. According to Professor Terman's instructions, a child passes this test if he says that "pity" is "to be sorry for some one"; the child fails if he says "to help" or "mercy." A correct definition of "justice" is as follows: "It's what you get when you go to court"; an incorrect definition is "to be honest."

A mental test, then, is established in this way: The tester himself guesses at a large number of tests which he hopes and believes are tests of intelligence. Among these tests those finally are adopted by him which sixty percent of the children under his observation can pass. The children whom the tester is studying select his tests.

There are, consequently, two uncertain elements. The first is whether the tests really test intelligence. The second is whether the children under observation are a large enough group to be typical. The answer to the first question—whether the tests are tests of intelligence—can be determined only by seeing whether the results agree with other tests of intelligence, whatever they may be. The answer to the second question can be had only by making a very much larger number of observations than have yet been made. We know that the largest test made, the army examinations, showed enormous error in the Stanford test of adult intelligence. These elements of doubt are, I think, radical enough to prohibit anyone from using the results of these tests for large generalization about the quality of human beings. For when people generalize about the quality of human beings they assume an objective criterion of quality, and for testing intelligence there is no such criterion. These puzzles may test intelligence, and they may not. They may test an aspect of intelligence. Nobody knows.

What then do the tests accomplish? I think we can answer this question best by starting with an illustration. Suppose you wished to judge all the pebbles in a large pile of gravel for the purpose of separating them into three piles, the first to contain the extraordinary pebbles, the second the normal pebbles, the third the insignificant pebbles. You have no scales. You first separate from the pile a much smaller pile and pick out one pebble which you guess is the average. You hold it in your left hand and pick up another pebble in your right hand. The right pebble feels heavier. You pick up another pebble. It feels lighter. You pick up a third. It feels still lighter. A fourth feels heavier than the first. By this method you can arrange all the pebbles from the smaller pile in a series running from the lightest to the heaviest. You thereupon call the middle pebble the standard pebble, and with it as a measure you determine whether any pebble in the larger pile is a subnormal, a normal or a supernormal pebble.

This is just about what the intelligence test does. It does not weigh or measure intelligence by any objective standard. It simply arranges a group of people in a series from best to worst by balancing their capacity to do certain arbitrarily selected puzzles, against the capacity of all the others. The intelligence test, in other words, is fundamentally an instrument for classifying a group of people. It may also be an instrument for measuring their intelligence, but of that we cannot be at all sure unless we believe that

Mr. Binet and Mr. Terman and a few other psychologists have guessed correctly when they invented their tests. They may have guessed correctly but, as we shall see later, the proof is not yet at hand.

The intelligence test, then, is an instrument for classifying a group of people, rather than "a measure of intelligence." People are classified within a group according to their success in solving problems which may or may not be tests of intelligence. They are classified according to the performance of some Californians in the years 1910 to about 1916 with Mr. Terman's notion of the problems that reveal intelligence. They are not classified according to their ability in dealing with the problems of real life that call for intelligence.

With this in mind let us look at the army results, as they are dished up by writers like Mr. Lothrop Stoddard and Professor McDougall of Harvard. The following table is given:

4½ % of the army were A men
9 % „   „   „   „   B „
16½ % „   „   „   „   C+ „
25 % „   „   „   „   C „
20 % „   „   „   „   C− „
10 % „   „   „   „   D− „
15 % „   „   „   „   D „

But how, you ask, did the army determine the qualities of an "A" man? For an "A" man is supposed to have "very superior intelligence," and of course mankind has wondered for at least two thousand years what were the earmarks of very superior intelligence. McDougall and Stoddard are quite content to take the army's word for it, or at least they never stop to explain, before they exploit the figures, what the army meant by "very superior intelligence." The army, of course, had no intention whatever of committing itself to a definition of very superior intelligence. The army was interested in classifying recruits. It therefore asked a committee of psychologists to assemble from all the different systems, Binet and otherwise, a series of tests. The committee took this series and tried it out in a few camps. They timed the tests. "The number of items and the time limits were so fixed that five percent or less in any average group would be able to finish the entire series of items in the time allowed." [1] It is not surprising, therefore, that five percent or less (4½ percent actually) of the army made a top score. It is not surprising that tests devised to pass five percent or less "A" men should have passed four and a half percent "A" men.

The army was quite justified in doing this because it was in a hurry and was looking for about five percent of the recruits to put into officers' train-

[1] Yoakum and Yerkes, Army Mental Tests, p. 3.

ing camps. I quarrel only with the Stoddards and McDougalls who solemnly talk about the 4½ percent "A" men in the American nation without understanding how these 4½ percent were picked. They do not seem to realize that if the army had wanted half the number of officers, it could by shortening the time have made the scarcity of "A" men seem even more alarming. If the army had wanted to double the "A" men, it could have done that by lengthening the time. Somewhere, of course, in the whole group would have been found men who could not have answered all the questions correctly in any length of time. But we do not know how many men of the kind there were because the tests were never made that way.[2]

The army was interested in discovering officers and in eliminating the feeble-minded. It had no time to waste, and so it adopted a rough test which would give a quick classification. In that it succeeded on the whole very well. But the army did not measure the intelligence of the American nation, and only very loose-minded writers imagine that it did. When men write as Mr. Stoddard does that "only four and a half millions [of the whole population] can be considered 'talented,'" the only possible comment is that the statement has no foundation whatsoever. We do not know how many talented people there are: first, because we have no measure of talent, and second, because we have never made the attempt to devise one or apply one. But when we see how men like Stoddard and McDougall have exploited the army tests, we realize how necessary, but how unheeded, is the warning of Messrs. Yoakum and Yerkes that "the case with which the army group test can be given and scored makes it a dangerous method in the hands of the inexpert. It was not prepared for civilian use, and is applicable only within certain limits to other uses than that for which it was prepared."

The Reliability of Intelligence Tests

Walter Lippmann

Suppose, for example, that our aim was to test athletic rather than intellectual ability. We appoint a committee consisting of Walter Camp, Percy Haughton, Tex Rickard and Bernard Darwin, and we tell them to work out tests which will take no longer than an hour and can be given to large numbers of men at once. These tests are to measure the true

[2] Psychological Examining in the United States Army, p. 419. "The high frequencies of persons gaining at the upper levels (often 100 percent) indicate for the people making high scores on single time the 'speed' element is predominant."

athletic capicity of all men anywhere for the whole of their athletic careers. The order would be a large one, but it would certainly be no larger than the pretensions of many well known intelligence testers.

Our committee of athletic testers scratch their heads. What shall be the hour's test, they wonder, which will "measure" the athletic "capacity" of Dempsey, Tilden, Sweetser, Siki, Suzanne Lenglen and Babe Ruth, of all sprinters, Marathon runners, broad jumpers, high divers, wrestlers, billiard players, marksmen, cricketers and pogo bouncers? The committee has courage. After much guessing and some experimenting the committee works out a sort of condensed Olympic games which can be held in any empty lot. These games consist of a short sprint, one or two jumps, throwing a ball at a bull's eye, hitting a punching machine, tackling a dummy and a short game of clock golf. They try out these tests on a mixed assortment of champions and duffers and find that on the whole the champions do all the tests better than the duffers. They score the result and compute statistically what is the average score for all the tests. This average score then constitutes normal athletic ability.

Now it is clear that such tests might really give some clue to athletic ability. But the fact that in any large group of people sixty percent made an average score would be no proof that you had actually tested their athletic ability. To prove that, you would have to show that success in the athletic tests correlated closely with success in athletics. The same conclusion applies to the intelligence tests. Their statistical uniformity is one thing; their reliability another. The tests might be a fair guess at intelligence, but the statistical result does not show whether they are or not. You could get a statistical curve very much like the curve of "intelligence" distribution if instead of giving each child from ten to thirty problems to do you have flipped a coin the same number of times for each child and had credited him with the heads. I do not mean, of course, that the results are as chancy as all that. They are not, as we shall soon see. But I do mean that there is no evidence for the reliability of the tests as tests of intelligence in the claim, made by Terman,[1] that the distribution of intelligence quotients corresponds closely to "the theoretical normal curve of distribution (the Gaussian curve)." He would in a large enough number of cases get an even more perfect curve if these tests were tests not of intelligence but of the flip of a coin.

Such a statistical check has its uses of course. It tends to show, for example, that in a large group the bias and errors of the tester have been cancelled out. It tends to show that the gross result is reached in the mass by statistically impartial methods, however wrong the judgment about any particular child may be. But the fairness in giving the tests and the reliability of the tests themselves must not be confused. The tests may be

[1] Stanford Revision Binet–Simon Scale, p. 42.

quite fair applied in the mass, and yet be poor tests of individual intelligence.

We come then to the question of the reliability of the tests. There are many different systems of intelligence testing and, therefore, it is important to find out how the results agree if the same group of people take a number of different tests. The figures given by Yoakum and Yerkes[2] indicate that people who do well or badly in one are likely to do more or less equally well or badly in the other tests. Thus the army test for English-speaking literates, known as Alpha, correlates with Beta, the test for non-English speakers or illiterates at .80. Alpha with a composite test of Alpha, Beta and Stanford–Binet gives .94. Alpha with Trabue B and C completion-tests combined gives .72. On the other hand, as we noted in the first article of this series, the Stanford–Binet system of calculating "mental ages" is in violent disagreement with the results obtained by the army tests.

Nevertheless, in a rough way the evidence shows that the various tests in the mass are testing the same capacities. Whether these capacities can fairly be called intelligence, however, is not yet proved. The tests are all a good deal alike. They all derive from a common stock, and it is entirely possible that they measure only a certain kind of ability. The type of mind which is very apt in solving Sunday newspaper puzzles, or even in playing chess, may be specially favored by these tests. The fact that the same people always do well with puzzles would in itself be no evidence that the solving of puzzles was a general test of intelligence. We must remember, too, that the emotional setting plays a large role in any examination. To some temperaments the atmosphere of the examination room is highly stimulating. Such people "outdo themselves" when they feel they are being tested; other people "cannot do themselves justice" under the same conditions. Now in a large group these differences of temperament may neutralize each other in the statistical result. But they do not neutralize each other in the individual case.

The correlation between the various systems enables us to say only that the tests are not mere chance, and that they do seem to seize upon a certain kind of ability. But whether this ability is a sign of general intelligence or not, we have no means of knowing from such evidence alone. The same conclusion holds true of the fact that when the tests are repeated at intervals on the same group of people they give much the same results. Data of this sort are as yet meager, for intelligence testing has not been practised long enough to give results over long periods of time. Yet the fact that the same child makes much the same score year after year is significant. It permits us to believe that some genuine capacity is being

2 Army Mental Tests, p. 20.

tested. But whether this is the capacity to pass tests or the capacity to deal with life, which we call intelligence, we do not know.

This is the crucial question, and in the nature of things there can as yet be little evidence one way or another. The Stanford–Binet tests were set in order about the year 1914. The oldest children of the group tested at that time were 142 children ranging from fourteen to sixteen years of age. Those children are now between twenty-two and twenty-four. The returns are not in. The main question of whether the children who ranked high in the Stanford–Binet tests will rank high in real life is now unanswerable, and will remain unanswered for a generation. We are thrown back, therefore, for a test of the tests on the success of these children in school. We ask whether the results of the intelligence test correspond with the quality of school work, with school grades and with school progress.

The crude figures at first glance show a poor correspondence. In Terman's studies[3] the intelligence quotient correlated with school work, as judged by teachers, only .45 and with intelligence as judged by teachers, only .48. But that in itself proves nothing against the reliability of the intelligence tests. For after all the test of school marks, of promotion or the teacher's judgments, is not necessarily more reliable. There is no reason certainly for thinking that the way public school teachers classify children is any final criterion of intelligence. The teachers may be mistaken. In a definite number of cases Terman has shown that they are mistaken, especially when they judge a child's intelligence by his grade in school and not by his age. A retarded child may be doing excellent work, an advanced child poorer work. Terman has shown also that teachers make their largest mistakes in judging children who are above or below the average. The teachers become confused by the fact that the school system is graded according to age.

A fair reading of the evidence will, I think, convince anyone that as a *system of grading* the intelligence tests may prove superior in the end to the system now prevailing in the public schools. The intelligence test, as we noted in an earlier article, is an instrument of classification. When it comes into competition with the method of classifying that prevails in school it exhibits many signs of superiority. If you have to classify children for the convenience of school administration, you are likely to get a more coherent classification with the tests than without them. I should like to emphasize this point especially, because it is important that in denying the larger pretensions and misunderstandings we should not lose sight of the positive value of the tests. We say, then, that none of the evidence thus far considered shows whether they are reliable tests of the capacity to deal intelligently with the problems of real life. But as gauges of the capacity to

[3] Stanford Revision of Binet-Simon Scale, Chapter VI.

deal intelligently with the problems of the classroom, the evidence justifies us in thinking that the tests will grade the pupils more accurately than do the traditional school examinations.

If school success were a reliable index of human capacity, we should be able to go a step further and say that the intelligence test is a general measure of human capacity. But of course no such claim can be made for school success, for that would be to say that the purpose of the schools is to measure capacity. It is impossible to admit this. The child's success with school work cannot be a measure of the child's success in life. On the contrary, his success in life must be a significant measure of the school's success in developing the capacities of the child. If a child fails in school and then fails in life, the school cannot sit back and say: you see how accurately I predicted this. Unless we are to admit that education is essentially impotent, we have to throw back the child's failure at the school, and describe it as a failure not by the child but by the school.

For this reason, the fact that the intelligence test may turn out to be an excellent administrative device for grading children in school cannot be accepted as evidence that it is a reliable test of intelligence. We shall see in the succeeding articles that the whole claim of the intelligence testers to have found a reliable measure of human capacity rests on an assumption, imported into the argument, that education is essentially impotent because intelligence is hereditary and unchangeable. This belief is the ultimate foundation of the claim that the tests are not merely an instrument of classification but a true measure of intelligence. It is this belief which has been seized upon eagerly by writers like Stoddard and McDougall. It is a belief which is, I am convinced, wholly unproved, and it is this belief which is obstructing and perverting the practical development of the tests.

The Abuse of the Tests

Walter Lippmann

We have found reason for thinking that the intelligence test may prove to be a considerable help in sorting out children into school classes. If it is true, as Professor Terman says,[1] that between a third and a half of the school-children fail to progress through the grades at the expected rate, then there is clearly something wrong with the present system of examinations and promotions. No one doubts that there is something wrong, and that in consequence both the retarded and the advanced child suffer.

[1] The Measurement of Intelligence, p. 3.

The intelligence test promises to be more successful in grading the children. This means that the tendency of the tests in the average is to give a fairly correct sample of the child's capacity to do school work. In a wholesale system of education, such as we have in our public schools, the intelligence test is likely to become a useful device for fitting the child into the school. This is, of course, better than not fitting the child into the school, and under a more correct system of grading, such as the intelligence test promises to furnish, it should become possible even where education is conducted in large classrooms to specialize the teaching, because the classes will be composed of pupils whose capacity for school work is fairly homogeneous.

Excellent as this seems, it is of the first importance that school authorities and parents realize exactly what this administrative improvement signifies. For great mischief will follow if there is confusion about the spiritual meaning of this reform. If, for example, the impression takes root that these tests really measure intelligence, that they constitute a sort of last judgment on the child's capacity, that they reveal "scientifically" his predestined ability, then it would be a thousand times better if all the intelligence testers and all their questionnaires were sunk without warning in the Sargasso Sea. One has only to read around in the literature of the subject, but more especially in the work of popularizers like McDougall and Stoddard, to see how easily the intelligence test can be turned into an engine of cruelty, how easily in the hands of blundering or prejudiced men it could turn into a method of stamping a permanent sense of inferiority upon the soul of a child.

It is not possible, I think, to imagine a more contemptible proceeding than to confront a child with a set of puzzles, and after an hour's monkeying with them, proclaim to the child, or to his parents, that here is a C— individual. It would not only be a contemptible thing to do. It would be a crazy thing to to, because there is nothing in these tests to warrant a judgment of this kind. All that can be claimed for the tests is that they can be used to classify into a homogeneous group the children whose capacities for school work are at a particular moment fairly similar. The intelligence test shows nothing as to why those capacities at any moment are what they are, and nothing as to the individual treatment which a temporarily retarded child may require.

I do not mean to say that the intelligence test is certain to be abused. I do mean to say it lends itself so easily to abuse that the temptation will be enormous. Suppose you have a school in which there are fifty ten year old children in the seventh grade and fifty eleven year old in the eighth. In each class you find children who would jump ahead if they could and others who lag behind. You then regrade them according to mental age. Some of the ten year olds go into the eighth grade, some of the elevens into the seventh grade. That is an improvement. But if you are satisfied to leave the matter there, you are doing a grave injustice to the retarded children and ultimately to the community in which they are going to live. You cannot, in other words, be satisfied to put retarded eleven year olds and average ten year olds together. The retarded eleven year olds need something besides proper classification according to mental age. They need special analysis and special training to overcome their retardation. The leading intelligence testers recognize this, of course. But the danger of the intelligence tests is that in a wholesome system of education, the less sophisticated or the more prejudiced will stop when they have classified and forget that their duty is to educate. They will grade the retarded child instead of fighting the causes of his backwardness. For the whole drift of the propaganda based on intelligence testing is to treat people with low intelligence quotients as congenitally and hopelessly inferior.

Readers who have not examined the literature of mental testing may wonder why there is reason to fear such an abuse of an invention which has many practical uses. The answer, I think, is that most of the more prominent testers have committed themselves to a dogma which must lead to just such abuse. They claim not only that they are really measuring intelligence, but that intelligence is innate, hereditary, and predetermined. They believe that they are measuring the capacity of a human being for all time and that this capacity is fatally fixed by the child's heredity. Intelligence testing in the hands of men who hold this dogma could not but lead to an intellectual caste system in which the task of education had given way to the doctrine of predestination and infant damnation. If the intelligence test really measured the unchangeable hereditary capacity of human beings, as so many assert, it would inevitably evolve from an administrative convenience into a basis for hereditary caste.

In the next article we shall examine the evidence for the claim that the intelligence tests reveal the fixed hereditary endowment.

Tests of Hereditary Intelligence

Walter Lippmann

The first argument in favor of the view that the capacity for intelligence is hereditary is an argument by analogy. There is a good deal of evidence that idiocy and certain forms of degeneracy are transmitted from parents to offspring. There are, for example, a number of notorious families—the Kallikaks, the Jukes, the Hill Folk, the Nams, the Zeros and the Ishmaelites, who have a long and persistent record of degeneracy. Whether these bad family histories are the result of a bad social start or of defective germplasm is not entirely clear, but the weight of evidence is in favor of the view that there is a taint in the blood. Yet even in these sensational cases, in fact just because they are so sensational and exceptional, it is important to remember that the proof is not conclusive.

There is, for example, some doubt as to the Kallikaks. It will be recalled that during the Revolutionary War a young soldier, known under the pseudonym of Martin Kallikak, had an illegitimate feeble-minded son by a feeble-minded girl. The descendants of this union have been criminals and degenerates. But after the war was over Martin married respectably. The descendants of this union have been successful people. This is a powerful evidence, but it would, as Professor Cattell[1] points out, be more powerful, and more interesting scientifically, if the wife of the respectable marriage had been feeble-minded, and the girl in the tavern had been a healthy, normal person. Then only would it have been possible to say with complete confidence that this was a pure case of biological rather than of social heredity.

Assuming, however, that the inheritance of degeneracy is established, we may turn to the other end of the scale. Here we find studies of the persistence of talent in superior families. Sir Francis Galton, for example, found "that the son of a distinguished judge had about one chance in four of becoming himself distinguished, while the son of a man picked out at random from the general population had only about one chance in four thousand of becoming similarly distinguished." [2] Professor Cattell in a study of the families of one thousand leading American scientists remarks in this connection: "Galton finds in the judges of England a notable proof of hereditary genius. It would be found to be much less in the judges of the United States. It could probably be shown by the same methods to be even stronger in the families conducting the leading publishing and banking houses of England and Germany." And in another place he remarks that "my data show that a boy born in Massachusetts or Connecticut has been fifty times as likely to become a scientific man as a boy born along the Southeastern seaboard from Georgia to Louisiana."

It is not necessary for our purpose to come to any conclusion as to the inheritance of capacity. The evidence is altogether insufficient for any conclusion, and the only possible attitude is an open mind. We are, moreover, not concerned with the question of whether intelligence is hered-

---

[1] Popular Science Monthly, May, 1915.

[2] Galton, Hereditary Genius (1869) cited by Stoddard, Revolt Against Civilization, p. 49.

itary. We are concerned only with the claim of the intelligence tester that *he reveals and measures* hereditary intelligence. These are quite separate propositions, but they are constantly confused by the testers. For these gentlemen seem to think that if Galton's conclusion about judges and the tale of the Kallikaks are accepted, then two things follow: first, that by analogy[3] all the graduations of intelligence are fixed in heredity, and second that the tests measure these different grades of heredity intelligence. Neither conclusion follows necessarily. The facts of heredity cannot be proved by analogy; the facts of heredity are what they are. The question of whether the intelligence test measures heredity is a wholly different matter. It is the only question which concerns us here.

We may start then with the admitted fact that children of favored classes test higher on the whole than other children. Binet tests made in Paris, Berlin, Brussels, Breslau, Rome, Petrograd, Moscow, in England and in America agree on this point. In California Professor Terman[4] divided 492 children into five social classes and obtained the following correlation between the median intelligence quotient and social status:

Social Group	Median IQ
Very Inferior	85
Inferior	95
Average	99.5
Very Superior	106
Superior	107

On the face of it this table would seem to indicate, if it indicates anything, a considerable connection between intelligence and environment. Mr. Terman denies this, and argues that "if home environment really has any considerable effect upon the IQ we should expect this effect to become more marked, the longer the influence has continued. That is, the correlation of IQ with social status should increase with age." But since his data show that at three age levels (5–8 years) and (9–11 years) and (12–15 years) the coefficient of correlation with social status declines (it is .43, .41 and .29 respectively), Mr. Terman concludes that "in the main, native qualities of intellect and character, rather than chance (sic) determine the social class to which a family belongs." He even pleads with us to accept this conclusion: "After all does not common observation teach

[3] cf. McDougall, p. 40.
[4] Revision, p. 89.

us that etc. etc." and "from what is already known about heredity should we not naturally expect" and so forth and so forth.

Now I propose to put aside entirely all that Mr. Terman's common observation and natural expectations teach him. I should like only to examine his argument that if home environment counted much its effect ought to become more and more marked as the child grew older.

It is difficult to see why Mr. Terman should expect this to happen. To the infant the home environment is the whole environment. When the child goes to school the influences of the home are merged in the larger environment of school and playground. Gradually the child's environment expands until it takes in a city, and the larger invisible environment of books and talk and movies and newspapers. Surely Mr. Terman is making a very strange assumption when he argues that as the child spends less and less time at home the influence of home environment ought to become more and more marked. His figures, showing that the correlation between social status and intelligence declines from .43 before eight years of age to .29 at twelve years of age, are hardly an argument for hereditary differences in the endowment of social classes. They are a rather strong argument on the contrary for the traditional American theory that the public school is an agency for equalizing the opportunities of the privileged and the unprivileged.

But Mr. Terman could by a shrewder use of his own data have made a better case. It was not necessary for him to use an argument which comes down to saying that the less contact the child has with the home the more influential the home ought to be. That is simply the gross logical fallacy of expecting increasing effects from a diminishing cause. Mr. Terman would have made a more interesting point if he had asked why the influence of social status on intelligence persists so long after the parents and the home have usually ceased to play a significant part in the child's intellectual development. Instead of being surprised that the correlation has declined from .43 at eight to .29 at twelve, he should have asked why there is any correlation left at twelve. That would have posed a question which the traditional eulogist of the little red schoolhouse could not answer offhand. If the question had been put that way, no one could dogmatically have denied that differences of heredity in social classes may be a contributing factor. But curiously, it is the mental tester himself who incidentally furnishes the most powerful defense of the orthodox belief that in the mass of differences of ability are the result of education rather than of heredity.

The intelligence tester has found that the rate of mental growth declines as the child matures. It is faster in infancy than in adolescence, and the adult intelligence is supposed to be fully developed somewhere between sixteen and nineteen years of age. The growth of intelligence slows up gradually until it stops entirely. I do not know whether this is true or not, but the intelligence testers believe it. From this belief it follows that there is "a decreasing significance of a given amount of retardation in the upper years." [5] Binet, in fact, suggested the rough rule that under ten years of age a retardation of two years usually means feeble-mindedness, while for older children feeble-mindedness is not indicated unless there is a retardation of at least three years.

This being the case the earlier the influence the more potent it would be, the later the influence the less significant. The influences which bore upon the child when his intelligence was making its greatest growth would leave a profounder impression than those which bore upon him when his growth was more nearly completed. Now in early childhood you have both the period of the greatest growth and the most inclusive and direct influence of the home environment. It is surprising that the effects of superior and inferior environments persist, though in diminishing degree, as the child emerges from the home?

It is possible, of course, to deny that the early environment has any important influence on the growth of intelligence. Men like Stoddard and McDougall do deny it, and so does Mr. Terman. But on the basis of the mental tests they have no right to an opinion. Mr. Terman's observations begin at four years of age. He publishes no data on infancy and he is, therefore, generalizing about the hereditary factor after four years of immensely significant development have already taken place. On his own showing as to the high importance of the earlier years, he is hardly justified in ignoring them. He cannot simply lump together the net result of natural endowment and infantile education and ascribe it to the germ-plasm.

In doing just that he is obeying the will to believe, not the methods of science. How far he is carried may be judged from this instance which Mr. Terman cites[6] as showing the negligible influence of environment. He tested twenty children in an orphanage and found only three who were fully normal. "The orphanage in question," he then remarks, "is a reasonably good one and affords an environment which is about as stimulating to normal mental development as average home life among the middle classes." Think of it. Mr. Terman first discovers what a "normal mental development" is by testing children who have grown up in an adult environment of parents, aunts and uncles. He then applies this footrule to children who are growing up in the abnormal environment of an institu-

[5] Revision, p. 51.
[6] Revision, p. 99.

tion and finds that they are not normal. He then puts the blame for abnormality on the germplasm of the orphans.

A Future for the Tests

Walter Lippmann

How does it happen that men of science can presume to dogmatize about the mental qualities of the germplasm when their own observations begin at four years of age? Yet this is what the chief intelligence testers, led by Professor Terman, are doing. Without offering any data on all that occurs between conception and the age of kindergarten, they announce on the basis of what they have got out of a few thousand questionnaires that they are measuring the hereditary mental endowment of human beings. Obviously this is not a conclusion obtained by research. It is a conclusion planted by the will to believe. It is, I think, for the most part unconsciously planted. The scoring of the tests itself favors an uncritical belief that intelligence is a fixed quantity in the germplasm and that, no matter what the environment, only a predetermined increment of intelligence can develop from year to year. For the result of a test is not stated in terms of intelligence, but as a percentage of the average for that age level. These percentages remain more or less constant. Therefore, if a child shows an IQ of 102, it is easy to argue that he was born with an IQ of 102.

There is here, I am convinced, a purely statistical illusion, which breaks down when we remember what IQ means. A child's IQ is his percentage of passes in the test which the average child of a large group of his own age has passed. The IQ measures his place in respect to the average at any year. But it does not show the rate of his growth from year to year. In fact it tends rather to conceal the fact that the creative opportunities in education are greatest in early childhood. It conceals the fact, which is of such far-reaching importance, that because the capacity to form intellectual habits decreases as the child matures, the earliest education has a cumulative effect on the child's future. All this the static percentages of the IQ iron out. They are meant to iron it out. It is the boast of the inventors of the IQ that "the distribution of intelligence maintains a certain constancy from five to thirteen or fourteen years of age, *when the degree of intelligence is expressed in terms of the intelligence quotient.*" [1] The intention

[1] Revision, p. 50.

is to eliminate the factor of uneven and cumulative growth, so that there shall be always a constant measure by which to classify children in class rooms.

This, as I have pointed out, may be useful in school administration, but it can turn out to be very misleading for an unwary theorist. If instead of saying that Johnny gained thirty pounds one year, twenty-five the next and twenty the third, you said that measured by the average gain for children of his age, Johnny's weight quotients were 101, 102, 101, you might, unless you were careful, begin to think that Johnny's germplasm weighed as much as he does today. And if you dodged that mistake, you might nevertheless come to think that since Johnny classified year after year in the same position, Johnny's diet had no influence on his weight.

The effect of the intelligence quotient on a tester's mind may be to make it *seem* as if intelligence were constant, whereas it is only the statistical position in large groups which is constant. This illusion of constancy has, I believe, helped seriously to prevent men like Terman from appreciating the variability of early childhood. Because in the mass the percentages remain fixed, they tend to forget how in each individual case there were offered creative opportunities which the parents and nurse girls improved or missed or bungled. The whole more or less blind drama of childhood, where the habits of intelligence are formed, is concealed in the mental test. The testers themselves become callous to it. What their footrule does not measure soon ceases to exist for them, and so they discuss heredity in school children before they have studied the education of infants.

But of course no student of human motives will believe that this revival of predestination is due to a purely statistical illusion. He will say with Nietzsche that "every impulse is imperious, and, as *such*, attempts to philosophize." And so behind the will to believe he will expect to find some manifestation of the will to power. He will not have to read far in the literature of mental testing to discover it. He will soon see that the intelligence test is being sold to the public on the basis of the claim that it is a device which will measure pure intelligence, whatever that may be, as distinguished from knowledge and acquired skill.

This advertisement is impressive. If it were true, the emotional and the worldly satisfactions in store for the intelligence tester would be very great. If he were really measuring intelligence, and if intelligence were a fixed hereditary quantity, it would be for him to say not only where to place each child in school, but also which children should go to high school, which to college, which into the professions, which into the manual trades and common labor. If the tester could make good his claim, he would soon occupy a position of power which no intellectual has held since the collapse of theocracy. The vista is enchanting, and even a little of the vista is intoxicating enough. If only it could be proved, or at least believed, that intelligence is fixed by heredity, and that the tester can measure it, what a future to dream about! The unconscious temptation is too strong for the ordinary critical defence of the scientific methods. With the help of a subtle statistical illusion, intricate logical fallacies and a few smuggled obiter dicta, self-deception as the preliminary to public deception is almost automatic.

The claim that we have learned how to *measure hereditary intelligence* has no scientific foundation. We cannot measure intelligence when we have never defined it, and we cannot speak of its hereditary basis after it has been indistinguishably fused with a thousand educational and environmental influences from the time of conception to the school age. The claim that Mr. Terman or anyone else is measuring hereditary intelligence has no more scientific foundation than a hundred other fads, vitamins and glands and amateur psychoanalysis and correspondence courses in will power, and it will pass with them into that limbo where phrenology and palmistry and characterology and the other Babu sciences are to be found. In all of these there was some admixture of primitive truth which the conscientious scientist retains long after the wave of popular credulity has spent itself.

So, I believe, it will be with mental testing. Gradually under the impact of criticism the claim will be abandoned that a device has been invented for measuring native intelligence. Suddenly it will dawn upon the testers that this is just another form of examination, differing in degree rather than in kind from Mr. Edison's questionnaire or a college entrance examination. It may be a better form of examination than these, but it is the same sort of thing. It tests, as they do, an unanalyzed mixture of native capacity, acquired habits and stored-up knowledge, and no tester knows at any moment which factor he is testing. He is testing the complex result of a long and unknown history, and the assumption that his questions and his puzzles can in fifty minutes isolate abstract intelligence is, therefore, vanity. The ability of a twelve-year-old child to define pity or justice and to say what lesson the story of the fox and crow "teaches" may be a measure of his total education, but it is no measure of the value or capacity of his germplasm.

Once the pretensions of this new science are thoroughly defeated by the realization that these are not "intelligence tests" at all nor "measurements of intelligence," but simply a somewhat more abstract kind of examination, their real usefulness can be established and developed. As examinations they can be adapted to the purposes in view, whether it be to indicate the feeble-minded for segregation, or to classify children in schools, or to select recruits from the army for officers' training camps, or to pick bank clerks. Once the notion is abandoned that the tests reveal pure intelligence, specific tests for specific purposes can be worked out.

A general measure of intelligence valid for all people everywhere at all times may be an interesting toy for the psychologist in his laboratory. But just because the tests are so general, just because they are made so abstract in the vain effort to discount training and knowledge, the tests are by that much less useful for the practical needs of school administration and industry. Instead, therefore, of trying to find a test which will with equal success discover artillery officers, Methodist ministers, and branch managers for the rubber business, the psychologists would far better work out special and specific examinations for artillery officers, divinity school candidates and branch managers in the rubber business. On that line they may ultimately make a serious contribution to a civilization which is constantly searching for more successful ways of classifying people for specialized jobs. And in the meantime the psychologists will save themselves from the reproach of having opened up a new chance for quackery in a field where quacks breed like rabbits, and they will save themselves from the humiliation of having furnished doped evidence to the exponents of the New Snobbery.

A POSTSCRIPT

This discussion has already provoked a lengthy correspondence which suggests the advisability of summarizing at this point the conclusions arrived at in the series of articles. The argument which I am prepared to defend is as follows:

1. The Statement that the intelligence of the American nation has been measured by the army intelligence tests has no foundation. Generalizations, like those of Mr. Lothrop Stoddard, that "the average mental age of Americans is only about fourteen" are in the strictest sense of the word nonsense.
2. There is reason to hope that for the purpose of more homogeneous classification of school children the intelligence tests may be of some practical benefit if administered with scepticism and sympathy.
3. This benefit is in great danger of being offset by dangerous abuse if the claims of the intelligence testers are not purged of certain fundamental assumptions.
4. The most important of these fundamental assumptions are:
   a. that the intelligence test measures "intelligence"

b. that "intelligence" is fixed by heredity, and that the intelligence test reveals and measures hereditary intelligence.

5. The attempt to construct a universal test of native intelligence on these assumptions may be an interesting theoretical experiment, but the claim that such a test exists, or is likely soon to exist, is scientifically unsound, is designed to lead to social injustice and to grave injury to those who are arbitrarily classified as predestined inferiors or superiors.

6. The claim that a universal test of native intelligence exists is not only unfounded and harmful, but it is also stultifying to the practical development of the tests themselves. Instead of aiming at a universal test of hereditary intelligence, psychological research should be directed towards the development of a multitude of specific tests for the use of administrators, industrial, scholastic or military, as the case may be, who have to deal with the practical problem of selecting and classifying groups of people. The aim should be to test, not the capacity of the germplasm of John Smith, for that cannot by any knowledge we possess be distinguished from his training, but the specific fitness of John Smith at this moment to do the work of the eighth grade, to run a freight locomotive or to sell medium priced automobiles. For tasks of modern life are much too varied to be measured by a single and universal test. One series of tests for intelligence is as meaningless as would be the attempt to measure time, space, weight, speed, color, shape, beauty, justice, faith, hope and charity, with a footrule, a pound scale and a speedometer.

The Great Conspiracy

or

The Impulse Imperious of Intelligence Testers,
Psychoanalyzed and Exposed by Mr. Lippmann

Lewis M. Terman

After Mr. Bryan had confounded the evolutionists, and Voliva the astronomers, it was only fitting that some equally fearless knight should stride forth in righteous wrath and annihilate that other group of pseudo-scientists known as "intelligence testers." Mr. Walter Lippmann, alone and unaided, has performed just this service. That it took six rambling articles to do the job is unimportant. It is done. The world is deeply in debt to Mr. Lippmann. So are the psychologists, if they only knew it, for henceforth they should know better than to waste their lives monkeying with those silly little "puzzles" or juggling IQ's and mental ages.

What have intelligence testers done that they should merit such a fate? Well, what have they not done? They have enunciated, ex cathedra, in the guise of fact, law and eternal verity, such highly revolutionary and absurd doctrines as the following; to wit:

1. That the strictly average representative of the genus homo is not a particularly intellectual animal;
2. that some members of the species are much stupider than others;
3. that school prodigies are usually brighter than school laggards;
4. that college professors are more intelligent than janitors, architects than hod-carriers, railroad presidents than switch-tenders; and (most heinous of all)
5. that the offspring of socially, economically and professionally successful parents have better mental endowment, on the average, than the offspring of said janitors, hod-carriers and switch-tenders.

These are indeed dangerous doctrines, subversive of American democracy. The crime of the "intelligence testers" is made worse by the fact that they have attempted to gain credence for their nefarious theories by resort to cunningly devised statistical formulae which common people do not understand. It is true that some of these doctrines had been voiced before, but as long as they were expressed in ordinary language they passed as mere opinion and did little harm. But to talk about mental differences in terms of IQ's, or to reckon mental inheritance in terms of a ".50 coefficient of resemblance between parent and offspring," is a far more serious matter. In the interest of freedom of opinion there ought to be a law passed forbidding the encroachment of quantitative methods upon those fields which from time immemorial have been reserved for the play of sentiment and opinion. For example, why should not one be allowed to take his political or social theory as he takes his religion, without having it all mixed up with IQ's, probable errors and coefficients or correlation?

At any rate, it will not do to let the idea get abroad that human beings differ in any such vital trait as ability to think, comprehend, reason; or, if such differences really exist, that there is the remotest possibility of anyone ever being able to measure them. If the psychologists should succeed in getting the intelligentsia to swallow this vanity-satisfying doctrine, who knows that they would not next succeed in putting over a system of plural voting based upon intelligence indices (to be determined by these self-same psychologists)? Absurd? By no means. Suppose, for example, they should somehow manage to give a test to the members of Congress (it might be done without their knowing it) and should then shrewdly award to each and every one a flatteringly high IQ. Sheer instinct on the part of the recipients could be depended upon to do the rest.

Let there be no misapprehension; the principle of democracy is at stake. The essential thing about a democracy is not equality of opportunity, as some foolish persons think, but equality of mental endowment. Where would our American democracy be if it should turn out that people differ in intelligence as they do in height; especially if the psychologist could make it appear that he had discovered a method of triangulating everybody's intellectual altitude? The argument of the psychologists that they would use their method in the discovery and conservation of talent, among rich and poor alike, is brazen camouflage. They don't care a twirl-o'-your-thumb about the conservation of talent. Their real purpose is to set up a neo-aristocracy, more snobbish, more tyrannical and on every count more hateful than any that has yet burdened the earth. Inasmuch as the psychologists know their little "puzzle" stunts better than anyone else can hope to know them, they are doubtless entertaining ambitious visions of themselves forming the cap stone of this new political and social structure. As Mr. Lippmann well says, "if the tester could make good his claim that his tests test intelligence he would soon occupy a position of power which no intellectual has held since the collapse of theocracy." In short, the whole thing is motivated by the Nietzschean Impulse Imperious.

It is high time that we were penetrating the wiles of this crafty cult. We have been entirely too unsuspecting. For example, the innocent-minded Germans are being shamefully taken in at this very moment. Hardly had the old government of Germany crashed, when the educational authorities of the newly established republic allowed the psychologists to launch a wild orgy of intelligence testing in the schools. The orgy continues unabated. The ostensible purpose is to sift the schools for superior talent in order to give it a chance to make the most of itself, in whatever stratum of society it may be found. The psychologists pretend that they are trying to break up the old Prussian caste system. They are not. It is the Impulse Imperious. If the German people don't wake up they will soon find themselves in the grip of a super-junker caste that will out-junker anything Prussia ever turned loose. England and the other European countries are in similar danger. The conspiracy has even spread to Australia, South Africa and Japan. It is world-wide.

Now it is evident that Mr. Lippman has been seeing red; also, that seeing red is not very conducive to seeing clearly. The impassioned tone of these six articles gives their case away. Clearly, something has hit the bull's-eye of one of Mr. Lippman's emotional complexes. From the concentration of attack upon me one would infer that I had caused all the trouble, even to the point of seducing such an eminent psychologist as William McDougall. If such is the case, my responsibility is very great, for a majority of the psychologists of America, England and Germany are now enrolled in the ranks of the "Intelligence testers," and all but a handful of the rest use their results.

The six articles are introduced by the editors of the New Republic as a critical "analysis and estimate of intelligence tests." As it turns out, the estimate is considerably more in evidence than the analysis. The former rings out clearly in every paragraph; the latter, when it is not downright loco, is vague and misleading. One gathers, however, that Mr. Lippmann thinks he has a mission to perform and that the end justifies the means. This is not an accusation; it is a charitable way of explaining his misuse of facts and quotations.

The validity of intelligence tests is hardly a question the psychologist would care to debate with Mr. Lippman; nor is there any reason to engage in so profitless a venture. It is only necessary to examine casually a few samples of his allegations in order to show what weight they should carry.[1]

Sample No. 1. *The belief that our draftees in the war had an average mental age of only fourteen years rests entirely upon the mental age standards embodied in the Stanford Revision of the Binet tests. These standards were based upon a mere handful of samplings and are entirely overthrown by the army results. The army tests have "knocked the Stanford Revision into a cocked hat."*

As a matter of fact, the belief in question does not rest at all upon the correctness of the Stanford mental age norms. Independent age norms have several times been derived for the army tests by applying them to large groups of unselected school children. I have presented some of these norms in the very report from which Mr. Lippmann quotes a few of the facts he is unable to interpret.[2] Such independently derived norms for the Alpha test, for the Beta test and for the Yerkes–Bridges Point Scale (all used in the army), agree with the Stanford–Binet in the verdict as to average mental age of our drafted soldiers. On every kind of test that was employed, even the most non-verbal, the average score earned by draftees was less than that earned by average fourteen-year-old school children. Psychologists are not entirely agreed as to how this fact should be interpreted, but that is beside the point. Those who accept the army data at

---

[1] His allegations are here stated in highly condensed form, as the text is much too verbose for literal quotation.

[2] Psychological Examining in the United States Army. Vol. 15, National Academy of Science Memoirs, p. 536 ff.

their face value think that the "Fourteen–Year" tests of the Stanford–Binet should be renamed "Average Adult" tests. The possible desirability of such renaming has no bearing whatever on the average mental age of soldiers or, for that matter, on the validity of the Stanford tests as a measure of intelligence.

Sample No. 2. *The intelligence rating earned by a soldier was determined chiefly by the time limits used in giving the tests.*

The effects of increased time limits were thoroughly investigated by the Division of Psychology, Surgeon General's Office. The results of the experiment, which was carried out under my direction by Dr. Mark A. May, are stated in the following words: "In general, then, we have no reason to assume that an extension of time limits would have improved the test or have given an opportunity to many individuals materially to alter their ratings." [3] In fact, scores earned by 510 men on regular time correlated with scores earned by the same group on double time to the extent of .965. This means, of course, that the top five percent of one method included almost exactly the same men as were in the top five percent by the other method, and similarly for a cross section in any range of the score distribution. These facts are to be found just three pages from a statement which Mr. Lippmann takes out of its setting and quotes in a manner certain to mislead.

Sample No. 3. *The symmetrical distribution of IQ's resulting from application of the Stanford–Binet to unselected children is no proof whatever of the validity of the test.*

Perfectly true and perfectly irrelevant. I have never made such a claim, although Mr. Lippman tries to give the impression that I have. It is true, as he asserts, that coin-tossing gives an even more symmetrical curve of distribution. Mr. Lippmann uses this illustration in order to suggest that intelligence score distributions, like those for coin-tossing, are mainly a product of chance. (He does admit they are "not quite as chancy as that.") What are the facts? Over and over again the experiment has been made of testing a large group of children twice, with an interval of several days, or months, or even years between the tests. Each pupil's original score is then paired with his later score, and a correlation coefficient is computed for the two series of tests. If the scores were due to chance, the resulting correlations would of course be .00. Actually they are nearly always above .80, and occasionally above .90. If Mr. Lippman will make two one-thousand series of coin-tosses and then correlate the results of the two series by pairing first toss with first toss, second toss with second toss, etc., he will get, not .80 or .90, but .00, plus or minus a small probable error.

[3] Psychological Examining in the U.S. Army, p. 416.

Sample No. 4. *The tests are doubtless useful in classifying school children, but this is no evidence that they test intelligence.*

Possibly it is not; or possibly it depends upon one's definition of intelligence. Most of us have uncritically taken it for granted that children who attend school eight or ten years without passing the fourth grade or surmounting long division, are probably stupider than children who lead their classes into high school at twelve years and into college at sixteen. Mr. Lippmann contends that we can't tell anything about how intelligent either one of these children is until he has lived out his life. Therefore, for a lifetime, at least, Mr. Lippmann considers his position impregnable!

Sample No. 5. *Although intelligence tests are capable of rendering valuable service in classifying school children, they are in great danger of becoming an "engine of cruelty" by being turned into "a method of stamping a permanent sense of inferiority upon the soul of the child." Nothing could be more contemptible than to—etc., etc.*

Mr. Lippmann does not charge that the tests have been thus abused, but that they easily could be. Very true; but they simply aren't. That is one of the recognized rules of the game. Isn't it funny what horrible possibilities an excited brain can conjure up? I recall a patient who had worked himself into a wretched stew from thinking how terrible it would be if butchers by concerted action all over the country, should suddenly take it into their heads to slaughter their unsuspecting customers. He was actually determined to get a law passed that would deprive these potential murderers of their edged and pointed tools.

Sample No. 6. *There is no proof that mental traits are inherited. Goddard thought he had proved it for mental deficiency, but Cattell questions his evidence. Galton thought he had proved it for genius, but Cattell doesn't seem to think much of that proof either.*

Note how cleverly Mr. Lippmann strives for effect by playing off one psychologist against another. He resorts to this frequently. The trick is very simple; all you do is to take an isolated statement out of its original setting and quote it in a setting made to order. In that way you can have all the expert opinion on your side. Mr. Bryan is said to use this method with telling effect against the evolutionists. Not that psychologists don't sometimes disagree, even as doctors do. It would be a sorry outlook for their young science if they did not. But when the outsider comes along and tries to make capital out of such differences, it is well to be on one's guard. In ninety-nine cases out of a hundred it means that an unfair advantage is being taken both of the reader and of the author quoted. Think, for example, of Mr. Lippmann's quoting Cattell in support of his tirade against intelligence testing—Cattell, the pupil of Galton, the father of mentality testing in America, the inventor of new methods for the study of individual differences, the author of important studies (in progress) on the inheritance of genius!

Sample No. 7. (Main Allegation, asserted at least three times in every paragraph, always with signs of greatly increased blood pressure.) *The intelligence tests don't test pure intelligence. Any appearance to the contrary is due to "a subtle statistical illusion." The psychologist's assumption "that his questions and his puzzles can in fifty minutes isolate abstract intelligence is vanity." It is worse than vanity; it is an attempt to restore the "doctrine of predestination and infant damnation" in favor of an "intellectual caste system,"* etc., etc.

It is evident that Jack has prepared an imposing giant for the slaughter. No matter that it is stuffed with straw or that it is set up in a fashion to make it the easy victim of a few vigorous puffs of superheated atmosphere. As a matter of fact, all the "intelligence testers" will readily agree with Mr. Lippmann that their tests do not measure simon pure intelligence, but always native ability plus other things, with no final verdict yet as to exactly how much the other things affect the score. However, nearly all the psychologists believe that native ability counts very heavily. Mr. Lippmann doesn't. He prefers to believe that more probably an individual's IQ is determined by what happens to him in the nursery before the age of four years, in connection with the "creative opportunities which the parents and nurse girls improved or missed or bungled"! After all, if our experiences in the nursery gave us our emotional complexes, as the Freudians say, why shouldn't they have determined our IQ's at the same time?

One wonders why Mr. Lippmann, holding this belief, did not suggest that we let up on higher education and pour our millions into kindergartens and nurseries. For, really and truly, high IQ's are not to be sneezed at. The difference between 150 IQ and 50 IQ is the difference between an individual who will be able, if he half tries, to graduate from college with Phi Beta Kappa honors at twenty, and an individual who at that age can hardly do long division, make change for four cents out of twenty-five or name the months of the year. Even the difference between 100 IQ and 75 IQ is the difference between the ability to graduate from high school or possibly from college, and inability to do even first year of high school work satisfactorily.

And just to think that we have been allowing all sorts of mysterious, uncontrolled, chance influences in the nursery to mould children's IQ's, this way and that way, right before our eyes. It is high time that we were investigating the IQ effects of different kinds of baby-talk, different versions of Mother Goose, and different makes of pacifiers and safety pins. If there is any possibility of identifying, weighting and bringing under control these IQ stimulants and depressors, we can well afford to throw up every other kind of scientific research until the job is accomplished. That problem once solved, the rest of the mysteries of the universe would fall easy prey before our made-to-order IQ's of 180 or 200.

Does not Mr. Lippmann owe it to the world to abandon his role of critic and to enter this enchanting field of research? He may safely be assured that if he unravels the secret of turning low IQ's into high ones, or even into moderately higher ones, his fame and fortune are made. If he could guarantee to raise certified 100's to certified 140's, or even certified 80's to certified 100's, nothing but premature death or the discovery and publication of his secret would keep him out of the Rockefeller-Ford class if he cared to achieve it. I know of a certain modern Croesus who alone would probably be willing to start him off with ten or twenty million if he could only raise one particular little girl from about 60 to 70 to a paltry 100 or so. Of course, if this man had only understood the secrets of "creative opportunity" in the nursery, he might have had all this and more for nothing. Who knows but if the matter were put to him in the right way he would be willing to endow for Mr. Lippmann a Bureau of Nursery Research for the Enchancement of the IQ?

If Mr. Lippmann gets this Bureau started there are several questions I shall want to submit to it for solution. Some of these have been bothering me for a long time. One is, why both high and low IQ's are so often found in children of the same family and of the same nursery. To be sure, parental habits change more or less as children come and grow up; nurse girls arrive and depart; toys wear out. The problem admittedly is complex, but by successive experiments in which one factor after another was kept constant while the others were varied, the evil and beneficent influences might gradually be sorted out.

Next, I should want to propose a minute comparative study of the influences operative in our California Japanese nurseries and those of our California Portuguese. Here is mystery enough to challenge any group of scientists Mr. Lippmann can get together, for notwithstanding the apparent similarity of nursery environment in the two cases, the IQ results are markedly different. Our average Portuguese child carries through school and into life an IQ of about 80; the average Japanese child soon develops an IQ not far below that of the average California white child of Nordic descent. In this case the nurse girl factor is eliminated; one might almost say, the nursery itself. But of course there are the toys, which are more or less differrent. It is also conceivable that the more liquid Latin tongue exerts a sedative effect on infants' minds as compared with the harsher Japanese language, which may be stimulating in comparison.

Another problem would relate to the IQ resemblance of identical twins as compared with that of fraternal twins. The latest and most extensive investigation of this problem[4] indicates a considerably greater IQ resemblance for the former than for the latter. This is a real poser; which I leave to Mr. Lippmann without attempting an explanation.

The Great Confusion
A Reply to Mr. Terman

Walter Lippmann

In last week's issue Professor Lewis M. Terman stated that it would be "profitless" to debate the validity of the intelligence tests with me. Nevertheless it seems that he felt impelled to pause in those labors, which he modestly compares with Darwin's, in order to write eight columns of print about the contemptible creature who had challenged his dogmas. I cannot imagine who Mr. Terman thinks is going to be fooled by this pretence.

Certainly I feel entitled to assume that Mr. Terman's reply contains the most damaging criticism of my articles which he is able to make. I assume that he has not spared me in his contempt. Therefore, I shall take no space to restate any of the conclusions which Mr. Terman has not challenged.

The first three columns of Professor Terman's reply come down to the charge that I criticized him because I think his arguments are subversive of the old naive theory of democracy. All that I can say to that is that I have written a book of over four hundred pages devoted to arguing the fallacy of the naive democratic theory. He must not think, therefore, that a criticism of the Terman dogmas constitutes a defence of this old theory. It often happens that an error is attacked in an erroneous and misleading way. Mr. Bryan's theory of creation, for example, is no doubt wrong, but it does not follow that everyone who answers Mr. Bryan is a sound biologist. In the same way it does not follow that Mr. Terman is a sound critic of democracy, because the democratic theory is open to criticism.

Nor does it necessarily follow, as Mr. Terman seems to imply, that because intelligence testing has spread all over the wide world, Mr. Terman's conclusions about these tests are valid. Popular success is not scientific evidence, and even the practical usefulness of the tests in schools is no evidence whatever that the theoretical assumptions are true or that the social generalizations are correct.

[4] By a Stanford student and not yet published.

At last after three columns of ridicule Mr. Terman stoops to argument. He denies that the talk about the average mental age of the army being fourteen rests upon the Stanford standardization of mental age. He refers me to p. 536 ff of the army report where he has presented what he calls "independent" age norms derived from large groups of unselected school children. Mr. Terman has missed the point of the matter entirely. An age norm is *internally standardized* according to the average performance of an age group. The army tests were given to the largest group ever collected. Therefore, the mental age of the army cannot be measured by norms, however "independent," which are derived from smaller and less representative groups. If the army tests were tests, you have to admit that they created their own norms. Otherwise you arrive at such logical absurdities as arguing that the average mental age of adults is less than the average mental age of adults.

The Stanford norms gave sixteen as adult. The army norms give a little less than fourteen on the Stanford scale. Either the army tests are unreliable or the Stanford norm is incorrect. Mr. Terman more or less realizes this, for he says that "Psychologists are not entirely agreed as to how this fact (this disparity between army "adults" and Stanford "adults") should be interpreted, but that is beside the point." I beg his pardon. It is the whole point when you are talking about "the average mental age" of Americans.

The second time Mr. Terman stoops to argument is on the factor of speed in the army tests. He refers me to an experiment conducted under his direction by Doctor Mark A. May as proof that time played no part in the army results. The only trouble with Dr. May's experiment is that it does not prove Mr. Terman's point. What is more the editors of the army report stated quite definitely that Dr. May's experiment did not prove the point.

Dr. May tested about a thousand men with double time, and found that "the order of abilities of various persons" was not materially altered. That is to say, the relative positions of the men remained about the same. The better men still graded ahead of the poorer. But in actual performance time *was* a very great factor, as Dr. May's own figures amply prove. Added time did not help the very poorest men much. Of those who scored zero on single time in each of seven tests, an average of even 17 percent made a better showing when the time was doubled. But of those who scored ten points in each of the seven tests over 80 percent gained by doubling the time. (p. 418) Naturally, then, the editors of the army report, who are men of quite different scientific temper from Mr. Terman, took good care not to let Dr. May's experiment be used for just such careless generalization as Mr. Terman has let himself in for. Therefore, after presenting Dr. May's data, they hasten to state that "the high frequencies of persons gaining at the upper levels (often 100 percent) indicate that for the people making high scores on single time the 'speed' element is predominant." (p. 419)

Mr. Terman's difficulty is a very simple one. Finding that the best men are still the best with double time, he notes triumphantly that the top five percent are almost exactly the same men under double as under single time. The top five percent are still the top five percent. I never denied it. What he fails to note is that although the relative positions are the same, the absolute performances are often radically different. "The top five percent" has no relevance to the argument. The relevant fact is that a very large percentage of men made much better scores when the time was doubled. And since the classification of any man as an "A," a "B" or a "C," was determined by his score, not by his relative position, there could have been more "A men" in the American nation if the army had thought it convenient to double the time.

Mr. Terman ought at the very least to interpret correctly work done by his own pupils under his own direction.

These are the only two instances where Mr. Terman ventures to debate. Throughout the rest of his reply he is consumed with laughter. It strikes him as enormously funny that data based on a few years out of the lives of a rather small number of school children should not be deemed proof that Mr. Terman has measured "native intelligence." It strikes him as enormously funny that I should argue that his tests do not provide convincing canons by which to distinguish hereditary from acquired ability. He jumps to the conclusion that I deny the hereditary factor. I did not deny it. I denied Mr. Terman's unproved claim that he had isolated the hereditary factor. Mr. Terman's logical abilities are so primitive that he finds this point impossible to grasp. But nothing seems to him so ludicrous as my argument that no testing which begins at four years of age can possibly claim that its results are uninfluenced by infantile education. The notion that the first four years of experience are highly formative arouses all his gifts of satire.

I said in my article that Mr. Terman was insensitive to childhood. I repeat the statement, and add that a psychologist who sneers at the significance of the earliest impressions and habits is too shallow to write about education.

Finally, a word about Mr. Terman's notion that I have an "emotional complex" about this business. Well, I have. I admit it. I hate the impudence of a claim that in fifty minutes you can judge and classify a human being's predestined fitness in life. I hate the pretentiousness of that claim. I hate the abuse of scientific method which it involves. I hate the sense of superiority which it creates, and the sense of inferiority which it imposes.

And so, while I honestly think that there is a considerable future for mental testing, if it is approached with something like the caution employed by the editors of the army report, I believe also that the whole field is destined to be the happy hunting ground of quacks and snobs if loose-minded men are allowed to occupy positions of leadership much longer.

Race and Immigration: The Politics of Intelligence Testing

Russell Marks

POLITICS AND THE NATURE-NURTURE QUESTION

Twentieth century America has made an ambitious attempt to bring human as well as physical resources under a pattern of rational control. The intelligence testing movement represents one attempt to standardize and stabilize the human resources of capitalism. This rationalizing of the social order has led in the direction of a meritocratic system, built on the principles of equality of opportunity and differential rewards based on individual ability and effort rather than birth and wealth. While equality of opportunity has not been achieved, and may be unattainable, given the grave economic differences in our society, nevertheless the meritocratic model has been a consistent driving ideal in American society. This ideal more than any other provides the essential area of consensus, the foundation for the existing status-quo.

The desirability of achieving a meritocracy is a goal that has unified many conservatives and liberals, hereditarians and environmentalists. Consensus on the meritocratic goal has turned the nature-nurture issue into a technical question, which the technique of intelligence testing is designed to resolve. As a technical question, a question of means and methods rather than ends, the nature-nurture issue has been stripped of any genuine political or ethical content. As it relates to the political spectrum, the nature-nurture issue has been reduced to a simple formula: the hereditarian position has been linked to a conservative political perspective and the environmentalist position to a liberal political perspective. From this simple formula, intelligence testers, as experts on the nature-nurture problem, have become powerful political spokesmen. Thus, virtually overnight, Arthur Jensen becomes an important social theorist whose psychological findings provide a welcome relief for conservatives and an eminent threat for liberals. Yet to accept this formula is to distort the relation between politics and the nature-nurture question; further, to participate in this battle over Jensen's findings is to accept the meritocratic vision of society.

The formulae itself is inadequate since it equates liberalism and environmentalism with a program promoting reform and conservatism and hereditarianism with a program opposed to change. This distinction is obviously false since reforms can be either hereditarian or environmentalist in nature. A more meaningful dichotomy therefore might be a distinction between reforms which encourage and endorse or discourage and question the development of the meritocracy.

From this perspective, the hereditary and environmental position can promote or negate the goal of rationalizing and standardizing the reward system and human resources of capitalism. The heredity position of course holds that the individual has fixed capacities which cannot be greatly altered through changing environmental factors. If this argument is accepted what are its societal implications? If heredity determines intelligence, then it might be argued, as it is today, that environmental reform should be seriously questioned or rejected. Or again, the heredity argument can be used as a rationale for hereditarian reform. From the hereditarian reform position, it has been argued that society should improve the population through implementing eugenic measures like sterilization, rewarding merit and intelligence, restricting the immigration of undesirable stocks, and classifying the populace for the purpose of maximizing social efficiency and control. On the other hand, given the heredity hypothesis it might be argued that the individual therefore is not responsible for his intellectual ability and should not be punished for his hereditary limits. This would seem to suggest a reward system where all would receive the same rewards or where rewards were based solely on effort since intelligence were hereditarily fixed and effort could be determined.

The same may also be said for the environmentalist position. It can be used as an argument challenging the efficacy of hereditarian reform or as a method for promoting environmental reform. But again, if reform implications are drawn, the meritocracy can be endorsed or challenged. Institutional change can be directed toward preserving and stabilizing the existing class structure or toward challenging and negating the reward structure and the authority of the state. The traditional model linking nature and conservatism, nurture and liberalism is therefore misleading.

Although no necessary political implications follow from the nature-nurture argument, nevertheless, it has been manipulated for specific political purposes. As such the nature-nurture controversy has served as a false and misleading issue; it has functioned as a veil that has concealed grave social and political issues. By abandoning the traditional alignment between conservatism and hereditarianism, liberalism and environmentalism, these political issues and the forces directing their solution become more readily discernible.

Illustrative of the principles that have been discussed were the Immigration Act of 1924 and the Brown decision of 1954. Upon first observation these influential decisions seem to be diametrically opposed since the former legislative act meant a closing of opportunity for Southern Europeans, while the latter judicial decision meant an opening of opportunity for Blacks. Further, while the Immigration Act was built on the hereditarian argument that Southern Europeans were innately intellectually inferior, the Brown decision was built on the environmentalist argument that Blacks were intellectually equal. Employing the traditional model, the former act was a triumph of conservatism, while the latter was a victory for liberalism.

Yet this was not the case. Rather in important respects both decisions were triumphs of liberal reform. More importantly, in both decisions the nature-nurture issue provided a convenient rationalization for policies that various interests in society wished to pursue. While several segments of American society played an influential part in these decisions, this discussion will focus on the role of intelligence testers, liberals and industrialists.

THE IMMIGRATION ACT OF 1924

The controversial aspect of the Immigration Act of 1924 was that it provided for a quota system that was unfavorable to Southern and Southeastern Europeans. Unlike the 1921 immigration act that was based on the 1910 census which gave these groups 45 percent of the total immigration, the 1924 act was based on the 1890 census that limited them to a quota of 15 percent. Passage of the 1924 act would therefore seriously limit the entry of Southern and Southeastern Europeans.

Proponents of Immigration Restriction

Among the supporters of the Immigration Act of 1924 were many intelligence testers. They indirectly supported immigration restriction through their findings linking intelligence and (or) character with particular racial traits. They directly aided the passage of the law through their active support of restriction. A wide variety of studies and observations by psychologists promoted the belief that there was indeed something uncommon about the Nordic. It could be expressed informally like the following expression of anti-semitism stated by Edward L. Thorndike in discussing an applicant for a teaching position: "Blair seems to be a pretty good man and he happens to be of some experience in the schools. But I am not sure that he will be a good enough teacher and I suspect that he is a Jew." [1] Or it could be found in scientific studies which supposedly

---

[1] Letter, Thorndike to Cattell, January 22, 1902, J. McKeen Cattell Papers, Library of Congress.

proved the inferiority of non-Nordics. In these studies psychologists found for example that the more white blood Indians and Negroes had the higher their intelligence and that Southern and Southeastern Europeans, Mexicans, Spanish Americans and Negroes among others were intellectually inferior to Nordics.[2] It did not follow however that intellectual superiority was always considered a virtue. When two Canadian psychologists found that the Japanese did very well on intelligence tests, they neatly reversed the rationale for discrimination:

> If these results are reliable the Japanese form the cleverest racial group resident in British Columbia. . . . The presence of so many clever, industrious and frugal aliens constitutes a political and economic problem of the greatest importance.[3]

Other psychologists not only demonstrated the racial inferiority of certain stocks but actively campaigned for immigration restriction. Among the most active in promoting restriction was the Chairman of the Division of Anthropology and Psychology of the National Research Council, Robert M. Yerkes, and his close associate, Carl C. Brigham.

Writing in 1924 as chairman of a special committee to investigate human migration for the Council, Yerkes stressed the importance of knowledge in solving the immigration problem. While optimistic that "important modification of our national immigration policy is imminent," he nevertheless warned that "prejudices arising from racial friction, dislike or hatred" were increasingly obscuring the important issues. His solution was disinterested knowledge:

> Knowledge of human traits and potentialities . . . is tragically inadequate. Wisdom dictates that every effort be made to secure the information which is requisite to intelligent, far-sighted, and wise action on practical matters. This needed information and the methods necessary to attain it are fundamental to the safe development of social biology.[4]

Presumably to meet the need for an informed public, Yerkes one year earlier had written an article for *The Atlantic* on "Testing the Human Mind." In Yerkes' words, his "excuse for turning from my scientific tasks to write a would-be popular article" on the results of the army tests was

[2] See e.g. T. R. Garth, "Intelligence of Mixed Blood Indians," *Journal of Applied Psychology*, 1927, p. 275; Kimball Young, "Intelligence of Certain Immigrant Groups," *Scientific Monthly*, Nov. 1922, p. 444; T. R. Garth, "The Intelligence of Mexican School Children," *School and Society*, June 30, 1928, p. 794; R. A. Schwegler, "A Comparative Study of the Intelligence of White and Colored Children," *Journal of Educational Research*, Dec. 1920, p. 846.

[3] P. Saniford and R. Kerr, "Intelligence of Chinese and Japanese Children," *Journal of Educational Psychology*, Sept. 1926, p. 367.

[4] Robert M. Yerkes, "The Work of Committee on Scientific Problems of Human Migration, National Research Council," *Reprint and Circular Series of the National Research Council*, #58, p. 189.

to clarify their meaning.[5] Among the most important results demonstrated by the testing program of the army was the low intelligence of Southern European immigrants. While some uniformed people, Yerkes observed, consider the "meagre intelligence" of immigrants an "industrial necessity and blessing," it is better understood as a national burden. "Certainly the results of psychological examining in the United States Army," Yerkes continued, "establish the relation of inferior intelligence to delinquency and crime, and justify the belief that a country which encourages, or even permits, the immigrations of simple-minded, uneducated, defective, diseased or criminalistic persons, because it needs cheap labor, seeks trouble in the shape of public expense." In fact, "it might almost be said that whoever desires high taxes, full alms-houses, a constantly increasing number of schools for defectives, of correctional institutions, penitentiaries, hospitals and special classes in our public schools," should, he concluded, "by all means work for unrestricted and non-selective immigration." [6]

It was Yerkes' colleague, Carl C. Brigham, however, who had particular impact in promoting immigration restriction. Brigham, a First Lieutenant in the Psychological Division during the war, used the findings of the army tests for a study on immigration. His book, *A Study of American Intelligence*, was a supplementary publication of the National Research Council. It originated from the activities of the Committee for Psychology of the National Research Council and the Committee on Classification of Personnel in the Army.[7]

Brigham's study divided the population of the United States into four ᵣacial groups: The Nordic, including people from Belgium, Denmark, Holland, Norway, Sweden, England, Scotland and Canada; the Alpine race from Austria–Hungary, France, Germany, Russia, Poland and European Turkey; the Mediterranean race from Greece, Italy, Spain, Ireland, Wales and Asian Turkey; and the Negro races. The army tests clearly indicated that the Nordic draftees were intellectually superior to the Alpine, Mediterranean and Negro races. German stock also performed well on the tests but Brigham attributed this exception to the fact that

[5] R. M. Yerkes, "Testing the Human Mind," *The Atlantic*, March 1923, p. 358.

[6] *Ibid.*, p. 365.

[7] Nor were Brigham's activities limited to analyzing the army tests. While working on *A Study of American Intelligence*, Brigham was appointed chairman of the committee on Internationalizing Mental Measurement. This committee was one branch of the Committee of Scientific Migration of the National Research Council. The organization and early activities of the Committee of Scientific Migration were made possible by an appropriation of $5,000 from the Russell Sage Foundation and $60,000 from the Laura Spelman Rockefeller Foundation. Brigham's committee did not file any reports until a couple years after the passage of the Immigration Act. Nevertheless his association with this committee no doubt added credence to his investigation of American Intelligence.

Germans had almost as much Nordic blood (40 percent) as Alpine blood (60 percent).[8]

Brigham was alarmed that immigration from Alpine and Mediterranean races constituted over 70 percent of the total immigration in the early 1920's. As a result American intelligence was declining and would continue to deteriorate with an accelerating rate of racial mixing. Steps must therefore be taken, Brigham argued, to preserve or improve the intellectual capacity of the nation, and "must of course be dictated by science and not by political expediency." It was thus essential that immigration become not only restrictive but highly selective.[9]

Brigham's study was enthusiastically received and considered by many people as the final word on the intelligence of immigrants. Not surprisingly among his most zealous supporters was Yerkes who considered Brigham's study the best "explicit discussion of immigration" ever written. It presented "not theories or opinions but facts" and according to Yerkes should be read since Americans can not "afford to ignore the menace of race deterioration or the evident relations of immigration to national progress and welfare." [10] Similarly Lewis M. Terman, author of the Stanford–Binet and Stanford Achievement Test, rated Brigham's work "excellent and convincing." Terman in fact was so impressed that he informed Yerkes that "we are offering Brigham an associate professorship in applied psychology." [11]

Opponents of Brigham's Study

On the other hand, Brigham's work was not without its critics. Although J. McKeen Cattell could boldly state that "there is in fact fair agreement on the scope and meaning of intelligence tests,"[12] the evidence, including Cattell's own work, indicated the contrary. Among Brigham's critics were psychologists Edwin G. Boring, Frank N. Freeman, Cattell and educator William C. Bagley.

Writing Terman in January of 1923, Yerkes observed that he was encouraging Boring to write a review of Brigham's book for the *New Republic*. Yerkes felt it would be an excellent opportunity "to help along

---

[8] C. C. Brigham, *A Study of American Intelligence*, (Princeton: Princeton University Press, 1923), pp. 159, 207.

[9] *Ibid.*, p. 210.

[10] Foreword to Brigham, pp. vii–viii.

[11] Letter, Terman to Yerkes, April 10, 1923, L. M. Terman Papers, Archives, Stanford University.

[12] J. McKeen Cattell, "The Interpretation of Intelligence Tests," *The Scientific Monthly*, May 1924, p. 516.

the cause." [13] Four months later Boring reviewed *A Study of American Intelligence* in the *New Republic*, although his review was hardly what Yerkes had anticipated. Rather than helping the "cause," Boring was critical of Brigham's study. Particularly, Boring was skeptical of the meaning of the army data. While they might mean, as Brigham argued, that certain racial groups were inferior, it was also plausible that the army had an inadequate sample of the foreign born, or that the racial differences were attributable to education, familiarity with examinations, etc. Although Boring believed the "indications are in the direction which Mr. Brigham points," it nevertheless seemed to him that "we are by no means ready to definitely recommend legislation" restricting immigration.[14]

Even less sympathetic than Boring, was Freeman. He argued that Brigham had seriously neglected to even consider other explanations for the poor performance of certain "racial" groups on the army tests. Rather, according to Freeman, it seemed likely that Brigham had merely used the facts of the army tests to prove his own theory. Had Brigham, Freeman noted, "started with the hypothesis that the race theory is doubtful instead of with the hypothesis that education cannot affect the test scores" he would have likely arrived at very different conclusions. In any case, Freeman argued "to defend himself from the charge of special pleading, an author of a scientific treatise must at least consider the various possibilities of explanation of his facts." [15]

While the reviews of Boring and Freeman were relatively straightforward about the dangers of racial stereotyping, the articles by Cattell and Bagley were much less so. Although Cattell did not specifically refer to Brigham's book, the timing and nature of his remarks in "The Interpretation of Intelligence Tests" were certainly applicable to it. Of particular interest were Cattell's observations about the Irish: "when Irish children do not do as well as some others, it may be due only to different interests in the home, but these differences may reflect real racial differences." In effect, Cattell was questioning Brigham's reliance on the doctrine of intellectual racial superiority, and substituting the hypothesis that certain racial groups might have different abilities not measured on the tests. The Irish, for example, might have other interests and abilities:

> The tests may predict that the Irish children will not do as well as American children in bookkeeping and stenography; but they do not directly measure the probable success of the two groups in keeping saloons, running Tammany Hall, writing poetic drama, or starting rows.[16]

[13] Letter, Yerkes to Terman, Jan. 2, 1923, Terman Papers.
[14] E. G. Boring, "Facts and Fancies of Immigration," *The New Republic*, April 25, 1923, pp. 245–246.
[15] F. N. Freeman, "An Evaluation of American Intelligence," *The School Review*, Oct. 1923, pp. 627–628.
[16] Cattell, p. 516.

Indeed, if the tests measured the genuine abilities of the Irish surely they would perform well!

Equally revealing was Bagley's treatment of Brigham's work. In "The Army Tests and Pro-Nordic Propaganda," Bagley, an environmentalist, attacked several of Brigham's hereditary assertions. Even more informative, however, was Bagley's areas of agreement with Brigham. Of particular significance was that the social implications drawn by Bagley, the environmentalist were similar to those of Brigham, the hereditarian.

Bagley concurred with Brigham that immigration restriction was absolutely necessary. "The dangers of immigration restriction" Bagley noted, "are unquestioned and the undesirable quality of much of our recent immigration is conceded." Yet Bagley insisted one can promote immigration restriction and still reject Brigham's "scientific" findings: "to recognize unrestricted immigration as an evil is one thing; to fan the fires of race-prejudice with alleged scientific findings is quite another" [17]

In discussing the weaknesses of Brigham's study, it was not surprising that Bagley, one of America's most prominent educators, continually emphasized Brigham's neglect and distortion of the schooling process. Bagley noted that Brigham's analysis was largely dependent upon his acceptance of the army tests as a valid index of native intelligence. "Professor Brigham's principal defense of the army tests as true measures of native intelligence" in turn for Bagley was "based upon the fact that the scores correlate highly with schooling." Brigham's assumption, Bagley continued, "is that native intelligence will determine the amount of schooling that one receives apparently to such an extent as to render negligible all other factors, including opportunity and stimulus for schooling." Such an assumption was inexcusable to Bagley, particularly since Brigham treated the impact of schooling in such a "brief" and "amateurish" fashion.[18]

Similarly, Bagley would agree with Brigham about the intellectual inferiority of Blacks but disagree about the influence of schooling in determining their performance on tests. Bagley believed "no one can seriously doubt the general superiority of the whites over the negroes in native intelligence." Yet at the same time, contrary to Brigham's findings, he felt the Army tests clearly demonstrated the "tremendous influence of good schools in stimulating the growth of intelligence. . . . " The fact that "literate negroes" from Illinois achieved a median score above the scores of both "literate negroes" and "literate whites" in the South was clear evidence for Bagley of the impact of schooling.[19]

[17] W. C. Bagley, "The Army Tests and Pro-Nordic Propaganda," *Educational Review*, April 1924, p. 79.

[18] *Ibid.*, p. 180.

[19] *Ibid.*, p. 184.

In addition, Bagley agreed with Brigham that racial purity was necessary to advance civilization, although he disagreed with him about the best means for achieving this goal. Bagley warned that Brigham's proposal would ultimately lead to inter-racial war. Bagley's alternative, which he called the position of the "rational equalitarian," emphasized forces that drew men together rather than divided them. Thus, "instead of intensifying biological differentiation" the rational equalitarian "would stimulate cultural integration." Further, the rational equalitarian believed that "diverse racial stocks can learn to live together and to work together without necessitating a blend of blood, and that undesirable blends of blood can be prevented through education." For Bagley, education quite naturally provided the foundations for the rational equalitarian's proposals for reform. Among the reforms Bagley supported were the following:

> (1) a vast extension of educational facilities and a far-reaching refinement of educational materials and methods; and (2) among other objectives, the direction of educational agencies toward (a) the establishment of the ideal of race-purity in all major races and (b) a voluntary acceptance of eugenic practices to the end that, *in all races*, the reproduction of less worthy stock may be reduced.[20]

He believed the ideal of race-purity needed to be established not only for the Nordic race but for all races. In effect Bagley was, if anything, advocating a more extensive policy of racial purity than Brigham.

Finally it should be noted that Bagley's support of eugenic reform was not inconsistent with his environmentalist position. Bagley's environmentalism roughly allotted a seventy percent role to nurture and thirty percent role to nature. In attributing a thirty percent role to heredity in the determination of intelligence, he was allowing eugenic reform to still play an important role. At the same time, he attributed a significant role to the environment, since he believed support for eugenic ends could be achieved through education. Thus, while they differed over the nature-nurture issue, some of the social goals of environmentalist Bagley, who advocated eugenic and environmentalist engineering, were very similar to the eugenic engineering objectives of hereditarian Brigham.

Passage of the Immigration Act

The promotion of eugenic ends was indeed a primary force in securing approval of the Immigration Act of 1924. As earlier noted, passage of the act would seriously curtail the quota of Southern Europeans entering America. Providing major testimony for the restriction of Southern

---

[20] *Ibid.*, p. 186.

Europeans before the Congress was eugenics expert H. H. Laughlin. Laughlin had long been associated with the privately financed Eugenics Record Office which, since its founding in 1910, had been active in sterilization.[21] In 1918 the Carnegie Institute of Washington assumed control of the Record Office. As a representative of the Carnegie sponsored Record Office, Laughlin filed his influential report, *An Analysis of America's Melting Pot*, before the House Committee on Immigration and Naturalization. Using statistics from the army tests, state and federal penitentiaries, and institutions for the insane, feebleminded, blind, epileptic and dependent, he concluded that a much greater proportion of the "new" immigrants were "socially inadequate" than were the "old immigrants and native born. He attributed the inferiority of the new immigrants to their racial characteristics. He recommended a quota base which would create a predominantly Northwest European immigration. When Laughlin was later challenged on his findings before the House committee he replied:

> ... my studies were made with no preselected theory or policy to support. There were no conclusions drawn before the data were in hand and analyzed, and the conclusions were in sound keeping with first hand facts.[22]

Laughlin's objective expertise was accepted by the committee as was his argument about the racial inferiority of Southern Europeans. When, however, the committee argued its case before the House the rhetoric was changed and the Southern Europeans were simply labeled non-assimilable as J. E. Connell of Rhode Island observed:

> The persons particularly sought to be excluded are not spoken as inferior or undesirable but as near non-assimilable, and on this ground are, in effect, discriminated against. The adjective is changed, but the subject is sought to be removed as a potential factor in our future national life.[23]

Although the emphasis had shifted, the assumptions and findings of the intelligence testers were clearly evident in the House. Grant H. Hudson of Michigan observed that "our American race . . . is now almost swamped" with the "hordes of eastern and southern Europeans." He was hopeful that immigration would be restricted since "we are slowly awakening to the consciousness that education and environment do not fundamentally alter racial values." S. D. McReynolds of Tennessee noted that the investigations made by the "army psychologists" of foreign born enlistments showed a

[21] See Mark H. Haller, *Eugenics*, (New Brunswick, N.J.: Rutgers University Press, 1963), p. 133.
[22] U.S. Congress, House Committee on Immigration and Naturalization, *Europe as an Emigrant—Exporting Continent and the United States as an Immigrant—Receiving Nation*, by H. H. Laughlin, 68th Cong., 1st sess., Mar. 8, 1924, p. 1311.
[23] *Congressional Record*, Apr. 8, 1924, p. 5836.

"much greater mental deficiency of foreign born." Another representative cited and agreed with a letter published in the *Boston Herald* which warned of neglecting the "iron certainties of heredity" and encouraged that men be "selected and bred as sacredly as cows and pigs and sheep." [24]

The opponents of the immigration act attacked these assumptions and ridiculed the objective expertise of Laughlin, spelled L-A-U-G-H by one representative.[25] Emanuel Celler of New York considered Laughlin's findings "redolent with downright and deliberate falsehoods." Laughlin, he continued, was "predisposed in favor of so called Nordic superiority," and was determined to demonstrate that the "Nordics are a super-human race." Among the most serious mistakes in his studies, Celler continued, was that his examination of institutional "defectives" was concentrated in areas with the highest percentages of new immigrants although Laughlin correlated his figures with the entire population.[26] The myth of racial superiority was a persuasive argument however and not easily defeated. One representative warned that if the bill should pass with the 1890 census, the House would be indirectly establishing the principle that Southern and Eastern European immigrants were inferior.[27] The bill was passed and the principle was established. Interestingly enough, not a single progressive in the Senate opposed the passage of the bill. In fact, progressives had played a very active role in securing immigration restriction, particularly in pre-war years when their numbers were much greater.[28]

The passage of the act was a victory from the testers' perspective as well. Immigration of supposedly inferior hereditary stocks had been seriously curbed. Yerkes, Brigham and other psychologists could claim a large, although indirect, responsibility for the immigration act. As one writer of the period stated: the "army tests had great weight with Congress and helped to crystalize the sentiment that finally resulted in the enactment of the Immigration Act of 1924." [29] Similarly psychological findings were referred to throughout the influential Laughlin Report and in the debate in Congress.

Yet immigration restriction was also seemingly a victory from the perspective of big business. But why did foundations representing industrial interests support Laughlin, Brigham and others who were campaigning for

[24] *Record*, Apr. 5, 1924, pp. 5641–42; Apr. 8, 1924, p. 5856, 5872.

[25] *Record*, Apr. 5, 1924, p. 5647.

[26] *Record*, Apr. 8, 1924, pp. 5913–4. For other criticism of Laughlin see Mr. Sabbath's remarks, Apr. 5, 1924, p. 5662; Mr. Jacobstein's remarks, Apr. 8, 1924, p. 5861.

[27] *Record*, Remarks of Mr. Perlman, Apr. 5, 1924, p. 5651; See James' remarks Apr. 5, 1924, p. 5667.

[28] William E. Leuchtenburg, *The Perils of Prosperity 1914–1932*, (Chicago: University of Chicago Press, 1958), p. 127.

[29] Roy L. Garis, *Immigration Restriction*, (New York: Macmillan Co., 1927), p. 239.

immigration restriction? Of course, it could be argued that restriction was contrary to their interests and that they had inadvertently supported restriction.[30] Yet, on the other hand, the evidence seems to indicate the contrary. Immigration restriction served the interests of big business in several different ways. First there was some recognition by big business that an ever expanding labor supply was no longer necessary. Edward A. Filene, a pioneer in employment management noted:

> Employers do not need an increased labor supply, since increased use of labor-saving machinery and elimination of waste in production and distribution will for many years reduce costs more rapidly than wages increase, and so prevent undue domination of labor.[31]

Further, the immigrant was viewed by many as a definite threat to social cohesion and unity. The war had stirred racial and ethnic grievances in America to the boiling point. Even the immigrants' ability to work was now questioned. Immigrant specialist Francis Kellor, an associate of many businessmen, including Coleman du Pont and Cyrus H. McCormick, expressed this sentiment well when he stated:

> The present immigrant is not so eager to do the kind of work which America most needs to have done. This changed attitude on his part may be due to several reasons. He may have become affected by the Bolshevist doctrine which pervades Europe, or by the independence granted to his home country.[32]

Finally some industrialists realized that there were valuable untapped sources of manpower already existing in the United States. Foremost of these untapped human resources was the Black. Ironically, the closing of opportunity for Southern Europeans forecast the eventual opening of opportunity for Black Americans. Although it would take another world war to convince many industrialists of the importance of fully utilizing Black labor, nevertheless there were some industrialists who recognized their value much earlier. Among them was Andrew Carnegie. Before turning to a discussion of Carnegie, it is important to note the shift occurring in the academic community over the nature-nurture issue.

The Nature-Nurture Question 1924–1954

From the dominant hereditarian position of the psychologists in the twenties the testers, by the early thirties, were becoming more sympathetic

---

[30] Laughlin in fact argued this position in his testimony before the House.

[31] As quoted by Robert De C. Ward, "Our New Immigration Policy," *Foreign Affairs*, September 1924, p. 104.

[32] Francis Kellor, *Immigration and the Future*, (New York: George H. Doran Co., 1920), p. 159.

to an environmentalist position. Indicative of this shift was Carl C. Brigham who, in 1930, boldly renounced his earlier position:

> This review has summarized some of the more recent test findings which show that comparative studies of various national and racial groups may not be made with existing tests, and which show in particular, that one of the most pretentious of these comparative racial studies—the writer's own—was without foundation.[33]

Four years later a questionnaire given to seventy-seven prominent psychologists revealed that only twenty-five percent believed that the Black was inherently mentally inferior to the white, while eleven percent felt he was equal and sixty-four percent felt the data were inconclusive.[34] This was a significant change from the strong hereditarian emphasis of the twenties.

Yet this shifting emphasis from nature to nurture in the thirties did not occur in a social vacuum. The undermining of genetic reform, the denunciation of Hitler's racial policies, the decline of post-war American fanaticism and overt racism, and the new emphasis on environmental social reform were important aspects shaping the psychologist's scientific perspective. Given such changes in social reality, psychologists, devoted to human engineering and professional interests, were likely to begin to interpret their data differently.

While new inconclusive data would be introduced, much of the controversy would continue to revolve around the interpretation of earlier studies. Some of these studies became scientific as well as political footballs which were batted about indiscriminately by environmentalists and hereditarians, liberals and conservatives. Perhaps the classic study of this kind was the World War I examination of soldiers, an examination which has been a subject of debate up to the present. The first forty years of the debate run roughly as follows.

Among the most important findings of the army tests was that the median test score of Blacks was much lower than the median score of whites.[35] For hereditarians this was a clear example of the innate inferiority of Blacks. Environmentalists, however were quick to point out that Northern Blacks performed much better on the tests than Southern Blacks, a fact which clearly demonstrated that superior schooling was the primary factor in determining test performance. The hereditarians retorted that it was the brighter Blacks who went North and thus heredity rather than environment was primary. To this assertion, the environmentalist coun-

---

[33] C. C. Brigham, "Intelligence Tests of Immigrant Groups," *Psychological Review*, 1930, p. 165.

[34] C. H. Thompson, "The Conclusions of Scientists Relative to Racial Differences," *J. of Negro Education*, 1934, p. 499.

[35] See Brigham, *American Intelligence*.

tered with the question: Why is it that the longer Blacks live in the North the higher they score on intelligence tests? Surely it can only mean that environment and not heredity is the determining factor.

Not dismayed, hereditarians would concede that schooling did make some difference yet even with equal schooling Blacks did not catch up to whites because of their inferior hereditary makeup. To such criticism, environmentalists responded that the tests themselves were so culturally biased that they could not give an accurate measurement of innate intelligence. Hereditarians either disagreed with this criticism or partially concurred and then scurried off to write that elusive culture free test to finally establish the innate differences between races. Environmentalists likewise scurried for more conclusive evidence or eagerly awaited the hereditarians' findings so the battle might resume.

From such heated, indecisive controversies emerged a strong emphasis in the thirties on environmentalism. As in other periods this did not mean there was an absence of opposing literature and research (in this case hereditarian research) but rather only that at this point the environmentalist position became dominant.

Like the environmentalists who were on the defensive in the twenties, the hereditarians in the thirties, forties and fifties appealed especially to "objectivity" in arguing the nature–nurture issue. Representative of this emphasis on objectivity were the statements of Columbia University psychologist H. E. Garrett. Writing in 1947 on "Negro–White Differences in Mental Ability in the United States," Garrett observed:

> The question of the existence of Negro–White differences in mental ability within the United States has of late been sadly confused with social and political issues of racial superiority, discrimination, and the like. As a result of this confusion, many writers seem to take the position that racial differences ought not to be found, or if found should immediately be explained away as somehow reprehensible and socially undesirable. With this attitude the present writer is in sharp disagreement. While he is heartily in favor of every genuine effort to aid the Negro in improving his status as an American citizen, he does not believe it is at all necessary to 'prove' the nonexistence of race differences in order to justify a fair policy toward the Negro. It cannot be said too often that the honest psychologist, like any other true scientist, has no racial bias; he does not *care* which race (if any) is the more intelligent or whether all races are potentially equal in mental ability. But he *is* interested in discovering whether differences in mental ability exist, and in making inferences concerning the origin of such differences. And this would seem to be an entirely legitimate enterprise.[36]

[36] H. E. Garrett, "Negro White Differences in Mental Ability in the United States," *The Scientific Monthly*, 1947, p. 329. In the mid-sixties, Garrett changed his approach and came out with vehement statements against the Black who he believed was at least 200,000 years behind the white. See Clarence Karier's discussion in "Testing For Order and Control in the Corporate Liberal State," *Educational Theory*, Spring 1972.

Not surprisingly, hereditarian Garrett's objective analysis led him to conclude that Blacks were inherently intellectually inferior. His argument was based on the fact that on tests of mental ability the Black, on the average, ranked consistently lower than the white. For Garrett "the regularity of this result from babyhood to adulthood makes it extremely unlikely . . . that environmental opportunities can possibly explain *all* the differences found." [37] Environmentalists, on the other hand, of course would prefer to believe that environmental factors could explain the differences. Both positions were more a matter of faith than of hard evidence.

For to prove equality or differences on the basis of intelligence testing required a culture free test. Given the diversity of ethnic, regional, racial, socio-economic, and educational backgrounds, such a test was probably a technical impossibility in racist, capitalistic America.

THE BROWN DECISION OF 1954

While the nature–nurture issue was shifting, industrialists were gradually beginning to realize the importance of fully utilizing Black labor. By the time of the Brown Decision in 1954, enlightened big business was in favor of granting greater opportunity for the Black. While the Brown Decision was ahead of many sectors of American society, if anything, it lagged behind big business. For the great finding in the mid-twentieth century was that racial discrimination was economically and socially inefficient. It was not the liberals' or businessmen's love of the Black that led them to give the Black greater opportunity, but rather, the demands of the socio-economic system. The demands of industrial efficiency and social control were the driving forces that largely changed the liberals' and businessmen's attitude toward the Black. Once the Black was recognized as a capable productive unit, whose economic potential could only be realized through more fully integrating him into the society, then prejudice and discrimination were wasteful. Among the first industrialists to realize the importance of fully utilizing Black labor was Andrew Carnegie.

The Myrdal Study

In the early twentieth century Carnegie gave generously to Negro institutions including Hampton and Tuskegee Institute. His motivation for giving such funds was intimately related to industry's manpower needs. In 1904, just one year after granting the Tuskegee Institute $600,000, Carnegie asserted that:

[37] Garrett, p. 333.

It is certain we must grow more cotton to meet the demands of the world, or endanger our practical monopoly of that indispensable article. Either the efforts of Europe will be successful to grow in other parts, even at greater cost for a time, or the world will learn to substitute something else for it. We can not afford to lose the Negro. We have urgent need of all and of more. Let us therefore turn our efforts to making the best of him.[38]

The Carnegie Corporation's continued interest in the Black was evident in the fact that between 1911 and 1938, they made grants of over two and one-half million dollars to these institutions.[39] While during much of this period, the Corporation viewed Blacks as a valuable source of unskilled labor, in later years the Blacks would be viewed as a potential source of skilled labor as well. Although the Corporation had of course done considerable research on the Black in America, it was not until 1938 that their classic study was launched. This study, which in part was designed to assess the ability of the Black, was completed six years later and cost the Corporation over $286,000.[40]

Conducting this ambitious study of the Black was Gunnar Myrdal and his staff of about 37 research specialists. The "Myrdal Study" produced numerous monographs and articles as well as its primary two volume work, *An American Dilemma: The Negro Problem and Modern Democracy*. Published in 1944, it was reviewed widely and generally favorably in all sections of the United States. It was, as the Carnegie Corporation *Report of the President* observed, "Generally regarded as definitive, comprehensive, and accurate in its portrayals and interpretation." [41]

The Negro problem, for Myrdal, was essentially not an economic, social or political problem but a moral one. The "American Dilemma" was, according to Myrdal, the "ever-raging conflict" between valuations held on the general plane where the "American thinks, talks, and acts under the influence of high national and Christian precepts," and valuations held on specific planes where "personal and local interests; economic, social and sexual jealouses; considerations of community prestige and conformity; group prejudice against particular persons or types of people; and all sorts of miscellaneous wants, impulses, and habits dominate his outlook." [42] In treating the Negro Problem as an American Dilemma, a moral issue, Myrdal tended to legitimize the social order without asking critical ques-

[38] Andrew Carnegie, "Proceedings of a Meeting Held in New York City Feb. 12, 1904 under the Direction of the Armstrong Association," Andrew Carnegie Papers, Library of Congress.

[39] Gunnar Myrdal, *An American Dilemma: The Negro Problem and Modern Democracy*, (New York: Harper and Brothers, 1944), p. vi.

[40] See the *Report of the President* of the Carnegie Corporation of New York for the years 1938–1945.

[41] Carnegie Corporation of New York, *Report of the President*, 1944, p. 25.

[42] Myrdal, p. xlvii.

tions about it. Rather than locating Black suffering in its primary cause, economic exploitation, Myrdal located it in the hearts and minds of white people. His solution to the Negro problem was to appeal to the higher ideals of whites and also to inform them, through essentially environmentalist explanations like the "vicious cycle" theory, why Blacks appeared inferior. In focusing on Black inferiority and white morality, rather than exploitation, Myrdal successfully evaded the task of asking hard questions about the social order. Writing in 1946, Herbert Aptheker fully realized this weakness, and, contrary to Myrdal, proposed that the Negro question was primarily material rather than moral. "The oppression and superexploitation of the American Negro," Aptheker argued, "exist and are maintained because they were and are profitable and useful to America's propertied interests." [43] As will be seen, it was probably socio-economic factors more than any others that were transforming the position of the Black in America.

The Negro problem for Myrdal was related to the nature-nurture issue. He treated the new emphasis on environmental causation in the thirties as a definite advancement of science. He described this triumph of science as follows:

> The wave of racialism for a time swayed not only public opinion but also some psychologists who were measuring psychic traits, especially intelligence, and perhaps also some few representatives of related social sciences. But the social sciences had now developed strength and were well on the way toward freeing themselves entirely from the old biologistic tendency. The social sciences received an impetus to their modern development by reacting against this biologistic onslaught. They fought for the theory of environmental causation. Their primary object of suspicion became more and more the old static entity, 'human nature,' and the belief that fundamental differences between economic, social, or racial groups were due to 'nature.' [44]

Happily for Myrdal, environmental causation was consistent with his belief that environmentalists were liberals and hereditarians were conservatives. Thus liberalism was scientifically rationalized with his argument.

Myrdal, of course, was not unaware that the new emphasis on environmental causation ran parallel to the conspicuous development, materialized in the New Deal, of environmental social reform. Myrdal was willing to entertain the idea, although he did not accept it, that the new environmental hypothesis was a rationalization of political valuations:

> As always, we can, of course, assume that basically both the scientific trend and the political development in a civilization are functions of a larger synchronized development of social ideology. A suspicion is, then,

[43] Herbert Aptheker, *The Negro People in America*, (New York: International Publishers, 1946), p. 66.
[44] Myrdal, p. 92.

natural that fundamentally the scientific trend in America is a rationalization of changed political valuation. This trend has, however, had its course during a remarkable improvement of observation and measurement techniques and has been determined by real efforts to criticize research methods and the manner in which the scientific inferences are made from research data. It has, to a large extent, been running against expectation and, we may assume, wishes. This is the general reason why, in spite of the natural suspicion, we can feel confident that the scientific trend is, on the whole, a definite approach toward truth.[45]

The only difficulty with Myrdal's analysis was that improved observation, measurement techniques, and critical research did not necessarily lead to an environmentalist explanation. Contemporary research and later evidence clearly demonstrated that an hereditary explanation was also a plausible result of improved research. Further, Myrdal seemingly overlooked the fact that the willingness and ability to criticize hereditarian research methods and data were greatly enhanced when the researcher ideologically disagreed with the findings.

Perhaps of greater significance than the publication of the *American Dilemma* were the research activities it set in motion and the supplementary publications it produced. Allison Davis, who had been an active participant in Myrdal's study, established an interdepartmental committee at the University of Chicago to examine the relationship between cultural learning and performance on mental tests. Joining Davis on this committee were Robert J. Havighurst, Ralph W. Tyler, W. Lloyd Warner, Lee Cronbach and others who would all play an important role in exposing the cultural biases of the tests.

Similarly, one of the four major supplementary publications of the Myrdal Study was Otto Klineberg's *Characteristics of the American Negro*. This work would be frequently cited in the school decisions in the 1950's. Klineberg completed his study of the American Negro by concluding that his findings indicated the lack of "proof of fundamental, inherited intellectual differences" between Negroes and whites. Where differences were found they appeared to be the "consequence of other than biological factors." This conclusion, he noted, had to be stated in negative terms. "There is not proof that the groups are inherently different," Klineberg argued, but "there is also no complete demonstration that the groups are entirely alike." Given the methods available, Klineberg noted, "it is legitimate to conclude that in all probability inherent intellectual differences between Negroes and whites do not exist." [46] Klineberg's conclusion that "in all probability" innate intellectual differences between the races do not

---

[45] *Ibid.*, p. 93.
[46] Otto Klineberg, *Characteristics of the American Negro*, (New York: Harper and Brothers, 1944), pp. 400–401.

exist was largely dependent on his assertion that "there is no proof that the groups are inherently different, but there is also no complete demonstration that the groups are entirely alike." Yet by interpreting the evidence slightly differently hereditarians could just as easily conclude the opposite and argue that there is no proof that the groups are inherently alike, but there is also no complete demonstration that the groups are different.

Among the more interesting insights of Myrdal was his recognition of the importance of having a happy and productive Black population. As Myrdal expressed it, Black aggression could have undesirable consequences for the white dominant group:

> Not only occasional acts of violence, but more laziness, carelessness, unreliability, petty stealing and lying are undoubtedly to be explained as concealed aggression. . . . The truth is the *Negroes generally do not feel they have unqualified moral obligations to white people.* . . . The voluntary withdrawal which has intensified the isolation between the two castes is also an expression of Negro protest under cover.[47]

Myrdal argued it was essential for Americans to realize that Black discontent was growing. Even before the outbreak of the Second World War he emphasized that America could *"never more regard its Negroes as a patient, submissive minority."* During the war he warned that "among common Negroes in the South and the North" there exists "much sullen skepticism, and even cynicism, and vague, tired, angry dissatisfaction." [48] These indeed were conditions for alarm.

Even more important for national security during the war was the need for America to demonstrate to other nations, particularly Asian ones, that she treated her Black population humanely. "For its international prestige, power, and future security," Myrdal noted the United States "needs to demonstrate to the world that American Negroes can be satisfactorily integrated into its democracy." Continuing, he observed that the "treatment of the Negro in America has not made good propaganda for America abroad and particularly not among colored nations." Indeed, the situation is actually such that "any and all concessions to Negro rights in this phase of the history of the world will repay the nation many times," while, on the other hand, "any and all injustices inflicted upon him will be extremely costly." While most Americans had not yet realized this fact, Myrdal believed it would "become increasingly apparent as the war goes on." [49] This recognition that discrimination against the Black was socially and economically inefficient and politically inexpedient grew rapidly during the Second World War and postwar years.

---

[47] Myrdal, p. 763.
[48] *Ibid.*, pp. 1004–1006. (Myrdal's emphasis.)
[49] *Ibid.*, pp. 1015–1016.

Social and Industrial Efficiency

During the war numerous articles called attention to the industrial inefficiency of discrimination. *Modern Industry*, commenting on the inefficient use of Black labor, observed that "there's a million-odd manpower now unused or improperly used that American industrial management can profitably put to work. . . . " [50] *Harper's Magazine* noted that "even if it were possible to ignore the moral significance of denying one-tenth of a nation—the Negro—a right to make an honest living on a basis of merit, America certainly cannot at this time afford to keep fifteen million of its citizens in economic bondage solely because of color." [51] Similarly, the avowedly conservative Baltimore *Evening Sun*, faced by the enormous shortages of white labor in Baltimore and the great surplus of unemployed Black labor in Baltimore, reflected as following on the "ironic" situation:

> We are thinking simply of the ironic situation Baltimore finds itself in right now: on the one hand a desperate shortage of skilled and semiskilled workmen for our war industries, and on the other hand, the existence of a large reservoir of labor which is rarely considered when there is need for skilled rather than unskilled workmen. It seems to us that in this emergency a dispassionate and objective examination of the situation of the Negro in Baltimore's industries is called for.[52]

Nor was industrial efficiency the only reason that more equal treatment of the Black was promoted during the war. Social control and social efficiency, many commentators observed, could only be safely maintained by giving the Black a fairer deal. Thus the Council for Democracy warned that when a nation prepares or engages in war "then embittered and disillusioned people, beyond being a burden, become a danger." For if any large group in the population, i.e., the Negro becomes convinced that "their citizenship is only 'second class,' that they are excluded from the benefits of the social order they are expected to give their lives to defend," then the Council warned, "they become fertile ground for subversive propaganda, for agitation and unrest." [53] At the same time, Black soldiers were not likely to fight vigorously for their country, as *Fortune* observed, unless they were treated more equally since "men do not die for causes they are cynical about; and they cannot conquer on behalf of a principle they discount." [54]

After the war, industrial efficiency and social control would continue to be primary factors for giving the Black greater opportunity. Comment-

[50] "Found: A Million Manpower," *Modern Industry*, May 15, 1942, p. 31.
[51] Earl Brown, "American Negroes and the War," *Harpers Magazine*, April 1942, p.552.
[52] As quoted in "The Negro's War," *Fortune*, June 1942, p. 80.
[53] Council for Democracy, *The Negro and Defense*, (pamphlet), 1941, p. 32.
[54] *Fortune*, p. 163.

ing on the factor of industrial efficiency, the President's Committee on Civil Rights in 1947 stated that "the United States can no longer afford this heavy drain upon its human wealth, its national competence." The Committee further noted the following:

> One of the principal economic problems facing us and the rest of the world is achieving maximum production and continued prosperity. The loss of a huge, potential market for goods is a direct result of the economic discrimination which is practiced against many of our minority groups. As a result, their purchasing power is curtailed and markets are reduced. Reduced markets result in reduced production. This cuts down employment, which of course means lower wages and still fewer jobs opportunity. Rising fear, prejudice, and insecurity aggravate the very discrimination in employment which sets the vicious circle in motion.[55]

Even more emphatic than this Committee was Elmo Roper in an article on "The Price Business Pays" in 1949. Roper noted that there is perhaps "no greater wastage today than our failure to make proper use" of Negro manpower. "A failure of this kind," Roper continued, "would be more understandable if the business community actually benefited and made greater profits from such discrimination." Yet existing discrimination for Roper was inexcusable since business suffered from not allowing Negroes to participate fully in the economy.[56]

This recognition that discrimination was socially and economically inefficient by liberals, businessmen and others would no doubt play an instrumental role in defining the social milieu from which the Brown decision emerged. From purely an economic standpoint, equal educational opportunity was not necessary for Blacks as long as they were regarded merely as a source of unskilled labor. It was necessary, however, to fully educate Blacks if they were to be used as skilled laborers and consumers. Correspondingly, the problem of social control shifted as the expectations and opportunities for Blacks increased.

Brown v. Board of Education

From this social milieu which gave priority to efficiency and productivity emerged the Brown decision. The *Brown v. Board of Education* decision climaxed hearings on four cases tried before the Supreme Court: *Briggs v. Elliott* (South Carolina case), *Davis v. County School Board*

---

[55] President's Committee on Civil Rights, *To Secure These Rights*, (Washington: U.S. Government Printing Office, 1947), p. 141, 146.

[56] Elmo Roper, "The Price Business Pays," *Discrimination and National Welfare*, ed., R. M. MacIver, (New York: Harper and Brothers, 1949), p. 16.

(Virginia case), *Gebhard v. Belton* (Delaware case), and the Brown case.[57] In the Brown decision, the Court ruled that separate educational facilities were inherently unequal, and therefore that racial segregation in the public schools violated the "due process" clause of the Fourteenth Amendment. In hearing the case, the Court admitted evidence from the social sciences.

The Court indicated, in its opinion, that purely juristic arguments were not sufficient to enable it to determine if segregated school facilities violated the Fourteenth Amendment. So it deemphasized juristic arguments and gave credence to arguments which embraced social science findings, leading some critics to denounce the Court for sustaining its conclusions on a "reasoning process which was heretofore unknown to jurisprudence." [58] Senator James Eastland, in a resolution before the United States Senate, declared that the decision was "based solely and alone on psychological, sociological, and anthropological considerations." [59] The decision, noted Eastland, was a "tragic commentary on the intelligence and judgment of the members of the United States Supreme Court. . . . " [60] Even some of those who agreed with the decision criticized it because it was not based on "ordinary constitutional law without benefit of sociology or psychology." [61] Not surprisingly those most pleased with the use of social scientific data were the social scientists. Kenneth B. Clark who gave major testimony in the school decisions was nothing less than exuberant over the use of the social sciences. For Clark evidence that "segregation inflicts injuries upon the Negro had to come from the social psychologists and other social scientists." [62] In arguing against segregation, the plaintiffs used social science evidence, to argue among other things that Blacks were innately intellectually equal to whites.

In the South Carolina case, the court granted permission to the plaintiff's testimony (which was originally given in the Sweatt v. Painter decision in 1950) of Robert Redfield, an anthropologist from the University of Chicago, to be included. During his testimony, Redfield had been asked if there were any recognizable differences in intellectual capacity between Negro and white students. Redfield replied that "We got something of a

---

[57] For a discussion of these cases and the types of evidence and argument employed see David B. Strother, "Evidence, Argument and Decision in Brown v. Board of Education," (unpublished Ph.D. dissertation, University of Illinois, 1958).

[58] Eugene Cook and W. I. Potter, "School Segregation Cases," *American Bar Association Journal*, April 1956, p. 313.

[59] *Record*, 84th Congress, 1st Session, 1955, p. 6963.

[60] *Ibid.*

[61] "Segregation was Doomed Before the Court Acted," an editorial in *Saturday Evening Post*, June 19, 1954, p. 10.

[62] K. B. Clark, "Desegregation: An Appraisal of the Evidence," *J. of Social Issues*, No. 4, 1953, p. 3.

lesson there." While we began with the common assumption of educators that there were inherent differences between the races, we "have slowly, but I think very convincingly, been compelled to come to the opposite conclusion, in the course of a long history of special research in the field." [63]

In the Delaware case, Klineberg would testify that there was "no racial difference in intellectual capacity" between the races.[64] Similarly, in the Brown decision, Horace B. English, a psychologist at Ohio State University, testified that on the basis of "color," one cannot predict how well a child will learn. "We don't have racial groups learning," English argued, "we have individuals learning and in both groups, white and Negro, we have some persons who are very good learners, and we have some medium learners." [65]

Finally to reinforce their argument that Blacks were intellectually equal and that segregation was discrimination, *per se*, the appellants submitted a social science statement as an appendix to their briefs. This statement was signed by thirty-two of the "foremost authorities" in sociology, anthropology, psychology, and psychiatry dealing with American race relations. Among the experts writing on "The Effects of Segregation and the Consequences of Desegregation: A Social Science Statement" were Clark, Davis, Klineberg, and Redfield.[66] Their statement, according to the appellants, represented a concensus of opinion among social scientists on the effects of racial segregation. It represented a summary of the best available scientific evidence relative to the effects of racial segregation on the individual." [67]

The content itself of the experts' statement was stated with conviction. Noting that "segregation is at present a social reality" the experts concurred that nevertheless "questions may be raised . . . as to what are the likely consequences of desegregation." One such question, the experts continued, asks whether "the inclusion of an intellectually inferior group may jeopardize the education of the more intelligent group by placing it in a situation where it is at a marked competitive disadvantage." Behind this question, they observed, was the assumption "that the presently seg-

[63] As quoted in Herbert Hill and Jack Greenberg, *Citizen's Guide to Desegregation*, (Boston: The Beacon Press, 1956), p. 71.

[64] As quoted in Strother, p. 106.

[65] As quoted in Strother, p. 90.

[66] The other social scientists were Floyd H. Allport, Gordon W. Allport, Charlotte Babcock, Viola W. Bernard, Jerome S. Bruner, Hadley Cantril, Isiodor Chein, Mamie P. Clark, Stuart W. Cook, Bingham Dai, Else Frenkel-Brunswick, Noel P. Gist, Daniel Katz, David Drech, Alfred McClung Lee, R. M. MacIver, Robert K. Merton, Gardner Murphy, Theodore W. Newcomb, Ira DeA. Reid, Arnold M. Rose, Gerhart Saenger, R. Nevitt Sanford, S. Stanfield Sargent, M. Brewster Smith, Samuel A. Stouffer, Wellman Warner, and Robin M. Williams.

[67] As quoted in Strother, p. 152.

regated groups actually are inferior intellectually." Citing Klineberg's studies as the basis for their "scientific evidence" they proceeded to argue that "much, perhaps all, of the observable differences" between racial and national groups could be "adequately explained in terms of environmental differences." For the committee, it seemed clear that "fears based on the assumption of innate racial differences in intelligence are not well founded." [68]

Critique of the Brown Decision

Interestingly enough this whole line of argument that the Black was innately intellectually equal would not be challenged by the defense. It was not for lack of evidence or witnesses that this assumption went unchallenged.[69] Rather it seems probable that the assumption that Blacks were intellectually equal was so thoroughly believed by the Court that it could only hurt the defense to argue the contrary.

In any case, the testimony of the social scientists was not much more conclusive that the earlier hereditarian findings of Laughlin, Yerkes and Brigham. While it could be demonstrated that existing tests were culturally biased, this did not prove that Blacks were innately intellectually equal (or inferior or superior) to whites. It did show that the subject was still very open and that to discriminate on the basis of alleged racial inferiority was unwise and unjust. Yet it did not show, as the plaintiffs alleged, that Blacks were intellectually equal to whites. Thus once again social scientific data had been misused.

Further, the use of social science data in the Brown decision posed many important problems. Edmund Cane, a lawyer writing in the *New York University Law Review*, asked the crucial question of whether it made any important difference if the Supreme Court relied on the psychologists' findings. His answer was that it did indeed make a difference:

> I submit it does. In the first place, since the behavioral sciences are so very young, imprecise, and changeful, their findings have an uncertain expectancy of life. Today's sanguine asseveration may be cancelled by tomorrow's new revelation—or new technical fad. It is one thing to use the current scientific findings, however ephemeral they may be, in order to ascertain whether the legislature has acted reasonably in adopting some

[68] "The Effects of Segregation and the Consequences of Desegregation: A Social Science Statement," *Minnesota Law Review*, Vol. 37, 1953, p. 435.

[69] Of those psychologists who no doubt would have been willing to testify that the Black was innately inferior was Henry E. Garrett. The defense used the Columbia University psychologist as a witness in the Virginia case but mainly only to testify that a Black could get a better education in a truly equal segregated school in the South than in an integrated one because of Southern social mores and customs. For his testimony see Hill and Strother.

scheme of social or economic regulation; deference here is shown not so much to the findings as to the legislature. It would be quite another thing to have our fundamental rights rise, fall, or change along with the latest fashions or psychological literature. Today the social psychologists—at least the leaders of the discipline—are liberal and egalitarian in basic approach. Suppose, a generation hence, some of their successors were to revert to the ethnic mysticism of the very recent past; suppose they were to present us with a collection of racist notion and label them "science." What then would be the state of our constitutional rights? Recognizing as we do how sagacious Mr. Justice Holmes was to insist that the Constitution be not tied to the wheels of any economic system whatsoever, we ought to keep it similarly uncommitted in relation to the other social sciences.[70]

If Cane had further historical background he would have realized that his fear of a "racist" science had been practiced thirty years earlier and that the "sagacious" Holmes had himself justified sterilization legislation on a scientific basis. Yet in his central point, Cane was surely correct. The acceptance of social scientific evidence in the courts was fraught with dangers. Not only could social science evidence be used to deprive an individual of freedom and constitutional rights but the professional interests of social scientists could lead them to manipulate their colleagues and the evidence.

The potential impact of these professional interests was evident in Kenneth B. Clark's discussion of "The Social Scientist as an Expert Witness in Civil Rights Litigation." With increasing collaboration between social science and the legal profession, Clark observed, "it will be necessary for the professional societies among the social and psychological sciences to develop safeguards against possible ethical abuses; e.g. flagrant manifestation of prejudice, distortion of data and deliberately misleading interpretation." The precise meaning of this statement became clearer when Clark proceeded to observe that:

> While it would be impossible to prevent honest disagreement among social scientists reflecting differences in interpretations and emphasis, it is nonetheless important to minimize the possibility of the presentation of conflicting testimony by equally competent scientists concerning the available facts. Professional organizations among social scientists now have the obligation to set up some kind of machinery which will prevent social scientists from being haunted by the same spectacle which has long bedeviled the field of psychiatry—two or more psychiatrists offering with equal certainty contradictory testimony concerning the sanity of a given defendant.[71]

[70] Edmund Cahn, "Jurisprudence," *New York University Law Review*, January 1955, p. 167.
[71] K. B. Clark, "The Social Scientist as an Expert Witness in Civil Rights Litigation," *Social Problems*, 1953, pp. 9–10.

While Clark's proposal for collaboration between social scientists would surely increase their professional power, it could hardly be justified scientifically.

CONCLUSION

Thus, the fact that many testers, liberals, and industrialists were generally supportive of the Immigration Act and Brown decision was not surprising. Viewed from the context of the traditional model linking politics and the nature–nurture issue, this alignment was indeed nonsensical. Yet as demonstrated there was no necessary relationship between liberalism and environmentalism or conservatism and hereditarianism. Although no necessary relationship existed, the nature-nurture question nevertheless was manipulated for specific political purposes. In both decisions the nature–nurture issue tended to veil important questions by turning political and ethical problems into technical ones, supposedly resolvable by intelligence tests. This process provided a convenient rationalization for policies that many industrialists, liberals, testers, and other interests wished to pursue.

For big business, their concern was in maximizing social control and industrial efficiency. To achieve these ends, the channeling of the nature–nurture issue was crucial. In choosing, for example, Myrdal to represent them, they were choosing a particular interpretation of the nature–nurture issue which was conducive for bringing Blacks into the labor market. This did not mean that Myrdal was not "objective," but rather only that his general findings on Blacks were predictable given his social framework. Had the foundations sought a different result, there were competent reactionary hereditarians who could have provided one.

While the argument can be made that liberals had to appeal to the interests of business to promote opportunity for Blacks, (i.e., that liberals were primarily motivated by their desire to help the Black) it is unconvincing. As pragmatists, liberals acted on the basis of national interest, as reflected in real and intended consequences, rather than on the basis of moral principles. Yet upon discerning the national interest, liberals invariably argued that their actions were based on moral principles. In the case of promoting the welfare of Blacks, it was especially hypocritical since many liberals had a history of racism.

Although the intelligence testers provided no conclusive evidence for resolving the nature–nurture issue, nevertheless they played an influential role in the decision-making process. They were generally supportive of the Immigration Act and Brown decision for a variety of extra-scientific reasons. While they also sought to promote the national interest, which in practice often meant supporting industrial efficiency and social control, they were also motivated by professional interests. The triple alliance of big business, liberals, and testers thus had interests in common which led them to cooperatively promote these two decisions.

Can Negroes Learn the Way Whites Do?

Findings of a Top Authority

Arthur R. Jensen

Are all men created equal in ability to learn the same thing the same way?

A noted professor of psychology—Dr. Arthur R. Jensen of the University of California—has reopened an old controversy by offering new arguments on that question. His study, entitled "How Much Can We Boost IQ and Scholastic Achievement?" has just been published by the "Harvard Educational Review." It brings into issue some of the fundamental teaching methods used in racially mixed schools.

The main points of his article are given below, as well as the reaction of other prominent authorities to his conclusions.

Shock waves are rolling through the U.S. educational community over a frank and startling reappraisal of differences in classroom performance between whites and Negroes.

In a lengthy article, taking up most of the winter issue of the "Harvard Educational Review," one of the nation's leading educational psychologists, Dr. Arthur R. Jensen of the University of California at Berkeley, presents these major findings:

Negro scores averaging about 15 points below the white average on IQ tests must be taken seriously as evidence of genetic differences between the two races in learning patterns.

Research suggests that such a difference would tend to work against Negroes and against the "disadvantaged" generally when it comes to "cognitive" learning—abstract reasoning—which forms the basis for intelligence measurements and for the higher mental skills.

Conversely, Negroes and other "disadvantaged" children tend to do well in tasks involving rote learning—memorizing mainly through repetition

—and some other skills, and these aptitudes can be used to help raise their scholastic achievement and job potential.

Unfortunately, big programs of "compensatory" education, now costing taxpayers hundreds of millions of dollars a year, are doomed to failure as long as they pursue old approaches stressing "cognitive" learning.

The Berkeley psychologist, who also is vice president of the American Educational Research Association, stressed his view that "the full range of human talents is represented in all the major races of man and in all socioeconomic levels." He added, however, that research clearly shows differing patterns of average intellectual skills among the races.

GENETIC FACTORS IGNORED

Dr. Jensen acknowledged that far more research is needed to define the extent and nature of these differences because "the possible importance of genetic factors . . . has been greatly ignored, almost to the point of being a tabooed subject." He strongly attacked the domination of educational theory by "environmentalists" who argue that all children except a rare few come equipped with the same learning mechanisms, and that differences in IQ scores are the result of social, economic, emotional and other pressures.

Cited by Dr. Jensen was the then U.S. Commissioner of Education, Francis Keppel, who proclaimed a few years ago that children "all have similar potential at birth—the differences occur thereafter."

There is now a growing realization among scholars in this field that discrepancies in performance "cannot be completely or directly attributed to discrimination or inequalities in education," Dr. Jensen said.

A REAPPRAISAL

Pointing to many admissions of failure in huge "compensatory" education programs for the poor, he asked:

"What has gone wrong? In other fields, when bridges do not stand, when aircraft do not fly, when machines do not work, when treatments do not cure . . . one begins to question the basic assumptions, principles, theories, and hypotheses that guide one's efforts. Is it time to follow suit in education?"

A fresh look at the whole problem of inequalities in the classroom, the Berkeley educator said, must begin with a re-examination of what "intelligence" really is. He stressed that the term "intelligence" is generally used by psychologists to apply to only a small part of the total range of mental ability, which also includes such qualities as acuteness of perception, motor behavior and memorizing skills.

As developed over the years, he said, the "intelligence test" is a sampling of abilities, oriented toward the middle-class child, by which testers can forecast likely performance in school and in occupational status and job capacities—not precisely, but within a small margin of error.

The crucial ability in this sampling is "cognitive" or "conceptual" learning—the capacity for abstract reasoning and problem-solving through classifying of similarities and dissimilarities. As observed by Dr. Jensen, it is this quality that has generated the world's great discoveries. It is this that enables children to proceed from rote learning to reasoning for themselves.

For most children, Dr. Jensen has found, this reasoning capacity begins to take hold in the first or second grade. But it does so at a varying pace and to varying degrees—and it is this variation that accounts in large measure for the differences in IQ test scores in any sampling of children.

RAISING INTELLIGENCE

Can intelligence centering on the "cognitive" factor be raised as much as environmentalists claim?

Dr. Jensen's reply is No. His article took up at length many tests of children whose origins and upbringing were thought to offer some clues on this issue.

Of especial interest were studies of identical twins—those who develop from a single fertilized ovum and therefore have identical genetic endowment. These studies, Dr. Jensen said, showed that such twins, even if reared apart in dissimilar environments, still tend to develop IQ's almost as similar as those of identical twins reared together.

Furthermore, he cited research indicating that children adopted shortly after birth are far more similar in IQ to their natural parents than to their adoptive parents.

Such studies, Dr. Jensen said, make it clear that "brain mechanisms which are involved in learning are genetically conditioned just as are other structures and functions of the organism." Altogether, his summation of studies on individual differences in IQ concluded that heredity accounts on the average for about 80 percent of those individual variations, as against only 20 percent resulting from environmental influences.

ENVIRONMENTAL INFLUENCES

Contrarily, he did find much evidence that environment can play an important role in modifying actual performance in the classroom or on the job, without much changing IQ itself. Studies of twins, he said, suggested that individual differences in scholastic performance are determined only about half as much by heredity as are IQ variations.

This means, said Dr. Jensen, that "many other traits, habits, attitudes and values enter into a child's performance in school besides just his intelligence, and these noncognitive factors are largely environmentally determined, mainly through influence within the child's family." IQ gains were described as being significant only when youngsters are removed from extreme, often bizarre, isolation and deprivation. Dr. Jensen found that the "disadvantaged" child often makes initial gain after a change for the better in environment, but then regresses toward his parents' level.

As an instance, he referred to a Milwaukee study last year of 586 children of 88 low-income Negro mothers living in a slum neighborhood which had only 5 percent of the city's school population—but one third of the retarded children, defined as those with IQ's of under 75. Of the 88 mothers, this study found, 45.4 percent were below 80 in IQ. Children of the low-IQ mothers suffered a systematic decline in intelligence testing, and in first grade accounted for four fifths of the children with under-80 IQ's in the total sampling.

This study and others were seen as underlining the influence of genetic factors in the relationship of IQ showings to social and economic status. Similarly, Dr. Jensen said, heredity probably plays some role in the heavy representation of Negroes in America's lower socioeconomic groups.

HEREDITY FINDINGS

After looking over the accumulated research on this subject, Dr. Jensen summed up the major findings as follows:

Negroes, on the average, test about 15 IQ points below the white average. This discrepancy is about the same in school achievement rather consistently in Grades 1 through 12.

One study found that IQ's below 75 have a much higher incidence among Negroes than among whites at every socioeconomic level. In the two highest of these levels, the Negro incidence was more than 13 times as high as for whites—an important statistic Dr. Jensen said, because "if environmental factors were mainly responsible for producing such differences, one should expect a lesser Negro-white discrepancy at the upper [socioeconomic] levels."

A 1967 survey of Negro and white children in a California school district found that Negroes lagged only 3.9 points in the lowest socioeconomic category—but the gap widened to 15.5 points in comparing white and Negro children from professional and managerial families.

Over all, Dr. Jensen said, one summation of the total literature on this subject up to 1965 found that in studies with subjects grouped by class, the upper-status Negro children averaged 2.6 points below the low-status whites. The author of this summary, Dr. Audrey M. Shuey, wrote:

"It seems improbable that upper and middle-class colored children would have no more culture opportunities provided them than white children of the lower and lowest class."

To buttress his argument that genetics—not environment—plays the major role in Negro IQ scores, Dr. Jensen mentioned the American Indians as actually being the most "disadvantaged" of racial groups included in the Coleman Report of the U.S. Department of Health, Education and Welfare in 1966. In almost every way, this report found, the environmental rating of Indians is as far below the Negro average as the Negro average is below that of whites.

Despite this, in scores on both ability and achievement tests, it was discovered that Indians averaged six to eight points above Negroes.

USES OF TESTS

Intelligence tests, Dr. Jensen said, satisfactorily measure intelligence as defined by the psychologists in line with "objective reality"—the educational and occupational demands of modern society. Even so, he believes, the findings open up many questions about the course that U.S. education should take in times ahead.

Mentioned in some detail were child-development tests that placed Negro infants considerably ahead of whites in motor skills and noncognitive abilities. One study found 60 percent of Negro infants—compared with 30 percent for white infants—doing well between the ages of 9 and 12 months in walking and "pat-a-cake" muscular co-ordination. Even in nonmotor items, Negro infants up to six months of age in the poorest section of Durham, N. C., scored six to eight points above white norms.

In still another study, Dr. Jensen told of repeatedly showing and naming to children about 20 unrelated but familiar objects, after which the youngsters were told to recall as many of the items as possible, in any order that came to mind.

Repeated testing, said the University of California psychologist, revealed that lower and middle-class children did about equally well, though their IQ's differed by 15 to 20 points.

The IQ differential, however, became clear when 20 familiar objects again were presented in a random order—but the objects this time could be grouped into conceptual categories such as food, furniture and clothing.

White children, in this test, tended to recall the items in "clusters" corresponding to the common categories. Negro children displayed significantly less of this conceptual clustering. Even though they recognized the concepts, the Negro children did not appear to respond as instinctively as white children did, Dr. Jensen said.

DIFFERENT REQUIREMENTS

A deficiency in conceptual ability, Dr. Jensen added, need not have the importance currently attached to it as the ultimate yardstick of fitness to play a productive role in modern society. Job descriptions, he suggested, should be reviewed to see whether the educational and mental-test requirements that now bar many "disadvantaged" persons are necessary.

Also recommended were smaller, more intensive and more carefully focused programs of "compensatory" education than those tried so far. Massive experiments such as New York City's "Higher Horizons" program were seen as disappointments because they tended merely to offer bigger doses of generalized "cognitive" learning. Dr. Jensen said such efforts should use as their basis instead the "associative" learning skills possessed by many poor children.

TIMETABLE OF LEARNING

Some basic skills can be acquired by rote learning at an early age—Dr. Jensen said—and ways should be found to transfer such memorized learning in a lasting way to the later stages of learning. He gave this explanation:

"Too often, if a child does not learn the school subject matter when taught in a way that depends largely on being average or above average on general intelligence, he does not learn at all, so that we find high-school students who have failed to learn basic skills which they could easily have learned many years earlier by means that do not depend much on general intelligence. . . . If a child cannot show that he 'understands' the meaning of 1 plus 1 equals 2 in some abstract, verbal, cognitive sense, he is in effect not allowed to go on to learn 2 plus 2 equals 4. I am reasonably convinced that all the basic scholastic skills can be learned by children with normal associative learning ability, provided the instructional techniques do not make general intelligence the *sine qua non* of being able to learn."

As one example of what can be done, he told of a preschool program at the University of Illinois which centered sharply on specific skills— language, reading and arithmetic—considered essential in developing the cognitive process. A high degree of pupil attention and participation was stressed in the experiment, along with emphatic repetition. In general, the

Illinois experiment put less stock on IQ gains than in scholastic performance. The result, Dr. Jensen said, was that achievement levels of the "disadvantaged" youngsters compared favorably with those of children whose IQs ranged 10 to 20 points higher.

OPPOSED TO SEGREGATION

Dr. Jensen made it clear that he is opposed to racial segregation. He said: "All persons must be regarded on the basis of their individual qualities and merits, and all social, educational and economic institutions must have built into them the mechanisms for insuring and maximizing the treatment of persons according to their individual behavior." While the article in the "Harvard Educational Review" did not specify how this could be accomplished in classrooms, Dr. Jensen on other occasions has mentioned such methods as small groupings of children and the use of computer-assisted teaching which could enable each child to learn through his own pattern of mental skills.

Required more than anything else, Dr. Jensen suggested, is for educational theorists to abandon "doctrinaire attitudes" on questions related to racial inequalities, and to undertake scientific inquiry—with "no holds barred." He concluded:

"Diversity rather than uniformity of approaches and aims would seem to be the key to making education rewarding for children of different patterns of ability. The reality of individual differences thus need not mean educational rewards for some children and frustration and defeat for others."

Behavior-Genetic Analysis and Its Biosocial Consequences

Jerry Hirsch

As a psychology student I was taught that a science was founded on the discovery of lawful relations between variables. During my student days at Berkeley, the true psychological scientist was preoccupied with the major learning theories. We read, studied, and designed experiments to test the theories of Thorndike, Guthrie, Hull and Tolman. Many of their verbally formulated laws of behavior were replaced by the mathematical models that have since come into vogue.

Afterwards I learned empirically the truth of what might be the most general of all behavioral laws. The Harvard law of animal behavior: "Under the most carefully controlled experimental conditions the animals do as they damn please." Still later I discovered the low esteem in which post World War II psychology was held by two of the best minds this century has seen. In 1947, John Dewey, eighth president of the American Psychological Association, wrote to discourage young Robert V. Daniels from studying psychology at Harvard:

> Psychology . . . is on the whole, in my opinion, the most inept and backwards a tool . . . as there is. It is much of it actually harmful because of wrong basic postulates—maybe not all stated, but actually there when one judges from what they do—the kind of problems attacked and the way they attack them. (5)

On the final page of the last book written before his death in 1951 Ludwig Wittgenstein, perhaps the most influential of the founders of modern philosophical analysis, observed:

> The confusion and barrenness of psychology is not to be explained by calling it a "young science"; its state is not comparable with that of physics, for instance, in its beginning. (Rather with that of certain branches of mathematics. Set theory.) For in psychology there are experimental methods and *conceptual confusion*. (As in the other case conceptual confusion and methods of proof.)
>
> The existence of the experimental method makes us think we have the means of solving the problems which trouble us; though problem and method pass one another by. (*34*)

LAWS OF GENETICS

It was then while overcome by feelings of disenchantment (obviously without laws behavior study could never be science) that I embraced genetics. There was true science. My passion became even more intense when I realized that like thermodynamics, genetics had three laws: segregation, independent assortment and the Hardy-Weinberg law of population equilibria. What a foundation they provided for my beloved individual differences.

Since both my teaching and research involved considerable work with *Drosophila*, I knew and would recount to my classes in somewhat elaborate detail the story of Calvin Bridge's classic experiments on sex determination as a function of a ratio between the sex chromosomes and the autosomes. As the important discoveries in human cytogenetics were made throughout the 1950's and 60's, and "abnormalities" like Klinefelter's, Turner's and Down's syndromes and the violence-prone males with an extra Y chromosome became genetically comprehensible, I began to realize that the so-called laws of genetics were no more universal than the so-called laws of behavior. Every one of the above-mentioned clinical conditions involved, at the very least, a violation of Mendel's law of segregation. Of course, so did Bridge's experiments, but it had been too easy to rationalize them as clever laboratory tricks.

BEHAVIORISM

Over the past two decades the case against behaviorist extremism has been spelled out in incontrovertible detail. The behaviorists committed many sins: they accepted the mind at birth as Locke's *tabula rasa*, they advocated an empty-organism psychology, they asserted the uniformity postulate of no pre-natal individual differences; in short they epitomized typological thinking. Many times we have heard quoted the famous boast by the first high priest of behaviorism, John B. Watson:

> Give me a dozen healthy infants, well-formed, and my own specified world to bring them up in, and I'll guarantee to take any one at random and train him to become any type of specialist I might select—doctor, lawyer, artist, merchant-chief and yes, even beggar-man and thief, regardless of his talents, penchants, tendencies, abilities, vocations, race of his ancestors.

However, it is only when we read the next sentence, which is rarely, if ever, quoted, that we begin to understand how so many people might have embraced something intellectually so shallow as radical behaviorism. In that all important next sentence Watson explains:

> I am going beyond my facts and I admit it, but so have the advocates of the contrary and they have been doing it for many thousands of years (p. 104). (*33*)

RACISM

Who were the advocates of the contrary and what had they been saying? It is difficult to establish the origins of racist thinking, but certainly one of its most influential advocates was Joseph Arthur de Gobineau, who published a four-volume *Essay on the inequality of the human races* (*10*) in the mid-1850's. De Gobineau preached the superiority of the white race, and among whites it was the Aryans who carried civilization to its highest point. In fact, they were responsible for civilization wherever it appeared. Unfortunately, de Gobineau's essay proved to be the major seminal work that inspired some of the most perverse developments in the intellectual and political history of our civilization. Later in his life, de Gobineau became an intimate of the celebrated German composer, Richard Wagner. The English-born Houston Stewart Chamberlain, who emigrated to the Continent, became a devoted admirer of both de Gobineau and Wagner. In 1908, after Wagner's death, he married Wagner's daughter, Eva, settled in and supported Germany against England during World War I, becoming a naturalized German citizen in 1916.

In the summer of 1923, an admirer who had read Chamberlain's writings, Adolf Hitler, visited Wahnfried, the Wagner family home in Bayreuth where Chamberlain lived. After their meeting, Chamberlain wrote to Hitler: "My faith in the Germans had never wavered for a moment, but my hope . . . had sunk to a low ebb. At one stroke you have transformed the state of my soul!" (*14*) We all know the sequel to that unfortunate tale. I find that our modern scientific colleagues, whether they be biological or social scientists, for the most part, do not know the sad parallel that exists for the essentially political tale I have so far recounted. The same theme can be traced down the main stream of biosocial science.

Today not many people know the complete title of Darwin's most famous book: *On the Origin of Species by Means of Natural Selection or the Preservation of Favoured Races in the Struggle for Life.* I find no evidence that Darwin had the attitudes we now call racist. Unfortunately many of his admirers, his contemporaries, and his successors were not as circumspect as he. In Paris in 1838, J.E.D. Esquirol first described a form of mental deficiency later to become well known by two inappropriate names unrelated to his work. Unhappily one of these names, through textbook adoption and clinical jargon, puts into wide circulation a term loaded with race prejudice. Somewhat later (1846 and 1866), E. Seguin described the same condition under the name "furfuraceous cretinism" and his account has only recently been recognized as "the most ingenious description of physical characteristics . . ." (2)

Unhappily that most promising scientific beginning was ignored. Instead the following unfortunate events occurred: In 1866, John Langdon Haydon Down published the paper entitled "Observations on an ethnic classification of idiots." (*6*)

> . . . making a classification of the feeble-minded, by arranging them around various ethnic standards—in other words, framing a natural system to supplement the information to be derived by an inquiry into the history of the case.
>
> I have been able to find among the large number of idiots and imbeciles which comes under my observation, both at Earlswood and the out-patient department of the Hospital, that a considerable portion can be fairly referred to one of the great divisions of the human family other than the class from which they have sprung. Of course, there are numerous representatives of the great Caucasian family. Several well-marked

examples of the Ethiopian variety have come under my notice, presenting the characteristic malar bones, the prominent eyes, the puffy lips, and
retreating chin. The woolly hair has also been present, although not always
black, nor has the skin acquired pigmentary deposit. They have been
specimens of white negroes, although of European descent.

Some arrange themselves around the Malay variety, and present in
their soft, black, curly hair, their prominent upper jaws and capacious
mouths, types of the family which people the South Sea Islands.

Nor have there been wanting the analogues of the people who with
shortened foreheads, prominent cheeks, deep-set eyes, and slightly apish
nose, originally inhabited the American Continent.

The great Mongolian family has numerous representatives, and it is to
this division, I wish, in this paper, to call special attention. A very large
number of congenital idiots are typical Mongols. So marked is this, that
when placed side by side, it is difficult to believe that the specimens compared are not children of the same parents. The number of idiots who
arrange themselves around the Mongolian type is so great, and they present such a close resemblance to one another in mental power, that I shall
describe an idiot member of this racial division, selected from the large
number that have fallen under my observation.

The hair is not black, as in the real Mongol, but of a brownish color,
straight and scanty. The face is flat and broad, and destitute of prominence. The cheeks are roundish, and extended laterally. The eyes are
obliquely placed, and the internal canthi more than normally distant from
one another. The palpebral fissure is very narrow. The forehead is
wrinkled transversely from the constant assistance which the levatores
palpebrarum derive from the occipito-frontalis muscle in the opening of
the eyes. The lips are large and thick with transverse fissures. The tongue
is long, thick, and is much roughened. The nose is small. The skin has a
slightly dirty yellowish tinge and is deficient in elasticity, giving the
appearance of being too large for the body.

The boy's aspect is such that it is difficult to realize that he is the child
of Europeans, but so frequently are these characters presented, that there
can be no doubt that these ethnic features are the result of degeneration.

And he means degeneration from a higher to a lower race. The foregoing
represents a distasteful but excellent example of the racial hierarchy theory
and its misleadingly dangerous implications. That was how the widely-
used terms Mongolism and Mongolian idiocy entered our "technical"
vocabulary. For the next century, this pattern of thought is going to persist
and occupy an important place in the minds of many leading scientists.

ALLEGED JEWISH GENETIC INFERIORITY

In 1884, Francis Galton, Darwin's half cousin, founder of the Eugenics
movement and respected contributor to many fields of science, wrote to
the distinguished Swiss botanist, Alphonse de Candolle: "It strikes me that
the Jews are specialized for a parasitical existence upon other nations, and

that there is need of evidence that they are capable of fulfilling the varied duties of a civilized nation by themselves" (p. 209). (*27*) Karl Pearson, Galton's disciple and biographer, echoed this opinion 40 years later during his attempt to prove the undesirability of Jewish immigration into Britain: ". . . for such men as religion, social habits, or language keep as a caste apart, there should be no place. They will not be absorbed by, and at the same time strengthen the existing population; they will develop into a parasitic race . . ." (p. 125). (*28*)

Beginning in 1908 and continuing at least until 1928, Karl Pearson collected and analyzed data in order to assess "the quality of the racial stock immigrating into Great Britain . . ." (p. 33). (*25*) He was particularly disturbed by the large numbers of East European Jews, who near the turn of the century began coming from Poland and Russia to escape the pogroms. Pearson's philosophy was quite explicitly spelled out:

> Let us admit . . . that the mind of a man is for the most part a congenital product, and the factors which determine it are racial and familial; we are not dealing with a mutable characteristic capable of being moulded by the doctor, the teacher, the parent or the home environment (p. 124). (*28*)
>
> The ancestors of the men who pride themselves on being English today were all at one time immigrants; it is not for us to cast the first stone against newcomers, solely because they are newcomers. But the test for immigrants in the old days was a severe one; it was power, physical and mental, to retain their hold on the land they seized. So came Celts, Saxons, Norsemen, Danes and Normans in succession and built up the nation of which we are proud. Nor do we criticize the alien Jewish immigration simply because it is Jewish; we took the alien Jews to study, because they were the chief immigrants of that day and material was readily available (p. 127). (*28*)

His observations led him to conclude: "Taken *on the average*, and regarding both sexes, this alien Jewish population is somewhat inferior physically and mentally to the native population" (p. 126). (*28*) Pearson proclaimed this general Jewish inferiority despite his own failure to find any differences between the Jewish and non-Jewish boys when comparisons (reported in the same article) were made for the sexes separately.

ALLEGED BLACK GENETIC INFERIORITY

Quite recently there has appeared a series of papers disputing whether or not black Americans are, in fact, genetically inferior to white Americans in intellectual capacity. The claims and counterclaims have been given enormous publicity in the popular press in America. Some of those papers contain most of the fallacies that can conceivably be associated with this widely misunderstood problem.

The steps toward the intellectual cul-de-sac into which this dispute leads and the fallacious assumptions on which such "progress" is based are the following: (1) A trait called intelligence, or anything else, is defined and a testing instrument for the measurement of trait expression is used; (2) the heritability of that trait is estimated; (3) races (populations) are compared with respect to their performance on the test of trait expression; (4) when the races (populations) differ on the test whose heritability has now been measured, the one with the lower score is genetically inferior, Q.E.D.

The foregoing argument can be applied to any single trait or to as many traits as one might choose to consider. Therefore, analysis of this general problem does *not* depend upon the particular definition and test used for this or that trait. For my analysis I shall pretend that an acceptable test exists for some trait, be it height, weight, intelligence, or anything else. (Without an acceptable test, discussion of the "trait" remains unscientific.)

Even to consider comparisons between races, the following concepts must be recognized: (1) the genome as a mosaic, (2) development as the expression of one out of many alternatives in the genotype's norm of reaction, (3) a population as a gene pool, (4) heritability is not instinct, (5) traits as distributions of scores, and (6) distributions as moments.

Since inheritance is particulate and not integral, the genome, genotype or hereditary endowment of each individual is a unique mosaic—an assemblage of factors many of which are independent. Because of the lottery-like nature of both gamete formation and fertilization, other than monozygotes no two individuals share the same genotypic mosaic.

NORM OF REACTION

The ontogeny of an individual's phenotype (observable outcome of development) has a norm or range of reaction not predictable in advance. In most cases the norm of reaction remains largely unknown; but the concept is nevertheless of fundamental importance, because it saves us from being taken in by glib and misleading textbook clichés such as "heredity sets the limits but environment determines the extent of development within those limits." Even in the most favorable materials only an approximate estimate can be obtained for the norm of reaction, when, as in plants and some animals, an individual genotype can be replicated many times and its development studied over a range of environmental conditions. The more varied the conditions, the more diverse might be the phenotypes developed from any one genotype. Of course, different genotypes should not be expected to have the same norm of reaction; unfortunately psychology's attention was diverted from appreciating this basic fact of biology by a half century of misguided environmentalism. Just as we see that, except for monozygotes, no two human faces are alike, so we must expect norms of reaction to show genotypic uniqueness. That is one reason why the heroic but ill-fated attempts of experimental learning psychology to write the "laws of environmental influence" were grasping at shadows. Therefore, those limits set by heredity in the textbook cliché can never be specified. They are plastic within each individual but differ between individuals. Extreme environmentalists were wrong to hope that one law or set of laws described universal features of modifiability. Extreme hereditarians were wrong to ignore the norm of reaction.

Individuals occur in populations and then only as temporary attachments, so to speak, each to particular combinations of genes. The population, on the other hand, can endure indefinitely as a pool of genes, maybe forever recombining to generate new individuals.

INSTINCTS, GENES AND HERITABILITY

What is heritability? How is heritability estimated for intelligence or any other trait? Is heritability related to instinct? In 1872, Douglas Spalding demonstrated that the ontogeny of a bird's ability to fly is simply maturation and not the result of practice, imitation or any demonstrable kind of learning. He confined immature birds and deprived them of the opportunity either to practice flapping their wings or to observe and imitate the flight of older birds; in spite of this, they developed the ability to fly. For some ethologists this deprivation experiment became the paradigm for proving the innateness or instinctive nature of a behavior by demonstrating that it appears despite the absence of any opportunity for it to be learned. Remember two things about this approach: (1) the observation involves experimental manipulation of the conditions of experience during development, and (2) such observation can be made on the development of one individual. For some people the results of a deprivation experiment now constitute the operational demonstration of the existence (or non-existence) of an instinct (in a particular species).

Are instincts heritable? That is, are they determined by genes? But what is a gene? A gene is an inference from a breeding experiment. It is recognized by the measurement of individual differences—the recognition of the segregation of distinguishable forms of the expression of some trait among the progeny of appropriate matings. For example, when an individual of blood type AA mates with one of type BB, their offspring are uniformly AB. If two of the AB offspring mate, it is found that the A and B gene forms have segregated during reproduction and recombined in their progeny to produce all combinations of A and B: AA, AB, and BB. Note that the only operation involved in such a study is *breeding* of one or more generations and then at an appropriate time of life, observation of the separate individuals born in each generation—controlled breeding with experimental material or pedigree analysis of the appropriate families with human subjects. In principle, only one (usually brief) observation is required. Thus we see that genetics is a science of *differences,* and the breeding experiment is its fundamental operation. The operational definition of the gene, therefore, involves observation in a breeding experiment of the segregation among several individuals of distinguishable differences in the expression of some trait from which the gene can be inferred. Genetics does not work with a single subject, whose development is studied. (The foregoing, the following, and all discussions of genetic analysis presuppose sufficiently adequate control of environmental conditions so that all observed individual differences have developed under the same, homogeneous environmental conditions, conditions never achieved in any human studies.)

How does heritability enter the picture? At the present stage of knowledge, many features (traits) of animals and plants have not yet been related to genes that can be recognized individually. But the role of large numbers of genes, often called polygenes and in most organisms still indistinguishable one from the other, has been demonstrated easily (and often) by selective breeding or by appropriate comparisons between different strains of animals or plants. Selection and strain crossing have provided the basis for many advances in agriculture and among the new generation of research workers are becoming standard tools for the experimental behaviorist. Heritability often summarizes the extent to which a particular population has responded to a regimen of being bred selectively on the basis of the expression of some trait. Heritability values vary between zero and plus one. If the distribution of trait expression among progeny remains the same no matter how their parents might be selected, then heritability has zero value. If parental selection does make a difference, heritability exceeds zero, its exact value reflecting the parent-offspring correlation. Or more generally, as Jensen says: "The basic data from which ... heritability coefficients are estimated are correlations among individuals of different degrees of kinship" (p. 48). (*18*) Though, many of the heritabilities Jensen discusses have been obtained by comparing mono- and di-zygotic twins. (*17*)

A heritability estimate, however, is a far more limited piece of information than most people realize. As was so well stated by Fuller and Thompson: "heritability is a property of populations and not of traits." (*9*) In its strictest sense, a heritability measure provides for a given population an estimate of the proportion of the variance it shows in trait (phenotype) expression which is correlated with the segregation of the alleles of independently acting genes. There are other more broadly conceived heritability measures, which estimate this correlation and also include the combined effects of genes that are independent and of those that interact. Therefore, heritability estimates the proportion of the total phenotypic variance (individual differences) shown by a trait that can be attributed to genetic variation (narrowly or broadly interpreted) in some particular population at a single generation under one set of conditions.

The foregoing description contains three fundamentally important limitations which have rarely been accorded sufficient attention: (1) The importance of limiting any heritability statement to a specific population is evident when we realize that a gene, which shows variation in one population because it is represented there by two or more segregating alleles, might show no variation in some other population because it is uniformly represented there by only a single allele. Remember that initially such a gene could never have been detected by genetic methods in the second population. Once it has been detected in some population carrying two or more of its segregating alleles, the information thus obtained might permit us to recognize it in populations carrying only a single allele. Note how this is related to heritability: the trait will show a greater-than-zero heritability in the segregating population but zero heritability in the non-segregating population. This does *not* mean that the trait is determined genetically in the first population and environmentally in the second!

Up to now my discussion has been limited to a single gene. The very same argument applies for every gene of the polygenic complexes involved in continuously varying traits like height, weight and intelligence. Also, only *genetic* variation has been considered—the presence or absence of segregating alleles at one or more loci in different populations.

(2) Next let us consider the ever-present environmental sources of variation. Usually from the Mendelian point of view, except for the genes on the segregating chromosomes, everything inside the cell and outside the organism is lumped together and can be called environmental variation: cytoplasmic constituents, the maternal effects now known to be so important, the early experience effects studied in so many psychological laboratories, and so on. None of these can be considered unimportant or trivial. They are ever present. Let us now perform what physicists call a Gedanken, or thought, experiment. Imagine Aldous Huxley's *Brave New World* or Skinner's *Walden II* organized in such a way that every individual is exposed to precisely the same environmental conditions. In other words, consider the extreme, but *un*realistic, case of complete environmental homogeneity. Under those circumstances the heritability value would approach unity, because only genetic variation would be present. Don't forget that even under the most simplifying assumptions, there are over

70 trillion potential human genotypes—no two of us share the same geno-type no matter how many ancestors we happen to have in common. (16) Since mitosis projects our unique genotype into the nucleus, or executive, of every cell in our bodies, the individuality that is so obvious in the human faces we see around us must also characterize the unseen components. Let the same experiment be imagined for any number of environments. In each environment heritability will approximate unity but each genotype *may* develop a different phenotype in every environment and the distribution (hierarchy) of genotypes (in terms of their phenotypes) must not be expected to remain invariant over environments.

(3) The third limitation refers to the fact that because gene frequen-cies can and do change from one generation to the next, so will heritability values or the magnitude of the genetic variance.

Now let us shift our focus to the entire genotype or at least to those of its components that might co-vary at least partially with the phenotypic expression of a particular trait. Early in this century Woltereck (7) called to our attention the norm-of-reaction concept: the same genotype can give rise to a wide array of phenotypes depending upon the environment in which it develops. This is most conveniently studied in plants where geno-types are easily replicated. Later Goldschmidt (11) was to show in *Droso-phila* that, by careful selection of the environmental conditions at critical periods in development, various phenotypes ordinarily associated with specific gene mutations could be produced from genotypes that did not include the mutant form of those genes. Descriptively, Goldschmidt called these events *phenocopies*—environmentally produced imitations of gene mutants or phenotypic expressions only manifested by the "inappropriate" genotype if unusual environmental influences impinge during critical periods in development, but regularly manifested by the "appropriate" genotype under the usual environmental conditions.

In 1946, the brilliant British geneticist J.B.S. Haldane (12) analyzed the interaction concept and gave quantitative meaning to the foregoing. For the simplest case but one, that of two genotypes in three environ-ments or, for its mathematical equivalent, that of three genotypes in two environments, he showed that there are 60 possible kinds of interaction. Ten genotypes in 10 environments generate 7.09×10^{144} possible kinds of interaction. In general m genotypes in n environments generate $\dfrac{(mn)!}{m!n!}$ kinds of interaction. Since the characterization of genotype-environment interaction can only be ad hoc and the number of possible interactions is effectively unlimited, it is no wonder that the long search for general laws has been so unfruitful.

For genetically different lines of rats showing the Tryon-type "bright-dull" difference in performance on a learning task, by so simple a change in environmental conditions as replacing massed-practice trials by distributed-practice trials, McGaugh, Jennings and Thomson (23) found that the so-called dulls moved right up to the scoring level of the so-called brights. In a recent study of the open-field behavior of mice, Hegmann and DeFries (13) found that heritabilities measured repeatedly in the same individuals were unstable over two successive days. In surveying earlier work they commented: "Heritability estimates for repeated measurements of behavioral characters have been found to increase (Broadhurst & Jinks, 1961), decrease (Broadhurst & Jinks, 1966), and fluctuate randomly (Fuller & Thompson, 1960) as a function of repeated testing" (p. 27). Therefore, to the limitations on heritability due to population, situation and breeding generation, we must now add developmental stage, or, many people might say, just plain unreliability! The late and brilliant Sir Ronald Fisher, whose authority Jensen cites (p. 34) (18) indicated how fully he had appreciated such limitations when he commented: "the so-called coefficient of heritability, which I regard as one of those unfortunate short-cuts which have emerged in biometry for lack of a more thorough analysis of the data" (p. 217). (8) The plain facts are that in the study of man a heritability estimate turns out to be a piece of "knowledge" that is both deceptive and trivial.

THE ROOTS OF ONE MISUSE OF STATISTICS

The other two concepts to be taken into account when racial comparisons are considered involve the representation of traits in populations by distributions of scores and the characterization of distributions by moment-derived statistics. Populations should be compared only with respect to one trait at a time and comparisons should be made in terms of the moment statistics of their trait distributions. Therefore, for any two populations, on each trait of interest, a separate comparison should be made for every moment of their score distributions. If we consider only the first four moments, from which are derived the familiar statistics for mean, variance, skewness, and kurtosis, then there are four ways in which populations or races may differ with respect to any single trait. Since we possess 23 independently assorting pairs of chromosomes, certainly there are at least 23 uncorrelated traits with respect to which populations can be compared. Since comparisons will be made in terms of four (usually independent) statistics, there are $4 \times 23 = 92$ ways in which races can differ. Since the integrity of chromosomes is *not* preserved over the generations, because they often break apart at meiosis and exchange constituent genes, there are far more than 23 independent hereditary units. If instead of 23 chromosomes we take the 100,000 genes man is now estimated to possess

(p. IX) (24) and we think in terms of their phenotypic trait correlates, then there may be as many as 400,000 comparisons to be made between any two populations or races.

A priori, at this time we know enough to expect no two populations to be the same with respect to most or all of the constituents of their gene pools. "Mutations and recombinations will occur at different places, at different times, and with differing frequencies. Furthermore, selection pressures will also vary" (p. 1441). (16) So the number and kinds of differences between populations now waiting to be revealed in "the more thorough analysis" recommended by Fisher literally staggers the imagination. It does not suggest a linear hierarchy of inferior and superior races.

Why has so much stress been placed on comparing distributions only with respect to their central tendencies by testing the significance of mean differences? There is much evidence that many observations are not normally distributed and that the distributions from many populations do not share homogeneity of variance. The source of our difficulty traces back to the very inception of our statistical tradition.

There is an unbroken line of intellectual influence from Quetelet through Galton and Pearson to modern psychometrics and biometrics. Adolphe Quetelet (1796–1874), the Belgian astronomer-statistician, introduced the concept of "the average man"; he also applied the normal distribution, so widely used in astronomy for error variation, to human data, biological and social. The great Francis Galton followed Quetelet's lead and then Karl Pearson elaborated and perfected their methods. I know of nothing that has contributed more to impose the typological way of thought on, and perpetuates it in, present-day psychology than the feedback from these methods for describing observations in terms of group averages.

There is a technique called composite photography to the perfection of which Sir Francis Galton contributed in an important way. Some of Galton's best work in this field was done by combining—literally averaging—the separate physiognomic features of many different Jewish individuals into his composite photograph of "the Jewish type." Karl Pearson, his disciple and biographer, wrote: "There is little doubt that Galton's Jewish type formed a landmark in composite photography . . ." (p. 293). (27) The part played by typological thinking in the development of modern statistics and the way in which such typological thinking has been feeding back into our conceptual framework through our continued careless use of these statistics is illuminated by Galton's following remarks: "The word generic presupposes a genus, that is to say, a collection of individuals who have much in common, and among whom medium characteristics are very much more frequent than extreme ones. The same idea is sometimes expressed by the word typical, which was much used by Quetelet, who was the first to give it a rigorous interpretation, and whose idea of a type lies at the basis of his statistical views. No statistician dreams of combining objects into the same genetic group that do not cluster towards a common centre; no more can we compose generic portraits out of heterogeneous elements, for if the attempt be made to do so the result is monstrous and meaningless" (p. 295). (27) The basic assumption of a type, or typical individual, is clear and explicit. They used the normal curve and they permitted distributions to be represented by an average because, even though at times they knew better, far too often they tended to think of races as discrete, even homogeneous, groups and individual variation as error.

It is important to realize that these developments began before 1900, when Mendel's work was still unknown. Thus at the inception of biosocial science there was no substantive basis for understanding individual differences. After 1900, when Mendel's work became available, its incorporation into biosocial science was bitterly opposed by the biometricians under Pearson's leadership. Galton had promulgated two "laws": his Law of Ancestral Heredity (1865) (27) and his Law of Regression (1877). (27) When Yule (35) and Castle (4) pointed out how the Law of Ancestral Heredity could be explained in Mendelian terms, Pearson (26) stubbornly denied it. Mendel had chosen for experimental observation seven traits, each of which, in his pea-plant material, turned out to be a phenotypic correlate of a single gene with two segregating alleles. For all seven traits one allele was dominant. Unfortunately Pearson assumed the universality of dominance and based his disdain for Mendelism on this assumption. Yule (36) then showed that without the assumption of dominance, Mendelism becomes perfectly consistent with the kind of quantitative data on the basis of which it was being rejected by Pearson. It is sad to realize that Pearson never appreciated the generality of Mendelism and seems to have gone on for the next 32 years without doing so.

TWO FALLACIES

Now we can consider the recent debate about the meaning of comparisons between the "intelligence" of different human races. We are told that intelligence has a high heritability and that one race performs better than another on intelligence tests. In essence we are presented with a racial hierarchy reminiscent of that pernicious "system" which John Haydon Langdon Down used when he misnamed a disease entity "mongolism."

The people who are so committed to answering the nature-nurture pseudo-question (Is heredity or environment more important in determining intelligence?) make two conceptual blunders. (1) Like Spalding's question about the instinctive nature of bird flight, which introduced the ethologist's deprivation experiment, their question about intelligence is, in fact, being asked about the development of a single individual. Unlike Spalding and the ethologists, however, they do not study development in single individuals. Usually they test groups of individuals comprising a population, not how much of whatever enters into the development of the observed expression of a trait in a particular individual has been contributed by heredity and by environment respectively. They want to know how instinctive is intelligence in the development of a certain individual, but instead they measure differences between large numbers of fully, or partially, developed individuals. If we now take into consideration the norm-of-reaction concept and combine it with the facts of genotypic individuality, then there is no general statement that can be made about the assignment of fixed proportions to the contributions of heredity and environment either to the development of a single individual, because we have not even begun to assess his norm of reaction, or to the differences that might be measured among members of a population, because we have hardly begun to assess the range of environmental conditions under which its constituent members might develop!

(2) Their second mistake, an egregious error, is related to the first one. They assume an inverse relationship between heritability magnitude and improvability by training and teaching. If heritability is high, little room is left for improvement by environmental modification. If heritability is low, much more improvement is possible. Note how this basic fallacy is incorporated directly into the title of Jensen's article "How much can we boost IQ and scholastic achievement? (18) That question received a straightforward, but fallacious, answer on his page 59: "The fact that scholastic achievement is considerably less heritable than intelligence . . . means there is potentially much more we can do to improve school performance through environmental means than we can do to change intelligence. . . . " Commenting on the heritability of intelligence and "the old nature-nurture controversy" one of Jensen's respondents makes the same mistake in his rebuttal: "This is an old estimate which many of us have used, but we have used it to determine what could be done with the variance left for the environment." He then goes on "to further emphasize some of the implications of environmental variance for education and child rearing." (p. 419). (3)

High or low heritability tells us absolutely nothing about how a given individual might have developed under conditions different from those in which he actually did develop. Heritability provides no information about norm of reaction. Since the characterization of genotype-environment interaction can only be ad hoc and the number of possible interactions is effectively unlimited, no wonder the search for general laws of behavior has been so unfruitful, and *the* heritability of intelligence or of any other trait must be recognized as still another of those will-o-the-wisp general laws. And no magic words about an interaction competent in a linear analysis-of-variance model will make disappear the reality of each genotype's unique norm of reaction. Such claims by Jensen or anyone else are false. Interaction is an abstraction of mathematics. Norm of reaction is a developmental reality of biology in plants, animals and people.

In Israel, the descendants of those Jews Pearson feared would contaminate Britain are manifesting some interesting properties of the norm of reaction. Children of European origin have an average IQ of 105 when they are brought up in individual homes. Those brought up in a Kibbutz on the nursery rearing schedule of 22 hours per day for 4 or more years have an average IQ of 115. In contrast, the mid-Eastern Jewish children brought up in individual homes have an average IQ of only 85, Jensen's danger point. However, when brought up in a Kibbutz, they also have an average IQ of 115. That is, they perform the same as the European children with whom they were matched for education, the occupational level of parents and the Kibbutz group in which they were raised (p. 420). (3) There is no basis for expecting different overall results for any population in our species.

SOME PROMISING RECENT DEVELOPMENTS

The power of the approach that begins by thinking first in terms of the genetic system and only later in terms of the phenotype (or behavior) to be analyzed is now being demonstrated by an accumulating and impressive body of evidence. The rationale of that approach derives directly from the particulate nature of the gene, the mosaic nature of the genotype and the manner in which heredity breaks apart and gets reassembled in being passed on from one generation to the next. We now have a well-articulated picture of the way heredity is shared among biological relatives.

That madness runs in families has been known for centuries. The controversy has been over whether it was the heredity or the environment supplied by the family that was responsible for the madness. Franz Kallmann and some others collected large amounts of data in the 1940's and 1950's showing that monozygotic twins were much more concordant than dizygotic twins. Since David Rosenthal of NIMH has provided some of the best criticism of the incompleteness, and therefore inconclusiveness, of the twin-study evidence for the role of heredity in schizophrenia, Rosenthal's own recent findings become especially noteworthy.

He has divided foster-reared children from adoptive homes into two groups: those with a biological parent who is schizophrenic and those without a schizophrenic biological parent. It was found by Rosenthal, (*31*) and by Heston (*15*) in a completely independent but similar study, that the incidence of schizophrenia was much greater among the biological children of schizophrenics. Most significantly, combining the two studies, the risk of schizophrenia in offspring is four to five times greater if a biological parent is schizophrenic. Still other recent studies support the Rosenthal and the Heston findings. Both Karlsson (*19*) and Wender (*30*) found a high incidence of schizophrenia in the foster-reared relatives of schizophrenics.

Thinking genetically first in terms of biological relationship has already paid off in the analytical detail revealed as well as in the mere demonstration of concordance with respect to diagnostic category. Lidz and co-workers (*20*) reported marked distortions in communicating among many of the non-hospitalized parents of schizophrenic hospital patients. Mc-Conaghy, (*22*) using an objective test of thought disorder, stressed the parents of 10 schizophrenic patients and compared them to a series of control subjects. Sixty percent of the patients' parents, including at least one parent in every pair, registered test scores in the range indicative of thought disturbance. In contrast, less than 10 percent of the controls had such scores.

The major features of McConaghy's findings have since been replicated by Lidz and co-workers. (*21*) More recently Phillips and co-workers (*29*) studied 48 relatives of adult schizophrenics and 45 control subjects using a battery of tests to assess thought disorder. They found cognitive disorders to be much more frequent among the relative of schizophrenics; 17 of 18 parents registered "pathological" scores, even though their social behavior had never been diagnosed as pathological.

In 1962, Anastasopoulos and Photiades (*1*) assessed susceptibility to LSD-induced "pathological reactions" in the relatives of schizophrenic patients. After studying 21 families of patients and 9 members of two control families, they reported ". . . it was almost invariable to find reactions to LSD in one of the parents, and often in one or more of the siblings and uncles and aunts, which were neither constant nor even common during the LSD-intoxication of healthy persons."

Analogous work has been done studying the responses of the relatives of patients with depressive disorders using anti-depressant drugs like imipramine (Tofranil) or an MAO inhibitor. Relatives tend to show a response pattern similar to that of their hospitalized relations.

Some very interesting human behavior-genetic analyses are currently being done on these affective disorders by George Winokur and his colleagues in St. Louis. (30) Out of 1,075 consecutive admissions to a psychiatric hospital, 426 were diagnosed as primary affective disorders. So far, these appear to fall into two subtypes, the first of which shows manic episodes; some first-degree relatives show similar manifestions. The other subtype is characterized by depressive episodes and lack of concordance among close relatives. Furthermore, evidence is now accumulating implicating a dominant factor or factors on the X-chromosome in the manic subtype: (1) the condition is considerably more prevalent in females than in males; (2) the morbid risk among siblings of male probands is the same for males and females, but the morbid risk among siblings of female probands is quite different—sisters of female probands are at a 21 percent risk while their brothers are only at a 7.4 percent risk. More detailed study in several appropriately chosen family pedigrees suggests that there is a dominant gene on the short arm of the X-chromosome. The condition has so far shown linkage with color-blindness and the Xg blood groups, both of which are loosely linked on the short arm of the X-chromosome.

To examine the structure of the phenotypic variation in a trait whose development is in no obvious way influenced by environment and which, though ostensibly a simple trait, has been sufficiently well-analyzed phenotypically to reveal its interesting complexity, we have chosen to study dermatoglyphics, or fingerprints, in my laboratory. For his doctoral dissertation, R. Peter Johnson is making these observations on both parents and offspring in individual families. His preparatory survey of the previous literature revealed one study which reported data on a cross-sectional sample of 2,000 males (32). Scoring them on all ten fingers with respect to four distinguishable pattern types, the following data reveal the interesting but sobering complexity that exists in such a "simple" trait: the same type of pattern was shown on all 10 fingers by 12 percent, on 9 of 10 fingers by 16 percent, and on 8 of 10 fingers by 10 percent of the men. In addition, 5 percent of the men showed all four pattern types. This included 1 percent of the individuals who had all four pattern types on a single hand.

While probably everybody has heard that there are some unusual hospitalized males who carry two Y chromosomes, are rather tall, and prone to commit crimes of violence, few people know that when a comparison was made between the first-order relatives of both the Y-Y chromosome males and control males hospitalized for similar reasons (but not carrying two Y chromosomes), there was a far greater incidence of a family history of crime among the controls. In this control group there were over six times as many individual first-order relatives convicted and many, many times the number of convictions.

In summary, the relationship between heredity and behavior has turned out to be one of neither isomorphism nor independence. Isomorphism might justify an approach like native reductionism, independence a naive behavorism. Neither one turns out to be adequate. I believe that in order to study behavior, we must understand genetics quite thoroughly. Then, and only then, can we as psychologists forget about it intelligently.

REFERENCES

1. Anastasopoulos, G., and Photiades, H. Effects of LSD-25 on relatives of schizophrenic patients. J. Ment. Sci. 108:95-98, 1962.

2. Benda, C. E. "Mongolism" or "Down's syndrome." Lancet. 1:163, 1962.

3. Bloom, B. S. Letter to the editor. Harvard Educ. Rev. 39: 419–421, 1969.

4. Castle, W. E. The laws of heredity of Galton and Mendel, and some laws governing race improvement by selection. Proc. Amer. Acad. Arts Sci. 39:223–242, 1903.

5. Dewey, J. Correspondence with Robert V. Daniels, 15 February, 1947. J. Hist. Ideas 20:570, 1959.

6. Down, J. L. H. Observations on an ethnic classification of idiots. London Hospital Reports, 1866. Reprinted in McKusick, V. A. (Ed.): Medical genetics, 1961. J. Chron. Dis. 15:417–572, 1962.

7. Dunn, L. C. A Short History of Genetics. New York, McGraw-Hill, 1965.

8. Fisher, R. A. Limits to intensive production in animals. Brit. Agr. Bull. 4:217–218, 1951.

9. Fuller, J. L., and Thompson, W. R. Behavior Genetics. New York, Wiley, 1960.

10. de Gobineau, J. A. Essai sur l' inégalité des races humaines. Rééd. intégrale en 1 vol., avec une préface de Hubert Juin. Paris, P. Belfond, 1967.

11. Goldschmidt, R. B. Theoretical Genetics. Berkeley, University of California Press, 1955, p. 257.

12. Haldane, J. B. S. The interaction of nature and nurture. Ann. Eugen. 13:197–205, 1946.

13. Hegmann, J. P., and DeFries, J. C. Open-field behavior in mice: Genetic analysis of repeated measures. Psychon. Sci. 13:27-28, 1968.

14. Heiden, K. Der Führer. London, Houghton, 1944, p. 198. Cited in Bullock, A. Hitler: A Study in Tyranny. Harmondsworth, Penguin, 1962, p. 80.

15. Heston, L. L. Psychiatric disorders in foster home reared children of schizophrenic mothers. Brit. J. Psychiat. 112:819–825, 1966.

16. Hirsch, J. Behavior genetics and individuality understood: behaviorism's counterfactual dogma blinded the behavioral sciences to the significance of meiosis. Science 142: 1436–1442, 1963.

17. Jensen, A. R. Estimation of the limits of heritability of traits by comparison of monozygotic and dizygotic twins. Proc. Nat. Acad. Sci. 58:149–156, 1967.

18. Jensen, A. R. How much can we boost IQ and scholastic achievement? Harvard Educ. Rev. 39:1–123, 1969.

19. Karlsson, J. L. The Biologic Basis of Schizophrenia. Springfield. Ill., Charles C. Thomas, 1966.

20. Lidz, T., Cornelison, A., Terry, D., and Fleck, S. Intrafamilial environment of the schizophrenic patient: VI. The transmission of irrationality. AMA Arch. Neurol. Psychiat. 79: 305–316, 1958.

21. ———, Wild, C., Schafer, S., Rosman, B., and Fleck, S. Thought disorders in the parents of schizophrenic patients: A study utilizing the Object Sorting Test. Psychiat. Res. 1:193–200, 1962.

22. McConaghy, N. The use of an object sorting test in elucidating the hereditary factor in schizophrenia. J. Neurol, Neurosurg. Psychiat. 22:243–246, 1959.

23. McGaugh, J. L., Jennings, R. D., and Thomson, C. W. Effect of distribution of practice on the maze learning of descendants of the Tryon maze bright and maze dull strains. Psychol. Rep. 10:147–150, 1962.

24. McKusick, V. A. Mendelian Inheritance in Man: Catalogs of Autosomal Dominant, Recessive, and X-Linked Phenotypes. Baltimore, Johns Hopkins Press, 1966.

25. Pastore, N. The Nature-Nurture Controversy. New York, King's Crown Press (Columbia University), 1949.

26. Pearson, K. On a generalized theory of alternative inheritance, with special reference to Mendel's laws. Phil. Trans. Roy. Soc. London A203:53–86, 1904.

27. ———, The Life, Letters and Labours of Francis Galton, Vol. II: Researches of Middle Life. Cambridge, Cambridge University Press, 1924.

28. ———, and Moul, M. The problem of alien immigration into Great Britain, illustrated by an examination of Russian and Polish Jewish children. Ann. Eugen. 1:5–127, 1925.

29. Phillips, J. E., Jacobson, N., and Turner, W. J. Conceptual thinking in schizophrenics and their relatives. Brit. J. Psychiat. 111:823–839, 1965.

30. Rose, R. J., Department of Psychology, University of Indiana, private communication, 1969.

31. Rosenthal, D., Wender, P. H., Kety, S. S., Schulsinger, F., Welner, J., and Østergaard, L. Schizophrenics' offspring reared in adoptive homes. J. Psychiat. Res. 6:377–391, 1968.

32. Waite, H. Association of fingerprints. Biometrika 10:421–478, 1915.

33. Watson, J. B. Behaviorism. Chicago, University of Chicago Press, 1959.

34. Wittgenstein, L. Philosophical Investigations (ed. 2). Translated by Anscombe, G. E. Oxford, Blackwell, 1963, p. 232.

35. Yule, C. U. Mendel's laws and their probable relation to intra-racial heredity. New Phytologist 1:193–207, 222–238, 1902.

36. Yule, G. U. On the theory of inheritance of quantitative compound characters on the basis of Mendel's laws—A preliminary note. Report 3rd Int. Conf. Genetics p. 140–142, 1906.

Heredity, Intelligence, Politics, and Psychology

Leon J. Kamin

This paper is concerned with two separate but clearly interrelated matters. First, I shall discuss briefly some of the social and political background out of which the intelligence testing movement in the United States took shape—and to which, in no small measure, it contributed. Then I shall examine in detail some of the empirical evidence which underlies the consensus view held by psychometricians and behavior geneticists—the view that something in the order of 80 percent of individual variation in intelligence test scores is attributable to genetic factors. The conclusions which I shall reach are these. First, that since its introduction to America the intelligence test has been used more or less consciously as an instrument of oppression against the underprivileged—the poor, the foreign-born, and racial minorities. And second, that a critical review of the literature produces no evidence which would convince a reasonably prudent man to reject the hypothesis that intelligence test scores have zero heritability.

First, then, a little social history. The first usable test of general intelligence was published by Binet in 1905. Though Binet protested against the "brutal pessimism" of those who regarded the test score as a fixed quantity, and prescribed corrective courses in "mental orthopedics" for those with low test scores, the orientation of the American importers of Binet's test was very different. The major translators and importers of the test in the decade following Binet's publication were Lewis Terman at Stanford, Robert Yerkes at Harvard, and Henry Goddard at Vineland, New Jersey. These pioneers of the mental testing movement shared a number of socio-political views, as exemplified by their joint involvement in the turn-of-the-century eugenics movements. Perhaps a few quotations from their writings will make the point.

Terman, in his 1916 book which introduced the Stanford–Binet test, after describing the poor test performance of a pair of Indian and Mexican children, wrote the following:

> Their dullness seems to be racial, or at least inherent in the family stocks from which they come. The fact that one meets this type with such extraordinary frequency among Indians, Mexicans, and negroes suggests quite forcibly that the whole question of racial differences in mental traits will have to be taken up anew . . . there will be discovered enormously significant racial differences . . . which cannot be wiped out by any scheme of mental culture.
> Children of this group should be segregated in special classes. . . . They cannot master abstractions, but they can often be made efficient workers. . . . There is no possibility at present of convincing society that they should not be allowed to reproduce . . . they constitute a grave problem because of their unusually prolific breeding (1).

Professor Terman should not be thought of as a racist. His stern eugenical judgment was applied even-handedly to poor people of all colors. Writing in 1917 under the heading "The Menace of Feeble-Mindedness," he declared,

1. Terman, L. M. *The Measurement of Intelligence*. Boston: Houghton-Mifflin, 1916.

. . . only recently have we begun to recognize how serious a menace it is to the social, economic and moral welfare of the state . . . it is responsible . . . for the majority of cases of chronic and semi-chronic pauperism . . . organized charities . . . often contribute to the survival of individuals who would otherwise not be able to live and reproduce. . . . If we would preserve our state for a class of people worthy to possess it, we must prevent, as far as possible, the propagation of mental degenerates . . . the increasing spawn of degeneracy *(2)*.

The squandering of charitable moneys on the degenerate poor similarly caught the attention of Henry Goddard, who lectured to a Princeton audience in 1919 on the new science of "mental levels." That new science, he pointed out, had invalidated the arguments of gentlemen socialists who "in their ultra altruistic and humane attitude" were embarrassed that their own shoes cost $12.00, while those of a laborer cost only $3.00.

Now the fact is, *that workman* may have a ten year intelligence while you have a twenty. To demand for him such a home as you enjoy is as absurd as it would be to insist that every laborer should receive a graduate fellowship. How can there be such a thing as social equality with this wide range of mental capacity? . . .

. . . The man of intelligence has spent his money wisely, has saved until he has enough to provide for his needs in case of sickness, while the man of low intelligence, no matter how much money he would have earned, would have spent much of it foolishly . . . during the past year, the coal miners in certain parts of the country have earned more money than the operators and yet today when the mines shut down for a time, those people are the first to suffer. They did not save anything, although their whole life has taught them that mining is an irregular thing and that . . . they should save . . . *(3)*.

To be diagnosed as "feeble-minded" was not a light matter in a period when discrimination between the criminal, the poor, the insane, and the dull were not clearly drawn. The public institutions to provide for such degenerates were in many states administered by a single functionary, the "Commissioner of Charities and Corrections." Further, prodded by the eugenicists, many states passed laws providing for the compulsory sterilization of the inmates of such taxpayer-supported institutions before their release. The preamble of the first such law, passed by Indiana in 1907, was typical in its assertion: "Whereas, heredity plays a most important part in the transmission of crime, idiocy, and imbecility." To this list of genetically determined traits, the New Jersey legislature added in 1911 "feeble-mindedness, epilepsy . . . and other defects," and Iowa in 1913 contributed

2. Terman, L. M. "Feeble-minded children in the public schools of California." *School and Society*, 5, 1917, 161–165.

3. Goddard, H. H. *Human Efficiency and Levels of Intelligence.* Princeton: Princeton University Press, 1920.

". . . lunatics, drunkards, drug fiends . . . moral and sexual perverts, and diseased and degenerate persons. . . . "

The lot of those officially diagnosed as feeble-minded was not enviable, and it is of interest to read Yerkes' caution:

> . . . never should such a diagnosis be made on the IQ alone. . . . We must inquire further into the subject's economic history. What is his occupation; his pay . . . we must learn what we can about his immediate family. What is the economic status or occupation of the parents? . . . When . . . this information has been collected . . . the psychologist may be of great value in getting the subject into the most suitable place in society . . . *(4)*.

The genetic interpretation of socio-economic class differences in test scores, fostered by Terman, Goddard, and Yerkes, could clearly serve to legitimate the existing social order. Perhaps the first major practical effect of the testing movement, however, lay in its contribution to the passage and rationalization of the overtly racist immigration law of 1924. This disgraceful chapter in the history of American psychology is not without contemporary relevance.

Prior to the first World War, though certain classes of undesirables were excluded, there was no numerical limitation on immigration to the United States, nor were geographic distinctions drawn among European countries. But as early as 1912 the U.S. Public Health Service invited Henry Goddard to Ellis Island to apply the new mental tests to arriving European immigrants. Goddard reported that, based upon his examination of the "great mass of average immigrants," 83 percent of Jews, 80 percent of Hungarians, 79 percent of Italians, and 87 percent of Russians were "feeble-minded" *(5)*. He was able to report in 1917 *(6)* that the use of mental tests "for the detection of feeble-minded aliens" had vastly increased the number of aliens deported.

The significance of these scientific findings was not lost upon the members of the Eugenics Research Association, who in 1917 appointed Yerkes as chairman of their "Committee on Inheritance of Mental Traits." The biologist Harry Laughlin, secretary of the Association and editor of its journal, "Eugenic News," wrote under the heading "The New Immigration Law": "When the knowledge of the existence of this science [mental testing] becomes generally known in Congress, that body will then be expected to apply the direct and logical test . . . " *(7)*.

4. Yerkes, R. M. and Foster, J. C. *A Point Scale for Measuring Mental Ability*. Baltimore: Warwick and York, 1923.

5. Goddard, H. H. "The Binet tests in relation to immigration." *J. Psychoasthenics*, 18, 1913, 105–107.

6. Goddard, H. H. "Mental tests and the immigrant," *J. Delinquency*, 2, 1917, 243–277.

7. Laughlin, H. H. "The new immigration law." *Eugenic News*, 2, 1917, 22.

Within months, American entry into the war had brought the science of mental testing to a new level of public recognition. Intelligence tests were applied to some 2,000,000 draftees—under the direction of Colonel Robert M. Yerkes, with the assistance of many of the leading experimental psychologists. The influence of Yerkes may perhaps be detected in the massive influx of leading experimentalists into the Eugenics Research Association in 1920. But in any event, the results of the Army's testing program were published, under Yerkes' editorship, by the National Academy of Sciences in 1921 (*8*). The data provided the first large-scale evidence that blacks scored lower than whites. But the chapter of most immediate significance in 1921 was that on the foreign-born. The test performance of immigrant draftees was analyzed by country of origin, as reproduced in Table 1. The data presented in Table 1 were succinctly summarized: "The Latin and Slavic countries stand low." The Poles, it was reported, did not score significantly higher than the blacks.

Table 1

The mean intelligence tests scores of immigrant draftees from various countries fell in the following order:

England
Holland
Denmark
Scotland
Germany
Sweden
Canada
Belgium
White Draft
Norway
Austria
Ireland
Turkey
Greece
All Foreign Countries
Russia
Italy
Poland

Source: Bar graph reprinted from Memoirs of the National Academy of Science, 1921.

8. National Academy of Sciences. *Memoirs*, 1921, 15.

These scientific data speedily became "generally known in Congress," with the considerable assistance of the scientists of the Eugenics Research Association, and of Yerkes, now employed by the National Research Council. The secretary of the E.R.A. was appointed "Expert Eugenics Affairs Agent" of the House Committee on Immigration and Naturalization of the U.S. Congress; and in 1923 the psychological and biological scientists of the E.R.A. elected as their organization's chairman the Honorable Albert Johnson. That gentleman, by a fortunate coincidence, was the congressman who chaired the House Committee on Immigration and Naturalization. Meanwhile, under Yerkes' leadership, the N.R.C.'s Division of Anthropology and Psychology established a Committee on Scientific Problems of Human Migration. That Committee, in an effort to take the national debate over immigration "out of politics," and to place it on "a scientific basis," began to support relevant research. The first research supported was that of Carl Brigham, then Assistant Professor of Psychology at Princeton. The Princeton University Press published in 1923 Brigham's "A Study of American Intelligence" with a foreword by Yerkes praising the book's contribution to the scientific study of immigration (9).

The unique contribution of Brigham's book was an intensive re-analysis of the Army data on immigrants. Brigham demonstrated that—pooling across all countries of origin—immigrants who had been in the country 16 to 20 years before being tested were as bright as native-born Americans; and that immigrants who had been in America only 0 to 5 years when tested, were virtually feeble-minded. "We must assume," Brigham wrote, "that we are measuring *native or inborn intelligence*." The psychologists who devised the tests had, after all, constructed special tests for the illiterate. The explanation for the correlation of test score with years of American residence proved to be simple. Twenty years ago, immigrants had flowed into the country from England, Scandinavia, Germany; five or ten years before the war, the massive "New Immigration" from southeastern Europe had begun—Italians, Poles, Russians, Jews. The decline of immigrant intelligence, Brigham noted, paralleled precisely the decrease in the amount of "Nordic blood," and the increase in the amount of "Alpine" and "Mediterranean" blood, in the immigrant stream—a nice example of the power of correlational analysis as applied to intelligence test data. The Jew, Brigham declared, "is an Alpine Slav." The concluding paragraphs of Brigham's book pointed out that ". . . we are incorporating the negro into our racial stock, while all of Europe is comparatively free

9. Brigham, C. C. *A Study of American Intelligence*. Princeton: Princeton University Press, 1923.

from this taint. . . . The steps that should be taken . . . . must of course be dictated by science and not by political expediency. . . . And the revision of the immigration and naturalization laws will only afford a slight relief. . . . The really important steps are those looking toward the prevention of the continued propagation of defective strains in the present population."

With this contribution behind him, Brigham moved on to the secretary-ship of the College Entrance Examination Board, where he devised and developed the Scholastic Aptitude Test; and at length, to the secretary-ship of the American Psychological Association.

The political usage of Brigham's book and of the Army data was immediate and intense. The book and the data figured prominently and repeatedly in Congressional committee hearings and debates on the new immigration law. I cite only a very few examples.

[Dr. Arthur Sweeney, to the House Committee, January 24, 1923] The fact that the immigrants are illiterate or unable to understand the English language is not an obstacle . . . "Beta" . . . is entirely objective. . . . We . . . strenuously object to immigration from Italy . . . Russia . . . Poland . . . Greece . . . Turkey. The Slavic and Latin countries show a marked contrast in intelligence with the western and northern European group . . . we shall degenerate to the level of the Slav and Latin races. . . .

[Mr. Francis Kinnicutt, to the Senate Committee, February 20, 1923] The immigration from [Poland and Russia] consists largely of the Hebrew elements . . . some of their labor unions are among the most radical in the whole country. . . . The recent Army tests show . . . these classes rank far below the average intelligence. . . . See "A study of American Intelligence" by Carl C. Brigham. . . . Col. Robert M. Yerkes . . . vouches for this book, and he speaks in the highest terms of Prof. Carl C. Brigham, now assistant professor of psychology in Princeton University.

[Mr. Madison Grant, to the Senate Committee, January 10, 1924] The country at large has been greatly impressed by . . . the Army intelligence tests . . . carefully analyzed by . . . Yerkes . . . Brigham. The experts . . . believe . . . the tests give as accurate a meaning of intelligence as is pos-sible. . . . The questions . . . were selected with a view to measuring innate ability . . . had mental tests been in operation . . . over 6,000,000 aliens now living in this country . . . would never have been admitted. . . .

The Congress passed in 1924 a law not only restricting the total *num-ber* of immigrants, but also assigning *"national origin quotas."* That is, immigrants from any European country would be allowed entry into America only to the proportionate extent that their countrymen were already represented in the American population—*as determined by the census of 1890.* The Congressional proponents of the law frankly asserted that the 1890 (rather than the 1920) census was used in order to curtail biologically inferior immigration from southeastern Europe. That is the law which led ultimately to the deaths of tens of thousands of victims of the Nazi terror, denied entry to the United States because the "German quota" was filled, though other quotas were undersubscribed.

The biological partitioning of the European continent did not appease some ardent intelligence testers, who continued to perform relevant research. Nathaniel Hirsch's work, under McDougall at Harvard, was also supported by the National Research Council. To demonstrate the genetic basis of low IQ's in immigrant stock, Hirsch tested the native-born *children* of immigrants. He reported in the 1926 Genetic Psychology Monographs:

> That part of the law which has to do with the non-quota immigrants should be modified. . . . All mental testing upon children of Spanish-Mexican descent has shown that the average intelligence of this group is even lower than the average intelligence of the Portuguese and Negro children . . . in this study. Yet Mexicans are flowing into the country. . . .
>
> From Canada . . . we are getting . . . the less intelligent of working-class people . . . the increase in the number of French Canadians is alarming. Whole New England villages and towns are filled with them. The average intelligence of the French Canadian group in our data approaches the level of the average negro intelligence.
>
> I have seen gatherings of the foreign-born in which narrow and sloping foreheads were the rule. . . . In every face there was something wrong —lips thick, mouth coarse . . . chin poorly formed . . . sugar-loaf heads . . . goose-bill noses . . . a set of skew-molds discarded by the Creator. . . . Immigration officials . . . report vast troubles in extracting the truth from certain brunette nationalities. *(10)*

That was the voice of Genetic Psychology Monographs in 1926. What shall we say of the voices of today's mental testers? The moral of this history seems to me sufficiently clear—and contemporary developments in mental testing too well known to us all—for explicit comment to be necessary. From this much, however, I cannot forebear. *The* domestic issue confronting the country in the 1920's was the problem of immigration. *The* domestic issue confronting us today—at least until the recent Watergate amusements broke upon us—is what our politicians euphemistically refer to as "the welfare mess." The intertwining of profound social, economic, and racial conflicts within each of these great issues is obvious enough. We know now that the psychologists who offered "expert" and "scientific" testimony relevant to explosive social issues in the 1920's did so on the basis of pitifully inadequate data, data which I believe all of us would now reject as irrelevant to the question of the possible inheritance of intelligence. We have to ask, how much more surely grounded are today's psychological equivalents to the "Expert Eugenics Affairs Agents" of the 1920's than were their predecessors? To that question—an examination of

10. Hirsch, N. D. M. "A study of natio-racial mental differences," *Genet. Psychol. Monogr.*, 1, Whole Nos. 3 and 4, 1926.

the empirical data purporting to support the idea that IQ test scores are highly heritable—I now turn.

The relevant literature is very large, and I shall be concerned here with only two classes of studies: those involving separated identical twins, and those involving adopted children. These two types of studies by general agreement provide the most powerful evidence for the heritability of IQ. They involve relatively few assumptions, and are conceptually simple to understand. The IQ correlation between separated MZ twins, e.g., itself provides an unbiased estimate of the heritability of IQ under the assumptions that such twins are representative of the population, and that the environments in which they have been reared are uncorrelated.

There have been four major studies of separated MZ twins. The essential data of these studies is presented in Table 2. Though the table indicates some discrepancy in the magnitudes of the reported correlations, the major conclusion is clear. The separated twins in all four studies do resemble one another in IQ very substantially, thereby suggesting a predominant role for heredity.

Table 2   IQ CORRELATIONS FOR SEPARATED MZ TWINS

Study	Test	Correlation
Burt	"Individual Test"	.86
		(N = 53)
Shields	Dominoes + [2xMill Hill]	.77
		(N = 37)
N, F, and H	Stanford–Binet	.67
		(N = 19)
Juel-Nielsen	Wechsler	.62
		(N = 12)

The most important of the four twin studies is that of the late Sir Cyril Burt, recipient in 1971 of the American Psychological Association's Edward Lee Thorndike Award. Burt's study involved the largest number of twin pairs, and reported the largest correlation; more important, it is the only study which purports to provide quantitative data on the socio-economic status of the homes in which separated twins were reared. For Burt's twins, at least, there was no detectable correlation between the statuses of the homes in which members of a separated pair were raised.

There are, it must be reported, a number of unresolved procedural ambiguities in Burt's published papers. The 1943 review of his work, e.g., presents a large number of relevant correlation coefficients, but virtually nothing is said of when or to whom tests were administered, or of what tests were employed. The reader is told only, "Some of the inquiries have been published in L.C.C. reports or elsewhere; but the majority remain buried in typed memoranda on degree theses" (11).

This lack of procedural detail is unfortunate, since a cross-check of several of Burt's papers, as Table 3 indicates, reveals a number of puzzling inconsistencies—as well as a number of astonishing consistencies. The table indicates that in 1943 Burt reported a correlation for a large sample between "intelligence and economic status." There was no clear indication of how either intelligence or economic status had been measured, but Burt took pains to indicate that the correlation involved economic, as opposed to cultural, status. The same survey was referred to again in 1956 (12); but now it becomes clear that the correlation—now involving "socio-economic status"—was based upon "adjusted assessments" of intelligence, rather than upon "crude test-results." Then, one year later, the *same* correlation from the *same* survey was described as involving "*cultural*" status, and an entirely *different* correlation was presented for "economic" status (13). From where did this latter correlation emerge? Why was it not utilized in 1943, when Burt wished to differentiate economic from cultural status? How did the measurement of one magically transmute to a measurement of the other over 14 years? We are not told.

Table 3

1943   "Intelligence and economic status" —————————— $r = .32$
        ("Economic" differentiated from "cultural")

1956   Intelligence and "socio-economic status"
        a. "adjusted assessments" —————————————— $r = .315$
        b. "crude test-results" ————————————————— $r = .453$

1957   "Adjusted assessments" of IQ and "economic and cultural conditions"
        a. with "cultural (i.e. educational and motivational) background" ———————————————————— $r = .315$
        b. with "material (i.e. financial and hygienic) conditions" —— $r = .226$

Source: Correlations from Burt.

11. Burt, C. "Ability and income." *Brit. J. educ. Psychol.*, 13, 1943, 83–98.

12. Burt, C. and Howard, M. "The multifactorial theory of inheritance." *Brit. J. statist. Psychol.*, 9, 1956, 95–131.

13. Burt, C. and Howard, M. "The relative influence of heredity and environment on assessments of intelligence." *Brit. J. statist. Psychol.*, 10, 1957, 99–104.

Burt collected correlations for various categories of kinship throughout a lengthy research career, continually cumulating cases. The correlations, based upon increasingly larger N's, were sporadically reported in a number of his papers. The correlations often exhibited an extraordinary stability. Table 4 presents correlations for the category "siblings reared apart," taken from Burt's 1955 (*14*) and 1966 (*15*) papers. The addition of 20 new cases over that 11-year period, it will be noted, did not change to the third decimal place three separate correlations for school attainments, or the correlations for height and weight. The correlations were similarly robust in the face of unexplained *decreases* in sample size, as Table 5 makes clear. The disappearance of 45 DZ twin pairs over the same period during which 20 separated sib pairs were located again failed to affect correlations for school attainments and physical traits, though intelligence correlations were affected.

This type of stability also characterized the unspecified "group test" of intelligence used by Burt in his studies of separated twins, which apparently formed a basis for his "final assessments" of the twins' IQ's. Table 6 adds to the two papers already cited two additional "interim reports"

Table 4   SIBLINGS REARED APART

	1955 (N = 131)	1966 (N = 151)
Intelligence		
Group test	.441	.412
Individual test	.463	.423
Final assessment	.517	.438
School Attainment		
Reading, Spelling	.490	.490
Arithmetic	.563	.563
General	.526	.526
Physical		
Height	.536	.536
Weight	.427	.427

Source: Correlations from Burt.

14. Burt, C. "The evidence for the concept of intelligence." *Brit. J. educ. Psychol.*, 25, 1955, 158–177.
15. Burt, C. "The genetic determination of differences in intelligence: A study of monozygotic twins reared together and apart." *Brit. J. Psychol.*, 57, 1966, 137–153.

Table 5   DZ TWINS REARED TOGETHER

	1955 (N = 172)	1966 (N = 127)
Intelligence		
Group test	.542	.552
Individual test	.526	.527
Final assessment	.551	.453
School Attainment		
Reading, Spelling	.915	.919
Arithmetic	.748	.748
General	.831	.831
Physical		
Height	.472	.472
Weight	.586	.586

Source: Correlations from Burt.

(*16, 17*). With the exception of a minor perturbation in late 1958, which simultaneously afflicted the correlations both for twins reared apart and for twins reared together, the IQ correlations for both categories remained identical to three decimal places over the entire series of Burt's cumulated researches.

There is considerable confusion in Burt's reports concerning the relation between "tests" and "assessments" of intelligence. Table 7 presents

Table 6   "GROUP TEST" OF INTELLIGENCE

	MZ Twins Reared Apart	MZ Twins Reared Together
1955	.771	.944
	(N = 21)	(N = 83)
1958a	.771	.944
	(N = "over 30")	(N = ?)
1958b	.778	.936
	(N = 42)	(N = ?)
1966	.771	.944
	(N = 53)	(N = 95)

Source: Correlations from Burt.

16. Burt, C. "The inheritance of mental ability." *Amer. Psychologist*, 13, 1958, 1–15.

17. Conway, J. "The inheritance of intelligence and its social implications." *Brit. J. statist. Psychol.*, 11, 1958, 171–190.

Table 7   HOW BURT ASSESSED THE INTELLIGENCE OF ADULTS

Burt and Howard, 1957	"But in each of our surveys, assessments were individually obtained for a representative sample of parents, checked, for purposes of standardization, by tests of the usual type." They refer the reader to a 1955 paper, p. 172.
Burt and Howard, 1956	They report correlations for 963 parent-child pairs and 321 grandparent-grandchild pairs. "The procedures employed, ard the results obtained have already been described in previous publications (Burt, 1955)."
Burt, 1955, p. 172, footnote	"For the assessments of the parents we relied chiefly on personal interviews; but in doubtful and borderline cases an open or a camouflaged test was employed."

three quotations, all referring to the same survey involving adult "IQ's." When the assiduous reader at length tracks down the 1955 footnote, it becomes clear that the IQ correlations discussed by Burt in 1956 and 1957 were based primarily upon "personal interviews" of adults. The spectacle of Professor Burt administering a "camouflaged test" of intelligence to a London grand-parent is an amusing one, but it does not inspire scientific confidence. That confidence is not bolstered by the observation that, over two years, Professor Burt's memory transformed "doubtful and border-line cases" to "a representative sample of parents"; and "an open or a camouflaged test" to "tests of the usual type."

We have a somewhat clearer picture of how the "final assessments" of children IQ's—including the twins—were arrived at. Burt wrote:

> The final assessments for the children were obtained by submitting the marks from the group tests to the judgment of the teachers . . . where the teacher disagreed with the verdict of the marks, the child was interviewed personally, and subjected to further tests, often on several successive occasions (16).

The rationale for depending upon such adjusted assessments, rather than raw test scores, was presented in some detail by Burt and Howard (18). They argued straightforwardly that, in testing the goodness-of-fit of a multi-factorial model of inheritance, the best possible estimate of

18. Burt, C. and Howard, M. "Heredity and intelligence: a reply to criticism." *Brit. J. statist. Psychol.*, 10, 1957, 33–63.

genotypic intelligence should be employed; and that the teacher's judgment was a more accurate estimate than that provided by an intelligence test score. This confidence in the teacher as a genotype-detector, however, was not always adhered to by Burt, as Table 8 indicates. The contradictory 1943 quotation (*19*) reflects Burt's concern that in post-war Britain the genetically most gifted should be selected for university preparation and training. For such an important practical purpose only the science of mental testing—and not the teacher—could be entrusted to sniff out the superior genotypes.

For the twin studies, however, Burt reported correlations based not only upon "group test" and "final assessment," but also upon "individual test." The most extended discussion of the tests given to the twins was provided in 1966 (*15*), and is reproduced in Table 9. The description is shrouded in ambiguities; and unfortunately it is impossible to know what group or individual tests were administered to which twins. The references supplied by Burt are of no help. One contains *no* group intelligence tests, while the other contains no fewer than seven; but each of these contains exclusively verbal items. With regard to these seven group tests, Burt wrote: "complete tables of age-norms would be unnecessary or even misleading . . . I give only rough averages calculated regardless of sex . . . I have not thought it worth the necessary time and space to elaborate and print a set of standardised instructions as to procedure or marking" (*20*).

Table 8

Burt and Howard, 1957	"We . . . are perfectly willing to admit that, as a means of estimating genotypic differences, even the most carefully constructed tests are highly fallible instruments, and that their verdicts are far less trustworthy than the judgments of the pupil's own teachers. . . ."
Burt, 1943	"But in regard to innate general ability there can be no question: the unaided judgments even of the most experienced teachers, shrewd as they are in many cases, are nevertheless far less trustworthy in the long run than the results obtained with properly applied intelligence tests."

(Underlining has been added to the original.)

19. Burt, C. "The education of the young adolescent: the psychological implications of the Norwood report." *Brit. J. educ. Psychol.*, 13, 1943, 126–131.
20. Burt, C. *Mental and Scholastic Tests*. London: King and Son, 1921.

**Table 9   WHAT "INDIVIDUAL TEST" DID BURT GIVE TO SEPARATED
MZ TWINS?**

Jensen, 1970   "Their IQ's were obtained from an individual test, the English
adaptation of the Stanford–Binet. . . ."

Burt, 1966   "The tests employed have been fully described elsewhere
(Burt, 1921, 1933). . . . They consisted of (i) a group test of
intelligence containing both non-verbal and verbal items, (ii)
an individual test (the London Revision of the Terman–Binet
Scale) used primarily for standardization, and for doubtful
cases (iii) a set of performance tests . . . standardized by Miss
Gaw (1925). The test results . . . were submitted to the teachers
for comment or criticism; and wherever any question arose,
the child was re-examined."

"[A critic's] main point is that the correlations we obtained
with our individual tests (.843 for identical twins reared apart
. . .) display a wider divergence than those reported by Newman . . . obtained with the old Stanford–Binet . . . the figures
he quotes from our own research were based on non-verbal
tests of the performance type."

Presumably it was the 1966 description which led Jensen to conclude
(21) that the twin "IQ scores" given to him by Burt were raw scores from
a Binet test. But as the figure indicates, Burt had earlier asserted (22)—in
apparent contradiction to his 1966 description—that the figures reported
in his tables under the heading "Individual test" were "based on non-verbal
tests of the performance type." There is no way out of this morass, except
possibly to examine Burt's raw data. That is what Professor Jensen has
now attempted to do, but he has recently reported: " . . . alas, nothing remained of Burt's possessions . . . unfortunately, the original data are lost,
and all that remains are the results of the statistical analyses. . . ."

There is somewhat more information available on the set of performance tests standardized by Miss Gaw in 1925 (23). The standardization
sample consisted of "100 pupils in London schools," none of them "of
scholarship or central school ability." There were "striking" differences
between the sexes in test scores. The reliability of the tests was .76 for
boys and .54 for girls.

21. Jensen, A. R. "IQ's of identical twins reared apart." *Behavior Genetics*,
1, 1970, 133–146.

22. Burt, C. "A note on the theory of intelligence." *Brit. J. educ. Psychol.*,
28, 1958, 281–288.

23. Gaw, F. "A study of performance tests." *Brit. J. Psychol.*, 15, 1925,
374–392.

The use in twin studies of tests which have not been adequately standardized for age and for sex is a *very* serious matter—particularly when, as in Burt's case, no information whatever is provided about the sexes or ages of the twins. Recall that identical twins are necessarily of the same age and same sex. Thus if the measure on which members of a twin pair are compared varies with either sex or age, and if twin pairs of both sexes and of varying ages are included, the IQ correlation between twins is utterly confounded with sex and age. The close resemblance of twins in IQ under such circumstances is scarcely an unambiguous testament to the genetic determination of IQ variation.

We should comment finally on the unique virtue of Burt's study— the provision of quantitative socio-economic class data. Here too there are problems. In 1959, (24) when only 42 separated twin pairs were available, it was clearly indicated that *at least four* children of "professional" parents had been reared in "orphanages"; but in 1966, with the same size increased to 53 pairs, it was reported that precisely two children of such parents had been reared in "residential institutions." Further, a comparison of the marginal totals in Burt's 1966 table with the individual socio-economic data for the *same* twins which Burt later gave to Jensen and Shockley, indicates that in *at least* six cases the classification of a twin was changed *after* 1966. There is also clear evidence that, at least in the case of two twin pairs, the "IQ's" reported were changed after 1966. The twin data were collected by Burt over a period of some 50 years, and it seems quite possible that assessments both of intelligence and of socio-economic class were subjected to a continuing process of revision and refinement.

The conclusion seems to me inescapable, and I can only regret that time does not permit fuller documentation—which exists in abundance. The numbers left behind by Professor Burt are simply not worthy of serious scientific attention.

The separated twin study by Shields (25), unlike Burt's, is replete with procedural details. The text (and especially the appendix), however, indicate some problems. Shields' correlations are not based upon IQ's as such, but upon a "Total Intelligence Score" which pooled the raw scores on two separate tests. The raw score on the Mill Hill vocabulary test was multiplied by two before being added to the raw Dominoes score, since the standard deviation of the Mill Hill was about half that of the Dominoes. The Dominoes had been standardized upon a British Army population, and not upon civilians or upon women. The majority of Shields' separated

24. Conway, J. "Class differences in general intelligence." *Brit. J. statist. Psychol.*, 12, 1959, 5–14.

25. Shields, J. *Monozygotic Twins Brought Up Apart and Brought Up Together*. London: Oxford Univer. Press, 1962.

twins were older females. The standardization of the Mill Hill indicated large age effects on raw score, but these were ignored by Shields. There is evidence within Shields' data for significant sex differences in Dominoes score, and for significant differences between separated and non-separated twins not only in mean test scores, but also in variances.

The appendix provides a considerably more detailed glimpse than does Burt of what kinds of cases constitute the category "separated twins." These examples, if a bit extreme, are not wholly atypical.

> [Benjamin and Ronald, separated at 9 months] Both brought up in the same fruit-growing village, Ben by the parents, Ron by the grandmother. . . . They were at school together. . . . They have continued to live in the same village.

> [Jessie and Winifred, separated at 3 months] Brought up within a few hundred yards of one another. . . . Told they were twins after girls discovered it for themselves, having gravitated to one another at school at the age of 5. . . . They play together quite a lot . . . Jessie often goes to tea with Winifred. . . . They were never apart, wanted to sit at the same desk. . . .

> [Bertram and Christopher, separated at birth] The paternal aunts decided to take one twin each and they have brought them up amicably, living next-door to one another in the same Midlands colliery village. . . . They are constantly in and out of each other's houses.

That is not, I fancy, the sort of separation conjured up by readers of secondary sources which present the twin data.

The Shields appendix makes possible a number of calculations which seem to me to have theoretical significance. Some examples are indicated in Table 10. Shields presents intelligence scores for 35 separated pairs in which he had personally tested each member; for 5 remaining pairs, the twins had been examined by two different psychologists (one usually Shields). The twin pairs tested by the same examiner resembled one

Table 10

Mean co-twin score difference

35 pairs tested by Shields	8.5
	(p < .025)
5 pairs *not* tested by Shields	22.4

Intelligence correlation

27 pairs reared in related families	.83
	(p < .05)
13 pairs reared in unrelated families	.51

Source: From Shields.

another more closely in intelligence, to a statistically significant degree. It is of some interest to note that, following Jensen's arbitrary procedure for converting Shields' scores to "IQ's," the mean IQ difference between twins tested by different examiners exceeds 17 points. That is the mean difference theoretically ‚expected when pairing individuals entirely at random. Thus it seems very likely that all separated twin studies are afflicted by an unconscious experimenter bias introduced during the administration and/or scoring of the tests. (The same tendency may be at work in the data of Churchill (26), who reported raw Wechsler IQ scores for 13 pairs of non-separated monochorionic twins. The correlation between twins can be computed as .995. When, again following Jensen, one corrects for unreliability of the test (assuming a .95 reliability), the true correlation between monochorionics stands revealed as 1.05.)

The Shields appendix also indicates that, in 27 cases, the two separated twins were reared in related branches of the parents' families; only in 13 cases were the twins reared in unrelated families. The twins reared in related families resembled one another more closely, to a statistically significant degree. That is scarcely evidence for an overwhelming genetic determination of IQ scores. Further, the relatively modest correlation of .51 observed in twins reared in unrelated families must in no sense be taken as an estimate of what might be observed if twins were assigned to families at random. The typical case of "unrelated families" was one in which the mother kept one twin, and gave the other to "friends of the family." For his study as a whole, Shields reported, "Large differences in social class do not occur often. . . . " This source of bias, of course, cumulates with biases introduced by imperfectly standardized tests and by experimenter expectation.

The only American study in this series, by Newman, Freeman, and Holzinger (27), was also the first to be reported. The study involved only 19 twin pairs, gathered largely by mail response to newspaper and radio appeals for volunteers. We shall pass over the bias introduced by exclusion from the study of volunteer pairs who, by mail, indicated that they were not "very much alike." The detailed analysis of the Newman et al. data affords a clear illustration of the way in which the confounding of IQ score with age may affect the interpretation of twin data.

For 100 *non-separated* MZ individuals located in the Chicago schools, Newman et al. reported a correlation of −.49 between Stanford–Binet

26. Churchill, J. A. "The relationship between intelligence and birth weight in twins." *Neurology*, 15, 1965, 341–347.

27. Newman, H. H., Freeman, F. N., and Holzinger, K. J. *Twins: a Study of Heredity and Environment*. Chicago: University of Chicago Press, 1937.

IQ and age. Their *separated* twins, however, were mostly adults, for whom an uncorrelated intraclass IQ correlation of .67 was reported. This correlation was doubly "corrected" by McNemar (*28*)—both for age and for restriction of range among the separated twins. The double correction raised the correlation from .67 to .77, with the latter figure by far more commonly cited in text-books. (The .77 figure has recently received a third correction from Jensen (*29*); when corrected for test unreliability, it rises to .81.)

Table 11 indicates, however, some of the problems associated with "correcting for age." The correlations between age and IQ are vastly different—significantly so—for the male and the female separated twins. This apparent sex difference is in turn confounded with the fact that the ages of most of the female twins lie outside the range of the seven male pairs. The table indicates that, within the age range included by the male twins, substantial IQ-age correlations can be detected for both males and females; but for the older subjects, all of whom happen to be female, the age-IQ correlation appears to drop substantially. Partial correlation "corrective" techniques are simply not justified in such a situation. There is no elegant way of removing the biasing effect of age in these data from the estimation of twin resemblance produced by identical genes—or by correlated environments.

Table 12 indicates an extraordinarily inelegant procedure which may serve at least some illustrative function. The ordinary intraclass correlational procedure used with twin data of course pairs the IQ scores of each set of twins. The "pseudo-pairing" procedure illustrated first sets down the scores of all twin pairs, with the order of entry corresponding exactly

Table 11 CORRELATIONS OF IQ WITH AGE

For 14 males, aged 13½–27 ——————————— $r = -.78$
$(p < .01)$
For 24 females, aged 11½–59 ——————————— $r = -.11$
For 6 females, aged 15–27 ——————————— $r = -.60$
For 14 females, aged 30–59 ——————————— $r = -.27$
For 20 (mixed-sex) individuals, aged 13½–27 —— $r = -.58$

Source: From Newman, Freeman, and Holzinger.

28. McNemar, Q., Newman, Freeman, "Holzinger's twins: A study of heredity and environment." *Psychol. Bull.*, 1938, 237–249.
29. Jensen, A. R. "How much can we boost IQ and scholastic achievement?" *Harvard Educational Review*, 39, 1969, 1–123.

Table 12   PSEUDO-PAIRING PROCEDURE

	Intraclass		Pseudo-pairings	
	IQ	IQ	IQ	IQ
Pair A, age 27	96	77	96	66
			77	78
Pair B, age 26.7	66	78	96	78
			77	66
Pair C, age 26	91	90	91	99
			90	101
Pair D, age 23	99	101	91	101
			90	99

etc.   etc.

Intraclass, 7 male NFH pairs ———————————— $r = .58$
Pseudo-paired intraclass, same group ————————— $r = .67$

Intraclass, 10 NFH pairs aged 13.5–27 ————————— $r = .65$
Pseudo-paired intraclass, same group ———————— $r = .47$

to the ages of the twins. The twins are then broken up into clusters, each cluster consisting of two twin sets immediately adjacent in age. (When the number of twin sets in the sample is odd, the set mid-most in age is discarded.) Then, within each cluster, four pseudo-pairings are made. Each score is paired with each other score in the cluster—*except that* pairings of the scores of actual twins are *omitted*. Finally, the intraclass correlation is computed for the pseudo-pairings.

The column of pseudo-pairings, it will be noted, contains precisely the same numbers as does the column of true pairings, but each number appears twice among the pseudo-pairings. The virtue of the pseudo-pairing procedure is obvious. The pseudo-pairings remove all genetic effects from the correlation, and the only systematic bias introduced is that all pseudo-pairings involve individuals quite close together in age. Thus, though the correlation computed from the pseudo-pairings cannot be assessed for statistical significance, it does provide—without the assumptions underlying partial correlation—an estimate of the resemblance between twins to be expected solely on the basis of their shared age. The figure indicates that, for the Newman et al. male sample, that estimate is in fact *higher* than the actual IQ correlation. For the mixed-sex sample consisting of pairs being within the same age range as the males, the estimate, though substantial, is lower than the actually observed correlation.

The final separated twin study, conducted by Juel–Nielsen in Denmark (30), involved only 12 pairs. The test employed was the Wechsler scale for adults. That test, as the author indicated, had never been standardized on a Danish population. Perhaps some of the peculiarities in her data, presented in Figure 13, reflect that unfortunate fact. Her male subjects had significantly higher IQ's than her female subjects. There were significant correlations between age and IQ for each sex—but the two significant correlations were opposite in sign! (This in turn is confounded with the fact that two of her three male pairs fell outside the age range of her 9 female pairs.) The pseudo-pairing technique is applicable only to the relatively "large" female sample. For that sample, the estimate of the correlation produced by age resemblance alone is identical to the actually observed IQ correlation.

The confounding of age with IQ score, it should be noted, is not confined to very old IQ tests employed in exotic foreign studies. Table 14 presents correlations computed from raw data presented in two relatively recent American studies (31, 32). The studies employed the latest versions of the Stanford–Binet and of the WISC, with samples of non-separated MZ twins. The agreement between the studies in the IQ correlation for twins is remarkable; but the agreement between them in the highly significant correlation between age and IQ is even more remarkable. The age–IQ correlation is also observed in the single sample of DZ twins. The pseudo-pairing technique again indicates that a substantial proportion of the IQ correlation between twins may be simply attributable to age. For the pooled MZ sample, the observed IQ correlation was .87. The estimate derived by the pseudo-pairing technique was .67.

From the four separated twin studies reviewed above, Jensen (21) concluded:

> The overall intraclass correlation . . . .824 . . . may be interpreted as an upperbound estimate of the heritability of IQ in the English, Danish, and North American populations sampled in these studies.

My own conclusion is different. I see no unambiguous evidence whatever in these studies for *any* heritability of IQ test scores. The studies do contain clear data which demonstrate the importance of correlated environ-

---

30. Juel-Nielsen, N. "Individual and environment: A psychiatric-psychological investigation of monozygous twins reared apart." *Acta psychiatrica et neurologica Scandinavica*, (Monogr. Suppl. 183), 1965.

31. Babson, S. G., Kangas, J., Young, N., and Bramhall, J. L. "Growth and development of twins of dissimilar size at birth." *Pediatrics*, 30, 1964, 327–333.

32. Willerman, L. and Churchill, J.A. "Intelligence and birth weight in identical twins." *Child Development*, 38, 1967, 623–629.

Table 14   RECENT DATA ON THE AGE-IQ CONFOUND IN TWINS

	Babson et al., 1964 (Stanford–Binet)	Willerman & Churchill, 1967 (WISC Verbal)
For Monozygotics		
Intraclass IQ correlation	.83 (9 pairs)	.82 (14 pairs)
Age × IQ correlation	.59 (N = 18)	.59 (N = 28)
Pseudo-paired intraclass	.28	.77
For Dizygotics		
Intraclass IQ correlation	.65 (7 pairs)	——
Age × IQ correlation	.75 (N = 14)	——
Pseudo-paired intraclass	.44	
Pooling All MZ's		
IQ correlation	.87 (23 pairs)	
Pseudo-paired correlation	.67	

ments in determining the IQ resemblance of so-called separated twins, and there are strong suggestions that unconscious experimenter expectations inflate the reported correlations. There is also in these studies very strong evidence that either our leading IQ tests are incredibly badly standardized, or that general population norms do not apply to twins, or that the twin samples studied by psychologists are bizarre—or all three.

The twin studies, however, are often said to be cross-validated by other types of evidence suggesting a high heritability of IQ. Particularly, the study of adopted children has been asserted by Vandenberg (*33*) to provide "the strongest evidence possible for hereditary factors in intelligence." We turn now to that strong evidence.

There have been four major IQ studies of adoptive children—Freeman, Holzinger, and Mitchell (*34*), Burks (*35*), Leahy (*36*), and Skodak

33. Vandenberg, S. G. "What do we know today about the inheritance of intelligence and how do we know it?" In R. Cancro (Ed.), *Intelligence: Genetic and Environmental Influences*. New York: Grune and Stratton, 1971.

34. Freeman, F. N., Holzinger, K. J., and Mitchell, B. C. "The influence of environment on the intelligence, school achievement, and conduct of foster children." *Nat. Soc. Study Educ.*, 27th Yearbook, Part I, 1928.

35. Burks, B. S. "The relative influence of nature and nurture upon mental development; A comparative study of foster parent–foster child resemblance and true parent–true child resemblance." *Nat. Soc. Study Educ.*, 27th Yearbook, Part I, 1928.

36. Leahy, A. M. "Nature-nurture and intelligence." *Genet. Psychol. Monogr.*, 17, 1935, Whole No. 4.

and Skeels (*37*). The four studies agree in one major particular. The IQ correlation observed between adoptive child and adoptive parent was invariably much lower than that normally observed between biological parent and child. That has been presumed to reflect the fact that biological parent-child pairs share not only a common environment, but also, and much more importantly, common genes.

The Freeman et al. study observed only adoptive families; there were, within the study itself, no natural families to which the adoptive families could be compared. This deficiency was corrected in both the Burks and Leahy studies, which included "matched" control groups of natural families. The Burks study, indeed, according to Jensen (*29*), contained "a perfectly matched control group of parents rearing their own children."

With reflection, however, it may seem doubtful whether adoptive and natural families could be "perfectly" matched for very many variables. The Burks study (like Leahy's) in fact matched families, imperfectly, only with respect to the following: father's occupation and "type of neighborhood," subject child's age and sex, non-separation of living parents, and exclusion of blacks, Jews, and south-Europeans. That matching was not sufficient to control for a number of theoretically relevant variables, as the comparisons in Table 15 make clear.

Though the Leahy report does not include equivalent data, Burks' data demonstrate the obvious—foster parents are older, and have fewer children in their homes, than do natural parents. They are also, in the

Table 15   COMPARISONS BETWEEN "MATCHED" ADOPTIVE AND CONTROL HOMES

	Adoptive	Control
From Leahy		
Home's "environmental status score" ____	137.9	118.7 ($p < .001$)
Correlation, husband and wife IQ ____	.57	.41 ($p < .05$)
Correlation, husband and wife education	.59	.71 ($p < .05$)
From Burks		
Father's mean age ____	45.9	41.0 (sig.)
Mother's mean age ____	41.0	36.1 (sig.)
Number children in home ____	1.5	2.3 (sig.)
Mean family income ____	$6,200	$4,100 (sig.)
Mean value of home ____	$13,200	$9,500 (sig.)

37. Skodak, M. and Skeels, H. M. "A final follow-up study of one hundred adopted children." *J. genet. Psychol.,* 75, 1949, 85–125.

Burks study, some 50 percent wealthier, and live in much more expensive homes—though they have been matched to the control parents for "type of neighborhood." Though Burks' adoptive parents lived in more expensive homes, and with more money, than did her control parents, she could detect no difference in the cultural environments of the homes. However, Leahy, who reported no financial data, did report a significant difference in the "environmental status scores" of the homes.

But the most interesting differences between the two types of families are those reported without significance tests by Leahy, involving correlations *between husband and wife*. The resemblance between spouses is significantly different in the two types of families—both for IQ, and for amount of education. For IQ, spouses in adoptive families resemble one another more than do spouses in control families; but for education, they resemble one another less! That is to say, the interrelations among variables which may themselves relate to child's IQ differ in the two types of families. The foster families are a very highly selected group and evidently provide a very special kind of family environment. The entire nexus of environmental IQ determinants appears to differ across the two types of families. To the extent that this is true, a comparison of parent-child correlations across the two types of families is simply inappropriate.

The studies do contain, however—without comment—some nuggets of very relevant data. There are some adoptive parents who have, in addition to their adopted child, a *biological child* of their own. The relevant question to ask is, what is the IQ correlation between *such* children and their parents? How does it compare to the correlation between the *same* parents and their adopted children, and how does it compare to the correlation between "control" children and parents?

The entirety of the available data is presented in Table 16. The correlations in the table are for child and mid-parent, since that is the only form in which data for the biological children of adoptive parents are presented in these studies. The mid-parent–child correlation is typically considerably larger than the correlation between child and a single parent.

The first point to be made about Table 16 is that, within each column, there is no significant heterogeneity among the correlations. Thus the correlations may reasonably be pooled. For the pooled data, it is clear that the correlation between adoptive child and adoptive parent is significantly lower than that between control child and biological parent. However, the correlation between biological child of an adoptive parent and its parent is *also* significantly lower than that observed in "control" families. Further, the correlations do *not* differ significantly between adoptive parent and, on one hand, adoptive child, and on the other hand, biological child. The latter two correlations do not differ significantly in either of the two studies which present data for each. The data of course confirm that the parent-

Table 16   IQ CORRELATIONS, ADOPTION STUDIES

	Control Child X True Mid-Parent	Adoptive Child X Adoptive Mid-Parent	Own True Child X Adoptive Mid-Parent
Freeman, et al	——	.39 (N = 169)	.35 (N = 28)
Burks	.52 (N = 100)	.20 (N = 174)	——
Leahy	.60 (N = 173)	.18 (N = 177)	.36 (N = 20)
Three studies pooled	.57 (N = 273)	.26 (N = 520)	.35 (N = 48) .35 (N = 48)

child correlation is higher in "control" than in adoptive families. They also indicate, however, that *within* adoptive families, it makes no difference whether the child is adoptive or biological; in either case, the correlation with parent is low. There is no evidence for heritability in these data; quite the opposite.

The final study, by Skodak and Skeels, involved only a single group of 100 adoptive children. The same children were compared both to their true mothers and to their foster mothers. The comparison, however, did not directly involve the parents' IQ's, since IQ's were not available for the foster parents. The child's IQ was correlated with the *number of years of education* of the true and the adoptive parent. The correlations were .32 with true mother's education, and a mere .02 with foster mother's. The contrast appears to suggest a powerful role for heredity; but as Table 17 indicates, there are complications.

There were enormous differences in the amount of education of the two types of mothers. More than half of the foster mothers had attended college, while very few of the true (illegitimate) mothers had. It seems doubtful whether *any* measure could be significantly correlated with number of years of college attended. The foster mothers, in short, were a very much more homogeneous group than the true mothers. The logic of a "scale" of educational attainment which equates the difference between completing 6 and 7 years of school with that between completing 12 and 13 is in any event questionable; one suspects that the decision to proceed from high school to college might be correlated with socio-cultural variables not reflected between Grade 6 and Grade 7 dropouts. There is, thus, little mystery in the fact that the adopted children's IQ did not correlate with their foster parents' education. The significant fact is that the child's IQ *did* correlate with its true mother's education, although

Table 17

True mother's education × child's IQ —————	r = .32	(N = 92)
		(p < .01)
Foster mother's education × child's IQ —————	r = .02	(N = 100)
Proportion of true mothers attending college ———	8.7%	
		(p < .0001)
Proportion of foster mothers attending college ——	51.0%	
For 8 true mothers > grade 12, *foster* mother's education ———————————————	13.9 yrs.	
		(p < .05)
For 12 true mothers < grade 8, *foster* mother's education ———————————————	11.8 yrs	
For 12 "college" foster homes, *true* mother's education ———————————————	11.3 yrs.	
		(p < .005)
For 22 "grade school" foster homes, *true* mother's education ———————————————	9.1 yrs.	

Source: From Skodak and Skeels.

the child had never lived with the true mother. What could this fact reflect other than a powerful genetic determination of IQ?

The most obvious fact which it might reflect is a policy of selective placement on the part of adoption agencies. The raw data in the Skodak and Skeels appendix can in fact be used to demonstrate clearly such selective placement. There were 8 true mothers who had attended college, and 12 true mothers who had failed to complete grade school. We can ask, were there differences in the types of homes into which illegitimate children of these two groups of mothers were placed? There were indeed; the foster mothers who received children of highly educated true mothers were significantly more highly educated than were the foster mothers who received children of poorly educated true mothers. The same kind of selective placement can be demonstrated in mirror image. There were 12 foster homes in which each parent had *completed* college, and 22 in which neither parent had completed high school. The true mothers of children placed into these two classes of homes differed significantly, in the expected direction, in the amount of their own education. The illegitimate child of a college-educated mother, it appears, is very likely to be placed in a college foster home; the probability is much less that the illegitimate child of a grade school drop-out will be so placed.

Perhaps it is instructive to note that Skodak and Skeels were unable to demonstrate selective placement in terms of the true mother's *IQ*. That suggests that adoption agencies, unlike psychologists, are guided in the real world by significant social facts such as amount of education, more than by such fanciful psychological constructs as the IQ.

The evidence indicates, in any event, that children were placed into foster homes on the basis of their true mother's education, or of variables correlated with it. We can assume that the children of highly educated true mothers were placed into "good" foster homes, homes conducive to the development of high IQ. The observed correlation between child's IQ and true mother's education follows directly from this fact. Further, on the assumption that foster parent's education correlated only moderately with "goodness" of the foster home, there would be little or no correlation between child's IQ and foster parent's education. The latter assumption is especially likely to be valid, as Skodak and Skeels themselves pointed out, in a farming state such as Iowa in the 1930's. They indicated in their report that many of the foster homes with the greatest cultural and environmental amenities belonged to successful farmers who had relatively little formal education.

The adopted child studies, like the separated twin studies, seem to me to offer no evidence sufficient to reject the hypothesis of zero heritability of IQ scores. The policy recommendations made by contemporary psychologists on the basis of these data seem no more firmly grounded in science than those made during the earlier eugenic and immigration debates. They seem to me to reflect the same elitism, and the same ethnocentric narrowness of vision and concern, which characterized our psychological ancestors during their anti-immigrant hysteria.

The assertion is abroad that compensatory education has been tried, and has failed; and that failure is an inevitable consequence of demonstrated genetic truths. Perhaps, however, it is we psychologists who have failed; perhaps again, it is the society in which we live that has failed. Those who care have a double task. We had better build a better psychology; and we had better help to build, quickly, a better society.

IQ Tests: Building Blocks for the New Class System

Noam Chomsky

In the following article Noam Chomsky discusses the controversial views of Harvard Psychologist Richard Herrnstein, which first received widespread attention when they were presented, under the laconic title "IQ" in the September 1971 Atlantic. Herrnstein stands as one of the more intellectually respectable of a recent crop of scientific apologists for social inequity, the more notorious exponents ranging downward through Berkeley Professor A. R. Jensen, to the lower depths occupied by William

Shockley, the Stanford electrical engineer. But if all these academics cannot be fairly lumped together without distinction, one thing they do share in common is the basic intellectual decrepitude of their arguments, which in essence they have merely dug up from the past and fitted out in terms that suit the current mode.

Class subordination and social privilege have never been the most promising subjects for ethical defense. Historically the defenses that have been mustered, and which could be espoused with any presentable show of disinterest or conviction, have turned out to be very few, and by now rather ancient. But since every system of social inequality craves to be legitimized, the same time worn apologia of privilege have had to be perennially resurrected. And in each case an attempt is made to draw renewed conviction from the particular epoch's most vital springs of faith.

Thus, in orthodox times the social order is sanctified by its conformity to the Divine Order, a sanctity which has been considered useful at one time or another by both the pedigreed noble and the successful bourgeois, by the annointed and the elect.

In a period (like our own) when rationalism casts doubt on divine testimonials on behalf of the ruling class, a substitute is usually found in science. Privilege is now shown to be in conformity with the Natural Order rather than the Divine. Class subordination is no longer "what God decreed," but "what Nature intended."

For those on top, whether their endorsement comes from science or religion, the main thing is that authority is on the side of power. Of course for people (like ourselves) who consider themselves hardheaded, the appeal to science has always been more persuasive, since any subjective inclination of the privileged in favor of the status quo will presumably be tested against objective data.

Aristotle, for instance, considering whether slavery was really natural and just, appealed to the evidence of biology: "all tame animals are better off when they are ruled by man; for then they are preserved. Again, the male is by nature superior, and the female inferior; and the one rules and the other is ruled," and he concludes, "this principle, of necessity, extends to all mankind."

The Greeks generally at this time relied on an objective criterion to indicate the naturally subordinate. The barbaros, *meaning those people who did not speak Greek, were set off almost as a distinct species by their deficient linguistic ability. Greek speaking served as a kind of IQ test for them, and those who flunked it were fair game to be conquered and enslaved.*

An appeal to science was also made by Thomas Hobbes in his defense of absolutist government and total submission to established power. These were necessary, he argued, as the only viable alternative to the intolerable state suffered by people lacking such an authority. So that we should not have to rely on his own speculative assessment of the dire alternative to absolutist rule, Hobbes resorted to what we now call anthropology, citing empirical data gathered by observers in the field: "The savage people in many places of America, except for the government of small families, the concord whereof depends on natural lust, have no government at all and live at this day in that brutish manner as I said before."

In the 19th century, Charles Darwin's depiction of Survival of the Fittest gave a tremendous scientific boost to those who wished to believe that the people on the top in society were there because they deserved to be. In Bertrand Russell's words, Darwin's model was popularly pictured as "a global free competition, in which victory went to the animals that most resembled successful capitalists."

Of course nowadays the self-serving interpretations and anecdotal methods that used to pass for science would influence no one. Today we give credence only to what impresses us as hard data, and we look for the authenticating signs: everybody recognizes that laboratories are scientific, and everybody knows that numbers are precise. It is natural then that the current attempts to legitimize class subordination and social privilege should employ these present day talismans of scientific authority as they are applied in the study of human psychology. So we have appeals first to the principles of behaviorist psychology, whose identification with the laboratory is so complete because they never found much in reality outside of it; and second to the statistics of the IQ which being numerical are thought to transform the amorphous concept of intelligence into something quantifiably precise.

Appeals to one or both of these are the basis of the new genre of scientific apologia for established privilege and the status quo. Although white racial chauvinism is not flatly expounded in the more respectable of the various arguments, it is always present. And it is clear that in the consciousness and unconsciousness of white America there exists a longing to have the socially repressed ugliness of candid racism vindicated and unleashed by prestigious professors using two dollar words. There is the feeling that if debator's points could be won in a few university classrooms, the great historical imperatives of racial justice that are straining and testing American society will somehow be eased, and continued suppression of black people will suddenly be morally sanctioned and socially tenable.

It is odd that these academicians and others ever got the idea in the first place that the roots of the intractable racial conflict in America could be searched out by probing for a statistical margin of racial difference. The manifest social reality that stares us in the face is just the opposite. It is precisely the tension between equality and inequity that is so agonizing and explosive. Hobbes understood the dynamic of equality and social conflict far better than today's computerized numerologists: "From this equality of ability arises equality of hope in the attaining of our ends. And therefore if any two men desire the same thing, which nevertheless they cannot both enjoy, they become enemies . . . and from hence it comes to pass that . . . if one plant, sow, build, or possess a convenient seat, others may probably be expected to come with forces united to dispossess and deprive him, not only of the fruit of his labor, but also of his life or liberty. And the invader again is in the like danger of another."

David Kolodney

In the ten months since Dr. Richard Herrnstein's article "IQ," first appeared in the *Atlantic*, it has become the focus of an intriguing controversy, predictably intense but surprisingly sustained. There is no question that Herrnstein's argument is provocative; he purports to show that American society is drifting inexorably towards a stable hereditary meritocracy, towards a social stratification determined by inborn differences and a corresponding distribution of "rewards."

Herrnstein's argument is based first of all on the hypothesis that differences in mental abilities are inherited and that people close to one another in mental ability are more likely to marry and reproduce so that there will be a tendency toward long-term stratification by mental ability (which Herrnstein takes to be measured by IQ). Secondly, Herrnstein argues that "success" requires mental ability and that social rewards "depend on success." This step in the argument embodies two assumptions: that it is so in fact; and that it must be so for society to function effectively. The conclusion is that there is a tendency toward hereditary meritocracy, with "social standing (which reflects earnings and prestige)" concentrated in groups with higher IQ's. This tendency will be accelerated as society becomes more egalitarian, that is, as artificial social barriers are eliminated, defects in prenatal (e.g. nutritional) environment are overcome, and so on, so that natural ability can play a more direct role in attainment of social reward. Therefore, as society becomes more egalitarian, social rewards will be concentrated in a hereditary meritocratic elite.

Herrnstein has been widely denounced as a racist for this argument, a conclusion which seems to me unwarranted. There is, however, an ideological element in his argument that is absolutely critical to it. Consider the second step, that is, the claim that IQ is a factor in attaining reward and that this must be so for society to function effectively. Herrnstein recognizes that his argument will collapse if, indeed, society can be organized in accordance with the "socialist dictum, 'From each according to his ability, to each according to his needs.'" His argument would not apply in a society in which "income (economic, social, and political) is unaffected by success."

Actually, Herrnstein fails to point out that his argument not only requires the assumption that success must be rewarded, but that it must be rewarded in quite specific ways. If individuals were rewarded for success only by prestige, then no conclusions of any importance would follow. It would only follow (granting his other assumptions) that the children of people respected for their achievements would be more likely to win respect by achievements of their own—an innocuous result even if true. It may be that the child of two Olympic swimmers has a greater than average chance of achieving the same success (and the acclaim for it), but no dire social consequences follow from this hypothesis.

The conclusion that Herrnstein and others find disturbing is that wealth and power will tend to concentrate in a hereditary meritocracy. But this follows only on the assumption that rewards of successful achievement must be wealth and power (not merely respect) and that these (or their effects) must be transmittable, that is, allowed to be passed on from parents to children. The issue is confused by Herrnstein's failure to isolate the specific factors crucial to his argument, and his use of the phrase "income (economic, social, and political)" to cover "rewards" of all types, including respect as well as wealth. It is confused further by the fact that he continually slips into identifying "social standing" with wealth. Thus, for example, he writes that if the social ladder is tapered steeply, the obvious way to rescue the people at the bottom is "to increase the aggregate wealth of society so that there is more room at the top"—which is untrue if "social standing" is solely a matter of acclaim and respect. (We overlook the fact that even on his tacit assumption, redistribution of income would appear to be an equally obvious strategy.)

Consider then the narrower assumption that is crucial to his argument: not just that transmittable wealth and power do presently accrue to mental ability, but that they must for society to function effectively. If this assumption is false and society *can* be organized more or less in accordance with the "socialist dictum," then nothing is left of Herrnstein's argument (except that it will apply to a competitive society in which his other factual assumptions hold). But, Herrnstein claims, the assumption is true. The reason is that an individual's ability "expresses itself in labor only for gain" and people "compete for gain—economic and otherwise." People will work only if they are rewarded in terms of "social and political influence or relief from threat." All of this is merely asserted; no justification is given.

What reason is there to believe the crucial assumption that, because people will work only for gain in (transmittable) wealth and power, society cannot be organized in accordance with the socialist dictum? In a decent society, everyone would have the opportunity to find interesting work, and each person would be permitted the fullest possible scope for his talents. Would more be required—in particular, extrinsic reward in the form of wealth and power? Only if we assume that applying one's talents in interesting and socially useful work is not rewarding in itself, that there is no intrinsic satisfaction in creative and productive work, suited to one's abilities, or in helping others (say, one's family, friends, associates, or simply fellow members of society). Unless we suppose this, then even granting all of Herrnstein's other assumptions, it does not follow that there should be any concentration of wealth or power in a hereditary elite.

For Herrnstein's argument to have any force at all we must assume that people labor only for gain, and that the satisfaction found in interesting or socially beneficial work or in work well-done or in the respect shown to such activities, is not a sufficient "gain" to induce anyone to work. The assumption, in short, is that without material reward, people will vegetate. For this crucial assumption, no semblance of an argument is offered. Rather, Herrnstein merely asserts that if bakers and lumberjacks "got the top salaries and the top social approval," [1] in place of those now at the top of the social ladder, then "the scale of IQ's would also invert," and the most talented would strive to become bakers and lumberjacks. This, of course, is not an argument, but merely a reiteration of the claim that, necessarily, individuals work only for extrinsic reward. Furthermore, it is an extremely implausible claim. I doubt very much that Herrnstein would become a baker or lumberjack if he could earn more money that way.

Similar points are made in the commentary on Herrnstein's article in the November, 1971 *Atlantic*.[2] In this response he merely reiterates his belief that there is no way "to end the blight of differential rewards."

---

[1] He does not specifically mention this assumption, but it is necessary to the argument.

[2] Note again Herrnstein's failure to distinguish remuneration from social approval, though the argument collapses if the only reward is approval.

Repeated assertion, however, is not to be confused with argument. Herrnstein's further contention that "history shows . . . " in effect concedes defeat. Of course history shows concentration of wealth and power in the hands of those able to accumulate it. One thought Herrnstein was trying to do more than merely expound this truism.

If we look more carefully at what history and experience show, we find that, where free exercise is permitted to the qualities of ruthlessness, cunning, and the other ingredients of "success" in competitive societies, then those who have these qualities will rise to the top and will use their wealth and power to preserve and extend the privileges they attain. They will also construct ideologies to demonstrate that this result is only fair and just. We also find, contrary to capitalist ideology and behaviorist doctrine, that many people often do not act solely, or even primarily, so as to achieve material gain, or even so as to maximize applause. As for the argument (if offered) that "history shows" the untenability of the "socialist dictum," this may be assigned the same status as an argument made in the 18th century that capitalist democracy is impossible, as history then showed. Evidently, from the lessons of history we can reach only the most tentative conclusions about basic human tendencies.

Suppose that Herrnstein's crucial and unargued claim is incorrect. Suppose that there is in fact some intrinsic satisfaction in employing one's talents in challenging and creative work. Then, one might argue, this should compensate even for a diminution of extrinsic reward; and "reinforcement" should be given for the performance of unpleasant and boring tasks. It follows, then, that there should be a concentration of wealth (and the power that comes from wealth) among the less talented. I do not urge this conclusion, but merely observe that it is more plausible than Herrnstein's if his fundamental and unsupported assumption is false.

The belief that people must be driven or drawn to work by "gain" is a curious one. Of course, it is true if we use the vacuous behaviorist scheme and speak of the "reinforcing quality" of interesting or useful work; the belief may also be true, though irrelevant to Herrnstein's thesis, if the "gain" sought is merely general respect and prestige. But the assumption necessary for Herrnstein's argument is that people must be driven or drawn to work by the quest for wealth or power. This obviously does not derive from science, nor does it appear to be supported by personal experience. I suspect that Herrnstein would exclude himself from the generalization, as already noted. Thus I am not convinced that he would at once apply for a job as a garbage collector if this were to pay more than his present position as a teacher and research psychologist. He would say, I am sure, that he does his work not because it maximizes wealth (or even prestige) but because it is interesting and challenging, that is, intrinsically rewarding; and there is no reason to doubt that this response would be correct. The statistical evidence, he points out, suggests that "if *very* high income is your goal, and you have a high IQ, do not waste your time with formal education beyond high school." Thus, if you are an economic maximizer with a high IQ don't bother with a college education. Few follow this advice, quite probably because they prefer interesting work to mere material reward. The assumption that people will work only for gain in wealth and power is not only unargued, but quite probably false, except under extreme deprivation. But this degrading and brutal assumption, common to capitalist ideology and the behaviorist view of human beings, is fundamental to Herrnstein's argument.

There are other ideological elements in Herrnstein's argument, more peripheral, but still worth noting. He invariably describes the society he sees evolving as a "meritocracy," thus expressing the value judgment that the characteristics that yield reward are a sign of merit, that is, positive characteristics. He considers IQ specifically, but of course recognizes that there might very well be other factors in the attainment of "social success." One might speculate, rather plausibly, that wealth and power tend to accrue to those who are ruthless, cunning, avaricious, self-seeking, lacking in sympathy and compassion, subservient to authority, willing to abandon principle for material gain, and so on. Furthermore, these less endearing traits might well be as heritable as IQ, and might outweigh IQ as factors in gaining material reward. Such qualities might be just the most valuable ones for a Hobbsean war of all against all. If so, then the society that results (applying Herrnstein's "syllogism") could hardly be characterized as a "meritocracy." By using the word "meritocracy" Herrnstein begs some interesting questions and reveals implicit assumptions about our society that are hardly self-evident.

Teachers in ghetto schools commonly observe that students who are self-reliant, imaginative, energetic and unwilling to submit to authority are often regarded as trouble-makers and punished, on occasion even driven out of the school system. The implicit assumption that in a highly discriminatory society, or one with tremendous inequality of wealth and power, the "meritorious" will be rewarded, is a curious one indeed.

Consider further Herrnstein's assumption that in fact social rewards accrue to those who perform beneficial and needed services. He claims that the "gradient of occupations" is "a natural measure of value and scarcity," and that "the ties among IQ, occupation, and social standing make practical sense." This is his way of expressing the familiar theory that people are automatically rewarded in a just society (and more or less in our society) in accordance with their contributions to social welfare or "output." The theory is familiar, and so are its fallacies.

To assume that society's rewards go to those who have performed a social service is to succumb to essentially the same fallacy (among others) involved in the claim that a free market leads to the optimal satisfaction of wants. In fact, when wealth is badly distributed, a free market will tend to produce luxuries for the few who can pay, rather than necessities for the many who cannot. Similarly, given great inequalities of wealth, we will expect to find that the "gradient of occupations" by pay is a natural measure, not of service to society but of service to wealth and power to those who can purchase and compel. The ties among IQ, occupation, and social standing that Herrnstein notes make "practical sense" for those with wealth and power, but not necessarily for society or its members in general.

The point is quite obvious. Herrnstein's failure to notice it is particularly surprising given the data on which he bases his observations about the relation between social reward and occupation. He bases these judgments on a ranking of occupations which shows, for example, that accountants, specialists in public relations, auditors, and sales managers tend to have higher IQ's (hence, he would claim, receive higher pay, as they must if society is to function effectively) than musicians, riveters, bakers, lumberjacks and teamsters. Accountants were ranked highest among 74 listed occupations, with public relations 4th, musicians 35th, riveters 50th, bakers 65th, truck drivers 67th, and lumberjacks 70th. From such data, Herrnstein concludes that society is wisely "husbanding its intellectual resources" [3] and that the gradient of occupation is a natural measure of value and makes practical sense.

Is it obvious that an accountant helping a corporation to cut its tax bill is doing work of greater social value than a musician, riveter, baker, truck driver, or lumberjack? Is a lawyer who earns a $100,000 fee to keep a dangerous drug on the market worth more to society than a farm worker or a nurse? Is a surgeon who performs operations for the rich doing work of greater social value than a practitioner in the slums, who may work much harder for much less extrinsic reward? The gradient of occupations that Herrnstein uses to support his claims surely reflects, at least in part, the demands of wealth and power; a further argument is needed to demonstrate Herrnstein's claim that those at the top of the list are performing the highest service to "society," which is wisely husbanding its resources by rewarding accountants and public relations experts and engineers (e.g., designers of anti-personnel weapons) for their special skills. Herrnstein's failure to notice what his data immediately suggest is another indication

[3] Misleading, Herrnstein states: "society is, in effect, husbanding its intellectual resources by holding engineers in greater esteem and paying them more." But if he really wants to claim this on the basis of the ties between IQ and social standing that his data reveal, then he should conclude as well that society is husbanding its intellectual resources by holding accountants and PR men in greater esteem and paying them more. Quite apart from this, it is not so obvious as he apparently believes that society is wisely husbanding its intellectual resources by employing most of its scientists and engineers in military and space R-and-D.

of his uncritical and apparently unconscious acceptance of capitalist ideology in its crudest form.

If the ranking of occupations by IQ correlates with ranking by income, this could be interpreted in part as indicating an unfortunate social bias leading able individuals toward occupations that serve the wealthy and powerful and away from work that might be more satisfying and socially useful. This would certainly seem at least a plausible assumption, but one that Herrnstein never discusses, given his unquestioning acceptance of the prevailing ideology.

There is, no doubt, some complex of characteristics conducive to material reward in a stable capitalist society. This complex may include IQ and quite possibly other more important factors, perhaps those noted earlier. To the extent that these characteristics are heritable (and a factor in choosing mates) there will be a tendency toward stratification in terms of these qualities. This much is obvious enough.

Furthermore, people with higher IQ's will tend to have more freedom in selection of occupation. Depending on their other traits and opportunities, they will tend to choose more interesting work or more remunerative work, these categories being by no means identical. Therefore one can expect to find some correlation between IQ and material reward, and some correlation between IQ and an independent ranking of occupations according to their intrinsic interest and intellectual challenge. Were we to rank occupations by social utility in some manner, we would probably find at most a weak correlation with remuneration or with intrinsic interest and quite possibly a negative correlation. Unequal distribution of wealth and power will naturally introduce a bias toward greater remuneration for services to the privileged, thereby causing the scale of remuneration to diverge from the scale of social utility in many instances.

From Herrnstein's data and arguments, we can draw no further conclusions about what would happen in a just society—unless we add the assumption that people labor only for material gain, for wealth and power, and that unless offered such a reward they would rather vegetate than seek interesting work suited to their abilities. Since Herrnstein offers no reason why we should believe any of this (and there is certainly some reason why we should not), none of his conclusions follow from his factual assumptions, even if these are correct. The crucial step in his "syllogism" in effect amounts to a bare assertion that the ideology of capitalist society accurately expresses universal traits of human nature, and that certain related implicit assumptions of behaviorist psychology are correct. Conceivably, these unsupported assumptions are true. But once it is recognized how critical their role is in Herrnstein's argument and how insubstantial their empirical support, any further interest in this argument would seem to evaporate.

I have assumed so far that prestige, respect, and so on might be factors in causing people to work (as Herrnstein implies). This seems to me by no means obvious, though, even if it is true, Herrnstein's conclusions clearly do not follow. In a decent society, socially necessary and unpleasant work would be divided on some egalitarian basis, and beyond that people would have, as an inalienable right, the widest possible opportunity to do work that interests them. They might be rewarded ("reinforced") by self-respect, if they do their work to the best of their ability, or if their work benefits those to whom they are related by bonds of friendship and sympathy and solidarity. Such projections are commonly an object of ridicule —as it was common, in an earlier period, to scoff at the absurd idea that a peasant had the same inalienable rights as a nobleman. There always have been, and no doubt always will be, people who cannot conceive of the possibility that things could be different from what they are. Perhaps they are right, but again one awaits a rational argument.

In a decent society of the sort just described—which, one might think, becomes increasingly realizable with technological progress—there should be no shortage of scientists, engineers, surgeons, artists, craftsmen, teachers, and so on, simply because such work is intrinsically rewarding. There is no reason to doubt that people in these occupations would work as hard as those fortunate few who can choose their own work generally do today. Of course, if Herrnstein's assumptions, borrowed from capitalist ideology and behaviorist belief, are correct, then people will remain idle rather than do such work unless there is deprivation and extrinsic reward. But no reason is suggested as to why we should accept this strange and demeaning doctrine.

Lurking in the background of the debate over Herrnstein's syllogism is the matter of race, though he himself barely alludes to it. His critics are disturbed, and rightly so, by the fact that his argument will surely be exploited by racists to justify discrimination, much as Herrnstein may personally deplore this fact. More generally, Herrnstein's argument will be adopted by the privileged to justify their privilege on grounds that they are being rewarded for their ability and that such reward is necessary if society is to function properly. The situation is reminiscent of 19th century racist anthropology. Marvin Harris notes:

> Racism also had its use as a justification for class and caste hierarchies; it was a splendid explanation of both national and class privilege. It helped to maintain slavery and serfdom; it smoothed the way for the rape of Africa and the slaughter of the American Indian; it steeled the nerves of the Manchester captains of industry as they lowered wages, lengthened the working day, and hired more women and children.[4]

We can expect Herrnstein's arguments to be used in a similar way, and for similar reasons. When we discover that his argument is without force, unless we adopt unargued and implausible premises that happen to incor-

[4] *Op. cit.*, p. 106.

porate the dominant ideology, we quite naturally turn to the question of the social function of his conclusions and ask why the argument is taken seriously.

Since the issue is often obscured by polemic, it is perhaps worth stating again that the question of the validity and scientific status of a particular point of view is of course logically independent from the question of its social function. But each is a legitimate topic of inquiry, and the social function takes on a particular interest when the point of view in question is revealed to be seriously deficient on empirical or logical grounds.

The 19th century racist anthropologists were no doubt quite often honest and sincere. They may have believed that they were simply dispassionate investigators, advancing science, following the facts where they led. Conceding this, we might nevertheless question their judgment, and not merely because the evidence was poor and the arguments fallacious. We might take note of the relative lack of concern over the ways in which these "scientific investigations" were likely to be used. It would be a poor excuse for the 19th century racist anthropolgist to plead, in Herrnstein's words, that "a neutral commentator . . . would have to say that the case is simply not settled" (with regard to racial inferiority) and that the "fundamental issue" is "whether inquiry shall (again) be shut off because someone thinks society is best left in ignorance." The 19th century racist anthropologist, like any other person, is responsible for the effects of what he does, insofar as they can be clearly foreseen. If the likely consequences of his "scientific work" are those that Harris describes, he has the responsibility to take this likelihood into account. This would be true even if the work had real scientific merit—in fact, more so in that case.

Similarly, imagine a psychologist in Hitler's Germany who thought he could show that Jews had a genetically determined tendency toward usury (like squirrels bred to collect too many nuts) or a drive toward antisocial conspiracy and domination, and so on. If he were criticized for even undertaking these studies, would it be sufficient for him to respond that "a neutral commentator . . . would have to say that the case is simply not settled" and that the "fundamental issue" is "whether inquiry shall (again) be shut off because someone thinks society is best left in ignorance?" I think not. I think that such a response would have been met with justifiable contempt. At best, he could claim that he is faced with a conflict of values. On the one hand, there is the alleged scientific importance of determining whether in fact Jews had a genetically determined tendency toward usury and domination (an empirical question, no doubt). On the other, there is the likelihood that even opening this question and regarding it as a subject for scientific inquiry would provide ammunition for Goebbels and Rosenberg and their henchmen. Were this hypothetical psychologist to disregard the likely social consequences of his research (or even of his undertaking such research) under existing social conditions, he would fully deserve the contempt of decent people. Of course, scientific curiosity should be encouraged (though fallacious argument and investigation of silly questions should not), but it is not an absolute value.

The extravagant praise lavished on Herrnstein's flimsy argument and the widespread failure to note its implicit bias and unargued assumptions[5] suggest that we are not dealing simply with a question of scientific curiosity. Since it is impossible to explain this acclaim on the basis of the substance or force of the argument, it is natural to ask whether the conclusions are so welcome to many commentators that they lose their critical faculties and fail to perceive that certain crucial and quite unsupported assumptions happen to be nothing other than a variant of the prevailing ideology. This failure is disturbing, more so, perhaps, than the conclusions Herrnstein attempts to draw from his flawed syllogism.

Turning to the question of race and intelligence, we are granting too much to the contemporary investigator of this question when we see him as faced with a conflict of values: scientific curiosity versus social consequences. Given the virtual certainty that even the undertaking of the inquiry will reinforce some of the most despicable features of our society, the authenticity of the presumed moral dilemma depends critically on the scientific significance of the issue that he is choosing to investigate. Even if the scientific significance were immense, we should certainly question the seriousness of the dilemma, given the likely social consequences. But if the scientific interest of any possible finding is slight, then the dilemma vanishes.

In fact, it seems that the question of the relation, if any, between race and intelligence has very little scientific importance (as it has no social importance, except under the assumptions of a racist society). A possible correlation between mean IQ and skin color is of no greater scientific interest than a correlation between any two other arbitrarily selected traits, say, mean height and color of eyes. The empirical results, whatever they might be, appear to have little bearing on any issue of scientific significance. In the present state of scientific understanding, there would appear to be little interest in the discovery that one partly heritable trait correlates (or does not) with another partly heritable trait. Such questions might be interesting if the results had some bearing, say, on hypotheses about the psychological mechanisms involved, but this is not the case. Therefore the investigation seems of quite limited scientific interest, and the zeal and intensity with which some pursue or welcome it cannot reasonably be attributed to a dispassionate desire to advance science. It would, of course, be foolish to claim, in response, that "society should not be left in igno-

[5] See the correspondence in the *Atlantic*, November, 1971.

rance." Society is happily "in ignorance" of an infinitude of insignificant matters of all sorts. And, with the best of will, it is difficult to avoid questioning the good faith of those who deplore the alleged "anti-intellectualism" of the critics of scientifically trivial and socially malicious investigations. On the contrary, the investigator of race and intelligence might do well to explain the intellectual significance of the topic he is studying, and thus enlighten us to the moral dilemma he perceives. If he perceives none, the conclusion is obvious, with no further discussion.

As to social importance, a correlation between race and mean IQ (were this shown to exist) entails no social consequences except in a racist society in which each individual is assigned to a racial category and dealt with not as an individual in his own right, but as a representative of this category. Herrnstein mentions a possible correlation between height and IQ. Of what social importance is that? None, of course, since our society does not suffer under discrimination by height. We do not insist on assigning each adult to the category "below six feet in height" or "above six feet in height" when we ask what sort of education he should receive or where he should live or what work he should do. Rather, he is what he is, quite independent of the mean IQ of people of his height category. In a non-racist society, the category of race would be of no greater significance. The mean IQ of individuals of a certain racial background is irrelevant to the situation of a particular individual, who is what he is. Recognizing this perfectly obvious fact, we are left with little, if any, plausible justification for an interest in the relation between mean IQ and race, apart from the "justification" provided by the existence of racial discrimination.

The question of heritability of IQ might conceivably have some social importance, say, with regard to educational practice. However, even this seems dubious, and one would like to see an argument. It is, incidentally, surprising to me that so many commentators should find it disturbing that IQ might be heritable, perhaps largely so. An advertisement in the *Harvard Crimson* (November 29, 1971), signed by many faculty members, refers to the "disturbing conclusion that 'intelligence' is largely genetic, so that over many, many years society might evolve into classes marked by distinctly different levels of ability." Since, as already noted, the conclusion does not follow from the premise, it may be that what disturbs the signers is the "conclusion that 'intelligence' is largely genetic." Why this should seem disturbing remains obscure. Would it also be disturbing to discover that relative height, or musical talent, or rank in running the 100 yard dash, is in part genetically determined? Why should one have preconceptions one way or another about these questions, and how do the answers to them, whatever they may be, relate either to serious scientific issues (in the present state of our knowledge) or to social practice, in a decent society?

CHAPTER 10

Dysgenics and Applied Raceology

Racial psychology reflected the broader, deep-seated racism which was a fundamental part of American culture. Drawing on more than half a century of racial- and class-bias testing, Henry E. Garrett, who for sixteen years headed Columbia's Department of Psychology and served for a shorter time as President of the American Psychological Association and member of the National Research Council, turned, in the twilight years of his life, to writing pamphlets for the Patrick Henry Press, including "How Classroom Desegregation Will Work," "Children Black and White," and "Breeding Down." [1] In these pamphlets one can once again hear the voices of H. H. Goddard, Lewis M. Terman, David Starr Jordan, and Edward L. Thorndike and see the ways in which their research was being applied in a culture burning with racial fears and hatreds. "Breeding Down" is an especially important pamphlet. Over 500,000 copies were distributed free of charge to teachers, school boards and P.T.A.'s in school districts that bordered the ghettos immediately after they had burned during the 1960's. Teachers, administrators and parents from those all white districts which surrounded smoldering ghettos such as those in Watts, Harlem, Rochester, Detroit, and Newark were reminded by Garrett that, indeed, what racial psychology has proven is that "wherever there has been mixed breeding with the Negro, there has been deterioration in civilization." The Negro, he asserted, represented a 200,000-year lag in the process of civilization building.

The testing movement and the racial psychology which it propounded was used by Garrett in "Breeding Down" to fan racial fears and hatreds in order to build a white backlash against the possibility that desegregation

[1] See Henry E. Garrett, *How Classroom Desegregation Will Work*. (Richmond, Virginia: Patrick Henry Press, 1967). Also *Children Black and White*. (Richmond, Virginia: Patrick Henry Press, 1966) and *Breeding Down* (Richmond, Virginia: Patrick Henry Press), undated.

might work.[2] Racial psychology was applied directly at this point to turn people away from the possibility of desegregation, just as shortly thereafter Arthur Jensen's racial psychology was used directly to turn people away from compensatory education programs designed to raise the cognitive ability of blacks. In a racially oriented America, the racial psychology of the academy was to have a profound effect on the course of American social and educational policy.

No sooner had Garrett retired from the scene of racial conflict when William Shockley took the lead. Shockley, a Nobel Prize laureate, adopted the term "raceology" to describe his philosophy. Just as Garrett, Thorndike, Terman and David Starr Jordan; Shockley also worried about contaminating the genetic pool with inferior black genes. Shockley proposed a "final solution" similar to what Terman, Jordan and Thorndike all had supported in their day. Shockley's proposal included a voluntary sterilization plan for those with low IQ's and, therefore, presumably inferior genes. His proposal incorporated a bonus plan which was graduated so that the lower the IQ, the greater the material reward one would receive for submitting to the operation. By the early 1970's, some state legislatures were seriously considering Shockley's proposal or a variant of it.

With the collapse of desegregation efforts as well as compulsory education programs, the dangers, for white racists, of an integrated American society passed as blacks were increasingly confined below the poverty level in economically segregated, decaying urban ghettos. Further, with the withdrawal of federal support for urban schools and the consequent deterioration of these schools as educational institutions, the future for black youth was sealed. As a result of these circumstances, more and more black youth would be channeled into unskilled areas of employment. At a time when automation was rapidly eliminating unskilled areas of employment, the possibility that blacks would spend much of their lives on welfare roles was predictable. As welfare roles swell and the backlash against the dole increases, Shockley's "final solution" could be expected to become more and more seriously entertained. In this kind of social context, Shockley and Garrett's racial psychology takes on profound social significance. If and when Shockley's "final solution" is acted upon and institutionalized, it will be yet another case of professors as professional experts acting out their role as servants of power rather than servants of truth. In the works of Garrett and Shockley, the responsibility of racial psychologists for providing ideological instruments through which racial repression is cultivated in the educational state in America is brought into clear focus.

[2] See Henry E. Garrett, "How Classroom Desegregation Will Work." Patrick Henry Press, 1967.

Dysgenics—A Social-Problem Reality Evaded by the Illusion of Infinite Plasticity of Human Intelligence?

William Shockley

RESOLVING THE ENVIRONMENT–HEREDITY UNCERTAINTY

My chief contribution to this symposium is to ask a question—an unpleasant question but one that I believe must not only be asked but answered if our generation of citizens is to fulfill its responsibility to the next generation. My question is:

Do important social problems arise from dysgenics—retrogressive evolution through the disproportionate reproduction of the genetically disadvantaged?

Underlying this question is the nature-nurture issue. I described it in 1966 as the environment-heredity uncertainty in order to draw parallels with those uncertainty principles in physics that are basic. My thesis today is that the environment-heredity uncertainty is not basic and indeed it has really been resolved—at least for one significant case that I shall discuss— but that an illusion or a delusion prevents the acceptance of the reality of this resolution and blocks its application to the social problems being faced by this symposium.

The resolution of the environment-heredity uncertainty that I shall describe is limited to the IQ's of individuals in one particular population; and further acceptable research is needed for a comparable resolution applicable to social problems for the U.S. population as a whole.

Because these limitations prevent evaluation of the dysgenic threat, I have demanded increased research on genetic aspects of human-quality problems. Four of the most frequent reasons given for rejection of my demands are these: (1) intelligence measured by IQ score is so complexly influenced by culture that genetic influences are not quantifiable, (2) IQ score has no relevance to successful living, (3) races cannot be meaningfully defined and all ethnic groups have the same genetic potential for intelligence and (4) even if the environment-heredity uncertainty, including its racial aspects, were resolved, the knowledge would be worthless because the needed remedies would inevitably require quality control applied to human reproduction on the basis of genetics. This is nothing less than eugenics—a repugnant concept.

As I shall demonstrate in the remainder of my presentation, none of these four objections stand up under objective analysis.

GENETICITY OF IQ AND THE SIGNIFICANCE OF THE GLADYS-HELEN CASE

Figure 1 is my answer to the first objection. I use published data to "predict" 122 "observed" IQ's. The root-mean-square error of prediction is only 8.5 IQ points for the 122 cases that are distributed with a standard deviation of 15 points. The "prediction" is possible because four studies have matched each "observed" IQ with the IQ of an identical twin reared apart. The other IQ is my "prediction"; each point is a twin pair. I maintain, but most psychologists deny, that the details of these studies assembled by A. R. Jensen from England, Denmark and the U.S.A. validate this assertion:

> Intelligence, measured by IQ, varies more than twice as much from genetic difference as from environmental ones for individuals from families like those that raise one of a pair of white identical twins. This assertion is conservative. The correlation coefficient between twins' IQs is 0.82: "geneticity" [i.e., my nondictionary word, like "culturology" of this symposium, for the fraction of population variance due to genes] is 82 percent; nongenetic factors cause only 18 percent of the variance.

If the results of Figure 1 are as obvious as I assert, why are they not accepted?

The twin data of Figure 1 can be differently—but not soundly—interpreted. In fact, one pair of twins in the study of Newman, Freeman and Holzinger have been repeatedly cited as evidence for what I label the *illusion of infinite plasticity of intelligence*. Gladys and Helen differed by 24 IQ points—much more than the average IQ difference between whites and Negroes. Obviously, it is asserted, environment has dominant control.

This reasoning, that is emphasized in many psychology tests, is superficial. Actually the Gladys–Helen case provides an exception needed to prove the 82 percent geneticity rule. Failure to interpret these results soundly seems to me an example of the myths about social problems that this symposium may dispel.

The correct reasoning is presented in Figure 2. In brief, what it shows is that nongenetic contributions to IQ differences between the twins are accurately distributed in a normal distribution. One striking result on this figure is that the famous pair of identical twins, Gladys and Helen of the well-known Newmann, Freeman and Holzinger study, do indeed supply the exception that proves the rule. In a distribution of 122 pairs of twins, *one pair differing by 24 IQ points should be found by the laws of probability if geneticity is 82 percent*.

The normal distribution of Figure 2 also warrants another important conclusion—one not previously presented at a scientific meeting so far as

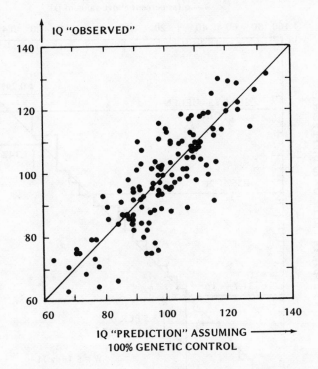

Figure 1.   Actually each "prediction" is the IQ of one of a pair of separately-reared, white-identical twins. The "observed" value is the other. The correlation coefficient is 0.82 implying that only 18 percent of the population variance is nongenetic. The "geneticity" or fraction of variance due to genetic difference is 82 percent.

I know. This new conclusion is an evaluation of the confidence that one can place in the 82 percent geneticity value—always, of course, for populations like those that raise one of a pair of white identical twins. My own research on this older research reveals that *if all the nongenetic factors that affected the IQ's added up to as much as 29 percent of the total variance, then there is less than one chance in two thousand that chance alone would have produced the smallness of the observed 122 IQ differences between the separately reared cotwins.* In other words, *the greater importance of genes compared to environment is established at a level of significance enormously higher than one in 2,000.* Geneticity is most unlikely to be less than twice as important as everything else—always for the limited population considered. Further research shows that this conclusion is not a spurious consequence of similar environments for both twins of a pair.

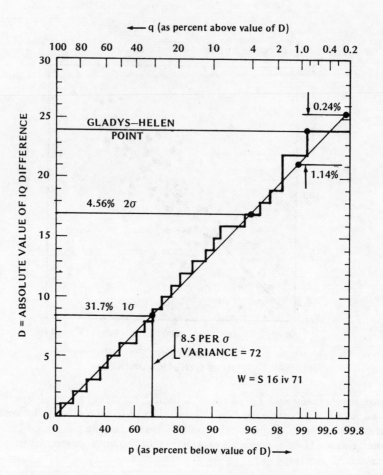

Figure 2. This figure shows that differences in IQ between identical twins reared apart obey a basic statistical law known as the normal distribution. If the data that give the "staircase" of heavy lines fell so that a straight line cut each step in half, the fit would be perfect—in fact, too perfect—like perfect alternation between heads and tails for a tossed coin. The figure shows that Gladys and Helen, the identical twins famous for differing by 24 IQ points, are the exception that proves the rule—the normal distribution predicts one such case among the 122 pairs of twins just as six heads in a row occurs once in 64 tries.

The data of the figure warrant the assertion that *intelligence, measured by IQ, varies more than twice as much from genetic differences as from environmental ones for individuals from families like those that raise one of a pair of white identical twins.* If genetic differences were less than twice as important as environmental ones, the probability is less than one in 2,000 that chance would have produced the good fit of the figure.

One prediction from 82 percent geneticity is that a difference of approximately 25 IQ points between identical twins should occur if one is raised in the worst 1 percent and the other in the best 1 percent of the normal distribution of environments. This may be relevant to the recently publicized results for young slum children reported by Professor Heber of Wisconsin.

Regarding the second objection—IQ means nothing—I observe that IQ is positively correlated with many socially-accepted measures of human quality. I refer you to A. R. Jensen's well-known article, H. J. Eysenck's recent book and Richard Herrnstein's article in the current *Atlantic Monthly* for data on traits that I calculate have correlation coefficients of about 0.2 to 0.5 with IQ.

RACEOLOGY AND THE MORAL OBLIGATION TO DIAGNOSE

The third objection—that race is meaningless—is refuted by T. E. Reed of Toronto who has determined with a precision of 1 percent that the Oakland, California, Negro population is 22 percent Caucasian in ancestry. I have refined Reed's studies and used them with Army preinduction test data to estimate that for low IQ Negro populations, each 1 percent of Caucasian ancestry raises average IQ by 1 point. I have suggested ways of controlling for the environmental differences to test the reliability of this estimate. An interesting question is the level at which diminishing returns set in; for example, at 40 percent Caucasian ancestry, would average IQ be 110?

In respect to this symposium's concern with "social problems" and its goal of "the reestablishment of stability, order and meaning," I express this warning: To fail to use diagnosis based on racial differences in blood types for fear of being called a racist is irresponsible. It may also be a great injustice to black Americans themselves. If those Negroes with the fewest Caucasian genes are in fact the most prolific and also the least intelligent, then genetic enslavement will be the destiny of their next generation. The consequences may be extremes of racism and agony for both blacks and whites.

The word "raceology" has been proposed for studies like mine. They are not racism. They are motivated by concern—not by fear and hate. My research focuses principally upon white-Negro comparisons for two reasons: (1) Our national racial problems primarily involve the Negro minority and (2) Negroes are the only racial group for which extensive published statistics are available. Therefore, my personal research on questions related to Negroes has far greater immediate promise of contrib-

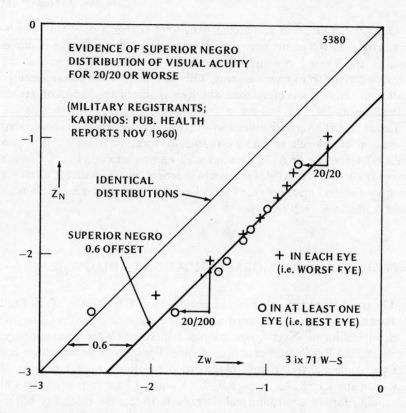

Figure 3. Evidence that increases in percentages of Caucasian genes in Negro populations improve mental performance and degrade physical performance is furnished by the preinduction test results reported by the Office of the Surgeon General, Department of the Army. The 1968 results show that Negroes in Georgia in the Third Recruiting District have a mental qualification rate of 47.3 percent or an IQ of about 80 compared to 17.5 percent and 90 for California in the Sixth District. The superior performance of Negroes in California compared to Georgia supports the theory that Negro IQ is raised by an admixture of white ancestry. California Negroes have twice as high a percentage of their genes from white ancestors as do Georgia Negroes according to an estimate based on measurements by Professor T. E. Reed of the University of Toronto of 22 percent Caucasian genes for Oakland, California and 11 percent for Evans and Bullock counties, Georgia. Reasoning from the trend shown by all the recruiting districts for both Negro and non-Negro inductees, Professor William Shockley estimates that the average IQ of Negro populations increases by about one IQ point for each 1 percent of added Caucasian genes and might match or even exceed the whites at 30 or 40 percent. The physical qualifications correspondingly drop. Professor Shockley urges that his hypothesis should be tested by determining the percentages of Caucasian genes for representative populations of Negro inductees. Such research might also permit evaluating the claim that Negro-white differences in medical disqualifications are biased by the poor medical counseling available to the economically disadvantaged.

uting to sound diagnosis of our human quality problems than, for example, would attempts to study hereditary factors for Appalacian whites, for whom I have found that statistical data is practically unobtainable. Although I emphasize the Negro area for these reasons, I continue to urge broad inquiry into hereditary aspects of human behavior for all racial groups.

As an example of raceology, I present in Figure 3 some new research results on Negro superiority that compares Negro and white visual acuity as based on Army tests. The points specify fractions of Negroes and whites having various levels of visual acuity. From 20/20 to less than 20/200, the points fall accurately along a line. The interpretation of this analysis is that whites and Negroes are distributed in their visual acuity according to the same basic underlying normal distribution but that the distribution for Negro visual acuity is offset upwards by approximately 0.6 of a standard deviation—a value that if applied for mental performance would be equivalent to about 9 IQ points.

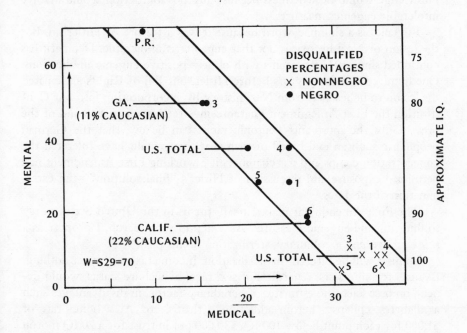

Figure 4. The Z_W values give normal distribution arguments that correspond to the percentage of white, military registrants who fail to meet the prescribed visual acuity. Z_N corresponds to Negroes. The unmarked visual acuities are in sequence 20/30, 20/40, 20/50, 20/70, 20/100. The extreme points that fall out of the pattern are 20/400. If the points fell perfectly on the line, it would imply identical normal distributions for both races except for an offset of 0.6 standard deviations.

Where data have been available, I have tried to compare other racial groups. My findings do not support a theory of white Aryan supremacy: I have found and published the observation that American orientals are about ten times more successful than the national average on a per capita basis in achieving the distinction of election to the National Academy of Sciences. They are also about ten times more successful in avoiding citations in the annual FBI uniform crime reports. My statistics also show that Jewish Nobel Prize winners in science occur about ten times more often than expected on the basis of the population as a whole.

THE "APPLE OF GOD'S EYE OBSESSION"—A CAUSE OF DELUSIONS ABOUT SOCIAL PROBLEMS?

I shall now attempt an analysis of psychological factors underlying the four objections to my research demands. I shall start with the fourth—that knowledge would be worthless because any possible action would involve intolerable eugenics measures.

Eugenics is a shunned word because it was a feature of Hitlerism. But the lesson of Nazi history is not that eugenics is intolerable. Denmark has continued since 1935 programs with clearly positive eugenic implications. One hundred and forty years before Hitler, our Bill of Rights anticipated the lesson to be learned from Nazi history by incorporating into our Constitution the First Amendment guaranteeing freedom of speech and of the press. Only the most anti-Teutonic racist can believe that the German people are such an evil breed of man that they would have tolerated the concentration camps and gas chambers if a working First Amendment had permitted exposure and discussion of Hitler's "final solution"—the extermination of the Jews.

The First Amendment makes it safe for us in the United States to try to find humane eugenic measures. As a step in such search, I propose as a *thinking exercise* a voluntary, sterilization bonus plan.

Bonuses will be offered for sterilization. Income tax-payers get nothing. Bonuses for all others, regardless of sex, race, or welfare status, would depend on best scientific estimates of hereditary factors in disadvantages such as diabetes, epilepsy, heroin addiction, arthritis, etc. At a bonus rate of $1,000 for each point below 100 IQ, $30,000 put in trust for a 70 IQ moron of twenty-child potential might return $250,000 to tax-payers in reduced costs of mental retardation care. Ten percent of the bonus in spot cash might put our national talent for entrepreneurship into action.

A motivation boost might be to permit those sterilized to be employed at below minimum standard wages without any loss of welfare floor income. Could this provide opportunity for those now unemployable?

I shall close with an hypothesis about the psychology of the critics of my concerns about dysgenics. I doubt neither the sincerity nor the good intentions of these critics. I diagnose their obtuseness as caused by a theologico-scientific delusion. I call it the "Apple of God's Eye Obsession"— God meaning for some the proper socio-biological order of the universe. True believers of this obsession hold that God has designed nature's laws so that good intentions suffice to ensure humanity's well-being—a belief that satisfies a human need for self-esteem. Any evidence counter to man's claim to be the apple of God's eye strikes a central blow at his self-esteem, and thereby provokes retaliation reminiscent of the prompt execution of a Greek messenger bearing ill tidings of defeat in battle. These parallels become clearer in the historical perspective of Galileo and Darwin. In each case they brought new knowledge that was incompatible with the then cherished interpretation of humanity's unique place in the universe. Either the new knowledge had to be rejected or else the "Apple of God's Eye Obsession" had to be painfully revised.

I propose that illusions and delusions are important in the rejection of the relevance of genetics to social problems because the theory that intelligence is largely determined by the genes and that races may differ in distribution of mental capacity offends equalitarian-environmentalism—an important feature of the contemporary form of the "Apple of God's Eye Obsession." The preponderance of the world's intellectual community resists the fact that nature can be cruel to the newborn baby. Babies too often get an unfair shake from a badly-loaded parental genetic dice cup. At the acme of unfairness are features of racial differences that my own research inescapably leads me to conclude exist: Nature has color-coded groups of individuals so that statistically reliable predictions of their adaptability to intellectually rewarding and effective lives can easily be made and profitably be used by the pragmatic man-in-the-street.

If, as many thinking citizens fear, our welfare programs are unwittingly, but with the noblest of intentions, selectively down-breeding the poor of our slums by encouraging their least foresighted to be most prolific, the consequences will be tragic for both blacks and whites—but proportionately so much worse for our black minority that, as I have said, the consequences may be a form of genetic enslavement that will provoke extremes of racism with agony for all citizens.

My position is that humanity has an obligation to use its intelligence to diagnose and to predict in order to prevent agonies that lack of foresight can all too easily create. The ambition of this symposium to dispose of "illusions and delusions" by "delving deeply into the social issues of our day" and seeking "solutions . . . which draw from man's basic core: his meaning system . . . " are in keeping with my position. I consider it a privilege to participate.

What Is the Answer

Henry E. Garrett

Q: Dr. Garrett, that Dr. Arthur Jensen of the University of California certainly made a splash, didn't he, with his findings? While I am glad to see the publicity given his opinions—that Whites are smarter than Negroes —what's so new about that? It seems to me others, you among them, have been presenting this sort of evidence for a long time.

A: What Dr. Jensen did was to find that Negroes have IQs about 15 points lower, on the average, than Whites. This, it is true, has been many times reported. What is interesting about the great amount of publicity given Dr. Jensen's published work is that publicity itself. Perhaps times are changing.

Q: Dr. Garrett, this past fall my son's high school was "massively integrated." He tells me the black children seem to be a drag. That is his way of putting it, meaning, I take it, they don't learn as rapidly as do white children. What about it?

A: Negroes can learn as readily as white children so long as the material given them involves only rote memory. But when the material demands reasoning, the Negroes lag behind. This is a common and often repeated finding. Moreover, it is a principal reason why "massive integration" should not be in effect—it is injurious to both races.

Breeding Down

Henry E. Garrett

Words such as "better," "superior," and the like, are relative words. Better than what? Superior (or inferior) to whom?

This is the nub of the race issue.

It is not argued there are no *differences* between races. No one argues that. Manifestly, there *are* differences. Caucasians, for instance, have a color peculiar to their race and in this they are indisputably *different*. The same applies to Negroes and to Orientals; each has his own color. Each race, then, *is* different.

Moreover, in the culture of the milieu native to any given race, *that* race is superior to all others. No White man can compete with an Indian who is native to the wilds of Brazil, not in those indigenous to the Indian's culture. Nor can either be expected to compete, say, with a snowbound Eskimo; a diet of blubber is not for them.

Similarly, in those things native to Caucasians, the White man is superior. He is superior precisely as a chicken is superior to a duck when both are in a chicken yard; as a duck is the superior on a millpond.

There is a simple logic in these truths that rings as clear as struck crystal. And were the various races of the world confined, as once they were, to their native habitat, the facts would be apparent, accepted by all, and would lie at rest.

But that elementary state no longer exists. Man, in one degree or another, and for whatever reason, has been nomadic. Sometimes he has traveled voluntarily. Sometimes he has moved, or was moved—as was the African Negro—under duress.

Consequently and through no fault of his own, the Negro in America finds himself caught up in a culture not of his making, like a chicken on a millpond. And as might be expected, he has not been able to compete. Therefore, he has become resentful and prey to those who would use him for devious ends.

Nor will he ever be able to compete, not so long as a White culture prevails. He can't compete and it is grossly unfair to expect him to shoulder the responsibilities of an "equal."

This fact, too, carries the clear ring of truth.

There are those, however, while admitting that a Negro, indigeneous to the Congo, cannot compete in America against White Americans, argue that those Negroes born in America has no such difficulty, or would not have, were there no such thing as invidious discrimination. Comparatively speaking, they argue that a chicken taken straight from his shell can be taught to swim, competitively, with a duck. Those who espouse this theory are known as Environmentalists. They believe *nature* the subordinate to *nurture*. Or so they argue.

Theirs is a false doctrine. And that it is false, that they themselves do not believe their own preachments is seen in their drive to destroy the concept of race. They urge racial inter-marriage.

Why, is there not a tacit admission inherent in their urgings? What other reason can there be for their push to mongrelize except that, in a White milieu, the White man is the Negro superior? The Environmentalists know, and it is true, White genes would be of benefit to the individual American Negro. Well enough, and if that were the extent of the problem, that would be the end of it for no reasonable person opposes the upgrading of any other person.

But it is not the end. For one thing, it presupposes Black genes for White people; you cannot give to one without taking from the other. You cannot upbreed the Negro without downbreeding the White. And there is the rub.

As Dr. Garrett has so graphically demonstrated (*How Classroom Desegregation Will Work*, see page 508), the average IQ of Negroes is about 80. That of Whites is 100. An admixture of the two, theoretically, would produce a race of 90s. And since the American culture is a White culture—the product of 100 IQ—to lower its intelligence level is to lower its culture. And it is this that spells the difference between maintenance of standards and their destruction.

Withal, this does *not* spell out the superiority of White over Black except, to repeat, in this limited sense: Within a White culture, the White man *is* superior. If ours were a Negro culture, the White man, within that culture, would be inferior.

This, then, is our choice. If we prefer a White culture, we must maintain it, that is, eschew race mixing. If we prefer a Negroid culture, even a cross-bred culture, one with radically different standards, then, we will accept the proposals of the Environmentalists and breed down.

Henry E. Garrett, Ph.D., by any criterion, is the best qualified man in America to write on this subject. His list of honors, those paid him over the years by his peers, is unequalled. He makes this point: Miscegenation would harm America, all of America, Negroes as well as Whites. For, as he says, if leadership is destroyed, all is destroyed. Take away 10 percent— our margin of cultural "profit"—and you have destroyed a viable, going, "profitable" way of life.

That is what *Breeding Down* is all about.

THE EDITORS

The Patrick Henry Press

About the Author

Henry E. Garrett received his doctorate (Ph.D.) from Columbia University in 1923, and spent the subsequent years, until his retirement in 1956, as a member of its faculty. For 16 years, Dr. Garrett headed Columbia's Department of Psychology.

At one time or another, Dr. Garrett has been visiting Professor at the University of California; The University of Florida; the University of Hawaii; The University of New Mexico; and The University of Virginia.

Dr. Garrett is Past President of The Eastern Psychological Association; the Psychometric Society; and the American Psychological Association. He is a Fellow, A.A.A.S., and a former member of the National Research Council. He is author of many books, articles and monographs; he is a member of the editorial board of Psychometrika and, for 20 years, was general editor of The American Psychology Series.

BREEDING DOWN

The Negro Revolution has as many aspects as there are spokes in a wheel: equal employment, equal pay, equal housing, equal this, and equal that, all nebulous terms not subject to clear definition. The hub that holds them all together, however, is definiable. What is being sought is the abolition of race differences, that is, the abolition of races. If there were no races, the argument runs, there could be no race differences. And that certainly is true.

The question, of course, is whether abolition of the races is a good end to seek or a bad end. That is the crucial question. Unfortunately, it is not as simple to answer as it is to ask. Put it another way and its complexities begin to emerge: Would civilization benefit through miscegenation? In what way? At what cost?

Make no mistake about it, this is the issue of our time and if it is going to be resolved, justly, such questions must be answered, the truth faced.

Begin, then, with this fact: There is inherent in the civil-rights movement the tacit admission that race differences themselves manifest the superiority of one race over the other. Nothing else makes sense. White people do not assault and defame one another over hair color, whether it be blonde, brown, or black. Nor do Negroes revolt because their skin is darker (or lighter) than their Negro neighbor's. For, while there are obvious differences among colors, there is no superiority inherent in the color white over the color black, of blonde over brunette. Therefore, such differences, not being important, are accepted.

SIGNIFICANT DIFFERENCES

Not so with race. There are significant differences between races, provable differences beyond the color of one's skin, and because these differences are recognized by both races, envy is bred, trouble ensues, and we have the Negro Revolution. Negroes are convinced, and with good reason, that if their Negro-ness were abolished or, conversely, if Whites were made Negroid (though it is rarely stated in this way), the problem they face as Negroes, *per se*, would be abolished. They know, instinctively, that miscegenation and nothing else will make them "equal."

And, in a sense, they are right. If we all had chocolate faces, race as a problem could not exist. Undoubtedly, other problems would arise—

human nature being what it is—between the long and the short, say, or the lean and the fat, but the Negro's problem of his Negro-ness would no longer worry him.

THE QUESTION

Be that as it may, since today's problem is not one of color but of race, and since Negroes are not the only ones snared in its coils, the solution is not necessarily to be found in common coloration, the superficiality, or in considering the emotions of only one race. White people are equally involved. As the slogan has it, they, too, demand—or should demand—equal rights.

Therefore, the question comes, would miscegenation be good for the White race? Indeed, would it be good for the Negro race? Is the ultimate end of the Negro Revolution a good end or a bad end?

THE ANSWER

There is not much argument about the first part of the question: No, miscegenation would not be good for White people because the Negro has nothing to offer that, on balance, would benefit White people. All scientific evidence points to this conclusion and history demonstrates its truth. The cathedral at Cologne placed in opposition to the mud huts of the Congo is a physical evidence of the fact. Shakespeare, Newton, Copernicus, Rembrandt, Edison, all placed against a void are further evidences.

White people, by and large, prefer not to discuss these things and their reticence is understandable. But, in today's climate, discussion is forced upon them. They are faced with an issue—to borrow a line—to be or not to be, and they must resolve it.

THE ARGUMENT

That being so, it is not fair, when the talk begins, to attribute Hitlerian aspirations to those who advocate racial purity. The argument for social segregation should not be mistaken to be an argument for racial superiority. God willing, the day will come when the Negro will have reached the plane the White man invests today, brought there as the White man arrived, through effort and evolution. Indeed it is not a plea for supremacy. It is, instead, an argument in support of the White man's right to maintain the level he has achieved after eons of struggle.

That is the White man's argument, that is what the White man has to lose through miscegenation: Not supremacy, but his own, hard-bought level of civilization. For you can no more mix the two races and maintain the standards of White civilization than you can add 80 (the average IQ of Negroes) and 100 (the average IQ of Whites), divide by two and get 100. What you would get would be a race of 90s, and it is that 10 percent differential that spells the difference between a spire and a mud hut; 10 percent—or less—is the margin of civilization's "profit"; it is the difference between a cultured society and savagery.

Therefore, it follows, if miscegenation would be bad for White people, it would be bad for Negroes as well. For, if leadership is destroyed, all is destroyed.

AN OLD PROBLEM

This is no new problem. That it is not is seen in the fact there are, today, 19 States—North and South—that have laws forbidding mixed marriages. And though the Supreme Court has skirted the issue a number of times, until now it has never declared such laws unconstitutional.

SPECIOUS REASONING

Those who oppose miscegenation laws do so, principally, on the grounds that they are insulting to the Negro and violative of his civil rights. In a recent article (*Interracial Marriage and the Law*, *Atlantic Monthly*, October, 1965), W. D. Zabel, a New York attorney, argues that such laws counteract the personal rights of the individual to marry whom he chooses. Some years ago, Mrs. Eleanor Roosevelt, using much the same argument, wrote that interracial marriage should be permitted if the couple "loved each other."

By the same logic, one supposes, incest, too, should be permitted.

Before scoffing at that parallel, consider the effects of interracial marriage from the same aspects one would consider the effects of incest. That is, biological and social.

BIOLOGICAL

Everyday observation confirms the judgment that the Negro-White hybrid (mulatto) is apparently a normal human specimen. And it is true, Negro-White crosses often are of exceptional physique. The prize fighters,

Cassius Clay and Joe Louis, are prime examples. Even so, the former repeatedly was deferred by Selective Service because of his low intellectual level ("I just said I was the greatest, not the smartest"). The latter, for many years, was "in trouble" with the Internal Revenue Service because of a seeming inability to keep straight his financial affairs.

Whatever the physical prowess of some mulattos, Davenport and Steggerda (*Race Crossing in Jamaica*, Carnegie Institute, Washington, 1929) reported certain physical disharmonies in their browns (hybrids) not found in either blacks or whites. Critics have pointed out that these anomalies, while sometimes important, are on the whole fairly trivial. And that may well be true. But the physique of a man is not the whole man and that is just the point.

200,000 YEAR LAG

From the standpoint of genetics, Negro genes lower the level of a racial cross. Studies of fossils (Coon, C. *The Origin of Races*, 1962) show the Negro, in an evolutionary sense, to be on the average at least 200,000 years behind the Whites. Moreover, the Negro brain, on the average, is some 100 cc smaller in volume, correspondingly lighter in weight, and less fissured than that of the White (although the overlap is 20–25 percent). Negro history confirms these physiological findings. In 5,000 years, the Black African did not build a literate civilization. Nor is there evidence, even now, to indicate the Negro, left to his own devices, is capable of rising above the mud-hut stage.[1] The Benin bronzes (greatly praised by African enthusiasts) are accepted as the acme of Negro art. But these objects d'art hardly compare with the renaissance genius of France and Italy that flourished during the same period.

THREE-TO-ONE

At least 50 studies of twins agree that heredity contributes to individual differences at least three times as much as does environment. Intelligence, therefore, is basically inherited, though it requires an adequate environment to fully express itself.

---

[1] During the 60 days prior to January 15, 1966, five "democratic" African nations —Upper Volta, Central African Republic, Dahomey, Nigeria and the Congo—were tumbled by coup d'etat. Since 1960, there have been at least 24 African rebellions, mutinies, assassinations or attempted assassinations, and coup d'etats. Sixteen of these were major disturbances. This record is a sad commentary on the naivete of those who thought Negroes capable of civilized self government.

THE IQ

The generally accepted means of determining an individual's intelligence is by way of his Intelligence Quotient (IQ). IQ measures abstractly one's ability to deal with symbols: words, numbers, diagrams, formulas. The average IQ of American Negroes, as repeated testings have demonstrated, is 80–85; that of American Whites, about 100. The effects of this IQ differential are seen in our schools. The Negro lags behind the Whites from 2–3 grades in elementary schools, more in high school. Only one percent of Negroes have an IQ sufficient to permit acceptable college level work (IQ 110). Thirty percent of Whites meet this standard.[2]

BREEDING DOWN

Owing to this gap in measured intelligence, Negro-White marriages, genetically speaking, represent a "breeding down." Brazil, Cuba, and Puerto Rico objectively reveal this to be the fact. These cross-bred countries are politically unstable, socially backward, and are crime and disease ridden. Their contributions to science and literature are minuscule. Haiti, once successfully governed by Whites and now ruled by Negroes, has reverted to savagery; Voodoo is widely practised.

Wherever there has been mixed breeding with the Negro, there has been deterioration in civilization. Egypt is a good example; so is Central America. There is no example to the contrary.

Genetically, therefore, it is clear that intermarriage of Negroes and Whites in the U.S.A. is undesirable.

SOCIAL

Undoubtedly, the most unhappy *immediate* effects of Negro-White marriage in the United States are psychological and social. At the least, the mixed couple can expect to be shunned, isolated and avoided. At most,

---

[2] The stability (and therefore the reliability) of IQ tests has been a constant source of concern to those who would deny inherited race differences. To by-pass or supplant the IQ, sociologists in the New York public-school system devised a "reading test" to be administered in lieu of the IQ. The result of this substitution was reported by *The New York Times*, May 2, 1965 (Mayer, Martin, *Close to Midnight for New York Schools*): "The real result of the acclaimed abandonment of the IQ test, then, is that Negro children in 1964–65 are more likely to be in the bottom classes of 'integrated schools' than they were (when the IQ tests were used) in 1963–64."

they will be insulted and perhaps physically mistreated—by both races. Most Whites resent and resist having Negro-White couples move into their neighborhoods, and refuse social contacts, while Negroes look upon the White unit of such a marriage as a curiosity. Mixed couples may be, and often are, sought out by professionally tolerant people—but such contacts, generally, are patronizing and supercilious. Negroes realize this and are doubly insulted by it.

MISEDUCATION

It is often said that Whites who marry Negroes are of low mental calibre to begin with, probably pathological, and hence of little social value to the community. This is sometimes true, but since low grades rarely bother with the marriage rite—generally they are content with illicit union—such marriages are neither frequent nor lasting. Marriage between college trained Negroes and Whites, on the other hand, is not unusual today, thanks to 40 years of miseducation by professional sociologists and cultural anthropologists. And it is at the door of these people much of our trouble should be placed. The modern sociologist, despite the "twin" studies, is usually a convinced believer in the power of environment over heredity; environment being his field, his reason for being. Because this is so, because his bread and butter depend upon the acceptance of his theories, he is blithely unconcerned by the absence of objective evidence to support them—and there is no such evidence.

ADOLESCENT PROTEST

The unsupported theories of such professors are manna to immature college students who exhibit what is termed "the adolescent protest." Such students resent constituted authority—that of their parents, their teachers and the police—and often take perverse delight in flaunting their "independence" through outlandish behavior. Not the least of such "protests" is inter-racial marriage. This is an age-old story. A very bright young man, son of a university professor, married an attractive Negro girl whom he had met in his progressive school. The outcome was tragedy for the young couple, for their friends, and for their family. When last heard from this boy had given up his plans for studying law, and was living in Harlem, working at a small job.

An Episcopal priest, who considers himself a Liberal, refuses to marry Negro-White couples. He deplores what he calls "prejudice and bigotry," but recognizes the existence of strong racial attitudes as a fact which cannot be explained away. Moreover, he believes the stresses and strains of marriage are great enough without deliberately compounding them. Consequently he confines the holy rites to those of identical races.

DEBT TO THE PAST

An offsetting force to these protests is "consciousness of kind." Some years ago, an Englishwoman of good family married a Nigerian chief replete with leopardskin coat. Many English protested this denial of a great heritage, saying that ancestors of present-day Britain deserve better than semi-savage descendants. In turn, Liberal newspapers ridiculed these Conservatives, alleging bigotry, prejudice and the rest. But the modern Englishman does owe a debt to the past which "breeding down" will not fulfill. England has a great history and mongrelism will not carry on this heritage. It is the sale of birthright for pottage.[3]

MISCEGENATION LAWS

There are two views as to the status of miscegenation laws. The first, advocated by lawyer Zabel, holds such laws to be unconstitutional. The other view holds that States—under their police power—can and should prohibit miscegenation, just as they ban marriage of the feeble-minded, the insane and various undesirables. Just as they outlaw incest.

The writer is no lawyer and hence makes no *legal* choice between the two. Zabel estimates that there are 1,000,000 Negro-White marriages in the U.S.A. today. And an educated guess is that the odds are long that given the present Supreme Court and the prevailing Liberal winds, miscegenation laws eventually will be struck down. Even so, the fact will remain there are good psychological and anthropological reasons for these laws to remain in effect.

However that may be, whether the laws remain or not, it will make little difference. Nothing ever has stopped co-habiting by partners of choice. Unless deterred by a change of opinion brought about by increased knowledge of genetics, history and psychology, there probably will be more of it, not less.

---

[3] Between 1945 and 1960, non-white immigrants to Britain numbered 1,000,000. This influx, mostly Jamaica Negroes, subsequently was curtailed by law. Though these 1,000,000 people constitute less than three per cent of England's population today, they are producing 75 percent of the waifs now being received in British orphanages. Most are illegitimate and are Negroid in varying degree. Only rarely, the orphanages report, are any of these children adopted. They are unwanted.

THREE CASTE SOCIETY

If mixed marriages occur often enough—if education does not prevail —we shall evolve into a three-caste society. At the top, will be the whites who refuse to mix; at the bottom will be the blacks who cannot mix; and in the middle will be a large group of negroids in a constant state of ferment. In general, American society will deteriorate, mentally and culturally, crime and political extravagance will increase. This has been the history of Negro-White mixing in other countries, at other times, whenever and wherever it occurred. It is not a pleasant prospect.

Pleasant or otherwise, miscegenation is the ultimate goal of the civil-rights movement, that Negro Revolution. And those who urge peace-at-any-price should know its cost—to their children's children: What we do, they cannot undo.

INDEX